BUILDING A
PEOPLE OF
POWER

Robert C. Linthicum

BUILDING A PEOPLE OF POWER

Equipping Churches to Transform Their Communities

Authentic

World Vision

Published in Partnership with World Vision Press

Authentic Media
We welcome your comments and questions.
129 Mobilization Drive, Waynesboro, GA 30830 USA authentic@stl.org
and 9 Holdom Avenue, Bletchley, Milton Keynes, Bucks, MK1 1QR, UK
www.authenticbooks.com

If you would like a copy of our current catalog, contact us at:
1-8MORE-BOOKS
ordersusa@stl.org

Building A People of Power
ISBN-10: 1-932805-51-6
ISBN-13: 978-1-932805-51-2

Published in partnership with World Vision
34834 Weyerhaeuser Way South, P.O. Box 9716, Federal Way, WA 98063 USA
www.worldvision.org

Scripture quotations are taken from the New Revised Standard Version Bible, copyright 1989,
Division of Christian Education of the National Council of the Churches of Christ in the United States
of America. Used by permission. All rights reserved.

Library of Congress Cataloging-in-Publication Data available

Cover design: Paul Lewis
Interior design: Angela Duerksen
Editorial team: K.J. Larson, Carol Pitts, Tom Richards

Printed in the United States of America

Dear Reader,

World Vision invites you to share your response to
the message of this book by writing to World Vision Press at
worldvisionpress@worldvision.org or by calling 800-777-7752.

For information about other World Vision Press publications, visit us at
www.worldvision.org/worldvisionpress.

Other Books by Robert C. Linthicum:

Transforming Power

Building a People of Power: A Video Course with Marilyn Stranske and
  Mike Miller

Are We a Church of the City? with Douglas Edwards and Roy Schlobohm

Revitalizando a Igreja (published in Brazil)

Signs of Hope in the City (editor)

Empowering the Poor

City of God; City of Satan

A Transformacao da Cidade (published in Brazil)

The People Who Turned the World Upside Down

The People Who Met God

The People's Bible Study

Church: Discover Your Calling

Christian Revolution for Church Renewal

CONTENTS

INTRODUCTION

Welcome to *Building a People of Power: Equipping Churches to Transform Their Communities*. This book will take you on a journey of discovering biblical principles enabling your church to become a community of relational power that can bring about significant transformation of its neighborhood, its city, and even in its own life. That journey is based upon a biblical understanding of power.

To most of us Christians, power is a dirty word. That is because we have experienced power as dominating, controlling, and unilateral. But the great biblical leaders such as Abraham, Moses, Joshua, Ruth, Samuel, David, Isaiah, Amos, Micah, Jeremiah, Nehemiah, Esther, Jesus, Paul, Mary Magdalene, and John discovered and used an entirely different kind of power—a power that was liberating, transforming, relational, and even redemptive. Learning how to access and use that power for the glory of Christ and the building of his Kingdom is what this book is about. So I hope you will be motivated to take this power tour with me.

This book is essentially about a praxis for the church as it seeks to engage the world. The word praxis is an easily misunderstood word. Most people believe that it is simply a synonym for "practice" or "application". It is not. Praxis is the intersection between theory and practice, the point where one's theoretical reflection (in our case, reflection on the biblical message) and one's acting out of that theory in practice meet. In effective praxis, reflection will result in action, but action will always result in deeper reflection. Thus, a continuing learning cycle occurs, so that the learning process is not complete until it has resulted in being acted out. Likewise, action is inadequate unless it results in an even deeper learning that, in turn, will lead to more substantive action. We will examine to a greater depth this pedagogical learning cycle in chapter eight. Meanwhile, let me simply assert that the purpose of this book is to have a conversation with you out of our mutual engagement with Scripture that will cause you to try out the strategies and tactics taught in this book. By this conversation and action between you and me, my hope is that you will take the steps that enable you to become a powerful change agent for God: blooming where you are planted.

I want to stress that what you will be reading here will not simply be theological, biblical, or sociological theory. Although I have taught at academic institutions, my career has been primarily a career of action, of experiencing praxis between my biblical studies and my everyday work as a pastor of inner city churches, as a mission executive, and as a community organizer in urban slums in Asia, Africa, and Latin America as well as in the United States. You'll read some of my stories in this book. But both my career and my life have been one of working as a follower of the Christ for justice among the world's poor and powerless. I have sought to do that by following the Iron Rule, "Never do for others what they can do for themselves" and its corollary, "When the people lack access to political or economic power, the power they have is each other!"

FROM *EMPOWERING THE POOR* TO *BUILDING A PEOPLE OF POWER*

This book is the successor to the work, *Empowering the Poor* (MARC Publications, 1991). *Empowering the Poor* came out of the work I did for World Vision, Christianity's largest humanitarian relief and development agency.

From 1985 through 1995, I was the director of World Vision's Urban Advance. The Urban Advance was a major ministry innovation that enabled World Vision to learn how to most effectively undertake work that would promote human transformation, seek justice, and bear witness to the good news of the kingdom of God among the poor in the major cities of the world. During its ten years, the Urban Advance worked with sixteen World Vision field offices in Asia, Africa, and Latin America, where we developed twenty-eight local community organizations, created over ninety economic development projects, built over six thousand homes, brought about significant health care, and contributed to the strengthening of hundreds of churches. Helping to provide leadership to this movement of transformation was one of the most exciting times in my life.

Obviously, the Urban Advance staff and I didn't do all this organizing ourselves. We trained World Vision staff, community residents, and pastors to do this organizing. Over 6200 pastors, community leaders, and World Vision staff participated in sixty-eight urban workshops that we conducted, where they honed their skills in community organizing, urban ministry, strategic planning, economic development, and urban biblical theology. These events were held in fifty-three cities in twelve Third World countries and six First World countries.

It became clear very soon that my colleagues and I could not shoulder this teaching load by ourselves. So I wrote a curriculum on the biblical principles, strategies, and primary tactics of community organizing that other World Vision staff and pastors could use. I was then asked by World Vision leadership to turn that curriculum into a book. Thus, *Empowering the Poor* was born.

Empowering the Poor was a small book—only 118 pages. But it proved to be a manual that was helpful to many. Intended primarily for an audience of Third World pastors and mission workers, it became instead one of MARC Publication's best-selling books for more than ten years, especially being picked up by seminarians and urban ministry students. But as time passed on, it became increasingly clear to me that it was showing its age (something I discovered happens to all of us!). When the successor to MARC Publications, World Vision Press, approached me about doing a third edition of *Empowering the Poor* for a new day, I realized it would be better to start with a clean slate than to try to pump vitamins into an aging body. Thus, *Building a People of Power* was envisioned.

Empowering the Poor sought to introduce the church and Christian mission agencies to the biblical principles and primary strategies of community organizing. *Building a People of Power* takes that exploration further by thoroughly exploring a biblical theology of power and applying the same to the latest innovations in organizing manifested in broad-based organizing. And *Building a People of Power* does this, not simply through the written word, but also through DVDs, videos, CD ROMs and curricula that can be used to both hone skills and to conduct biblical research (see "Next Steps in Building a People of Power" in the appendix).

The advances made in organizing over the past decade have been significant. Ten years ago, most organizing was community or citywide organizing, concentrating on the organizing of specific neighborhoods within a city or, at the most, organizing throughout a city. Such organizing was always focused upon a specific ethnic or racial group, upon poor people or working class people, or within a given slum or squatter settlement. That was the nature of World Vision's organizing in Asia, Africa, and Latin America under the Urban Advance. And that was the style of organizing throughout the United States.

But over the past ten to fifteen years, organizing began to change. It was increasingly recognized that society could not be significantly changed unless both workers and management, both poor and middle class, both inner city and suburbanite, black and brown, yellow and white shared in building power together. And that power had to be built relationally—by discovering our common issues and pains, and by caring what happened to each other.

Thus, community organizing began to be replaced by broad-based organizing—broad in every way. That meant building organizations that were institutionally-based rather than based in individuals, that were comprised of institutions from suburbs as well as from inner-cities, that covered the denominational spectrum, that included both churches and organizations who might build their power relationally but might not be Christian or even religious institutions, and who wielded significant power simply because of their size. Thus, United Power for Action and Justice was born in 1997 throughout the Chicago metropolitan area, with over 330 member institutions rather than the usual twenty-five to forty institutions that make up a traditional community organization. And ONE LA (the organization to which my church belongs and in which I participate), at its founding convention in 2004, gathered over 12,000 delegates from more than 120 institutions to organize a metropolitan area larger than the states of Rhode Island, Connecticut, and Massachusetts combined.

By their sheer size and the enormous economic and political power they represent, such organizations need not prove themselves to the politically and economically powerful; rather they are, ipso facto, powerful and therefore can get down to business to negotiate decisions with power, that work directly for justice for their constituencies. Any book presenting biblical principles and strategies for building a people of power that does not appreciate such trends in organizing today will not guide its readers into the realities of how to work for the transformation of their cities. Therefore, *Empowering the Poor* is out, and *Building a People of Power* is in!

My Approach to Scripture

The biblical theology of power developed in this book may seem a different way of reading Scripture. So a word needs to be said about varied approaches to interpreting Scripture.

There have been two primary approaches to the study of Scripture throughout much of the twentieth century. The first has been that of seeking to discern the sources of Scripture in order to have as definitive a text as possible from which to interpret the faith. The second has been that of seeking to discern the discourse of the biblical message, approaching Scripture from the perspective of listening to how the text spoke to its original readers. The first one was the overwhelming approach to Scripture in the latter part of the nineteenth century and much of the twentieth century. The emphasis on the second approach didn't begin until midway through the century, but has now, in the twenty-first century, become the dominant approach to interpreting Scripture.

The foundation for the source discernment of Scripture lies in the Enlightenment period, and particularly in its emphasis on the rational and logical. Thus, with this approach, one is always trying to prove the faith ("It's illogical to not be a Christian"). The vehicles that biblical scholarship has used to prove the Scripture, returning it as close as possible to its original autographs, have been form criticism, redaction criticism, and historical criticism. Form criticism concentrated upon seeking the accuracy of the specific text. Redaction criticism sought to discern how specific Scripture passages have been put together, including layers of editing to bring it to what it is today (e.g., Moses obviously didn't write of his own death in Deuteronomy 34; so who did, when did he write it, and what else might he have written or edited in Deuteronomy?). Historical criticism sought to discern the original documents upon which Scripture is based (e.g., those propounding the documentary hypothesis suggest that the Torah is built upon four documents—J, E, D and P—and not upon the writing of Moses, or that the Synoptic Gospels are built around a common pre-Gospel source called Q).

Our view of inspiration tends to influence the vehicle in which we work, with those holding to a verbal or plenary inspiration of Scripture gravitating toward form criticism (because they want as accurate a text as possible from which to work) and those holding to a non-literal theory of inspiration or no theory at all gravitating toward historical criticism. The importance of this approach to Scripture, however, regardless of one's theological convictions, is the desire to determine the most accurate text from which one can study and interpret the Bible. What proponents of this school of thought did not see, however, is that even in their pursuit of the most accurate text, their understandings of society (e.g., the dominance of individualism over the collective) and of theology (e.g., the Calvinists who argued that Paul's baptism of the family of the Philippian jailer in Acts 16:33 is a biblical indication that the early church practiced infant baptism) significantly influenced their interpretation of the text.

The discourse discernment school has followed an entirely different approach to working with Scripture. It believes that seeking the source of Scripture is to miss the point of Scripture itself. How Scripture developed is not, finally, that important. What is important is dealing with what we now read. The church doesn't read Q; it reads Matthew, Mark, and Luke. It doesn't read D; it reads Deuteronomy. What is crucial is not how that Scripture got to us; what is crucial is what it says to us. We must let the text as it is, and only the text as it is, speak to us. It is not so much that we, as Christians, should read the Scripture, as it is that we must allow the Scripture to read us.

To let the Scripture read us requires us to do three things. First, we must discern to whom that particular Scripture passage was written. For whom was it intended? Second, we must understand what were the major events and the major movements occurring at that time and to the people to whom this Scripture was intended (especially what was happening politically, economically, and religiously in that society). Third, in the light of the message the writer was seeking to communicate to the people to whom he was writing, what is that Scripture saying to us? Thus, the task of working with Scripture is to ask three questions: What was going on at the time this Scripture was written? What did it say to the people to whom it was written? What does it say to us?

For example, it is universally accepted by both the most conservative and the most liberal biblical scholars that the gospel of Mark was written at or before the time of the defeat of Israel by the Roman Empire in AD 70. Recognizing that fact, those working with Scripture from a source-orientation would then work with the stories of the gospel of Mark from their understanding of what they believe Christian faith is and what they believe about Jesus. However, those working with Scripture from the discourse-discernment school would approach the gospel of Mark quite differently. They would be concerned about understanding clearly what was going on politically, economically, and religiously in Israel at the time Mark was writing and what were the essential issues with which both the people and the Jewish leaders were wrestling. Then they would be interested in discerning how Mark reached back into the story of Jesus so that what he was writing spoke clearly to Christians about how they faced these essential issues in their time consistent with what Jesus was seeking to do and to teach for his time. Finally, they would seek to let the Scripture coming out of Mark's time "read" our situation so that we would have a sense of what Christ is calling us to do in the twenty-first century.

How does this methodology work in Mark? That gospel was likely written in the interim between Israel's initial revolt against Rome in AD 65 (when they drove all Roman forces from the land) and Rome's counter offensive in AD 70 that would decimate Israel. In essence, during that interim, the nation had become divided into two positions. The zealots and revolutionaries (which included some of Israel's leaders) were calling for continued all-out revolt against Rome until the Empire would be pushed permanently out of Israel and the Jews could win their independence. The majority of Israel's leadership (the high priest, the priests, Sadducees, Pharisees, and scribes), all of whom had fared well by cooperating with Rome, was calling upon the nation to surrender and to sue for peace.

What would the church do? On which side would they fasten? The gospel of Mark is written to counsel Christians to look back and see what Jesus did when faced with these two alternatives in his time. What he did was to insist upon a third way—not to become revolutionaries seeking the overthrow of Rome or to join with Israel's aristocratic elite in cooperating with Rome. Rather, the church should, like Jesus, proclaim and work for the kingdom of God by seeking to peacefully (but astutely) re-form society on the Jubilee principles of a reversal of fortune, where wealth is equitably distributed, poverty is eliminated, all politics are just, and all are reconciled to each other because they are reconciled with God.

The approach I will use to study the Bible throughout this book will be that of discourse discernment, permitting the Bible to read us as we seek to understand the political, economic, and religious realities for the writer's time and in that light, seeking to discern what the scriptures are calling us to be and do as God's contemporary people.

So now it's time to begin building a people of power. May God speak power-fully to you as you seek to be faithful in building such a people.

Chapter One

_____

WHERE TO BEGIN:

THE SHALOM COMMUNITY AS THE DREAM OF SCRIPTURE

At seven years of age, I watched my father die of a burst aorta. He was only forty-eight. A year later, my mother unintentionally stepped in front of a fast-moving trolley car and was struck. She was paralyzed from the waist-down. My mother, recognizing she was in no condition to continue to care for my brother and me, asked a close friend what to do. "Enroll your boys in Girard College," he responded.

Girard College is a residential elementary and secondary school in Philadelphia that was founded by Stephen Girard, America's first multimillionaire. Upon Girard's death in 1832, he left his entire estate to the city of Philadelphia for the creation and maintenance of a school for the education of "poor, fatherless, male orphans." That school continues to the present, giving from eight hundred to fifteen hundred boys and girls from destitute homes a superior education and hope in life.

So it was that in September 1945, my younger brother and I entered Girard College. For the next ten years, I lived in that orphanage until graduating from high school.

In one sense, Girard was very good for me. At the time I was there, it was rated near the top of all Pennsylvania's private and parochial schools—and I loved to learn! Classes were small and teachers were motivated. I can remember spending many afternoons reading in the school's two-story library. The school used Philadelphia as a laboratory that made history come alive. The school brought out my speaking abilities through drama, debate, and reporting for several years on the campus radio station. Girard taught me discipline and self-control in its highly competitive and organized environment, where excellence was de rigueur. So I owe much to Girard.

But there was much I disliked about Girard. Besides its regimentation and discipline, I missed growing up in a family and home. But most of all, there was no room at Girard for the spiritual dimensions of life. Stephen Girard was an agnostic and required that his school neither observe religion nor allow any clergy on campus.

When I became a Christian, it was outside the Girard environment. And in my confinement behind the walls of this orphanage, I nurtured my faith in Christ simply by reading the Bible and listening to radio preachers.

As I listened to the radio preachers, I became increasingly convinced that I needed to live a life that would be a testimony to the world that I belonged to Jesus Christ. The radio preachers told me what that life would look like: I wouldn't smoke, drink, belong to secret societies, dance, or go to movies. Well, Girard didn't allow its students to smoke or drink. I didn't have any idea what a "secret society" was. Since it was an all-boys school at the time, I wasn't about to dance with any of them! So all that was left to give up for Christ was movies. And therein lay a problem.

Every Friday night was movie night at Girard College. The entire student body, from first through twelfth grades, would gather in the school's auditorium to watch a current film playing in Philadelphia theaters. Everyone was to be there; there were no exceptions. So here was where—at fifteen years of age—I could take my stand for Christ!

I went to my house manager and told him I couldn't watch the film. "Why not?" he asked. "Because it's against my religion," I replied. "My church doesn't believe in watching movies!" What could he do? He fussed and fumed, and then reported me to his superior. So I went to see the superior, and used the same argument. He fussed and fumed, and then moved me up the ladder. On and on it went until I arrived in the president's office.

"I can't go to the Friday night film," I told the president. "Why not?" he innocently asked. "Because it's against my religion. My church believes it is a sin to watch Hollywood films."

"Well that's too bad," replied the president. "All the students have to attend the movies."

"Sir, with all due respect," I responded, "I'm not going to do it. You can't make me do something that my church and I believe is a mortal sin!" (I didn't know about the "mortal" stuff, but it sounded impressive.)

"You will do it," he replied.

"No, I won't. Do you really want to have it known that Girard insists I do something my church and I believe is a mortal sin? What would this do to the image of the school?"

He looked hard at me for the longest time. And then he responded in a way I never expected. "Young man, what do you expect to be doing while everyone else is watching this film?"

"I would like to do class work or to read."

"And where would you do that?"

"This office looks as good as any place to me."

So it was that every Friday night, I walked into the president's office as all the other students filed into the auditorium down the hallway. There I would sit in his big leather chair behind his desk and read. Soon, other students whom I had won to Christ also joined me in the president's office. And so, each Friday night we had church in the President's office, sitting in his leather chairs and sofa, singing hymns and studying the Bible together—while Stephen Girard frowned down upon us from his full-length portrait high on the office wall! It was a victory as sweet as St. Paul's must have been when, under house arrest in Rome and awaiting trial before the emperor, he won his guards to Christ and started a church in their midst. I had experienced the use of biblical power for the first time in my life.

The writer of Genesis called it the Garden of Eden (Genesis 2:7–8). According to the author of Exodus, God called it "a priestly kingdom and a holy nation" (Exodus 19:3–6). Moses called it "a people of God's very own possession" (Deuteronomy 4:12–20). The Psalmist called it "Zion," "the city of our God," "the holy mountain" (Psalm 48:1, 12–14a). Isaiah called it the "house of the God of Jacob," "Zion," and "Jerusalem" (Isaiah 2:2–3). Like the Psalmist, Zechariah the prophet called it "the holy mountain" (Zechariah 8:3). Jesus called it "the kingdom of God" (Luke 17:20–21). Paul called it "the kingdom of Christ" (1 Corinthians 15:23). John called it "the kingdom of our Lord and of his Messiah," "the holy city," and "the new Jerusalem" (Revelation 21:1–2). From the first chapters of Genesis to the last chapters of Revelation, what all these biblical leaders professed in common was a single, clear-cut vision of God's intentions for the world.

What the Scriptures call us to be about is: grasping God's intentions for humanity, understanding what makes the world the way it actually is, and then working in the world as it is in order to draw it toward what God intends. All three tasks are strategic. Without grasping God's intentions for the world, we have no vision. Without appraising the world as it actually is, we lack a realistic context. And without the effort to work with God for the transformation of the world, we have no mission.

That is the intent of this book—to enable you to embrace the biblical vision of the world as God intended it, to make a frank appraisal of the world's corporate sin, and to carry out your mission so that you build your people into a people of power who can effectively seek the transformation of your community or city into at least a partial approximation of the kingdom of God. This chapter will deal with the first two tasks: to examine Scripture in order to understand the world as God intends it to be and the world as it actually is, ravaged by individual and societal sin. Chapters two through twelve will then concentrate upon the third task, as we work together to build a people of power capable of transforming the world.

THE WORLD AS GOD INTENDED

As we noted earlier, there are many images used in Scripture to describe the world as God intended it to be, such as the "Garden of Eden," a "priestly kingdom and a holy nation," "Zion," "the mountain of the Lord," or "the kingdom of God." These terms represent the specific ways each writer has attempted to articulate God's intentions for the world. But when we get behind the specific image to examine its vision, we begin to note the significant commonalities running through all these images. In essence, whether we use the term of "Zion" or "kingdom of God" or "the new Jerusalem," we are talking about essentially the same vision.

Let me suggest a word that I think best encapsulates the world as God intended. This word is the word most often used throughout Scripture to describe God's intentions for the world. It is the word *shalom*. It is a description of the people of God as *the shalom community.*

What does shalom mean? When one works with the original Hebrew in the Old Testament, one is stunned by how often the word *shalom* is used and how rich the nuances of that word are. *Shalom* is used a total of 397 times in the Hebrew Bible. Its Greek counterpart, *eirene,* is used 89 times in the Christian Bible (New Testament). Such heavy usage is a clear indication of how important a word it was—that it was a concept that permeated both Hebrew and early Christian society.

The second striking reality is the many ways shalom is translated into English. In order to capture the unique nuance of the Hebrew word as it is used in specific contexts, translators have had to use the following English words: *weal, welfare, completeness, to cause to be at peace, to make peace, peace offering, at rest, at ease, secure, safe, to finish well, to prosper, to be whole, to be perfect, to be victorious.* In other words, in any given context, shalom can mean any of the above English words.

The same is true to a lesser degree of the Greek equivalent of shalom, *eirene.* While not as rich a word as shalom, eirene still requires other English words besides *peace* to translate it, including *unity, concord,* and *to desire peace.*

What this comparison reveals to us is that shalom and eirene do not simply mean what the English word peace means. The English word is essentially a negative word—that is, the word peace is expressing the absence of something—war, conflict, violence, or confrontation. Therefore, *peace* exists in conflict's place. But the Hebrew word *shalom* goes far beyond that.

Shalom can be used simply as a greeting or a wish to a friend or loved one ("Shalom to you, my friend"). But at its fullest, shalom captures the Hebrew vision of human society, the non-human world, and even the environment in an integrated and relational whole where "the wolf and the lamb shall feed together and the lion shall eat straw like the ox" (Isaiah 65:25). Shalom is the theology of hope of Israel and of the early church, its vision of what the world some day will be.

Shalom for the Haves and the Have-Nots

Shalom can best be understood as being presented in Scripture for two distinct groups of Israelites—those who are in positions of power and influence (the haves) and those who have faced in the past or who are presently facing oppression and exploitation by those in power (the have-nots).[1]

The tradition of the have-nots begins with Moses and moves from him through Joshua, Samuel, and most of the prophets, and then culminates in the New Testament in the person of Jesus. This is a shalom for people who live in a precarious place, who are economically exploited, politically oppressed, or religiously controlled. Their shalom is understood in terms of their crying out in their pain and of being delivered—whether that deliverance is from slavery in Egypt, from precariousness in a new land, from the injustice of dominating and exploitive Jewish kings, from the persecution and humiliation of Babylonian exile, or from domination by Rome and the Jerusalem clerical aristocracy. That shalom is captured in such Scripture as: "The Israelites groaned under their slavery and cried out. Out of the slavery their cry for help rose up to God. God heard their groaning, and God took notice of them" (Exodus 2:23–25). Or consider this instance of shalom:

> When he (Bartimaeus, a blind beggar) heard that it was Jesus of
> Nazareth (walking past him), he began to shout out and say, "Son
> of David, have mercy on me!" . . . Then Jesus said to him, "What
> do you want me to do for you?" The blind man said to him, "My
> teacher, let me see again." Jesus said to him, "Go; your faith has
> made you well." Immediately he regained his sight and followed him
> on the way. (Mark 10:47, 51–52)

Such shalom is an action of liberation, of salvation, of setting free—whether such setting free is from political oppression and economic exploitation (Egyptian slavery), physical deformity (Bartimaeus' blindness), or was yet another domination. In all instances of shalom for the have-nots, the theme is one of being set free, of being liberated. It is therefore a tradition of liberation and salvation.

But there is a second, and equally valid, tradition in the Hebrew and Christian traditions. That is shalom for the haves. This tradition can be traced through Noah, Abraham, David, the wisdom literature, Isaiah, and the rabbis culminating in Paul (who was a former rabbi). This tradition is for people who are essentially secure and who are consequently concerned about the appropriate management of the resources God has placed at their disposal as well as celebrating the good things of life provided for them from a generous God. A clear example of this second shalom tradition is God's promise to King David:

> Thus says the LORD of hosts; I took you from the pasture, from
> following the sheep to be prince over my people Israel; and I have
> been with you wherever you went, and have cut off all your enemies
> from before you; and I will make for you a great name, like the name
> of the great ones of earth. . . . Moreover the LORD declares to you
> that the LORD will make you a house [dynasty]. When your days are
> fulfilled and you lie down with your ancestors, I will raise up your
> offspring after you. . . . Your house and your kingdom shall be made
> sure forever before me; your throne shall be established forever.
> (2 Samuel 7:8–9, 11–12, 16)

This is a shalom, not of a tyrannized people but of a secure people, not of a people living under oppression, but a people of well being. Therefore, it is a shalom, not of liberation, but of celebration and of the wise management of the resources God has invested in you (in this case, management of the kingdom God has invested in David). Thus, this shalom is carried out in the recognition that when a community is economically or politically well-off, that is an indication of God's blessings upon it. Therefore, with such a shalom, the community's task becomes the wise use of those resources (stewardship), which are an investment made in that community by God and thus are to be managed in such a way that justice and economic equality will result for everyone. People in this tradition do not want a disruptive act of liberation—"God's outstretched arm" freeing them, but rather the continuance of a social order that will continue to benefit them and those around them. They want security, not liberation.

Although shalom for the haves and have-nots are two separate traditions in the Scriptures, they are not mutually exclusive traditions. There is at least one author in the Old Testament and one person in the New Testament who combine both traditions into a single larger tradition.

The book of Deuteronomy integrates the two traditions into one new tradition. The writer of Deuteronomy begins from the liberationist position. What Israel's history was about, he insists, was God's saving of and then the building of a people who had begun as have-nots—as slaves in Egypt. But God, through his mighty acts and his "outstretched arm" had rescued them, had freed them from Pharaoh's tyranny and had honed them as a people in the wilderness. But for what purpose? So that they could gain possession of a homeland, Palestine, where they could build a people and shape a nation (Deuteronomy 26:1–10).

How was Israel to build its people into a nation? The people were to do that by understanding that all that they possessed had been given to them as a gift from God and that their chief task was to subdue that land and to then manage its resources so that God's intentions in freeing them from Egypt would be realized. Israel was to become a people who would live relationally with God and each other, practice justice politically, and share their wealth so that the poverty in their midst would be eliminated (Deuteronomy 7:7–14).

Thus, in the Old Testament, it is Deuteronomy that combines the two shalom traditions of liberation of the have-nots and the thankful stewardship of the haves into a new tradition, a tradition that applies to all Israelites—king and commoner alike—united in the building of God's kingdom on earth, the shalom community.

But it is in the New Testament that the shalom community reaches its apex—a worldwide kingdom of Gentiles and Jews, of all nations, races, and conditions of humans and of their societies and even their environment. That zenith of shalom is brought about by Jesus of Nazareth.

It is clear that Jesus' main emphasis was on shalom or "Jubilee"[2]—on the liberation of both the poor (the peasants of Israel) and the poor in spirit (the rabbis and land-owners of Israel who had been seduced by the systems and yet were pure in heart). But it is also clear that Jesus placed a heavy emphasis on awakening the rich and powerful to the responsibility of their position. He saw them as being blessed in order to be a blessing, with the responsibility not to be protective of their wealth and power but to be primarily concerned with reclaiming for Israel the vision of society as God intended it to be—relational, just, and equitable. That reclamation was to occur both by the political and economic policies they should pursue and in the personal exercise of their wealth and power. This was what his confrontations of the rich young ruler (Luke 18:18–25), the tax collector Zacchaeus (Luke 19:1–10) and the Pharisees (Matt. 23:1–36) were all about. It wasn't so much that they were more evil than the peasants or even his disciples. It was that, because of their power, prestige, and money, they had so much potential for good—and they were squandering that advantage by building a society that would maintain themselves and their compatriots in power, wealth, and control.

The biblical message on shalom is that it is for both the haves and the have-nots. It is both for those who lack power and are in need of liberation and for those who hold power and seek to appropriately manage the resources God has placed at their disposal. Both kinds of people are in every church. One of the essential tasks of the church is to bring together through Christ those searching for liberation or salvation and those who are the mangers of society and seek security, so that they might work together to build a shalom that is truly just and equitable for all, that brings people into an ever-deepening relationship with God and each other, and consequently contributes to the formation of society as God intended it to be lived.

A Shalom of Public Justice

What the Bible is essentially about when it is dealing with shalom and eirene is public justice, not private morality. Although it is concerned about morality, it is far more concerned with public life, and especially how the political, economic, and religious powers seek or deny justice and economic equity and how the people avoid or unite in engagement in public life

In this section, we will examine some of the most pivotal examples of the use or abuse of shalom and eirene in the public life of Israel and the Roman Empire, and we will demonstrate that the emphasis is on public justice, not private morality.

Shalom as the Foundation of the Peaceable Kingdom: The family of Jacob (also named Israel) moved to Egypt to escape a famine. Over the course of that family's four hundred-year sojourn in Egypt, the pharaohs increasingly viewed the Israelites as a threat. Therefore, they enslaved the Israelites and used them as slave labor to build the treasure cities of the Egyptian Empire. "God looked upon the Israelites, and God took notice of them" (Exodus 2:25). God selected Moses to confront Pharaoh, gain the release of the Israelites, and then lead them to liberation and freedom. God made a promise to Israel while they were encamped in the Sinai Desert, heading toward the land promised to Abraham and thus to them.

> If you follow my statutes and keep my commandments and observe
> them faithfully, I will give you your rains in their season, and the
> land shall yield its produce, and the trees of the field shall yield their
> fruit. . . . And I will grant [*shalom*] in the land, and you shall lie
> down, and no one shall make you afraid; . . . I will walk among you,
> and will be your God, and you shall be my people. I am the Lord
> your God who brought you out of the land of Egypt, to be their slaves
> no more; I have broken the bars of your yoke and made you walk
> erect. (Leviticus 26:3–4, 6, 12–13)

This passage captures magnificently the priorities that God would have for the Israelites. Their culture is to be a relational culture—and that is to be most evident in their relationship with God. God will live in their midst as their great king. He will walk among them. He will be their God; they will be God's people. He freed them from Egypt, liberated them from slavery, and enabled them to stand unbowed with the weight of the burdens Egypt heaped upon their backs.

As a society in relationship with God, if Israel will be faithful to him, then God promises them fertility of the land (Leviticus 26:4–5, 10), security (26:6), triumph over their enemies (26:7–8), and prosperity (26:9–10).

It is verse six that captures the very essence of God's promise to Israel, fulfilled if they remain faithful to him. "And I will grant [*shalom*] in your land, and you shall lie down, and no one shall make you afraid." If they live out the practice of justice in their public life, God will give them the assurance of shalom.

This is God's peaceable kingdom, promised to any nation or society that centers its public life on relationship with God and relationship with each other.

The Shalom Community and Judah's Decline: The profound prophecy of God's intentions for Israel were declared and written by the prophet Isaiah in the final centuries of Judah's independent existence as a nation.

> [When] a spirit from on high is poured out on us,
> and the wilderness becomes a fruitful field,
> and the fruitful field is deemed a forest.
> Then justice will dwell in the wilderness,
> and righteousness abide in the fruitful field. (Isaiah 32:15–16)

In this passage, the prophet describes the world and human society as God intends it to be when God's Spirit is poured out upon humanity. It presents a vision of a fruitful and abundant earth filled with a people living in peace and in the security of doing the will of God.

What is particularly significant about this passage is not that it suggests economic reform and social legislation will bring in this new society. It is that a profound moral and spiritual transformation will occur through God's Spirit being poured out on them, which activates a political, social, and economic transformation. God's new act of grace will enable humanity to meet God's moral demands for society.

When God's Spirit comes upon humanity, . . .

> Then justice will dwell in the wilderness,
> and righteousness abide in the fruitful field.
> The effect of righteousness will be [*shalom*]
> and the result of righteousness, quietness and trust forever.
> (Isaiah 32:16–17)

The social responsibility of Israelite society, as presented in this passage, is described as justice and righteousness. It is important to comprehend the Hebrew understanding of these two words, rather than the English meaning of them. Righteousness, in its English usage, is defined as "acting in accord with divine or moral law; free from guilt or sin" or "morally right or justifiable."[3] Therefore, righteousness means, in English, private or moral behavior.

But that is not what righteousness means in the Hebrew language. Rather the same Hebrew word is used *(tsedeq)* for both righteousness and justice.[4] It is the arbitrary decision of the translator that determines whether *tsedeq* should be translated *justice* or *righteousness* in any given passage. The word, therefore, has much more of a meaning of compensatory equality, public justice, clemency, and compassion about it than does our English equivalent.[5] When *tsedeq* is used in tandem as it is in Isaiah 32:16 ("Then justice will dwell in the wilderness, and righteousness abide in the fruitful field"), it is to intentionally give us the nuance of the word so that its first usage is implying its legal usage (i.e., compensatory equality) and the second, its ethical usage (i.e., compassionate mercy toward the poor and the victims of the misuse of power). But with either usage, shalom is being equated with public justice and not private morality.

Jesus and Shalom: It is important, when reading in the four gospels, to keep in mind that Jesus did not speak Greek. Although the entirety of the New Testament is written in Greek, Jesus spoke the language of the ordinary people of Israel—Aramaic. Thus, whereas the four gospels use the Greek word *eirene* for shalom, the word Jesus actually used was *shelam.* Shelam meant exactly what shalom meant. Therefore, in order to capture the power of what Jesus was actually saying, I will use the word *shalom* rather than *peace* in the passage we will be examining together.

Jesus used the word shelam repeatedly, and almost always in conjunction with the phrase, "the kingdom of God" or "kingdom of heaven." We will examine just two such usages. The first is Luke 10:1–12.

Jesus has begun his final journey to Jerusalem. He sends out seventy followers in pairs as advance teams to prepare for his coming through Galilean towns (Luke 10:1). He instructs the seventy in the work they are to do preparing for his arrival. What is of particular interest to us, however, is the emphasis he makes upon their giving or withholding of shalom to the households and villages they enter, and the connection he makes between this shalom and the advance of the kingdom of God.

The seventy are instructed to stay in only one home for the duration of their work in each town (Luke 10:4). When they enter that house, they are to place the blessing of shalom upon it and its occupants. If there are those in that house who have committed themselves to living in shalom (that is, follow Jesus), then that blessing of shalom will rest upon them. If there is no one in the house who follows the Jesus shalom, then the blessing will be retracted and returned to the one who blessed. Whether the people of the house or of the village receive or reject Jesus' gospel, the fact is "the kingdom of God has come near to you" (Luke 10:9).

One could interpret Luke 10:5, "Whatever house you enter, first say, '[Shalom] to this house!'" simply as a wish that one person gives to another person—comparable to our "Have a good day!" But Luke 10:6 takes it much further than that. It states, "And if anyone is there who shares in [shalom], your [shalom] will rest on that person; but if not, it will return to you." Here, Jesus sees shalom as an entity that can be transmitted from one person to another, received and possessed by the other or rejected and returned to the sender. It is a gift of God that is distributed by people appointed by Jesus to distribute it. It is a tangible essence, not simply a fond wish.

And what is that shalom that can be transmitted to people, to a house or to a town? It is the embracing, on the part of people and their community, of society as God intended it to be—a Godly society of justice, equitable distribution of wealth, elimination of poverty, and of intimate and committed relationship to God and each other. It is that entity that can be transmitted to people by Jesus and by Jesus' followers. It is the "kingdom of God." Therefore, when that entity entered a village through the two who had been sent by Jesus, the kingdom of God had come near. It was in their very midst. And the people of that household or town decided whether to receive that entity or to reject it. But either way the shalom, the kingdom of God, "has come near."

Paul and Shalom: The New Testament writers substitute the Greek word *eirene* for the Hebrew word *shalom.* Like the English word *peace*, the Greek *eirene* is a primarily negative word, simply meaning an absence of war or conflict. But the surprising thing the writers of the New Testament did was to fill the Greek word with the Hebrew meaning of shalom, so that *eirene* also came to mean God's intentions for humanity, the ideal state of life. Thus, the authors of the New Testament redefined the word *eirene*, and for all time changed its meaning.[6] Paul was among the writers and Christian leaders to do this.

Like Jesus, Paul often used the word *shalom* to connote God's intentions for humanity (except that Paul spoke Greek as his primary language on his mission journeys and therefore would have used the Greek *eirene* rather than the Aramaic *shelam*.) Let's examine one use of that word.

In Paul's letter to the Church in Rome, the apostle is concerned about issues that had the potential to tear the church apart. Chief among those issues was the eating of meat offered to idols.

In the Roman Empire, temple worship and the food industry were closely linked, especially the meat offered to idols. Thousands of cattle, sheep, pigs, and poultry were sacrificed each day in temples to various gods. Usually only the blood of the slain animal was sprinkled on the altar and sometimes choice pieces of meat were taken by the priests. But what would happen to the remainder? It would be sold to butchers, who would then sell it in turn to customers. Because only spotless animals would be sacrificed to the gods, meat that was labeled as offered to the gods was premium meat—the most prized for purchase from the local butcher.

The controversy that arose in the church was whether it was appropriate for Christians to eat meat offered to idols. Would not eating such meat indicate tacit approval of Greek and Roman gods? Would it not endorse this trade in sacrificed meat? Would eating such meat compromise one's faith and/or one's witness—especially to pagans? What should the church do? What would Paul advise?

In Romans 14:13–20, Paul deals with this issue, but not by choosing one side over the other. Instead, he draws the Roman Christians' attention to the primary emphasis of the gospel: "The kingdom of God is righteousness and peace and joy in the Holy Spirit" (Romans 14:16). That is, Christianity is essentially about compassionate and just behavior toward the poor ("righteousness" or *tsedeq*), working for God's intentions for society ("peace" or *shalom*), and a vital, dynamic and spontaneous relationship with God ("joy in the Holy Spirit"). It is "not food and drink."

Therefore, what should be of primary importance to you as a Christian is the spiritual formation of your brother or sister in Christ. Therefore, if the relationship of your Christian brother or sister and Christ and his church is hurt because you eat meat offered to idols—don't eat it. It is not a question of who's right or wrong. It is a question of whether your actions "makes your brother or sister stumble" (Romans 14:22). If it does, don't do it. That is how to live out the kingdom life, to practice shalom in the kingdom of God.

The Primary Indicators of Shalom In Society

There are three primary indicators that God's intentions for a community, a city, or a nation are actually being carried out. These three indicators of shalom occur in the economic, political, and social/spiritual systems of a community. "A system is an organized body of people gathered around three components: *values* that are held in common, *structures* that institutionalize those values, and *individuals* who manage and operate those institutions."[7] Since shalom has to do more with public justice than private morality, what does God intend for the political, economic, and social/spiritual systems that society is built on? How does God want a political system, an economic system or a social/spiritual system to operate? Intriguingly, the Scripture is both universal and specific in its answer.

The Social/Spiritual Indicators of Shalom: What should be the focus of the systems that shape the spirituality and social dimensions (education, health care, childcare, etc.) of a shalom society? What are God's intentions for the religion of a community, a city, a nation? The Scripture is full of a common response to these questions. But it is beautifully encapsulated in one of the best-known prayers found in the Bible.

> The Lord bless you and keep you;
> the Lord make his face to shine upon you,

And be gracious to you;
the Lord lift up his countenance upon you,
And give you [shalom]. (Numbers 6:24–26)

When one first reads this prayer, one immediately concludes that it is an individual prayer—that I am to be blessed and kept. But the context makes it clear that this is a prayer for all of Israel. It begins with an instruction to Aaron and his sons to bless all Israel (Numbers 6:22–23), and concludes with the words, "So they shall put my name on the Israelites, and I will bless them" (6:27). This is a prayer for a nation, not its individuals.

In essence, what this prayer communicates is that the indicator of a "right religion" in a society is whether it brings people and the society itself into an active, dynamic relationship with God. God wants to bless, keep, and be present and gracious to the people, so that God's shalom comes upon them. God's primary intention is that humanity be in an ongoing relationship with God. What God wants is a relational society built around his love relationship with us.

The same thing is stated in the New Testament. What more powerful testimony can there be of a relational Christianity than Paul's moving witness to what God did to him? He wrote to the Philippians, "I want to know Christ and the power of his resurrection and the sharing of his sufferings by becoming like him in his death, if somehow I may attain the resurrection from the dead" (Philippians 3:10).

"I want to know Christ"—that is, to be in the most intimate relationship with Christ. That was Paul's wish. And that is God's wish for all humankind.

So how do we know that a community is truly living in shalom? The primary indicator is whether or not the people exhibit a dynamic, personal relationship with God that is manifested in their relationships with each other.

Political Indicators of Shalom: Perhaps the most pithy statement of God's political expectations for his people is presented in Micah 6:8.

He has told you, O mortal, what is good;
and what does the Lord require of you
but to do justice,
and to love kindness,
and to walk humbly with your God?

What is not immediately self-evident from the English translation of this famed passage is its intriguing parallel construction. It actually says "and what does the Lord require of you but to do *mishpat* (justice), and to do *chesedh*, and to walk humbly with your God." The NRSV has attempted to capture that parallelism, but in doing so has sacrificed the depth of the word *chesedh*, reducing it to "love kindness" (in one sense the old KJV was closer to the original sense by translating it "mercy").

Mishpat (justice) we understand. But what is *chesedh*? There is no single English word that is the equivalent of the Hebrew word *chesedh*. Therefore, it can only be translated by using several English words in tandem that are closest to the Hebrew. Consequently, the English words most often used to approximate *chesedh* are "steadfast love" or "loving kindness." *Chesedh* is normally used in Scripture to refer to God's love for us. It is God's redeeming love, unconditional love, totally embracing love that is directed toward us and is against all logic and even against all dignity.

What is being laid out in this magnificent summary of the Hebrew Bible is that the political task is twofold. Whether it is the ordering of a family, a church or synagogue, a neighborhood, a city or a nation, God intends that the primary political task is both to do *mishpat* and to do *chesedh* within the context of "walking humbly" with God. All that God wants out of people and their systems is three things: to do justice, to do *chesedh,* and to be in relationship with God. That's all he wants—no sacrifices, no liturgies, no rituals, no slavish practices, no observances. All God wants is a relational people, relational systems, a relational culture.

But consider the parallel between "justice" and *chesedh*. *Chesedh* is the Hebrew word to describe God's love for us, his people. It is very comparable (but not identical) to the New Testament understanding of "grace." But what Micah is doing in this passage is quite extraordinary—because what he is doing is taking the way God loves his people and turning that around so it becomes the kind of love with which we are to love one another *in public life.*

In other words, what Micah is saying is neither justice nor love alone is adequate for building the public life of a Godly society. Both are needed because both must work in tandem. Justice without love will become a harsh demand, a society that might be eminently fair but would have no compassion in its decisions about its public life. Graceful love without justice would create a mushy society, a society that would keep on forgiving and caring but would not call for accountability nor require expectations from the people. Justice without love would be arbitrary and soulless. Love without justice would be gutless and without demand or expectation. What Micah is saying is that it requires both justice and grace-filled love working in concert with each other in order to create a truly relational culture. And it is the humble relationship with God that would keep such public life from becoming humanistic and secularist, but would center all of that society's justice and love in what ought to be the ground of its existence—God.

The political task is presented even more profoundly by Paul in his letter to the church in Colossae:

> [Christ] is the image of the invisible God, the firstborn of all creation; for in him all things in heaven and on earth were created, things visible and invisible, whether thrones or dominions or rulers or powers—all things have been created through him and for him. He himself is before all things, and in him all things hold together. . . . For in him all the fullness of God was pleased to dwell, and through him God was pleased to reconcile to himself all things, whether on earth or in heaven, by making peace through the blood of his cross. (Colossians 1:15–20)

On the face of it, this seems to be a theological statement about the importance of Jesus Christ. But in reality, it is a very political statement.[8] What Paul is arguing is the supremacy of Jesus Christ. He is the *arche* of reality, the very first principle or essence of life (in the words of the Nicene Creed, "God from God, Light from Light, true God from true God, begotten, not made"). As the *arche*, Paul is teaching here, Jesus is the creator of all things. And his creative work has included "all things in heaven and on earth, things visible and invisible, whether thrones or dominions or rulers or powers."

That formula of "thrones, dominions, rulers, and powers" is political language. Since Jesus is the *arche* and has created all things on earth, he has therefore created all earthly thrones (the seat of a government), dominions (the territory of a government), rulers (the individuals who run each government) and "powers" (the vehicles of a government by which it enforces its will). Thus, Paul is developing the argument that Jesus is the creator of the Roman Empire and the Israelite nation, they are accountable to him, and he has determined their task of working for justice and mercy as an integral part of molding life into God's intentions for it. Therefore, Jesus is the true Caesar, is head over the state, and is working "to reconcile to himself all things, whether on earth (political entities) or in heaven (angelical/demonic entities), by making peace through the blood of his cross."

Christ's death, therefore, is the act by God that will bring about a reconciliation of all governments and states into one holy kingdom of God—the shalom community. And the work of the church is to be engaged in public life as Christ's reconciling body, seeking by its intervention to bring about the conversion of the

Caesars of this world to Christ (Colossians 1:24–29; 2:8–15; Ephesians 1:15–22; 2:11–22; 3:7–13).

The political message throughout Scripture, therefore, is not only that politics and religion *do* mix. They *must* mix if society is ever to experience itself as the shalom community. The indicator that the political arena of a society is following God's intentions for it is that it is acting justly and mercifully. The church, as a mediating institution in society, is to be about the task of seeking to pressure its society's political institutions to be truly just in their management of public life while being particularly compassionate toward those who could become power-less. In this way, the church contributes toward bringing each throne, dominion, ruler, and power under the lordship of Christ and fulfilling that role that God intends it to fill.

Economic Indicators of Shalom: A nation and culture built on relationship with God and a politics of justice for all in the nation must inevitably deal with how wealth is generated and distributed.[9] It is in the book of Deuteronomy that the clearest economic indicators are given for a nation that truly desires to live under God.

> When the Lord your God has brought you into the land that he swore
> to your ancestors, to Abraham, to Isaac, and to Jacob, to give you—a
> land with fine, large cities that you did not build, houses filled with
> all sorts of goods that you did not fill, hewn cisterns that you did
> not hew, vineyards and olive groves that you did not plant—and
> when you have eaten your fill, take care that you do not forget the
> Lord, who brought you out of the land of Egypt, out of the house of
> slavery. (Deuteronomy 6:10–12)

Deuteronomy reminds the Israelites that Palestine existed, with all its wealth and power, before they were born and before they entered the land (Deuteronomy 6:10). He reminds them that it was God who took them out of Egypt "with a strong hand and a mighty arm," it was God who rescued them from slavery, it was God who protected them in the desert for forty years and there molded them into a mighty nation, and it was God who brought them into the Promised Land and gave them all of its wealth. "[You live, Israel, in] fine large cities *that you did not build,* houses . . . *that you did not fill,* hewn cisterns *that you did not hew,* vineyards and olive groves *that you did not plant"* (Deuteronomy 6:10–11, emphasis mine).

In other words, Deuteronomy is reminding Israel that all that they possess as a nation and as individuals is a gift from God. The wealth the nation possesses is a free gift from God, a wealth that God has chosen to invest in them, a result of

God's own *chesedh* toward Israel. What, then, does God expect of Israel? God expects that they will use this wealth they have been given by God for the benefit of all the people (Deuteronomy 6–8). Because their wealth is a gift from God, they are to perceive it not as a private wealth to be used by them as they choose, but as a *common wealth* that God has invested in them so they can be good trustees or stewards of it. The nation must keep before them the recognition that all that they have is a gift. Since it belongs to God and is only temporarily invested in God's people, they are to use it for the common good by being wise trustees of it.

Toward what end are they to manage this wealth? Here Deuteronomy presents its most radical insight—as radical for its time as it is for ours.

> "There will, however, be no one in need among you, because the
> Lord is sure to bless you in the land that the Lord your God is
> giving you as a possession to occupy, if only you will obey the Lord
> your God by diligently observing this entire commandment that I
> command you today. . . . Since there will never cease to be some in
> need on the earth, I therefore command you, "Open your hand to the
> poor and needy neighbor in your land." (Deuteronomy 15:4–5, 11)

There is only one reason why wealth is given to a nation, Deuteronomy states. God makes a nation wealthy for the purpose of eliminating its poverty. *The elimination of poverty is to be the primary agenda both of the systems and of each individual Israelite.*

Deuteronomy 15 actually states three things about poverty. First, poverty is wrong and should be eliminated from God's nation (Deuteronomy 15:4). Second, no matter how hard you work to eliminate poverty, "there will never cease to be some in need on the earth" (15:11).[10] Finally, "I command you, 'Open your hand to the poor and needy neighbor in your land'" (15:11).

Deuteronomy is replete with instructions as to how the nation can guarantee that the economy is managed in such a way that poverty will be eliminated. One such way is to observe *the sabbatical year.* "Every seventh year you shall grant a remission of debts. And this is the manner of the remission: every creditor shall remit the claim that is held against a neighbor, not exacting it of a neighbor who is a member of the community, because the Lord's remission has been proclaimed" (Deuteronomy 15:1–2).

Every seven years, all debts of all Israelites were to be forgiven (Deuteronomy 15:1–11). Those who through misfortune or even poor management had sunk into poverty over that seven-year period would have all their debts forgiven.

That, in essence, brought about a transfer of wealth so that people formerly in debt could start all over again.

The sabbatical year also contained provisions regarding slavery (Deuteronomy 15:12–18). Deuteronomy commands that no slave could be held beyond six years except by his or her consent. On the sabbatical year, each slave was to be set free. Intriguingly, Deuteronomy is quite specific in stating that these regulations applied to female as well as male slaves.

The final regulation of the sabbatical year does not appear in Deuteronomy but in Exodus, and later became associated with the sabbatical year. The land was to lie fallow for one year so that it could renew itself (Exodus 23:10–11). With no fertilizers except animal dung to renew the earth, it had to "rest" in order to be able to continue to provide sufficient crops for the Israelites.

A significant refinement of the sabbatical year was the Jubilee—legislation that is presented in Leviticus 25. The Jubilee was the Sabbath of the sabbatical year. That is, it occurred on the 49th year (or the seventh sabbatical year). The observance of the Jubilee included the three sabbatical requirements: the land lay fallow, all debts were forgiven and all slaves were freed (Leviticus 25:11, 25–55). But Jubilee added a fourth stipulation that was the most remarkable social and economic legislation in the Bible.

Wealth in ancient Israel was held in the land one owned. Every Israelite tribe, clan, and family had been assigned a designated portion of land when Israel conquered Palestine under Joshua. That land was each family's birthright; it was to be the foundation upon which that family's financial existence would be built. But as the years went by, poor families would sell their birthright in order to eliminate their debt.

Jubilee was designed to put an end to this practice. It decreed that if a poor family had to sell its birthright, the new owner was required to return that family's birthright to them *at no charge* on the Jubilee (Leviticus 25:23–34). Thus, by this legislation, Israel had built into its society a means to periodically redistribute wealth. It was a radical reversal of fortune designed to keep wealth from steadily increasing in the hands of the wealthy few at the expense of the poor. No matter how much land the powerful could accumulate, they had to surrender all of it every 50 years and return it at no cost to its original owners.

Besides the sabbatical year and Jubilee, the Israelites had other laws designed to eliminate poverty through the redistribution of income. One such regulation was that all loans were to be made without charging interest (Deuteronomy 23:19–20).

Another regulation was three tithes of a family's annual income in which one tithe was to go the king and judiciary, a second tithe to the Levites and religious leaders, and a third tithe to the poor (Deuteronomy 14:22–29; 16:1–17). The tithe to the poor was to be given at the Festival of First Fruits (Deuteronomy 26:1–15), and was to be distributed directly to the poor themselves.

There are many other instructions within Deuteronomy regarding the responsibility of the rich and middle class toward the poor of the land. But these are some of the most surprising and intriguing requirements. We see demonstrated, in even this brief synopsis of Deuteronomy's economic policies, Israel's commitment to *compensatory economic justice*, for all the instructions are designed to bring to reality the assertion that "there will . . . be no poor among you!"

It is intriguing to note that the commitment to the sabbatical and to compensatory economic justice was not only a part of Israelite culture. It was also central to the life and mission of the early Christian church (Acts 4:32–35).

It has long been recognized that the early Christians were an intentional communitarian community. What is not equally recognized was that such a practice was not simply due to the level of commitment and trust they had in each other or even obedience to the teachings of Jesus (e.g., the Sermon on the Mount). They were a communitarian culture because that was the acting out of Jewish religious, political, and economic beliefs and actions about how the shalom community should live.

The premise of the earliest Christian church was that it was the "New Israel"—Israel as God had originally intended it to be. They had a new Moses (Jesus), a new law (the law of love as exemplified in the Sermon on the Mount), twelve founders of the nation (the twelve disciples rather than the twelve tribes). And as the new Israel, the Church was to carry out the Deuteronomic economic reforms that were designed to eliminate poverty. The Christians had become the practitioners of the sabbatical year.

But those Christians added a new twist to that year. Instead of practicing every seven years, they practiced it continuously. They created an economic system based upon the *value* of wealth as being a common wealth rather than private wealth ("everything they owned was held in common" Acts 4:32) in order to eliminate poverty ("there was not a needy person among them" Acts 4:34). They devised the *structure* of a continuing assembly or gathering of people (they all lived together). And they determined the *people* to provide the rule and leadership of the system (the apostles and, later, the deacons). Thus, they created a continuous community rather than a society that had to be "righted again" every seven years.

The other reality of the book of Acts is that nowhere in that book or in any of the letters of Paul or other apostles is it ever recorded that this community was disbanded during the apostolic era. We simply assume that it was disbanded because it is a style of corporate life so foreign to anything we can envision or tolerate. But Acts never records any deviation from this practice of holding goods in common, supporting one another economically as well as spiritually, or working to reduce or eliminate poverty. Obviously, adjustments were made as the gospel moved out into the Gentile world. But there is no recorded dismantling of the economic community the earliest Christians created in order to implement the economic policies of Israel to their existence as the church.

The Shalom Community: A Summary

One of the most concise and yet visionary descriptions of the world as God intended it to be is found in Isaiah 65:17–25. It is an intensely practical description. But it also magnificently captures the vision expressed throughout the warp-and-woof of the Hebrew and Christian Scriptures. In this passage, God is sharing with the reader God's vision for what life in God's earth ought to be like. It begins:

> I am about to create new heavens
> and a new earth;
> the former things shall not be remembered
> or come to mind.
> But be glad and rejoice forever
> in what I am creating;
> for I am about to create Jerusalem as a joy,
> and its people as a delight. (Isaiah 65:17–18)

Then begins a magnificent description of society as God intends it to be.

Characteristics of the Shalom Community: According to Isaiah 65, God's intentions for human society are as follows:

- Decent, safe, sanitary, secure, and affordable housing for everyone (65:21–22)

- Jobs that provide adequate income and bring meaning and focus to people's lives (65:21–22)

- Health care that adequately provides for all people, contributes to longevity, and ends infant mortality (65:20)

- Neighborhoods that are stable, safe, and mutually supportive (65:25)

- Environments that are healthy and are not dangerous to people's health and safety (65:20)

- Wealth relatively and equitably distributed, so that there are no great disparities in income, wealth, position, or status between people (65:21–23)

- People living in peace with one another (65:19, 25)

Now take a look at the entirety of this summary and please note that the shalom community is no *"pie in the sky by and by"!* God's intentions for our world are a very concrete, realistic, and perhaps even achievable vision. It was not created by God to be unreachable, but to provide for us clear indicators of what God intends human society to be. As the people of God, therefore, our responsibility is both to work for the achieving of such a dream while recognizing that it will not be reached in its totality until Christ returns to claim his kingdom. As a seminary professor of mine said to us more than fifty years ago, "Young men and women, the kingdom of God will come in God's good time and with God's good intervention. But we are to work for that kingdom as if its very coming depended upon us!" We will begin exploring in the fourth chapter how we can build a people of power to work toward the transformation of the world into the kingdom of our Lord.

THE WORLD AS IT ACTUALLY IS

But the shalom community is not the world we experience today. Far from it! In order to be effective in seeking the transformation of our community, city, or nation, we as children of God not only need to hold to a *vision* as big as the world itself. We must also have a frank and honest appraisal of the world, as it actually is—the *context* in which God calls us to do ministry.

They Did Not Know How to Blush!

The prophet Jeremiah wrote,

> For from the least to the greatest of them,
> everyone is greedy for unjust gain;
> and from prophet to priest,
> everyone deals falsely.
> They have treated the wound of my people carelessly,
> saying, "[Shalom, shalom],"
> when there is no [shalom].
> They acted shamefully, they committed abomination;

yet they were not ashamed,
they did not know how to blush[!] (Jeremiah 6:13–15)

Chapter six of Jeremiah foretells a great invasion of Judah that will crush the government, level Jerusalem, destroy the nation, and will bring Israel under total domination by Babylonia. Why would God so thoroughly annihilate his nation? Jeremiah tells us why.

"They did not know how to blush!" Judah's political, economic, and religious leaders have been acting in such a dominating and exploiting manner for so long that both they and the people of the nation have become so infected with greed and the lust to control that everyone has forgotten how to blush. That is, they have become so used to being greedy and lusting for power that neither national leader nor ordinary citizen are even aware any longer that they are doing wrong. Rejecting and disobeying God while covering it over with a veneer of liturgically-correct worship has become so commonplace that they don't even know how to be embarrassed any longer by their own actions.

Therefore, their leaders cry "*Shalom, shalom*"—when there is no *shalom*. Their religious leaders say, "All is well, all is secure, all is prosperous, all is at peace"—while the very foundations of their life as a nation and as a people have been rotted away with their own greed. So Jeremiah tells them, "The entire structure of your rotted-away nation is now about to collapse!" Their destruction is so very close at hand—and neither leaders nor people can see it.

Throughout its entirety, the Bible presents a profound analysis of what went wrong and what keeps going wrong in society that seems so often to thwart God's intentions for the world. We will look briefly at some samples of this analysis[11] in order to understand the forces that we will have to face in society (that will also try to seduce us) in our efforts to build a people who will seek the shalom community.

Economic Systems Gone Bad

To build the shalom community, God intends economic systems to perceive themselves as stewards of the wealth God has invested in them in order to eliminate poverty. But to what purpose did those in the economic systems of Israel actually give themselves that caused them to turn their back on God's vision and to go bad? Jeremiah tells us in no uncertain words: "From the least to the greatest, everyone is greedy for unjust gain. From prophet to priest, everyone deals falsely" (Jeremiah 8:10).

According to Jeremiah, the corruption of Israel begins with money. The collapse of the shalom community begins with the abuse of wealth—of acting out one's greed, and thus seeking wealth at the expense of others. Corruption begins to occur at the point of moving from a perception that one's economic task is to be a *steward* (trustee) of the *common* (or people's) wealth to seeing oneself as the *owner* of *private* wealth. When one sees his role as owner of wealth, one's natural inclination is both to accumulate as much wealth as possible and to be motivated out of greed. "Everyone is greedy for unjust gain." And particularly in a static economy[12] as was Israel's, one only accumulates more wealth by finding ways to deprive it from others. Thus, an economics of greed readily deteriorates into an economics of exploitation as one seeks to take advantage of those around him.

Jesus captured the same thought in his famous statement, "It is easier for a camel to go through the eye of a needle than for someone who is rich to enter the kingdom of God" (Mark 10:25). What prompted this statement was Jesus' encounter with the rich young man. In that encounter, the rich man asked, "What must I do to inherit eternal life?" Jesus gave the traditional Rabbinic answer to that question, but the man pressed him by saying, "Teacher, I have kept all these since my youth" (obviously implying that he didn't feel obeying the Law was sufficient). Jesus then replied, "You lack one thing; go, sell what you own, and give the money to the poor, and you will have treasure in heaven. Then come and follow me" (10:21). But when the rich man "heard this, he was shocked and went away grieving, for he had many possessions" (10:22).

What happened in this story was that the rich young man was willing to accept all sorts of religious disciplines and requirements in order to be right with God. But he wasn't willing to part with his money. He wasn't willing to follow the stipulations of the Torah regarding being a steward of that portion of God's wealth invested in him for the elimination of poverty. So he "went away grieving." It was not so much that he possessed great riches, as it was that his great riches possessed him.

Political Systems Gone Bad

To build the shalom community, God intends political systems to maintain a just order in society, with a primary purpose to resist tyranny and oppression. But to what purpose did the political systems of Israel and of the world actually give themselves that caused them to turn their back on God's vision and to go bad? In the same passage, Jeremiah reminds us with these words: "From prophet to priest everyone deals falsely."

Yielding repeatedly to economic greed that becomes exploitive of the poor and powerless inevitably affects public life. An unjust economics will lead to a politics of the unilateral use of power that will result in the oppression of the people. A perfect example of this is found in 1 Kings 21:1–24—the story of Naboth's vineyard.

This incident begins with the greed of King Ahab. He lusts after Naboth's vineyard. "Give me your vineyard, so that I may have it for a vegetable garden, because it is near my house," Ahab demands of Naboth (21:2). Naboth refuses because it is his birthright, his inheritance from his ancestors, and the inheritance of his children; he doesn't have the right to give it up. But this will not dissuade Ahab. He seeks to get it legally. And then when that fails, he obtains it illegally. Working through his wife Jezebel, Ahab has Naboth accused of a serious infraction of Hebrew law, and he is stoned to death by a mob (and without a trial) (21:8–14). Then Ahab simply takes possession of the vineyard (21:15–16)

This is a clear example of economic greed leading to political oppression. Ahab used the power at his disposal as king to engineer the situation and thus obtain the prize after which he lusted. But he did so at the cost of Naboth's life. Economic exploitation, driven by greed, inevitably leads to the abuse of political power resulting in the oppression of those so exploited.

This same abuse of power is presented by the author of the gospel of John in John 11:45–53. To thoroughly understand this passage from the gospel of John, one must recognize that the Jewish religious leaders were also the political and economic leaders of Israel, subject to the authority of Rome. It was their task to keep Judah and Galilee calm and stable under Rome. For that, they were amply rewarded, both economically and with political power.

Jesus posed a threat to them. His actions were stirring the people and were creating agitation. The result was the steadily eroding power of the priests and Pharisees. If this agitation continued, they could see that they would lose control of the situation, rebellion might occur, "and the Romans will come and destroy our nation" (and, incidentally, ourselves as well) (John 11:48). So the high priest, exercising his power, declared that Jesus must die and did so with what would become a famous statement, "It is better for one man to die for the people than to have the whole nation destroyed" (11:50). Thus, the next verse that follows this story states, "Jesus therefore no longer walked about openly among the Jews" (11:54).

In this case, it is the religious system (high and chief priests, Pharisees) that is also the functioning economic system of the nation conspiring together to placate the reigning political system (Rome) by arranging for Jesus to be killed. Economic exploitation and religious control lead to political oppression.

Religious Systems Gone Bad

To build the shalom community, God intends religious systems to draw humanity both to himself and to one another. The task of religion is to build the values of a society around the relationality of life. But to what purpose did those in the religious systems of Israel and of the world actually give themselves that caused them to turn their back on God's vision and to go bad? Once again, Jeremiah tells us.

> The word that came to Jeremiah from the Lord: Stand in the gate of
> the Lord's house, and proclaim there this word, and say, Hear the
> word of the Lord, all you people of Judah, you that enter these gates
> to worship the Lord. Thus says the Lord of hosts, the God of Israel:
> Amend your ways and your doings, and let me dwell with you in this
> place. Do not trust in these deceptive words: "This is the temple of
> the Lord, the temple of the Lord, the temple of the Lord."
> (Jeremiah 7:1–4)

This, of course, is the beginning of the famed Temple Speech of Jeremiah—perhaps the best known portion of his book of prophecies. Both the rulers and the people of Israel have adopted the exploitive and oppressive actions of the nations around them. Out of their steadily increasing greed and lust for power, they live as they so choose. They steal, murder, commit adultery, enter into illegal contracts in order to heighten their profit, and even worship other gods (7:9–10). Then they come to the Jerusalem temple with the words, "This is the temple of the Lord, the temple of the Lord" (7:4). By going through the rituals, sacrifices, and liturgies of temple worship, they think they assuage their guilt and keep God happy with them. But God is not amused. And so through Jeremiah he calls them to do three things: to repent of their sin, to give up their exploitive and oppressive activities, and begin to do justice (7:5–7). Will they respond? Will they convert? Will they once again embrace an authentic relationship with God and with each other, so that they become again the shalom community?

What is happening here is the end result of an economics of greed that leads to the exploitation of the poor and of a politics of power that leads to the oppression of the powerless. In order to build their respective powers, the political and economic systems will collude together to seduce the religious system to use the trust they have built with the people to control the people's responses. The objective of the political and economic systems is to get conformity (and even, hopefully, agreement) from the people. But to do that, they need the support of the system that shapes the values of the people and in whom the people most trust—the religious system. So the religious system uses its power of trust to gain control over the minds and hearts of the people, convincing them that participating in the greed of the economic systems and the unilateral power of the political system will lead to the enrichment of their lives, not their exploitation and oppression. Thus, it is the religious system that seduces the people.

So what will happen to Israel? In his temple sermon, Jeremiah shares the instructions he received from God. "As for you, Jeremiah, do not pray for this people, do not raise a cry or prayer on their behalf, and do not intercede with me, for I will not hear you. Do you not see what they are doing in the towns of Judah and in the streets of Jerusalem?" (7:16–17). What the people are doing is imitating the political leaders of the nation, the economic powers, the priests, and prophets of the religious establishment (7:18–19). The people are now following their leaders. They are embracing the lifestyle of greed, lust for power, and control so that they are joining in becoming the exploiters of the poor, the oppressors of the powerless, the controllers of society.

The end result of a people who have so rejected shalom for their lives and embraced the greed, power, and domination of their leaders and of the heathen nations is they must be destroyed by God. Thus God says to Jeremiah,

> The days are coming, says the Lord, when it will no more be called
> Topheth . . . but the valley of Slaughter; for they will bury in Topheth
> until there is no more room. The corpses of this people will be food
> for the birds of the air, and for the animals of the earth. . . . And I
> will bring to an end the sound of mirth and gladness, the voice of
> the bride and bridegroom in the cities of Judah and in the streets of
> Jerusalem; for the land shall become a waste. (Jeremiah 7:32–34)

And that is exactly what happened. The nation that abandoned its shalom community was abandoned by God. The nation that was built on the vision of a people in love with God and each other, and thereby building a politics of justice and an economics of equality had become the nation of economic exploitation, political oppression, and religious domination. And the people would not repent. So God's only choice was to destroy them and begin all over again with a remnant. And when that, too, failed then God chose only One who would build a new people of God that would seek to become a people of Godly power working for the transformation of the world.

We have now explored the vision of the world as God intended: the shalom community. We have examined the world as it actually is, ruled by systems that exploit, oppress, and control. But we also perceive ourselves as God's people, called to work for shalom in a hostile world. What are the biblical principles by which we can build such a people of power and work for shalom? That will be the subject of the remainder of this book.

SUMMARY

Christians have three responsibilities. First, we need to have a vision for the world as God intended it to be. Second, we need to have a realistic understanding of the world as it actually is. And third, we are to work in the world as it actually is in order to draw it toward becoming the world as God desires it to be. This chapter sought to explore the world as it should be and the world as it actually is.

The Hebrew word that best captures God's intentions for the world is the word *shalom*. *Shalom* is a rich word, variously translated into the English words "welfare, completeness, security, prosperity, to be whole, to be perfect, at rest" as well as "peace." At its fullest, *shalom* captures the Hebrew vision of human society, the non-human world, and even the environment as a relational whole.

There are three primary indicators that *shalom* is being practiced by the people. Those indicators are lived out in the religious, political, and economic systems of any society. The first indicator is that "right religion" is being practiced when its beliefs, values, and religious practices bring people and the society itself into an active, dynamic relationship with God.

The second indicator is whether the people and their political system are acting justly and mercifully. The church, as a mediating institution in society, is to be about the task of pressuring its society's political institutions to be truly just in their management of public life while being particularly compassionate toward those who could become powerless.

The final indicator is the elimination of poverty. Israel and the Church were to perceive their wealth as a gift from God, a common wealth God has invested in them so that they could be good trustees of it. The end for which they were to manage that wealth was the elimination of poverty for everyone in that society.

But the shalom community is not the world as we experience it today. The primary corruption of society begins with money. Whereas God calls a nation to be a steward of wealth in order to eliminate its people's poverty, spiritual collapse begins when it becomes greedy for wealth and therefore uses it to exploit the people. Second, yielding to economic greed that exploits the poor and powerless inevitably leads to the practice of a politics of unilateral power that results in the oppression of the people.

But the practice of an economics of exploitation and a politics of oppression are always in danger of generating rebellion on the part of the people. Therefore, the Bible tells us, the political and economic systems collude with the religious system to use the trust that the exercise of religion has built with the people to manage and control their responses. Thus, imitating their leaders, the people become the exploiters of each other, the oppressors of the powerless, the controllers of their societies. And *shalom* is rejected by the nation and its people.

QUESTIONS

1. What new insights came to you as the result of reading this chapter? What ideas gain a response from you that would cause you to want to act them out in your life? What ideas do you need to do a lot more thinking about before you act on them?

2. How would perceiving *shalom* as public justice rather than private morality inform your work for economic equity for the poor, justice for the powerless, and religion that is centered in right relationships rather than right doctrine?

3. How do you see your society acting oppressively, exploitively, and in domination toward its weakest, poorest, and most marginalized people?

Chapter Two

HOW JESUS BUILT A PEOPLE OF POWER:

A JOURNEY THROUGH THE FOUR GOSPELS

Who did the disciples believe Jesus was, and how did they see his words and actions as consistent with his vision of the kingdom of God and his claims about the unique role he saw himself playing in the inauguration of that kingdom?

One of the remarkable realities of Christianity through the ages has been our capacity to remake Jesus in our own image. This capacity to interpret Jesus in the light of the priorities of those who worshiped and proclaimed him began at the very origins of Christianity.

The amazing capacity of the disciples to remake Jesus in their image is one of the primary themes of the four gospel accounts. A most obvious example was Peter's confession of Jesus as Messiah and his almost immediate redefining of what *messiah* meant. When Jesus asked the disciple band, "Who do you say that I am?" Peter responds, "You are the Messiah, the Son of the living God" (Matthew 16:15–16). Jesus commends Peter for his spiritual discernment: "Blessed are you, Simon son of Jonah! For flesh and blood has not revealed this to you, but my Father in heaven" (Matthew 16:17).

This amazing story of discernment is immediately followed by a story of Peter's spiritual obtuseness. Matthew tells us,

> From that time on, Jesus began to show his disciples that he must go
> to Jerusalem and undergo great suffering at the hands of the elders
> and chief priests and scribes, and be killed, and on the third day be
> raised. And Peter took him aside and began to rebuke him, saying,
> "God forbid it, Lord! This must never happen to you." But Jesus
> turned and said to Peter, "Get behind me, Satan! You are a stumbling

block to me; for you are setting your mind not on divine things but on human things." (Matthew 16:21–23)

Poor Peter—from being called "blessed" to being named a "Satan" in just a few minutes. But there is a reason for Jesus' violent response. Peter's rebuke of Jesus' prediction that he would be crucified was not simply motivated by Peter's love for Jesus or his desire to save his friend suffering. It was based upon Peter's incredulity that any such thing could happen to the Messiah. Peter accepted the popular Jewish notion of his day—that Messiah was to be a conquering hero of Rome who would create a new Jewish empire that would far surpass that of King David. He had no concept of Messiah as being a suffering servant. Therefore, he could only react incredulously to Jesus' prediction. Because of his lack of biblical discernment and his unreflective embrace of contemporary Hebrew belief, Peter was guilty of seeking to remake Jesus in his own image.

This tendency was not peculiar to Peter or to the disciples of the first Christian century. It has been the bane both of biblical scholarship and of popular Christianity ever since. Thus, in a medieval age fixated on suffering, death, and the struggle of life, religious art invariably portrayed the adult Christ as the suffering, nail-pierced savior or the child Jesus as an infant playing on Mary's lap. Thus the church concentrated almost exclusively upon either the birth or crucifixion of Christ while ignoring his life, ministry, or even his resurrection.

Likewise, early twentieth century Christianity was often naïve in its belief that the world was getting better and better through the influence of a loving, gentle Christ that was more Anglo than Hebrew. Thus, Ralph W. Sockman, a famous preacher of the early years of that century and pastor of the Madison Avenue Methodist Church of New York City, rhapsodized on a painting of a blue-eyed, blond, light-skinned Christ by H. Stanley Todd,

> One day recently . . . I entered a darkened room where, in solitary
> impressiveness hung Colonel Todd's picture of the Galilean Christ.
> The figure so arrestingly modern, with its light hair and blue eyes
> transported me into another world . . . a world of noisy men made
> quiet, a world of worried men made calm, of sinful men made pure,
> of hopeless men made confident. And when I came out again into the
> confusion of the New York streets it was not quite the same as when
> I entered.[1]

How, then, can we gain a relatively accurate understanding of who Jesus perceived himself to be and what he understood as his essential mission? And how can we understand those who wrote about him within decades of his death as they discerned Jesus' person, message, and mission for their respective worlds? There are two means at our disposal that can help us understand Jesus in the context of his times. And both, combined together, provide a firm grounding to better understand what Jesus was all about.

The Conceptual Framework of Israel

One way to perceive Jesus' mission and intent is to understand the beliefs, convictions, and priorities of the Jewish people at the time when Jesus and his disciples were alive. As we explored in the first chapter of this book, Israel had at least a twelve hundred year commitment to a vision of the world as God intended it to be—a corporate society in which humanity (or at least the Jews) were centered on God and each other in a relational culture, practicing a politics of compensatory justice, and working to rid the nation of poverty through equitably distributed wealth. To understand that this was the conceptual framework out of which Jesus and his followers came—what Jesus called "the kingdom of God"— and consequently to read the gospel narratives out of that perception, brings a rich understanding to Jesus' mission and intent.

There is a second means that can be used to better understand the intentions of Jesus and his followers. That is to understand the context of Jesus' time.

The Context of First Century Israel

The overwhelming reality of first century Israel was that it was under the political and economic dominance of Rome. The reality of the Roman Empire dominated every conversation, every decision, and every action taken by Jewish priest and peasant alike. Rome was the most powerful empire that had existed to that point, and it bestrode the world like a giant colossus. It provided the framework of law and governance to the Mediterranean world. Its "Pax Romana" enforced by its military presence guaranteed a thousand-year peace. Its roads knit the empire together and upon those roads and seaways moved the economy of the world. The Roman presence dominated the Mediterranean world—including Israel.

But the Roman Empire was not a monolithic dictatorship. Rome essentially governed around the principle of subsidiary—that is, that decisions need to be made at the lowest possible level. Whenever possible, Rome governed through devolving authority to the local, even non-Roman leadership—whether it was a puppet king, priests, or locally selected leadership. Thus, what was formerly the state of Israel had been divided by Rome into three basic political entities: Galilee, Trans-Jordan, and Judea (which included Israel's capital city, Jerusalem).

Galilee was ruled by King Herod Agrippa, a descendant of King Herod the Great (the Idumean monarch of former Israel). Trans-Jordan was ruled by Philip, also a descendant of Herod but only holding the rank of tetrarch (a subordinate prince). Judea was ruled by a rather uncomfortable combination of a Roman procurator appointed by the Roman governor of Syria, the High Priest of Israel (who was also a Roman appointee), and the Sanhedrin (a legislative body of Jewish priests, Pharisees, and Sadducees).

To understand Jesus, one must realize that the Jewish religious system was not primarily a religious institution. It was an *apparently* religious body granted by Rome the responsibility to govern the nation. That religious community was to share that responsibility in Judea with the Roman procurator, and in Galilee with the Herodian nobility. But their primary role was to be the on-the-ground political operatives of Israel, controlling the legislative and judicial systems of Israel, maintaining peace among the people, and administering justice. And they were to exercise this control through the religious vehicles of synagogue, the temple, and the Mosaic Law. We cannot appreciate what was occurring in Jesus' continuing opposition to the Pharisees, Sadducees, and the Jerusalem Clerical Aristocracy without understanding this fact.

Further, we must understand that these "religious" leaders, along with the Herodian nobility and the land-owners, controlled the vast percentage of the wealth of the nation. These native-born leaders of the people made up only 2 percent of the population, but they owned around 60 percent to 70 percent of the wealth. Between 83 and 93 percent of the people were peasants (according to whether economic times were good or bad), made up primarily of farmers (like Peter and Andrew, who were "farmers of the sea") and artisans (like Jesus, a carpenter). They perennially lived on the edge of economic disaster. Farmers, for example, didn't own the land they farmed but rented it from landowners (the farmers lived in nearby towns, not on the land). Typically, 50 percent of their harvest would be paid to the landowner, 25 percent would be paid in taxes to the Herodian nobility and to Rome, 10 percent went to the Jewish authorities in Jerusalem, and 3 percent would go to their village. Thus, the typical Israelite farmer realized only about 12 percent of his harvest as his family's annual income *and* the monies to purchase next year's seed.

Every peasant family lived in fear that one day they would slip over the edge into economic disaster and become one of the "expendables." The expendables of Israelite society included the beggars, the excess children of peasant farmers, the widows and orphans, the unclean, and the shepherds. The ranks of the expendables would be made up of from 5 percent of the population (if times were good) to 15 percent (if times were bad). To have fallen into the expendable class meant that you were without predictable income, were dependent upon the generosity of the peasants (or, rarely, the elite), and were facing almost certain starvation and death. Most of the people Jesus healed were the expendables.[2]

The vehicle the Jewish leaders used to control the populace and to maintain this grossly unbalanced economic and political structure was their interpretation of the Mosaic Law. The Pharisees taught the Law to the people, the scribes adjudicated and interpreted the Law, the temple priests conducted public life and the affairs of both the temple and the state under the guidelines of the Law, and the nobility, landowners, and the religious establishment all benefited from the Law.

But the Law they taught and obeyed was considerably adjusted from the full Law. That is, they interpreted the Law to require obedience on the people's part in such ways that it would not jeopardize the aristocracy's maintenance of themselves in power and wealth. Thus, for example, they taught the importance of each Israelite to keep jubilee. But whereas the Law presented four stipulations of jubilee (the land is to lie fallow; all debts are to be cancelled; all Hebrew slaves are to be set free; all land is to be returned to the ancestral owner's family—Leviticus 25:8–55), Israel's religious leaders taught that maintaining jubilee was solely to allow the land to lie fallow (which would hurt only the peasants, shoving many into the expendable class). No wonder Jesus called them "hypocrites," "blind guides," and "brood of vipers" (Matthew 23).

If we understand both the conceptual framework of the shalom community and the context in which Jesus and the gospel writers lived with the mammoth power of the state, the political and economic roles of Israel's priesthood, and the crushing poverty of 98 percent of the people, then we can understand what Jesus was about. He was about building a people of power.

THE JUBILEE JESUS

There is only one place in the narratives of the four gospels where Jesus tells us clearly what he perceived as his essential mission:

> The Spirit of the Lord is upon me,
>> because he has anointed me to bring good news to the poor.
> He has sent me to proclaim release to the captives
>> and recovery of sight to the blind,
>> to let the oppressed go free,
> to proclaim the year of the Lord's favor. (Luke 4:18–19)

Jesus combined Isaiah 61:1–2 and 58:6 in this Sabbath reading of Scripture in his synagogue to announce Jubilee. Both Scriptures were recognized by all Jewry as jubilee passages. Jesus is doing something more here than simply proclaiming that he is going to preach good news to the poor, free captives, and heal the blind. He is declaring that his arrival is signaling the coming of jubilee upon Israel. The jubilee he is calling Israel to keep is the entire jubilee, and not just one regulation of it.

In the previous chapter, we looked at the jubilee legislation of Leviticus and the sabbatical year legislation of Deuteronomy as legislation intentionally created to redistribute wealth. In reality, jubilee is a legislated reversal of fortune in which society is economically rebalanced so that wealth can't accumulate nor power accrue in the hands of a self-selected few (in Jesus' context—the Herodian nobility, land-owners, and clergy aristocracy). With this announcement, Jesus is placing Israel's leadership on notice that his coming is God's action to reverse Israelite society so that wealth and power cannot be built up in their hands while all the rest are thrust ever deeper into poverty. Messiah is here to bring in the jubilee.

The gospel of Luke is a gospel about jubilee. There are many such examples. Consider these few:

The Lukan Christmas story, so beloved by children and adults alike, is actually a story of jubilee declaration. Consider these elements of the story, particularly when contrasted with Matthew (who had an entirely different purpose in his telling of that story, as we will develop later in this chapter).

The Christmas story begins with the angel Gabriel being sent to Nazareth to tell a teenage virgin that she is about to become pregnant without having sexual intercourse with a man—and that her baby "will be called the Son of the Most High, and the Lord God will give to him the throne of his ancestor David" (Luke 1:32).

This story is filled with astounding themes of liberation. First, the angel speaks to a woman about this most awesome event—not to a man. In Matthew, conversely, Mary is not even consulted; the angel speaks with Joseph, her fiancé. Further, she is not even a mature woman, but a mere girl, just entering adolescence, and still a virgin. Finally, she is given the privilege and right to refuse the angel's proposal—that is the honor bestowed upon her. And in faith believing, she accepts it. "Here am I, the servant of the Lord; let it be with me according to your word" (Luke 1:38).

Mary sings a hymn of praise to God in her visit with her cousin Elizabeth, who is also experiencing a miracle pregnancy. We tend to read the Magnificat (Luke 1:46–55), concentrating on its opening lines because those lines center on God's graciousness in selecting Mary to be the mother of the Messiah. But note the last lines of the Magnificat:

> The Mighty One . . . has shown strength with his arm;
>> he has scattered the proud in the thoughts of their hearts.
>
> He has brought down the powerful from their thrones,
>> and lifted up the lowly;
>> he has filled the hungry with good things,
>> and sent the rich away empty.
>
> He has helped his servant Israel,
>> in remembrance of his mercy,
>> according to the promise he made to our ancestors,
>> to Abraham and to his descendants forever. (Luke 1:49–55)

Here is the jubilee reversal of fortune—the powerful brought low, the oppressed freed from tyranny; the wealthy emptied, the destitute "filled with good things." The upside-down kingdom is being proclaimed through Mary's song.

The story then moves to Jesus' birth. Government tyranny forces his pregnant mother and his stepfather to travel from Nazareth to Bethlehem at the height of Mary's pregnancy. There, they find no room and so must bed down in a stable as Mary begins her labor. The savior of the world is wrapped in "swaddling cloths" and laid in a manger. It is a romantic picture, but it was not a romantic reality. Luke means to paint as harsh a picture as possible. It is shepherds, it is women and orphans, it is the destitute, it is the expendables, the untouchables who bed down in a stable, whose babies are born there and who are laid in a manger, wrapped with whatever cloth might be at hand. Jesus, the king of the world, is being born as the lowliest of peasants. The cognitive dissonance of this story must have struck the first Christians with unbelievable force.

Then comes the high point of the Christmas story. Angels appear to shepherds in the fields and proclaim "good news of great joy" for "born this day in the city of David is a Savior who is the Messiah, the Lord." The angels sing, "Glory to God in the highest heaven and on earth, peace among those whom he favors!" The shepherds, obviously, leave their flocks and run to the manger to view their Messiah (Luke 2:8–16).

The two important players in this portion of Luke's birth narrative are the shepherds and the angels. These actors are crucial for grasping the jubilee theme. Shepherds of Jesus' day were considered among the expendables of society; they were located near the bottom of the power scale, ranked only above lepers. Yet it is to shepherds that the angel appears to announce the birth of the one who will turn the kingdom upside-down. They are to be understood in contrast to the Emperor Augustus and Quirinius, the governor who had ordered the census. The high-and-mighty have unintentionally brought the Son of David to David's city for his coronation (birth). But the angels are appearing to the lowest of the low, announcing to them the good news of the coming of the Messiah. Good news comes to peasants; it doesn't come to the powerful. The words of Mary's Magnificat, "God has brought down the powerful from their thrones and lifted up the lowly" is being literally fulfilled through the birth of this baby.

The angels proclaim, "Glory to God in the highest heaven, and on earth peace among those whom he favors!" And whom does God favor? Shepherds. A peasant mother. A carpenter father. Ox and ass, sheep and doves. The powerful are being ignored, and the lowly given access to the liberator king.

Poor and Rich: The gospel of Luke is filled with stories about Jesus' identification with the poor, his call to the rich to deal with their money that stands between them and God, and his confrontation of the systems. Thus, the gospel is filled with stories of miraculous healings, exorcisms, and transformation of people—a leper, a paralytic, a man with a withered hand, a widow's son. And those healed are primarily the expendable ones and peasants. Isaiah 61 is being literally fulfilled in front of everyone.

It is informative to contrast Luke's beatitudes with Matthew's beatitudes. Whereas Matthew has Jesus say, "Blessed are the poor in spirit, for theirs is the kingdom of heaven," Luke has Jesus say, "Blessed are you who are poor, for yours is the kingdom of God." Whereas Matthew says, "Blessed are those who hunger and thirst after righteousness," Luke says "Blessed are you who are hungry now." Whereas Matthew says, "Blessed are those who mourn, for they shall be comforted," Luke writes, "Blessed are you who weep now, for you will laugh" (cf. Matthew 5:3, 6; Luke 6:20–23). "Poor in spirit; hunger after righteousness; mourn . . . [and] comforted." "Poor, hungry, weep now, laugh then (when the Great Reversal happens)." Luke's Jesus is concerned about those in need—the poor, the hungry, the crying; Matthew's Jesus is concerned about the spirituality of the people (vis-à-vis the Jewish Law).

And just so we, the readers, don't miss his point, Luke adds some woes: "Woe to you who are rich; woe to you who are full now; woe to you who are laughing now. . . ." Your day will come when the Jubilee occurs, so that you will "have received your consolation" (in other words, you've received all the wealth you're going to get), "you will be hungry, you will mourn and weep" (Luke 6:24–26). What Luke is clearly presenting is the great reversal of the jubilee.

One of the most brilliant juxtapositions of poor and rich about which Luke writes is the story of the rich young ruler (18:18–25) and the tax collector, Zacchaeus (19:1–10). In these two stories, Luke demonstrates how one rich man can have all the right theology and community respect, and yet so worship his money that he is condemned to hell, while the other rich man can have all the wrong theology, be ostracized by the community, and yet be delivered of his money's domination of him through his repentant response to the poor. Jesus' lesson to the theologically orthodox, liturgically correct Pharisees, scribes, and priests is obvious.

Jubilee Parables: No gospel is as rich in parables as is the gospel of Luke. The parables of the good Samaritan (10:25–37), the rich fool (12:13–21), the place of honor at a feast (14:7–14), the prodigal sons (15:11–32), the unjust steward (16:1–13), the rich man and Lazarus (16:19–31), the unjust judge (18:1–18) and the Pharisee and the publican (18:9–14) are all stories that appear only in the gospel of Luke. Each one of them deals with money. Each one of them deals with the responsible or irresponsible response of the rich to the poor. And each one of them consequently deals with a jubilee theme.

In the parable of the good Samaritan, Jesus adroitly shifts from the self-justifying question of the rich man, "Who is truly my neighbor?" to the recognition that we are all neighbor to anyone in need. The parable of the rich fool is a call to social responsibility, while the place of honor at a feast commands the powerful, "When you give a banquet, invite the poor, not the powerful." Jesus' parables of the prodigal son, the unjust steward, the rich man and Lazarus, the unjust judge and the Pharisee and publican all deal with the priorities of those who are occupied by holding onto power and wealth, and the need for a commitment to the poor and marginalized.

Women as the Marginalized: One of the most helpless group of people in Israelite society were women, especially those who were not married, were widowed, or who had no protector. One of the remarkable elements in Luke's gospel is that Jesus pays particular attention to women, taking them seriously. We have already seen the place of honor both the mother of Jesus and her cousin Elizabeth hold in the birth narratives. But that is simply a foretaste of what is yet to come in the gospel. In Luke, "a woman of the city, who was a sinner" is defended by Jesus before the Pharisees and forgiven of her sin (7:36–50). As well, Jesus ministers to both Mary and Martha, and takes quite seriously Mary's hunger after spirituality (10:38–42).

This is an extraordinary story. It is a flaunting of all womanly convention. Luke tells us that "Mary sat at the Lord's feet and listened to what he was saying" (10:34). That is the position of a disciple. To sit at the master's feet did not so much mean that one literally sat at his feet but rather sat in an expectant way, waiting to learn from him. It was a sign of submission to the master's authority and knowledge. To "listen to what he was saying" was to be his student, absorbing the wisdom flowing from him to such a degree that the disciple could teach such wisdom to others. In other words, Mary had assumed the role of a disciple, a primary follower of Jesus—and Jesus had let her do that. In fact, Jesus even commends Mary for choosing "that better part," thus declaring that a woman could be a disciple of Jesus and therefore eventually become a teacher of men and a practitioner of the gospel alongside Peter and James, Andrew and John. Thus, by this drastic change in roles, Jesus is freeing women to become the leaders they were created by God to be in the jubilee community, despite the constraints of both Jewish and Roman societies![3]

The gospel of Luke is clearly a gospel that announces jubilee to the world, and Jesus as being the purveyor of that jubilee. But is the message of jubilee liberation that permeates the gospel of Luke a message that is peculiar to that book alone? Or does it move throughout all the gospel narratives? Is the Jesus portrayed in Matthew, Mark, and John a gentle man who loved children, healed the sick, and brought salvation to the spiritually bankrupt? Or was he more than that? Who was this Jesus of Nazareth, as portrayed throughout the four gospels?

THE MARGINALIZED MESSIAH

The gospel of Matthew is a document focused upon reaching the Jews of the first century with the claims of Jesus the Messiah. Toward that end, the author of that gospel stresses the Jewish foundation of Christianity in everything he writes.

But there is a second theme in Matthew—an equally important theme. That is its emphasis that if Jesus is indeed the Messiah, he is a marginalized Messiah. He is the one on the outskirts, among the rejected ones and himself rejected, bringing a salvation that comes from the margins and not the center.[4]

At the Margins in Ministry

Matthew 4:12–17 tells us that, after John was arrested in Judea, Jesus went north into "the territory of Zebulun and Naphtali" to begin his ministry, far from the reach of the Jewish leaders. Zebulun and Naphtali are in "Galilee of the Gentiles"—the extreme margins of Israel. Thus, Matthew tells us, Jesus began his ministry in the far corners of Galilee with the proclamation, "Repent, for the kingdom of heaven has come near" (4:17). The gospel is first preached at the literal margins of Israel's life, and will come from those margins to turn the center upside down.

Healings play a strategic role in the gospel of Matthew. For example, Matthew 9 presents four healings: the raising of a dead girl who is the daughter of "a leader of the synagogue" (9:18–19, 23–26), the healing of a woman who had been hemorrhaging for twelve years (9:20–22), the restoring of sight to two blind men (9:27–31), and the healing of a man who was demon-possessed and mute (9:32–34). These healings demonstrate that Jesus is indeed who the church claims him to be—Lord and Christ.

It is intriguing to note the marginalization implied in these four healings. Being in a house of death was to make one's self unclean. A woman having her period was perceived to be unclean, and since that woman had not stopped her period for twelve years, she was constantly unclean. A person who was possessed by a demon was particularly seen as unclean. And if the two men were blind from birth, they were also unclean. So all were marginalized, and all were warmly received by Jesus.

It is also intriguing to note that Jesus touched the dead girl and the two blind men, and he accepted being touched by the woman with the issue of blood. A touch in each instance, whether by Jesus or to Jesus, rendered Jesus contaminated, according to the Law. But there is no indication that this bothered him at all.

In this collection of four healings, Matthew notes that it is the marginalized to whom Jesus ministers. It is the elite who distance themselves from Jesus and who criticize.

Parables: Throughout Matthew, the telling of parables is the primary means Jesus uses to communicate his vision of the world as God intended it to be, the world as it keeps going wrong, and what God is doing to bring human society back to God's intentions. A magnificent example of that strategy is presented in a series of parables in Matthew 13.

The Parable of the sower as told by Jesus in Matthew 13:1–23 is not so much about the sower as it is about four types of earth. What Jesus is teaching is that his call to embrace the world as God intended it to be is a call that is offered to everyone—poor and rich, powerless and powerful, Jews and Gentile alike. Some won't receive it. For others it will come as liberating good news. But what will those to whom it comes as good news do with that news?

For some to whom this good news comes, it comes as truth, but their allegiance to the dominant culture will overwhelm that good news and it will be snatched away—like birds scooping up the seed as soon as it falls on the ground. For others, that good news will take root, but when the opposition of the systems occurs—whether it comes politically, economically, or religiously—these people will be intimidated and immediately surrender their newfound good news. For still others, "the cares of the world and the lure of wealth choke the word and it yields nothing"—the priorities of the systems simply choke off the possibility of new life.

But for a few—a precious few—they will hear the good news of the shalom way of life, and they will embrace it. They will not be intimidated or overwhelmed or seduced by the systems. Instead, they will hold on tenaciously to the new work God is doing in and through them. And they will be the ones who will birth this new society with results that will "yield, in one case a hundredfold, in another sixty, and in another thirty."

The next parable—the parable of the weeds among the wheat (13:24–30)—presents the insidious nature of exploitive systems. It is like weeds intentionally sown among a crop of wheat. Those weeds look similar to the wheat as they mature, and the weeds can't be removed from the wheat until harvest because it would uproot the wheat. So the system of domination, sown in society by Satan, is insidious. It looks good. It is appealing. But it grabs hold of even the most relational culture, permeating and corrupting it.

But, on the other hand, the world as God intended it to be is also insidious. In the parable of the Mustard Seed (13:31–32), Jesus teaches that the shalom community is like a mustard seed that begins small but flourishes into a large tree-like bush. So the kingdom of God begins small in society. It enters into even the most domineering system with just a handful of people. But it is so appealing that, as those people organize, build relationships, develop leadership, confront the systems, and build a culture on relational and justice values, it grows and grows throughout society until it governs.

Confrontation: It is essential, if one is clearly to understand the gospel of Matthew, to perceive the central place Jesus' confrontation of the Pharisees holds. That confrontation is a microcosm of Jesus' conflict with the entire religious (priests, elders), political (Herod, Rome, high priest), and economic (Sadducees, land-owners) systems of Israel and of Rome. Let's look at one such instance of that conflict.

In this instance, the Pharisees say to the people, "It is only by Beelzebul, the ruler of demons, that this (Jesus) casts out the demons" (12:24). Jesus understandably takes considerable offense at their statement. He responds to their accusation by showing the inconsistency of their argument. "If Satan casts out Satan, he is divided against himself; how then can his kingdom stand? . . . But if it is by the Spirit of God that I cast out demons, then the kingdom of God has come to you" (12:26, 28).

Jesus then warms to his task. When you say I cast out demons by the power of Satan, he asserts, then you are blaspheming the One who has called me to cast down Satan's sway (12:31, 32). The Pharisees are committing a sin against the Holy Spirit when they accuse Jesus of being demonically influenced. They need to understand they are turning God's intentions upside-down when they say that. They, as religious leaders, were called by the Torah to bring both society's systems and each person to God. But, instead, they have used their office to build power and wealth and position for themselves while obscuring their actions in religious talk. Then, they have the utter nerve to take God's anointed—who is doing the work they ought to be doing—and accuse him of the very crime they are committing and attributing the same to the influence of Satan.

As the gospel account moves toward its inevitable end, the intensity of Jesus' conflict with the Pharisees accelerates. And it is hard-hitting! The names he calls them, the rage he displays, the accusations he makes against them, and especially in chapter 23, his profound expression of a desperate love for them that sees them blindly leading the nation into inevitable destruction is an essential theme of this gospel. The intentions of Matthew cannot be understood apart from Jesus' intense opposition to the people and systems of power while intensely loving them as unrepentant children of God.

The fulcrum of the gospel of Matthew is chapter 16. The Pharisees and Sadducees are unwilling to perceive and be responsive to what God is doing in their midst (16:1–4). Likewise, the disciples are people of "little faith" (16:5–12), unbelievably obtuse about what Jesus is teaching about the yeast of the systems.

It is in the light of this refusal to see (the Pharisees) or inability to see (the disciples), that the next story takes place—Peter's declaration about Jesus (16:13–20). "[Jesus] said to them, 'But who do you say that I am?' Simon Peter answered, 'You are the Messiah, the Son of the living God' " (16:15–16).

Peter finally gets it! Peter is finally open to see things as they really are. But no sooner does the door of insight swing open than it slams shut again. Jesus, thrilled with Peter's breakthrough of faith, shares with the disciples that, as Messiah, Jesus must be the Suffering Servant of Isaiah and die. This requires for the disciples as large a paradigm shift as it took for them to proclaim Jesus as Messiah. They had been taught all their lives that Messiah was to be a conquering hero. They could not envision him as anything else than that.

Having so directly confronted Peter, Jesus then goes on to teach the new paradigm of death and sacrifice as the key to bringing about world transformation (16:24–28). Victory will not come for the shalom community by accepting and using the conditions and structures of the exploitive systems. Unilateral means cannot be used to bring about relational ends. The Messiah can't conquer by using the force of arms or political intrigue or wealth. He will conquer only by using the force of relationships fostered in love and trust, exemplified and acted out by a man hanging on a cross (16:24–27).

Thus, Jesus begins the teaching of the new paradigm that will now dominate the remainder of the book of Matthew. Now that the disciples—"you of little faith"—have learned and received the first radical paradigm shift (Jesus is Messiah), Jesus begins conditioning them for the next paradigm shift they must embrace—that Messiah is the Marginalized One who will inaugurate God's shalom society only by using God's means—the way of the cross.

At the Margins in Death

The gospel of Matthew now moves relentlessly to the stories of the Last Supper, the betrayal, the denial by Peter, the trial and the crucifixion. The story is told in terms of the continuing struggle between the kingdom of a marginalized Messiah and the Israelite political, economic, and religious systems. Whereas in the gospel of John, Pilate is portrayed as a co-conspirator, in Matthew he is clearly reluctant to execute Jesus. He is confused at Jesus' unwillingness to defend himself, his wife tells him to release Jesus, and he calls Jesus "innocent"—indicating that he doesn't see the crime of which Jesus is accused as being punishable by death. But the elders and chief priests are relentless in their insistence, and finally,

Pilate acquiesces with the words "I am innocent of this man's blood; see to it yourselves" (27:24).

The story then contains three strategic statements peculiar only to Matthew. First, the crowd responds to Pilate's profession of innocence, "His blood be on us and on our children" (27:25). With these words, "the people as a whole" (27:25) join themselves with their nation's political, economic, and religious systems in rejecting Jesus; the seduction of the people by their own systems is now complete.

Jesus is then led off to Golgotha and is crucified. And there occurs the second strategic statement, unique in its entirety to Matthew:

> In the same way the chief priests also, along with the scribes and elders, were mocking him, saying, "He saved others; he cannot save himself. He is the King of Israel; let him come down from the cross now, and we will believe in him. He trusts in God; let God deliver him now, if he wants to; for he said, 'I am God's Son.'" (Matthew 27:41–43)[5]

This is not simply a mocking of Jesus. It is far more than that. Each of the three statements recalls a previous claim Jesus made about himself. The speaker then asserts that Jesus' death invalidates that claim. "He saved others; he cannot save himself"—Jesus claimed to be the Savior; now we see that he not only cannot save anyone else; he can't even save himself. "He is the King of Israel; let him come down from the cross and we will believe in him"—Jesus claimed to be Messiah, yet whoever heard of a crucified Messiah? "He trusts in God; let God deliver him now, if he wants to, for he said, I am God's Son"—Jesus claimed to be divine (the Son of God); well, you don't see God delivering him, do you? The taunting of the Jewish leaders, therefore, is very specific, seeking the invalidation of each of Jesus' claims about himself as Messiah, savior, and the Son of God.

This, then, is God's darkest hour—for the very systems he created are now the systems that reject Jesus politically (Messiah), economically (savior), and religiously (Son of God).[6]

No Longer Marginalized

As is true of the other gospel narratives, the gospel of Matthew doesn't end with a cross but with an empty tomb. Jesus rises from the dead. It is the women—themselves the most marginalized of the marginalized disciples—who go to the tomb and meet the risen Jesus (Matthew 28:8–10). Sent by the risen Christ, the women go to the disciples to tell them the good news that Jesus is alive.

But then a story occurs in this gospel narrative that appears only in Matthew. It is the third of the unique and crucial Matthean stories:

> While [the women] were going [to tell the disciples that Jesus was risen from the dead], some of the guard went into the city and told the chief priests everything that had happened. After the priests had assembled with the elders, they devised a plan to give a large sum of money to the soldiers, telling them, "You must say, 'His disciples came by night and stole him away while we were asleep.' If this comes to the governor's ears, we will satisfy him and keep you out of trouble." So they took the money and did as they were directed. And this story is still told among the Jews to this day. (Matthew 28:11–15)

Consider what this story is saying. The soldiers were Roman soldiers, posted at the tomb by Pilate specifically at the Jewish priests' request (27:62–66). They were not temple guards. Yet when security is breached by the resurrection, *the guards go to the Jewish priests and elders*, not to their military commander, Pilate. And they tell the priests "everything that had happened"—that is, *the guards' eyewitness to the resurrection*.

In other words, what Matthew is telling us is that the chief priests and elders *knew from the eyewitnesses at the tomb that Jesus had risen from the dead*. The Jewish system had tried to put a halt to Jesus' exposure of them and his call to practice the jubilee kingdom of God. And they thought they had won by executing him. But it is at this point that the systems reach their hour of decision. They now know, based on the testimony of the guards, that Jesus has risen from the dead. What shall they do? The priests and elders can now choose to confess Christ as Lord, admit their own culpability, and begin using their power to create the jubilee kingdom. Or they can choose to cover it up.

The Jewish political, economic, and religious elite chose to cover up their most profound act of injustice. It is what today would be called "damage control." So the Hebrew elite bribed the guards to lie about what happened at the tomb and to manipulate the Roman political system to guarantee there would be no repercussions.

The ending is a tragic tale. Those in power are so committed to their power and to maintaining the status quo that they lie, cover up, and protect their interests. They choose to "save their life" and thereby "lose it" (16:25). And with this action, the mainstream Jewish system becomes marginalized in the gospel of Matthew, and the marginalized Jesus and his church become the center of the world.

THE RADICAL RABBI

It is universally recognized that the gospel of Mark was the first of the gospel narratives written. It was likely written in that margin of time between Israel's seemingly successful revolt against Rome in 66 A.D. and that nation's total destruction by the Roman military machine in 70 A.D. In that interim period, Jewish Christians, like all Jews, were being pressured to make a choice: to either remain loyal to Rome and the Jewish systems (chief priests, elders, Pharisees and Sadducees) or to join with the zealots in revolution. However, the writer of the gospel of Mark suggests that Jesus' life, ministry, death, and resurrection calls the church to a third way—to a *radical* approach to the world and its institutions that goes far beyond either the maintenance of the status quo or revolution. For to be radical means that one goes to the "root" (from the Latin *radix* or "root") in both one's social analysis and in one's actions.[7]

Unlike the gospels of Matthew and Luke that begin with the birth of Jesus or John that begins with the creation of the world, the story of the radical rabbi of Mark begins immediately with his ministry. In a series of quick vignettes, we are introduced to John the Baptist (Mark 1:2–8), Jesus' baptism (1:9–11), his temptation in the wilderness (1:12–13), the beginning of his Galilean ministry (1:14–15), and his calling of his first disciples (1:16–20). We are virtually panting for breath by the time the first substantive story begins. But that story is crucial to the entirety of the book of Mark, because it introduces us to the essential theme of the remainder of the book. It is the story of the man with an unclean spirit (1:21–28).

In this story, Jesus enters a synagogue in Capernaum on the Sabbath. In essence, he has entered sacred space at a sacred time, and that place and time are symbols of Israel's dominant political, economic, and religious order—its "systems." Entering that space, Jesus quickly dominates it by effectively assuming what is the normal responsibility of the religious authorities. The very repetition of Mark's description underscores Jesus' domination of the situation: "he entered the synagogue and taught" (Mark 1:21), "they were astounded at his teaching" (1:22), "he taught them as one having authority, and not as the scribes" (1:22), "What is this? A new teaching—with authority!" (1:27).

Such an invasion and then domination of "sacred space" and "sacred time" gets a predictable response. Mark tells us that there was "in the synagogue a man

with an unclean spirit" (1:23). Note that this man didn't enter the synagogue because he heard Jesus was there. *He was already in the synagogue* when Jesus
arrived. In other words, he was part of the synagogue congregation, part of the
normal Sabbath crowd. And he takes Jesus on!

His opening words to Jesus are particularly intriguing. According to Ched
Myers, his words "What have you to do with us, Jesus of Nazareth?" (Mark 1:24)
are better translated, "What do we have in common?" or "Why do you meddle
with us?"[8] In essence, the demoniac is saying, "Why are you coming in here,
taking over our teachings and taking away our power?"

With that challenge, the battle between the demon and Jesus begins. The
demon exposes Jesus for who he is: "I know who you are, the Holy One of God"
(1:25). First century Jews believed that if you named a person, you had control
over him because you knew his inner essence. Thus, the demon seeks to gain
control over Jesus by naming him. But Jesus exerts his authority with the words,
"Be silent, and come out of him!" (1:25).

The text then tells us, "And the unclean spirit, convulsing him and crying
with a loud voice, came out of him" (Mark 1:26). Jesus demonstrates that he is
more powerful than the demon and the political, economic, and religious systems
(i.e., the synagogue) that demon possesses.

Finally, "at once his fame began to spread throughout the surrounding region
of Galilee" (Mark 1:28). People understood what was going on. This story is the
inauguration of the battle between Jesus and the systems for control of Israel and
its people. It is therefore a typology of what will be the continuing struggle that
permeates the entirety of the book of Mark.

What is the continuing choice before God's people? Is it obedience to the
established political, economic, and religious order of chief priests, Pharisees, and
Rome? Is it to join in revolution? Or is it to follow in the footsteps of the radical
rabbi, Jesus?

What Jesus Was About

First, Jesus confronts the dominant Jewish systems of his day, calls them
to accountability, and often defeats them. Perhaps one of the clearest examples of
Jesus' conflict with the systems in Mark is the story of Jesus' cursing of the fig
tree.

Mark 11:11–26 consists of three stories. 11:11–14 is the cursing of the fig
tree; 11:15–19 is Jesus' cleansing of the temple; and 11:20–26 is the lesson

learned from the withered fig tree. For the Jew of Jesus' day, the fig tree was a clear symbol for Israel, so used in the Hebrew Bible (e.g., Jeremiah 8:13, Isaiah 28:3, Hosea 9:10–16, Micah 7:1) as an emblem of peace, security, and prosperity both in Israel's past and in God's coming kingdom. The fruitfulness of the fig tree is the symbol of God's blessings upon the nation. The withering of the fig tree, conversely, is a sign to Israel of God's judgment upon them!

> Then [Jesus] entered Jerusalem and went into the temple; and when he had looked around at everything, as it was already late, he went out to Bethany with the twelve. On the following day, when they came from Bethany, [Jesus] was hungry. Seeing in the distance a fig tree in leaf, he went to see whether perhaps he would find anything on it. When he came to it, he found nothing but leaves, for it was not the season for figs. He said to it, "May no one ever eat fruit from you again." And his disciples heard it. (Mark 11:11–14)

This is an "acted-out parable"—that is a parable that is told by Jesus' action rather than by his words. He has just visited the temple—the most high-profile symbol of Israel's political, economic, and religious powers. Now, through this acted-out parable, Jesus is about to make commentary on the temple and all it stands for.

Jesus is illustrating that the Jewish nation, created by God to be "a blessing to all the nations of the world" has, instead, not produced fruit. It has not reached its potential at all ("it was not the season for figs"). Therefore, it is cursed by Jesus for not only not reaching its potential, but also refusing to do so. And this is primarily due to the refusal of temple leadership to seek the shalom of the nation and its people because of their own greed and lust for control. Therefore, having received God's curse through Jesus, the nation has become withered and the system rotten "to its roots" (Mark 11:20).

This acted-out parable is then followed by Jesus' visit to the temple (Mark 11:15–19) where he drives out the money-changers, overturns the tables, sets free the sacrificial doves, and declares, "My house shall be called a house of prayer for all the nations, but you have made it a den of robbers." (11:17) Called by God to build a society of justice, equitable distribution of wealth, and a shalom community, the religious, political and economic establishment of Israel have built a society of lust for power, oppression, exploitation, and domination. And the temple has become its chief symbol.

If the symbol of Israel's aristocracy is overthrown, upon what can we build God's kingdom, the disciples in essence ask Jesus. He points to the withered fig tree (Mark 11:21) and teaches them, "Truly I tell you, if you say to this mountain (that is, the temple), 'Be taken up and thrown into the sea,' and if you do not doubt in your heart but believe that what you say will come to pass, it will be done for you" (11:22–23). In other words, faith will outlast the temple. If your faith depends upon the temple and the systems behind the temple, it will soon be destroyed. But if your faith rests upon the radical rabbi, then you will move mountains.

The point of this entire sequence is that the symbolism of the fig tree and Jesus' cursing of it would not be lost on any Jewish audience. They would understand immediately what Mark was saying here. And the sandwiching of the "cursing" of the temple by Jesus in 11:15–29 between the two stories of the fig tree would make it obvious to any Jew that Jesus was commenting about the Jewish systems of his time and in what kingdom the listeners should ultimately place their trust.

Second, Jesus is for the poor and oppressed. This is a constantly recurring message in the book of Mark, as Jesus heals the sick, exorcises demons, feeds the poor, and comforts and teaches the powerless. He is clearly on the side of the poor, the exploited, and the powerless of both Israel and the Gentile nations. One of Mark's stories that most clearly (even embarrassingly) demonstrates this reality is the story of the Syrophoenician Woman (Mark 7:24–30).

In this story, Jesus is at the geographical limits of Jewish political control. Tyre is a Gentile town. Jesus was there in secret, "yet he could not escape notice" (Mark 7:24). One of those who took notice was a Syrophoenician woman, a Gentile who has a demon-possessed daughter. She interrupts Jesus in his home at private retreat with his disciples; she begs him to cast the demon out of her daughter. Jesus' response is "Let the children be fed first, for it is not fair to take the children's food and throw it to the dogs" (7:27). But she is tenacious, declaring, "Sir, even the dogs under the table eat the children's crumbs." Jesus, rebuked, responds, "For saying that, you may go—the demon has left your daughter." And the child is instantly healed.

What is not immediately apparent to twenty-first century eyes is the unbelievable effrontery of this woman's actions. In that day, no woman would approach a man without his permission. No Gentile would approach a Jew. And no one, under *any* circumstances, would invade the privacy of a rabbi when he was on retreat in a private home.

Yet the woman breaks all three codes of behavior out of her great desperation. Jesus' response to her is, in reality, quite mild. He, in essence, says to her, "Wait a while until I am finished here and then I will come out and tend to your problem." But the woman will not let Jesus go until he blesses her. Sensing her desperation, he acquiesces and heals her daughter.

To understand the full implications of Jesus' action, we must realize that for him to accede to this woman's demands was for him to be shamed in that society. He lost face! Sensing her desperation, Jesus allowed himself to lose all status in the eyes of every man and every Jew gathered at that retreat with him. His disciples must have been shocked beyond imagination! He had shown himself to be totally without principle to allow a woman and a Gentile and a stranger to do this to him.

But that was precisely the point. Jesus did let a woman and a Gentile and a stranger treat him this way. By agreeing to her demand, he in essence willingly suffered the indignity of her importunity, included her in the community of those gathered for that retreat, and became "least" to minister to her need (and her daughter's need), welcoming her as his equal. The lesson to the church could not have been more profound!

Third, Jesus is about the task of creating a new "nation of Israel." In the gospel of Mark, Jesus does more than confront the Israelite systems and carry on ministries of compassion and justice. Jesus also calls into being a new "nation of Israel."

In 3:13–19, Mark tells us that Jesus initiates three provocative actions. First, in the midst of ministering to multitudes of people, he ascends a mountain, just as Moses did in Exodus 19:3. Second, he calls the people to him and then "appoints" disciples; the word used here is the word used in the Septuagint version of the Hebrew Bible for the selection of the Levitical priests as well as Moses and Aaron (1 Kings 12:31, 13:33; 2 Chronicles 2:15; 1 Samuel 12:6). Third, the number of disciples he appoints is twelve—obviously reminding everyone of the twelve tribes of Israel. In other words, what Jesus is doing is creating a new "nation of Israel" to follow him in authentically implementing the Deuteronomic code and thus, God's intentions for the world.

And what is that new covenant people to be like?

Jesus' Third Way

The root of Israel's problem, Mark is teaching, is its understanding of power (Mark 10:32–42). Both conservative and revolutionary, both Roman governor and Zealot, both Jewish priest and Pharisee understand power as domination, as control, as enforced. But what if Godly power is something entirely different? What if true power is relational?

This is what Jesus is proposing in his radical statement to his disciples. "[W]hoever wishes to become great among you must be your servant, and whoever wishes to be first among you must be slave of all. For the Son of Man came not to be served but to serve, and to give his life a ransom for many" (10:43–45).

The image of a *servant* captures the essence of true power, Jesus teaches. The image of the one "who gives his life as a ransom for many" captures the power of Jesus' third way. Such a person who exercises servant power is "the man or woman for others." This is Jesus' "third way"—the radical solution that will keep the Jewish and Roman worlds from destroying each other.

But was Jesus right? Or was he a victim of his own delusion? The "realists" in Israel, whether of the Jewish or Roman persuasion, would say he was a dreamer, naïve, one who threw himself against the unyielding phalanx of Roman swords, high priest's law codes, and a procurator's cross.

So was the third way no way? Did the exercise of relational power reveal itself to be as useless as revolutionary power? For all his good intentions, had the radical rabbi lost?

> As [the women] entered the tomb, they saw a young man, dressed
> in a white robe, sitting on the right side; and they were alarmed.
> But he said to them, "Do not be alarmed; you are looking for Jesus
> of Nazareth, who was crucified. He has been raised; he is not here.
> Look, there is the place they laid him. But go, tell his disciples and
> Peter that he is going ahead of you to Galilee; there you will see him,
> just as he told you." (Mark 16:5–7)

Thus the gospel of Mark draws toward its end. But its end is no end. Jesus is going before them—before the women, to whom he appears as the only ones who stood faithfully beside him through his crucifixion, before the disciples who had fled in terror, before Peter who had denied him. He is going before all of them, back into Galilee, back to where the story first began, back to where it is always beginning, back to where God's people always keep engaging Jesus. We keep experiencing the *relational power of Jesus*—a power that could not be killed by even the greatest powers of Rome or Jewish high priests. As each person meets the resurrected Jesus and comes into relationship with him, the new covenant community keeps being recreated, and we follow Jesus into our "Galilees" as we each answer his ongoing call to discipleship.

THE COUNTER-CULTURAL CHRIST

In the beginning was the Word,
and the Word was with God,
and the Word was God.
He was in the beginning with God.
All things came into being through him,
and without him not one thing came into being.
What has come into being in him was life,
and the life was the light of all people.
The light shines in the darkness,
and the darkness did not overcome it. (John 1:1–5)

John's Magnificent Prologue

With these dramatic words, the gospel of John begins. And it begins in magnificent poetry that presents the profound foundation upon which this gospel is built.[9]

"In the beginning was the Word." The gospel of John opens with identical words to Genesis 1:1—"In the beginning." Through the Hebrew creation story runs a profound theme, repeated eight times (Gen. 1:3; 6–7, 9, 11, 14–15, 20–21, 24, and 26–30). That theme is "And God said. . . . And it was so."

Genesis tells us that God *spoke* the world into existence. So, John is declaring the same truth. The Word—in Greek, *logos*, in Hebrew *dabar*—is not just *a word* spoken by human beings. It is *the word*, for the *dabar* or *logos* is the conduit by which Yahweh invades humanity and writes sacred history into our history. The *logos* of God *is* God, the voice of God speaking the creation into life. Without the Word, there is no world.

For whom is this Word intended? The Word, John is telling us, is intended for the world. The Greek word used here for *world* is *cosmos*. The cosmos is not simply the geographical world—our sphere. The cosmos, to the Greeks, was the entire created order, the universe. The Word, John tells us, has entered the cosmos that God created, bringing to that cosmos "life," "light," and "power."

But how did the cosmos and its people respond? "The *cosmos* did not *know* him." "His own *people* did not *accept* him." Rejection of the Word (and therefore of God) occurred at two levels—societally (i.e., the cosmos) and individually (i.e., people). The "cosmos" and its "people" had refused to come into an intimate relationship with its creator because "darkness" had kept it and its people from the "light."

However, such rejection of the Word is not universal. "But to all who received [the Word], . . . he gave power to become children of God" (John 1:12). There are those who have responded to the Word and have become right with God. But how do they do that, John asks?

God's people are to be shaped around their embracing of the free gift of God's redemptive love (1:13), and making that "amazing grace" the foundation for their life together. God's shalom, the cosmos as God intended it to be will come into existence through "all who received him, who believed in his name" and who therefore create together a new community, an alternative society built upon God's love and grace.

The magnificent prologue of the gospel of John now rushes toward its climax, as it gives to the reader the essential theme of the remainder of the gospel of John.

"*The Word became flesh.*" The Word—the *dabar* of God, the *logos* of God, has become an actual, living human being. The Word "lives" among us within a human being! The Son of God, the enfleshment of the "Word," is journeying through the human experience, John is telling us, as the personification of "grace and truth."

But what does John mean by "grace and truth"? What John is doing here is using two Greek words to capture the essence of one Hebrew word—*chesedh*. Chesedh is the depth of God's love expressed towards us, a love that accepts us as we are and yet calls us to become all that God has created us to be. John is telling us that God has "tabernacled" among us so that we might become God's people as we live out *chesedh* in both our private and public lives and in the very ways we carry out the political, economic, and religious functions of our society.

Now the prologue reaches its climax. It names the Word. The "father's only son, full of grace and truth" is Jesus Christ. "The law indeed was given through Moses; grace and truth came through Jesus Christ" (John 1:17).

God's chesedh is not going to come to humanity and the cosmos any longer through Moses (that is, the Jewish system). The Law created by God to incarnate God in humanity's structures has become the exact opposite, for it has become the oppressive system of the first century that is designed to maintain power for the few while holding the populace in economic, political, and religious slavery. The Law has become so exploitive and dominating that it is beyond redemption.

But "grace and truth came through Jesus Christ." God has had to find another way. And that way is Jesus!

What John is proposing here is radically revolutionary. Is he right? The remainder of the gospel of John is his effort to demonstrate through the life and ministry, the death and resurrection of Jesus Christ the authenticity of what he has here proposed. And it is to demonstrate that authenticity against the landscape of the horrendous oppression of the Jewish and Roman systems.

Journeying Through John

The body of the gospel of John deals with three primary themes, woven through story after story. Each of those themes supports the primary assertions of the prologue, demonstrating those assertions through Jesus' life, ministry, and teachings. One theme is the blindness of the religious, political, and economic systems of Israel and of Rome, called by God to build the shalom community but instead committed to their domination of the people. The second theme is of the alternative community that Jesus is building, a counter-cultural effort that is seeking to capture for that century the social structure God has always desired for humanity. The third theme is of Jesus as "God-in-the-flesh" in order to incarnate God's presence in this corrupt world by transforming people and bringing them into God's counter-cultural community.

An example of the first theme occurs almost immediately in the gospel narrative, in the story of the cleansing of the temple (John 1:19–51). Jesus' first major action is his clearing of the temple of the moneychangers, the setting free of the sacrificial animals, and his driving the Jerusalem religious establishment out of the temple with a whip. This cleansing occurs in order to dramatically expose the depth of the exploitation, oppression, and domination being exercised by the Judeans.[10]

An example of the second theme is found in Jesus' command to his followers, "Just as I have loved you, you also should love one another. By this everyone will know that you are my disciples, if you have love for one another" (John 13:34–35). This is the single commandment for a new community, more important than the original Ten Commandments that now are used to support that false community that has been formed around the political, economic, and religious alliance of the Pharisees, priests, and Judeans.

An example of the third theme is found throughout the gospel of John in the "I Am" statements ("I am the Bread of Life," "I am the Way, the Truth and the Life," "I am the Good Shepherd," "I am the Resurrection and the Life," etc.). All of these "I Am" statements are one of the unique features of the gospel of John, because all of them appear only in the fourth gospel and in no other. What is particularly important about all these "I Am" statements, however, is that they say far more in Greek than can be translated into English. When Jesus used the Greek expression, *ego eimi* (I am), he was speaking a formula—the Greek translation of the Hebrew word, *Yahweh*.

Thus, every time Jesus spoke of himself, "I am . . . (the door of the sheep, the bread of life, etc.)," he was in essence declaring "I am YHWH." No wonder the religious leaders of Israel were so enraged at him.

The Climax of John

All the stories that make up the body of the gospel of John, whether they are themes of blind systems or the new community or the Saving Word, move the reader toward the inevitable climax of John—this author's unique interpretation of the arrest, trial, crucifixion, and resurrection of Jesus.

Who Arrests Whom? The Over-reactive Detention: The narrator of John writes, "So Judas brought a detachment of soldiers together with police from the chief priests and the Pharisees [to arrest Jesus]" (18:3). Who came to arrest Jesus? The words seem simple enough: Judas, a detachment of soldiers, police from the chief priests. But it is not as simple as it seems.

Whereas the English translation seems mildly ambiguous, the Greek is not. The Greek original tells us that the "soldiers" who came out to arrest Jesus were a *speiran* (translated in the NRSV as "detachment"). *Speiran* is a technical term. It was only used in the first century AD for a Roman military unit of between two hundred and six hundred soldiers.

This is not a small band. Nor is this a "detachment" from the local constabulary. It is the Roman garrison in Jerusalem—and Pilate would likely not have more than a single unit of *speiran* with him in Jerusalem. That means that the entire Roman military presence in Jerusalem had come to arrest Jesus. And it was impossible for them to come to perform this task unless commanded to do so by Pilate.

The term translated "police" is the Greek word *hyperatas*. That, too, is a technical term. It is the official military body under the authority of the high priest, which guarded the temple.

What John is telling us, therefore, is that an immense military force—somewhere between 300 and 800 soldiers—had come to arrest one man. And he is also telling us that these troops were both Roman and Judean. In other words, the political power of Rome and the religious authority of the Sanhedrin were already collaborating together to eliminate Jesus. Thus, Pilate was not a reluctant, manipulated Roman leader because *the speiran could not be there without Pilate's express order.*

What happens next in John's telling of the arrest story is amazing. When this military detachment of 300 to 800 armed men arrive in front of Jesus, *they do nothing!* They simply stop, dumfounded before Jesus. Then, the text tells us, "Jesus, knowing all that was to happen to him, came forward and asked them, 'Whom are you looking for?' They answered, 'Jesus of Nazareth'" (John 18:4–5). Neither these soldiers nor Judas are going to do anything but stand there, dumfounded. *And it is Jesus who must seize control of the situation and engineer his own arrest!*

Who Is On Trial Before Whom? The Judean Trial: Unlike the Synoptic Gospels, Jesus' Judean trial is before Annas—not the Sanhedrin. There is no mention of others gathered for the hearing. The text tells us, "They took [Jesus] to Annas, who was the father-in-law of Caiaphas, the high priest that year" (John 18:13).

Further, it implies that the hearing before Annas is illegal. That hearing is at night—since the cock crowed *after* the completion of the hearing (John 18:27). That made that trial illegal because the Law stated that trials could occur only in daylight and only before the entire Sanhedrin. Jesus makes note of this illegal hearing by saying to Annas, "I have spoken openly to the world; I have always taught in synagogue and in the temple, where all the Judeans come together. I have said nothing in secret" (18:20).

Jesus is, in essence, saying, "I have spoken openly; you have not. I have taught in public; you have conspired in private. I have said nothing in secret; everything you do to dominate and make profit off the people you do in secret. And this illegal trial is just another example of how deceitful and manipulative you are." The text doesn't record Annas' response, but he must have been livid as he realized he had just been both exposed and rebuked by his prisoner. He had just been placed on trial by that prisoner, and had been found guilty.

Who Is On Trial Before Whom? The Roman Trial: The trial scene now shifts to the direct meeting between Pilate and Jesus. Pilate intends it to be his interrogation of Jesus. Before the trial is over, Jesus has turned it into the trial of Pilate—and of Roman authority.

The trial begins with Pilate asking Jesus, "Are you the king of the Jews?" (John 18:33). In essence, Pilate is exclaiming, "Are you the man that the Judeans had gotten me to commit all my Jerusalem *speiran* to arrest?"

Jesus responds to Pilate's sarcastic (and perhaps incredulous) comment with a statement that makes the procurator realize that this is a more worthy opponent than he originally surmised. "Do you ask this on your own, or did others tell you about me?" (John 18:34).

Part of Rome's capacity to govern the world effectively was based upon the myth of its objectivity and unimpeachable authority. Roman law was supposed to be objective, independent of malice or manipulation, far above the fray of local petty politics. Rome was the great lawgiver of the world.

Jesus shatters that façade of unimpeachable authority with these few words. In this sentence, Jesus reveals that he knows that the troops sent to arrest him were, in reality, Pilate's troops, and rather than Rome being the objective, unbiased power it pretends to be, it is an integral part of the plot to eliminate him. Jesus exposes Rome for the manipulative, dominating power it truly is, locked in a deadly embrace with all the Judean political, economic, and religious systems and leaders to maintain control over the people, and to economically exploit and politically oppress them. Nothing has gotten by Jesus.

Pilate, astounded, seeks to distance himself and Rome from the Judean leaders. "I am not a Jew, am I?" he rhetorically asks. "Your own nation and the chief priests have handed you over to me" (John 18:35). But his attempt to evade Jesus' exposure of him by trying to redirect blame onto the Judean systems doesn't work. Jesus, instead, moves to the heart of the issue.

"My kingdom is not from this world. If my kingdom were from this world, my followers would be fighting to keep me from being handed over to the Judeans. But as it is, my kingdom is not from here" (John 18:36).

This is one of the most misinterpreted of the passages in John. It is usually interpreted as saying that Jesus' kingdom is a heavenly kingdom, not an earthly kingdom and therefore the angels would not defend him when he is killed by the earthly authorities. However, that interpretation makes no sense in the light of the context of this passage—which is the conflict between the Roman-Judean conspiracy (Pilate's world) and Jesus' jubilee community (Jesus' world). Nor is it consistent with John's use of the word *world* throughout his gospel (e.g., John 1:9–29; 14:17–31; 15:18–19; 17:6–25), where it is normally used to refer to the Judean/Roman political, economic, and religious systems.

What Jesus is actually saying in this response to Pilate is this: "My kingdom is not made up of society's systems that seek to oppress, exploit, and dominate people to accumulate wealth and power. If my kingdom were this kind of society, then of course, my followers would rise up in revolt and seek to overthrow you by force. But it is not that kind of kingdom. It is a kingdom totally outside your capacity to understand, because you understand power only as being unilateral and dominating, and you do not understand the power of relational love in community. So you and I, Pilate, come from two entirely different kingdoms, two entirely different ways of understanding life."

Pilate is confused and exasperated. This conversation began with Jesus on trial. And now, Jesus has deftly turned the tables so that Pilate finds himself—and the Roman Empire he represents—on trial before this Jewish peasant! So all Pilate can do is return to his old argument: "So you are a king?" (John 18:37).

Jesus isn't through with Pilate yet. He replies, "You say that I am a king. For this I was born and for this I came into the world, to testify to the truth. Everyone who belongs to the truth listens to my voice" (John 18:37). In other words, what Jesus says to Pilate is this: "I am here—even now, Pilate, and on trial before you—to testify to the truth. I am one who reveals the world as God intended it to be and calls people like you to use your influence to return society to God's intentions. And anyone who responds to this message and receives God's intentions for our life together is a part of this new kingdom—this beloved community of truth."

Pilate responds with his now famous line, peculiar only to the gospel of John. "What is truth?" (18:38) He simply does not understand that Truth is standing in front of him.

Pilate's moment of salvation, his opportunity as both a human being and as a high government official to embrace an entirely different way of life passes by. The door slams shut. The conversation is ended. And Pilate is found guilty.

Who Wins? Who Loses? The Crucifixion as Enthronement: "So [Pilate] handed [Jesus] over to them to be crucified" (John 19:16). The story of Jesus' crucifixion is uniquely nuanced by John.

John notes that the chief priests, rather than the soldiers, receive Jesus for crucifixion (John 19:16). But the Roman soldiers are there to execute the priests' orders (19:23). Thus, the complicity of both Rome and the Judean aristocracy continues to the very end.

It is intriguing to note that John uses the Greek word for "title" to refer to the inscription above Jesus' head, "Jesus of Nazareth, the King of the Jews." The term for "title" is specifically used for kings, particularly at their enthronement.

Dying on the cross, Jesus even takes the time and is in control sufficiently to make arrangements for the continued care of his mother by his beloved disciple.

Finally, Jesus declares, "It (i.e., his work, his mission) is completed," and "he hands over his spirit" to God (19:30). Jesus chooses his moment of death, just as he chose the method. The Judeans haven't won, for Jesus could have been rescued if he so chose (18:36). His enthronement has now occurred at the cross, for the cross is to John the symbol of Jesus' victory, not his defeat.

Why did Jesus have to die? John interprets Jesus' death as a sacrifice for and liberation of humanity, an act of atonement (John 19:36). And he indicates that those responsible for his death are the leaders of Israel's systems and the Romans (19:37) who conspired together to rid the nation of the man whose death would become redemptive and liberating to the people oppressed by those systems.

Resurrection as the End and Beginning of the Story: The gospel of John presents more on the resurrection than any of the other gospel narratives. We will look at only one of those stories, because it is so pivotal to the purpose of the book of John. That story is found in John 21:1–14.

The story begins at daybreak, with the disciples in their boat, having fished all night but having caught nothing. The risen Jesus appears on the shore, calling to them and asking if they have caught anything. They report they have not. He tells them to cast their nets on the other side of the boat, which they obediently do. The result is that they catch a great school of fish—so much they can't haul in the net. Peter leaps into the sea to swim to shore, because he recognizes the figure on the shore as Jesus. The others bring in the boat, dragging the great catch to Jesus.

On shore, they seem to forget about the catch in their eagerness to be with Jesus. He has prepared a breakfast for them of bread and fish (cf. John 6:1–15), and they add some of their own catch to the meal. Then this story concludes, "Jesus came and took the bread and gave it to them, and did the same with the fish. This was now the third time that Jesus appeared to the disciples after he was raised from the dead" (21:13–14).

The story is full of meaning, particularly at this location in the gospel narrative. The boat is obviously the church, Jesus' little community of believers. Then, as light slowly dawns, we see on the shore the risen Christ. He calls to us, and we "cast our nets" into the chaotic sea of the world, seeking to make a difference, seeking to win people to that Lord who stands on the beach, seeking to work for the transformation of the world. When we do that work in obedience to Jesus' command, then God blesses and our nets are filled to the breaking point with a bountiful harvest (John 4:35–38).

As Jesus' body, the church performs this mission for Jesus. As we do, we find the Lord awaiting us, a morning banquet prepared for us. He accepts for that banquet the offerings we add to it. And then, as his community gathered around our Lord, Jesus takes the bread and breaks it, he takes the cup and shares it, and we commune together as one joyous family that is now reunited forever! Thus the countercultural Christ has created his countercultural community, and through it transformed the world.

SUMMARY

The primary question of this chapter has been, "What did Jesus come to do?" We have begun answering that question by looking carefully at Jesus as represented by Matthew, Mark, Luke, and John in the four gospels. We have seen Jesus presented as one who was committed to the realization of jubilee for Israelite society, a radical who was creating a culture counter to the dominant culture of control, oppression, and exploitation, and who was marginalized from that dominant culture because he was calling for God's alternative to the world as it is. We were introduced to a Jesus who saw himself as God's means to bringing about the transformation of society, the one who through his life, ministry, death, and resurrection would act to inaugurate God's kingdom. We were introduced to a Jesus who was engaged in the pain and struggle and radicalization of society, a Jesus who confronted the political, economic, and values-forming leaders and systems of his day and sought to change them, a Jesus who knew the powers of the world would reject him and therefore set himself to building those who followed him into a people of power who could join with him in seeking the transformation of the world.

The church we know has most often represented Jesus to us as the Son of God who has died to "save us from our sins." But what are our sins? Are they the naughty things we do or the nasty thoughts we think? To make that our sins is to trivialize the death of Jesus. So what are our sins? Are not our sins the rejection of God as the daily ruler of our lives, the refusal to deeply care and commit to all humanity? Is not our sin to use the political process as a means to protect our interests at the expense of others, to seek security in money and investments and stock portfolios? What do "the naughty things we do" have to do with gang warfare that is threatening the lives of children, or being declared "redundant" as one's company downsizes, or living in deteriorated housing conditions, or experiencing constant racial prejudice? A Jesus that has been represented to Christians as God's answer for solely our personal sin gives precious little direction or offers precious little hope to Christians who are being sinned against by the political, economic, and values-creating systems of our society.

What would happen if the church would reclaim for itself the Jesus of Matthew, Mark, Luke, and John? How would the church be different if it believed that Jesus worked for both the transformation of people and the transformation of their society so that people and their systems would both embrace authentic relationship with God, exercise a politics of justice, and practice a stewardship of their common wealth so that poverty would be eliminated from that society? What would happen if we believed that God's work of salvation was as big as the totality of sin—corporate as well as individual, economic and political as well as spiritual—and that Christ had come to die for that entire world? How would the church be different if it saw itself as working with Christ for the building of the shalom community? And what could Christian people accomplish to right the wrongs in their city, and view such work as being the logical extension of the work that their Lord and Savior had come to do?

What would happen if the savior truly visited our cities? That's what we will explore in the next chapter, as we ask the question, "How has God come in Jesus Christ to save us, both as individuals and as a society?"

QUESTIONS

1. How does this chapter answer the question, "What did Jesus come to do?" What is the significance of labeling each of the gospel narratives with a particular way of understanding Jesus (the Jubilee Jesus, the Marginalized Messiah, the Radical Rabbi, the Countercultural Christ)?

2. What most speaks to you in these interpretations of the life, ministry, death, and resurrection of Jesus?

3. How would it impact the ministries of our churches if this kind of Jesus were to visit our cities?

Chapter Three

GOD'S WORK OF SALVATION AS FOUNDATION

FOR BUILDING A PEOPLE OF POWER

On Thanksgiving Day 1950, I had an experience that would radically shape the rest of my life. During that holiday, my sister invited me to accompany her to an evangelistic meeting in an Episcopal church. I was 13 at the time. Dorothy was dating a young Episcopalian who was an ardent Christian, and he had shared his faith with her. As a result, she had received Christ as her Savior and wanted me to receive him as well. That led to a series of arguments between her and me extending over about six months. The debates finally stopped when I declared, "Dot, I simply don't believe there is a God. But if you can prove to me that God exists, then I will consider what you have to say about Jesus Christ."

That squelched the argument (or so I thought), but in reality, Dot was merely biding her time. On that Thanksgiving Day, knowing that I was all "mellowed out" with a full stomach of turkey and all the fixings, she invited me to that evangelistic service. She got me to attend by telling me that a missionary would be speaking who worked in the Amazon River basin, and that he was going to show a film on his travels up that giant river. Since I was fascinated at the time with Brazil and the Amazon, I readily agreed to go. But I was going to get more than a vicarious trip up the Amazon River.

Before he showed the film, the missionary spoke. His topic was, "How you can know there is a God." I expected a philosophical argument. What I got was something entirely different.

The missionary held up a chair and said, "I could present you with an esoteric argument for the existence of God, and it might convince you that an object named 'God' exists in the universe—just as this chair exists. But what would I have accomplished by such an argument? I would have simply convinced you that there is an object in this universe we call 'God,' just as there is an object in the universe we call 'chair.'

"But," he continued, "God is not an object like this chair to be proved. God is a person to be known, loved, and experienced, and he is experienced in the man Christ Jesus. Think of a person whom you know and who loves you; think of the person sitting next to you." (I thought of my sister.) "You know him or her. But how do you know that person? Do you have to have that person's existence proven to you? Of course not. And why not? Simply because you experience that person everyday in your life, and that person is already very real to you."

Then he brought it home. "Well, just as this person is one you experience and love, so God in Christ is a person you can experience in your everyday life. And once you have experienced him and come to know him, you no longer need to have his existence proven to you. And why? Because you already know him."

That did it! This missionary had presented an argument for the existence of God I couldn't deny. To meet and experience God is to know God. But to refuse to experience him would mean that to have his existence proven to me would be meaningless—because even though I might know about him, I wouldn't know him.

At that point, the missionary ended his sermon and gave an altar call, asking those in the audience who had never met God face-to-face to come down the aisle and meet God at the altar. And I found myself thinking, "If God exists, and I refuse to meet him, then I have lost everything. If, on the other hand, he doesn't exist and I discover that by going to meet someone who isn't there, I may feel somewhat foolish, but I have actually lost nothing. It's worth the risk to find out whether God exists or not." Without realizing it, I had stumbled onto Pascal's Wager, and I was about to take it.

Down the aisle I went. The missionary's wife took me into a back room to prepare me to pray the sinner's prayer, and there I received Christ as my Lord and Savior. I discovered that day that God is real. And I have never doubted the reality of God again.

Incidentally, I never did get to see the movie, but on that Thanksgiving Day, I began a trip down a much bigger river than the Amazon will ever be. And the amazing justice of God is that years later, even though I missed that film, I got to travel twice up the real Amazon River, meet many of the villagers, visit creative ministries of the church, and see that river's majesty from the deck of the hospital ship that I was traveling on.

Why did I tell you this story? For two reasons. First, I want to explore in this chapter a much wider biblical perspective of the doctrine of salvation than one we are accustomed to articulate—and this story provides a way into that topic. Second, in this chapter we will be dealing with the corporate and social dimensions of salvation. As we do so, I do not want us to lose sight of the reality that God's work of salvation is individual as well as corporate, personal as well as social. And the best way to do that is to give witness to the way God acted in my life to redeem even me.

WHAT DID JESUS COME TO DO?

Thus far in this book, we have examined God's intentions for human society, its nations and its cities, and we have found that intention in the biblical concept of shalom. God is about the task of building a shalom community (the kingdom of God, in Jesus' words) in which the political system is using justice to compensate those who are most powerless, the economic system is equitably distributing the wealth it is generating so that poverty is eliminated, society is built around relationships rather than hierarchy so that all are in a right relationship with God and their neighbors, and the people are living out in their daily lives and in their relationships with each other the love, justice, and economic equitability that the systems are to be practicing. "He has showed you, O mortal, what is right. And what does the Lord require of you but to love justice, to treat each other mercifully, and to walk humbly with your God" (Micah 6:8).

We have looked not only at the world as it should be, but the world as it is. We have looked at the nature and extent of sin in human society, and we have discovered that, like God's intended world, it is corporate and social as well as individual and personal. The full depth and extent of evil cannot be appreciated unless we understand its systemic depth. The systems are as evil—if not more profoundly evil—than are individuals. We have discovered that the Bible presents a "world gone bad" because of systems that have gone bad. The political system, called by God to practice compensatory justice, instead seeks to accrue power to its own institutions and people and thus acts oppressively toward the weakest and most marginalized of its subjects. The economic system, called by God to perceive themselves as stewards of the city's and nation's common wealth in order to equitably distribute that wealth, instead seeks to grasp the wealth for itself and its institutions and systems and thus ends up exploiting the poorest and most powerless in its midst. The religious system, called by God to bring humanity into relationship with God and each other, instead seeks to build its own power, prestige, and parochialism as it seeks to control the thinking and the responses of the people. And finally, the people become seduced by the values and ethics of the systems and they themselves become corrupted by the same lust for power, prestige, possessions, and parochialism and thus become exploiters, oppressors, and controllers of one another.

We examined the ministry that Jesus undertook in the first century to call the systems to accountability and to provide an alternate way. We conducted that exploration by looking at the four primary source documents on Jesus' ministry and teachings—the Gospels of Matthew, Mark, Luke, and John. There we discovered an essentially common message about Jesus. Whether the writer perceived Jesus as the Radical Rabbi, the Marginalized Messiah, the Counter-cultural Christ, or the Jubilee Jesus, all these authors understood Jesus' ministry as one of seeking to recapture for Israel (and then the church) the shalom community—or what Jesus called "the kingdom of God." He was seeking to return Israel and his followers to the world as it should be in the midst of the world as it is. And to recapture the kingdom of God for Israel would require both the leadership of Israel and his followers to embrace the principles of a relational culture, a liberating politics, and equitable distribution of wealth.

Our reason for taking such a careful look at a biblical theology of God's intentions for humanity and the nature of systemic evil, as well as Jesus' commitment to the principles of the jubilee, will become apparent in this chapter—because in this chapter, we will explore a biblical understanding of the salvific work which God did through Jesus Christ. Or to put it another way, one's theory of salvation must be as big as one's understanding of the extent of evil. Otherwise, if it is not, then you will have sin that is, in essence, unforgivable and unforgiven.

So the essential question we must deal with in this chapter is the question, "What did Jesus come to do?"

Jesus' Redemptive Work for the City

> From that time on, Jesus began to show his disciples that he must go
> to Jerusalem and undergo great suffering at the hands of the elders
> and chief priests and scribes, and be killed, and on the third day be
> raised. (Matthew 16:21)

It is important to pay attention to the specific words used in this highly strategic passage. These words demonstrate how importantly Jerusalem—*the* city—figured in Jesus' understanding of God's plan of salvation. Consider these words:

Jesus "began to show (or make it clear)"—by stating the phrase in a repetitive manner, the author wants us to understand the compulsion Jesus felt to communicate clearly to his disciples.

" . . . that he *must* go"—that Jesus was destined to go, compelled to go, driven to go; this was not an optional activity on Jesus' part.

" . . . go to Jerusalem and undergo great suffering at the hands of the elders and chief priests and scribes, and be killed, and on the third day be raised." Note, again, the strong language. Jesus is compelled to go to Jerusalem. There, he will suffer and be executed by the leaders of Israel's economic, political, and religious systems. But there, he will also be raised from the dead.

What the author of this Scripture is seeking to communicate is compulsion. Jesus is driven and even destined to go to Jerusalem to suffer and die. His going there is not optional. It must be Jerusalem and nowhere else. He must undergo suffering and execution there. That suffering and death will come at the hands of the systems. But he will be "raised on the third day."

What Matthew wants to make us ask is the question, "Why did Jesus have to go to Jerusalem to die?" There may be many answers. It was the religious center of the Jewish faith. It was the political center of the Jewish nation. It was the economic center of Israel's economy. But the principal reason why Jesus had to go to Jerusalem to die was because, to the Jews, Jerusalem was the archetypal battlefield between God and Satan for control of the world.

Jerusalem was the gathering place of all the systems—the religious, political, and economic systems of Israel and of Rome, the symbolic center of the law and of sin and death (Romans 7–8), the city brooded over both by God and by Satan. It is caught up in the very etymology of the name "Jerusalem," which literally means "City of Yahweh; City of Shalem" (or Satan).[1] *To the Jews, to die in Jerusalem was to die in the spiritual center of the universe—the very center of the principalities and powers, the systems and structures.*

The Jews of Jesus' day literally believed that Jerusalem was the spiritual center of the universe. Popular Jewish belief at the time of Jesus insisted that the temple, symbol of that centrality, had been built upon a rock that was the entrance into Sheol or the Jewish afterlife. The temple, as the center and the principle symbol of Jewish faith, was the capstone holding Sheol at bay, and controlling entrance into the afterlife of either heaven or hell.[2] Jerusalem was the spiritual center of the universe—and that was why Jesus had to die there, and nowhere else.

What Did Jesus Come to Do?

The New Testament Scriptures are replete with an understanding of the essential work of salvation that Jesus came to do. Let's look at one of those Scriptures.

> Jesus said to them, "Jerusalem, Jerusalem, the city that kills the prophets and stones those who are sent to it! How often have I desired to gather your children together as a hen gathers her brood under her wings, and you were not willing! See, your house is left to you. And I tell you, you will not see me until the time comes when you say, 'Blessed is the one who comes in the name of the Lord.'" (Luke 13:34–35)

This passage lays out four insights that underlie our development of a theology of salvation that redeems more than people.

First, this passage demonstrates the patient love of God. Jesus' statement in Luke 13:34 reminds us of the broad spectrum of Jerusalem's sin for over 1,000 years—a sin that is individual, corporate, and systemic, even of the principalities and powers. Yet God went on loving her, forgiving her, and patiently starting all over again with this city.

Second, this Scripture exposes the broken heart of Jesus. It is one of the most poignant moments of Jesus' ministry, when we are enabled to see into his very soul and sense how deeply he is grieving over this city. Society always kills its prophets and stones its truth-tellers. Jesus longs to see the city come to him. But the city's refusal breaks Jesus' heart—for he knows the spiritual, social, and physical desolation towards which the city inevitably is propelling itself. He longs for it to choose him and his social order of the kingdom of God. So his heart is broken over the city's blindness and stubbornness, and its unwillingness to accept the outstretched hands of love and appeal.

Third, this Scripture reveals the calloused refusal of humanity. Jesus weeps over Jerusalem precisely because the potential for their salvation came to them, and they refused it. This is why salvation does not come to the city. It is not that God does not provide for the salvation of the city, for God has done so through Jesus. It is that humanity refuses it; the city will not accept its proffered salvation.

It is particularly important to note that the rejection is corporate. Jesus does not address people here. He addresses the city itself. He is not weeping over the people, but over the city. And he addresses the city directly. "How often have I longed to gather your children together as a hen gathers her brood under her wings, and you were not willing." (Luke 13:34) Jesus does not say, "they were not willing" but rather "you"—that is, the city, the systems of that city—"were not willing."

According to this Scripture, it is the city that Jesus longs to gather to him as a hen gathers her chicks, it is the city Jesus desires to save (that is, its systems, its principalities and powers, its interior spirituality). But it will not. It is the city that refuses to receive Christ as Lord of its corporate life. And therefore, it is the city that is to be rejected. There is simply no other way to read this passage without doing damage to its intent. Jesus is not engaging in hyperbole or symbolic speaking here; he is presenting an accurate critique of the spiritual condition of this particular corporate entity—the city of Jerusalem. And this is consistent with an emphasis throughout the entirety of the gospel—Jesus' call to cities and to nations to repent and be saved.

The final theme sounded in this Scripture deals with the results of the city's rejection. "They will crush you to the ground, you and your children within you, and they will not leave within you one stone upon another, because you did not recognize the time of your visitation from God" (Luke 19:44). The city will be destroyed because the city refused to recognize the redemptive events occurring within it. Because it rejected its moment of salvation, its salvation would have to wait.

Thus, Jerusalem is doomed in these words by Jesus to a continuing cycle of destruction, restoration, and destruction once again. And thus it has been, even unto today. It still cannot see "the time of its visitation from God"—nor even seek to discern it—but gives itself more fully than ever to oppression, exploitation, and control both of its own people and of the Palestinians.

These four emphases provide for us the frame in which we can now think about what it is that Jesus has done, not only for us as individuals or for the city of Jerusalem, but for every political, economic, and religious system and structure from the nation and the world's cities down to the smallest of social units: the family, the neighborhood, the church, and even ourselves.

GOD REDEEMS MORE THAN PEOPLE

An essential theme of Scripture is that Jesus has died in order to bring about the redemption of individuals. But an equally powerful theme throughout the Scripture is the salvation of the corporate structures of society. American Christianity seems to avoid these texts that deal with corporate or societal salvation, or we make symbolic interpretation of them. But if we are to understand the profundity and complexity of the biblical message, we cannot afford to ignore these Scriptures or trivialize them. Instead, we *must* take them seriously and *at face value*. We must be intellectually honest enough to allow the biblical writers to speak for themselves, rather than to reinterpret what they are saying in order to get them to fit into our preconceived understanding of the work God was doing through Christ for the redemption of the world. Let us look at a few of those disturbing texts:

Romans 8:18–25

The apostle Paul wrote to the church in Rome these startling words: "The creation waits with eager longing for the revealing of the children of God; for the creation was subjected to futility, not of its own will but by the will of the one who subjected it, in hope that the creation itself will be set free from its bondage to decay" (8:19–21). What on earth is Paul talking about?

The context of this startling passage is Paul's analysis of why human beings can't make and maintain consistently good systems (Romans 7:7–24) and why God's intervention through Jesus Christ is necessary to make systems act as God intended (7:25—8:17). (This passage will be explored in detail in the next major section of this chapter.) So Paul, dealing with the transformation of the world's systems through Christ, in this passage takes it a step further by speculating on what Christ's death has done for the entire cosmos—the created order.

Paul asserts here that the entire created order is in bondage to decay; it is, in other words, "running down" (the second law of thermodynamics). Therefore, Paul asserts, it is subject to decadence and sin. But such collapse is not inevitable. God, the creator of the cosmos, is still at work in the cosmos. And he is at work in the cosmos through Jesus Christ. "Creation will be set free from its bondage to decay and will obtain the freedom of the glory of the children of God" (Romans 8:21). The created order will be saved. It will someday be set free from its own entropy and decay. And when it is set free from its seemingly inevitable running down, it will experience the same "freedom" and "glory" as do "the children of God."

It is, Paul suggests, as if creation is in the process of childbirth, "groaning in labor pains" to bring forth that which none of us has the capability to understand. But it will be a new creation, a new universe, and a new cosmos, as God would have it be. And the only way we can begin to glimpse this magnificent work of redemption and liberation that God is doing through Christ with the entire created order is to examine that work in the light of the work God is doing in us—for our redemption witnesses to us of "the first fruits of the Spirit." As God has done a miracle in our lives, so God will do a miracle in all of creation.

Colossians 1:15–20

Paul states what is implied and hinted at in Romans clearly and unequivocally in the book of Colossians. He writes, "(Jesus) is the image of the invisible God, the firstborn of all creation; for in him all things in heaven and on earth were created, things visible and invisible, whether thrones or dominions or rulers or powers—all things have been created through him and for him" (1:15–16).

This is a statement about Jesus Christ. But as Paul tells us in this passage about who Jesus is and what he came to do, he also tells us a great deal about the scope of the salvation given through Jesus Christ.

Jesus, Paul is telling us, is the incarnation of God—God in the flesh. As an integral part of the godhead, Jesus was one with God in the creation of the heavens and the earth. He created both the world and the galaxies (the "visible") and the spiritual dimensions of reality (the "invisible"). He created "thrones, dominions, rulers, powers."

It is important to understand that this terminology of "thrones, dominions, rulers, powers" was established political-economic-religious[3] nomenclature at the time of Paul. We touched on this in chapter one, but let's look more carefully at this concept. A "throne" was the symbol of power [i.e., the seat of authority]; "dominions" were the lands held by the king; a "ruler" was the individual monarch currently occupying the "throne" and ruling his "dominion"; the "powers" were the legal statutes, ordinances, and covenants and the military force that would legitimize the "ruler." So these were all political/economic terms any Jewish or Gentile reader of Paul's day would clearly understand.

Paul thus contends in this passage that Jesus gave to the monarchs of the earth their authority to rule. These monarchs were created to serve Jesus by serving the people with justice and the wise stewardship of the nation's resources for benefit of all the people. This, of course, was an astounding (and when being used in reference to Rome, a treasonous) claim.

Further, Paul states, Jesus is the "ruler" of the church, "the head of the body." He is the first (but not the last) of the church to rise from the dead. Creation began in him. Creation will end in him. Therefore, in him "all the fullness of God was pleased to dwell." But that indwelling of God's presence in the Son is for one purpose—"to reconcile to himself all things, whether on earth or in heaven, by making peace through the blood of his cross."

It is the sacrificial death of Jesus that reconciles a sinful universe to a sinless God. But notice with what care Paul crafts this statement of the redemptive work of Christ. Jesus "reconciles to himself *all things*"—not just individuals, not just humankind, but also *all things*. And what are those "all things"? They were listed above. Christ has reconciled the Church, the political and economic systems of the world, and even creation itself to God. And to make sure the reader gets the point, Paul adds "whether on earth or in heaven"—the entire created order is reconciled to God. God through Christ saves more than people.

John 3:16–17

We now come to what must be the most misinterpreted passage in the Scripture.

> God so loved the world that he gave his only Son, so that everyone
> who believes in him may not perish but may have eternal life. Indeed,
> God did not send the Son into the world to condemn the world, but in
> order that the world might be saved through him. (John 3:16)

When I was a child in Sunday School, I once had a teacher have me read John 3:16 this way: "For God so loved Bobby Linthicum that he gave his only begotten Son, so that Bobby Linthicum believing in him may not perish but may have everlasting life." Is that true? Absolutely! Is that what John 3:16 says? No, it does not!

The story that reaches its zenith in John 3:16 begins with the text telling us, "Now there was a Pharisee named Nicodemus, a leader of the Jews. He came to Jesus by night" (John 3:1–2). This passage tells us three things about Nicodemus. First, he belonged to the Pharisee movement of Israel—one of the nation's principle power groups Jesus opposed. Second, he was a "leader of the Jews"—in other words, he was a member of the Sanhedrin and therefore a part of the ruling body in Israel. Third, he came to Jesus "by night." Normally, we think of Nicodemus as being an honest seeker after truth, but the text doesn't imply that. In fact, the text implies the opposite, noting in particular that he came "by night." Nicodemus came under cover of darkness, hoping not to be recognized.

This "leader" never gets to tell Jesus the purpose for which he has come. Instead, he opens with words of flattery, which was an appropriate way of beginning a conversation with a teacher at that time. Jesus interrupts and cuts to the chase with the words, "Very truly, I tell you, no one can see the kingdom of God without being born again" (John 3:3). The words the author has Jesus use for "born again" are intriguing. It can correctly be translated either "born from above" or "born again"; either translation is equally correct. The church has filled that word with all kinds of theological content ("Brother, are you born again?" "He's a born-again Christian."). But consider to whom Jesus is speaking, and what he is demanding of him.

Nicodemus is highly positioned in the political and economic establishment. He is a part of "the world" that John has previously described as "darkness." He is a part of the dominating hierarchy of Israel that has made itself powerful at the expense of the peasants. Now Jesus is telling him, "You cannot experience the kingdom of God—the shalom community—unless you are born again, born from above."

In other words, Jesus is saying to him, "Nicodemus, if you really want to embrace the kingdom of God for yourself, then you have to start all over again. You have to be willing to die to your dominating way of life, and be 'born again'—as if you were a fresh, new baby—living the kingdom life. And that can't happen except that you are 'born from above'; you must allow God to work in your soul and life to liberate you from your commitment to all that makes you powerful and be willing to join this relational community of my disciples. And you can't do that, Nicodemus, by coming 'at night.' You can't do it and escape notice. You can only do it by openly embracing a personal and public life of a politics of justice, an economics of equitable sharing of wealth, and 'to walk humbly with your God' as a member of my community. You must be born again, Nicodemus."

Then either Jesus or the narrator moves on to a commentary on Jesus' challenge to Nicodemus: "For God so loved the world that he gave his only Son, so that everyone who believes in him may not perish but may have eternal life" (John 3:16). This is a summary of Jesus' gospel. God loves "the world," "the cosmos," the "created order," the "social structures," "humankind" so much that he gave his Son so that humanity might come to redemption. Even those who are God's enemies receive God's unmerited love. God's love, manifested in Jesus, is so powerful that it brings everyone and everything into the circle of his love (even the Roman Empire).

The basis for judgment is not God's act but each person's and each system's decision. "Indeed, God did not send the Son into the [cosmos] to condemn the [cosmos], but in order that the [cosmos] might be saved through him" (John 3:17).

But if it is not God that condemns us, then what causes the cosmos—the universe, the earth, the systems of the world, humankind, individuals—to be lost? Jesus or the narrator continues: "And this is the judgment, that the light has come into the [cosmos], and people loved darkness rather than light because their deeds were evil" (John 3:19).

The judgment is that people like Nicodemus (or you or me) choose to join with the political system, their businesses and industry, their religion and value systems in the practice of domination, oppression, and exploitation. It is their actions that lead to rejection. Their deeds betray them, for those deeds reveal whether one's heart belongs to the "light" or to the "darkness." It's up to you, Nicodemus? Whom will you choose?

Here we see in John 3:16–17 a magnificent blending of the personal and the corporate, the individual and the systems. John is proclaiming that Jesus has come to set free the entire cosmos from "darkness" (i.e., domination, oppression, and exploitation). Whether individuals, the systems and structures of society, and humankind as a totality ever experience being set free depends entirely upon us—and whether we embrace the new world Jesus is bringing to us in all its capacity to transform all of human existence.

2 Corinthians 5:17–20

In what is one of the most beautiful statements in Paul's writings, the apostle sums up the entire work of Christ in this pithy statement, "In Christ, God was reconciling the world to himself" (5:19).

Paul suggests that the primary work in which God is involved through Christ is the work of reconciliation. When one considers that Paul is writing this letter to one of the most divided churches in first-century Christendom, this is a particularly poignant statement. The work of Christ, Paul is saying, is the work of reconciliation. Consequently, we should be living as a reconciled and not divided fellowship. And we should assume Christ's work of reconciliation, both between each other and to a hostile world.

What are of particular note in the context of this chapter, however, are the parameters that Paul presents on God's work of reconciliation. The work of healing, of pulling together factions and binding up the wounds they have inflicted upon each other, of making whole again, is the essential work in which God is involved in Christ. And the arena of such binding up and making whole again is the "world." Again, this is the word "cosmos," with all of the meaning explored earlier in John 3:16. God is at work seeking to bring together oppressed and oppressor, exploited and exploiter, the controlled and the controllers. But this is done, not by becoming resigned to the misuse of power, wealth, and status by the political, economic, and religious leaders but by their surrender of such forces of domination, as they seek the common good. Reconciliation can occur only when that which has caused the breach is dealt with. When that breach is caused by the misuse of power, wealth, and privilege, that means a resolution of such misuse and a willingness to embrace justice, equitability, and a relational culture by the offenders.

The community that is given the responsibility of working for such reconciliation by God is the Christian community. Of all people, they should know God's desires for all society. But they can't take on such a ministry with any authenticity unless they have dealt with the divisions that lie between themselves. As long as one says, "I am of Peter's party," and another, "I am of Paul," and another, "I keep my allegiance to Apollos" (1 Corinthians 1:10–17), then none of them are of Christ. They are obligated, as people of "the Way," to overcome their differences and act as one community of faith.

The task to which all Christians are called, according to this passage, is to be "ambassadors for Christ" and that means "since God is making his appeal through us, we entreat you on behalf of Christ, be reconciled to God" (2 Corinthians 5:20). We cannot do the work of reconciliation; only God can ultimately do that work as people and the systems respond to the vision of the shalom community. But we are to be ambassadors—representatives of the king who share his message and seek reconciliation.

Revelation 11:15–19

The final Scripture we will explore in this section, "God Redeems More Than People," is from the final book of the Bible: The writer of Revelation proclaims, "The kingdom of the world has become the kingdom of our Lord and of his Messiah, and he will reign forever" (11:15).

Many of us have had the joy of singing in a mass choir George Frideric Handel's magnificent "Hallelujah Chorus."[4] For many who have had little encounter with Scripture, it has introduced them to the moving words of Revelation 11:15 as they sing, "The kingdom of this world will become the kingdom of our Lord and of His Christ." Unfortunately, most singing it believe that the text should read "the kingdoms of this world will become the kingdom of our Lord," and are transported to a vision of the nations of the world streaming to the throne of God where they will be united into one. It is a magnificent and moving vision, and I've heard it articulated by many. Unfortunately, it is a vision not accurate to the text.

The Greek does not say, "The kingdoms of this world will become the kingdom of our Lord and of His Christ." The Greek says, "The *kingdom* of this world has become the kingdom of our Lord" (Revelation 11:15). It is singular—kingdom, not kingdoms. What is it that John is saying in this passage?

What John is proclaiming is that human society, as we know it, will be transformed into God's society. The "kingdom of this world," in the book of Revelation, is not individual nations. The "kingdom of this world" is the current world order. And what is that world order?

The current world order, the "kingdom of this world," is a society dominated by the politically and militarily powerful who are practicing a politics of power and oppression. It is an international, national, regional, and local business community whose bottom line is the accumulation of wealth, doing whatever is necessary to gain that wealth, even if it is at the expense of the community. It is the systems of society that create and maintain the values of that society—including the media, educational systems, the sports world, the world of entertainment as well as the religious community and the "spin doctors" of the political and economic systems—all who are concerned with controlling and conventionalizing the thinking of people. To the writer of the book of Revelation, that is "the kingdom of this world."

What he is declaring, therefore, is that "the kingdom of this world" will get converted. Somehow, God-in-Christ is going to break through to them—as impossible as it sounds. They will hear. And they will respond. Even the current world order will "become the kingdom of our Lord and of his Messiah." And when that happens, all of reality will burst into song even greater than the Hallelujah Chorus, singing, "We give you thanks, Lord God Almighty, for you have taken your great power and begun to reign" (Revelation 11:16).

As we look at these selected passages from the New Testament, it is obvious that to the earliest Christians, the work of Christ encompassed more than the salvation of individuals. It included their salvation, but it went far beyond that. Christ's salvific work, as developed throughout the Scripture is both individual and corporate, both private and systemic, both for people and for the political, economic, and religious systems of society, for the city, the nation, the world, the universe—the entire created order.

CLAIMING A DOCTRINE OF SALVATION
AS BIG AS THE WORLD ITSELF

The most comprehensive statement found in Scripture describing the breadth of salvation is Romans 7:7–8:4. But the key to comprehending Paul's description of salvation is first to understand what he means by the law.

In the book of Romans, Paul presents his trilogy of the forces that separate humanity from God. That trilogy is sin, death, and the law. His definitions of sin and death are obvious, but what does Paul mean by "the law"? Obviously, he does not mean Roman law, nor does he simply mean the Torah and its accompanying traditions, because his description of the law is too comprehensive to simply mean the written Jewish law.

What Paul meant by "the law" is the religious, cultural, political, and economic mosaic of rules and regulations that ordered all of life throughout worldwide Judaism. It includes the essential values by which Jewish life is to be lived, the structures by which those values are to be enacted into everyday life, and the offices (e.g., high priest, Levitical priesthood, scribes) and parties (the Pharisees, the Sadducees, the Sanhedrin)—or, in other words, the people by which these values and structures are to be implemented throughout worldwide Jewry. In other words, by the very definition of a system as consisting of values, structures, and people, what Paul means by "the law" is the primary system of worldwide Judaism. Understanding Paul's definition of the law is extremely strategic to our understanding of the book of Romans, and of Paul's message contained therein.

Why Humans Can't Build Consistently Good Systems

In Romans 7:7–13, Paul presents his perspective as to why human beings can't make and maintain consistently good systems—or, in other words, why humans can't build the shalom community by themselves. Paul had earlier contended that the Christian is free from the demands of the law (i.e., the system of worldwide Judaism), sin, and death, because we have been set free by the sacrifice of Christ. Now it is incumbent upon Paul to support that argument. To do so, the apostle writes, "What then should we say? That the law is sin? By no means! Yet, if it had not been for the law, I would not have known sin. . . . Did what is good, then, bring death to me? By no means! It was sin, working death in me through what is good, in order that sin . . . might become sinful beyond measure" (Romans 7:7, 13).

In order to understand the depth of what Paul is saying here, we must keep in mind that every reference by Paul to "the law" is a reference to an all-encompassing, controlling structure of systems—what Paul called the "Principalities and Powers." Keeping in mind that what Paul is referring to when he speaks of "the law" is what we mean today by the systems of the Jewish religion and society, consider what the apostle is actually saying here.

When there were no systems ordering life (i.e., the Garden of Eden), humanity was "alive" in God. But when the systems of Israel (and, by inference, all nations and cities) came into existence, sin (or the lust for power, wealth, or control) sprang to life and we spiritually died. It was not because the systems are evil that society became corrupt. To the contrary, the need to create political, economic, and religious systems was placed in humanity by God to provide structure, order, and direction to human society. But the very existence of such systems killed— and still kills—humanity. The very existence of that which we need to focus us, give meaning to life, and which is consequently good for us, leads inevitably to the decay and destruction both of our society and of ourselves. And here is the reason that is true.

The very nature of our humanity will inevitably seek to take advantage of any system that structures our lives. Our very proclivity as human beings towards protecting our own interests and taking advantage of any weakness in our competitors—that is, our very proclivity toward sinfulness and lawlessness—will inevitably destroy even the best systems we might invent. By our very nature as sinful (that is, self-serving) creatures, we corrupt the very systems we create to structure life.

A good example of this tendency in us can be seen in the common phenomena of pastors who have committed themselves to the ministry of a single congregation for much of their careers. They may build that church into a strong and large congregation from a small and weak one. But then they can't let go. They begin hurting people, using every means at their disposal to maintain control and essentially identifying themselves with that church. The church begins to suffer. It stops growing and moves into stasis. The lay leadership becomes increasingly critical of the methods and tactics of the pastor. As they do, that pastor becomes even less flexible, increasingly dictatorial, and increasingly ineffective. So it is that this pastor ends up unintentionally tearing down and even destroying that church and ministry (that is, that system) that he has spent decades building.

So those systems, created to bring order to life, bring us death instead. That is why human beings can never create a good society. We are, in essence, our own worst enemy.

Why We Are Our Own Worst Enemy

"I do not do what I want, but I do the very thing I hate. . . . Wretched man that I am! Who will rescue me from this body of death" (7:15, 24)? In these words, Paul speaks for "Everyman," for we cannot help but recognize ourselves in his admission of his own sinfulness. Paul recognizes the importance of the systems for ordering life and acknowledges they have great capacity for social good. But he tells us in Romans 7:14–24, there is something demonic in him—and in fact, in every one of us—that always wants to "beat the system," to use the system for one's own ends. That attitude, acted out over and over again by each person, century after century, person after person after person, family after family after family, organization after organization after organization, system after system corrupts both one's self and the systems we create and maintain.

A simple experience which all of us have had illustrates Paul's point. Either by accident or by intent, you drive through a red light. What do you instinctively do, once you realize that you have broken the law? You look in the rear-view mirror. Why? In order to check whether a police car is pursuing you. And if you see no pursuing police, if you see no flashing light or hear no blaring siren, how do you feel? Sorry? Crestfallen for having broken the law? In deep remorse? Come on—be honest. What you feel is exactly what I feel—exaltation! I've broken the law—*and I've gotten away with it! I've beaten the system!*

The point Paul is making is this. The enemy is not, in the final analysis, the systems themselves. The enemy is not simply "them"—the maintainers and creators of the systems. The enemy is not simply "those politicians," the "owners of the market," the "religious or academic elite." *The enemy is us!*

If we do not see this, then we will operate out of a dichotomy that divides the world into good guys and bad guys. We will see other institutions and their people as being evil and ourselves as being good. The reason why we will do that is because we will be judging others by their actions while judging ourselves by our intentions.

If, on the other hand, we recognize the great capacity for evil that lies within ourselves, the more realistic we will be in understanding the world. It is imperative for us as Christians, Paul is essentially saying in this passage, to understand that the systems are not evil and we are good, but that evil lies in each of us, that evil compels all of us to attempt to beat the very systems we create, and that consequently we destroy everything we touch even when our intentions are good and honorable.

One percent of the population of the United States owns 40 percent of the wealth, and 5 percent of the population owns 60 percent of the wealth of this nation.[5] In fact, the world's *three richest individuals* have as much wealth as the world's 43 poorest countries combined.[6] Yet all the hungry, sick, dying people of the world could be fed, adequately housed, clothed, and given adequate health care if these three individuals or that 1 percent of America's richest families would contribute only 5 percent of their annual income.[7] And our reaction to such news is to ask, "What's the matter with these people? Why do they have to be so greedy? What kind of human beings are they, anyway?"

What kind of human beings are they? They are human beings just like us. The only difference between the powerful and us is that we have lacked their opportunity. If we were worth a billion dollars, our concern would be to protect it. If we were president of the United States, we would be concerned about preserving and exercising our power. Given a reversal of roles, we would likely act in situations comparable to the way the powerful and wealthy act, to preserve our power, accumulate wealth, and seek to control the thinking and obedience of our "subjects."

The enemy is not "them"; the enemy is "us." It is our own deeply ingrained and perfidious nature that will keep on corrupting every system that we create or in which we participate. Because of our own need to use to our own advantage every system in which we find ourselves—and because every single human being who is also in that system is seeking to use it in every way that he can for his advantage—we will destroy every structure, every institution that we touch—even when our intentions are good.

So the inevitable conflict in the human/societal condition, according to Paul, comes down to this: "I can will what is right, but I cannot do it. For I do not do the good I want, but the evil I do not want is what I do." What hope is there, then, for me, for my family, for my community, for my church, for my city, for my nation, for the world—*if even I am the enemy?*

The Solution: "Thanks Be to God for Jesus Christ our Lord!"

"Thanks be to God for Jesus Christ our Lord!" (Romans 7:25). Paul concludes that only Jesus can release us as individuals, can release the systems we create, and can release all of the created order from the powers of sin, death, and the law. Salvation does not lie in our political designs, our economic systems, even in the religion in which we might believe. Salvation does not lie in any person—whether ourselves or a great leader, since both that leader and we who follow him will be corrupted by our own self-service. It is only by the intervention of God in our political, economic, and religious systems and into our individual lives that we can be released from our own perfidious nature to corrupt everything we touch. And that intervention has already happened through the death and resurrection of Jesus Christ.

But how has Christ's death and resurrection enabled both us and the systems that we create to be delivered from the powers of "sin, death, and the law"? Here Paul's theology reaches its most profound level in an analysis far more sophisticated than the writing of any other New Testament author.

"God has done what the law, weakened by the flesh, could not do: by sending his own Son in the likeness of sinful flesh, and to deal with sin, he condemned sin in the flesh, so that the just requirement of the law might be fulfilled in us" (Romans 8:3–4). The "systems" of God—that is, the "law (or systems) of the spirit of life in Christ Jesus"—is able to liberate us from the systems ordering the world. God has done what neither our systems nor we can do, because we so pervasively corrupt and demonize every system in which we find ourselves.

It is through the intervention of Jesus' death that God has fulfilled all the obligations of all systems. That is, it was only Jesus who as God in the flesh would not and did not corrupt every system in which he was placed, because he was the only human being never to proceed from self-service, manipulation, or control. And because he could live sinless before the systems, and to do so in our stead, all the demands our systems place upon us, all the demands the specter of death, and the very corruptibleness of our own personalities make upon us—have been met and satisfied in Christ.

In his death, Christ met all the conditions of the law (the systems); he faced the worst of death for us at the hands of the political, economic, and religious systems of Israel and of Rome. He plunged the depth of human corruption *in our stead and in the systems' stead.*

This is what the Apostles Creed means by that mysterious teaching, "He descended into hell." Jesus descended in his death into the hell of the worst humanity and human society could throw at him. He plunged the greatest depths of human corruption. He has received all that corruption could throw at any human being, not just the corruptions of individuals or of groups, but of the systems themselves. In the most profound act of redemption and forgiveness, Paul tells us, Christ had plunged the very depths, not only of our sin but also of the systems, because God wants transformed systems, redeemed creation. In that plunge, Jesus took upon himself all the evil—personal, corporate, and systemic evil—could ever do, and thus he liberated us *and our systems* from the necessity of evil's complex grasp. We are redeemed. And the systems have also been set free by the sacrificial death of Christ.

It is in that light of what Christ has done for us and our systems that we can then join with him in working to bring the world's systems in fact as well as in spirit and in truth under the authority and control of God. Doing that, on our part, recaptures for all humanity the shalom community. Jesus has made it possible. That is why he died, according to the apostle Paul.

As we draw to the end of this chapter, I do not want any reader to interpret what I have written to suggest that I do not value individual salvation. If I did that, I would be denying the power of how Christ has saved me and, consequently, denying the importance for my life of the story with which I began this chapter. Rather, what I am seeking to do is to reclaim for the church the full-orbed doctrine of salvation that is at the very heart of the New Testament.

SUMMARY

Salvation is personal and individual. But it is also social, corporate, and even cosmic. This chapter has sought to thoroughly explore selected scriptures that teach a salvation that is greater than the conversion of individuals. Through their exploration, we have discovered that salvation is both individual and corporate, both private and systemic, both for people and for the political, economic, and religious systems of society, for the city, the nation, the world, the universe—the entire created order.

If we believe that God is actively at work through Jesus Christ to redeem the structures and systems of our city and nation, that God is seeking to transform society's values into relational and just values, then we will have a much more holistic and comprehensive understanding of God's work in our midst. If we claim the apostle Paul's theology as our own, then our God will become a God who is in love with His creation and is actively seeking to transform it, not abandon it as he seeks to spirit individual souls out of a rejected world and into a personal nirvana. Further, if we believe that God is actively at work through Christ to redeem the world's systems as well as its people, we will be able to move into ministries that affirm the world and work for its full transformation.

The truth is simply this. Our Lord was not crucified on a golden cross placed upon a marble altar between two silver candlesticks in a Gothic cathedral. He was crucified on a rugged cross between two thieves, on the city's garbage heap, at the kind of place where the powers conspire and systems dominate, and the people become powerless victims.

That is where he died. And that is what he died about. And that is where his people should be. And that is what his people should be about.

QUESTIONS

1. What difference would it make in our ministry and practice of our faith for us to believe that God saves more than people—that God is actively at work seeking to redeem the structures, the systems of the city or nation—or even the city or nation itself?

2. How do you see God actively at work today in your city, redeeming more than solely its people?

3. Holding to such a doctrine of salvation, what would you suspect Christ would call the church to be and do in the city?

Chapter Four

WORKING FOR THE SHALOM
OF YOUR SOCIETY:

GOD'S CALL TO THE CHURCH

What is the work of the church to which the Bible calls us? In the light of the biblical vision of the shalom community that presents God's intentions for all human society, and in the face of society-controlling systems operating out of the value of domination, what is the work that the church is to be about in today's world? Let's look at one biblical answer.[1]

What Jeremiah prophesied would happen did indeed happen. The southern kingdom of Judah was conquered by the Babylonian empire. The political, economic, and religious systems of the nation had collapsed, and with them, the nation. The city of Jerusalem had been burned to the ground and the temple destroyed. The political, economic, and religious leaders of Jerusalem had been dragged off as captives to the city of Babylon by the invading king, Nebuchadnezzar. There, in the city of their captors, the former Israelite leaders lifted up their voices and wept. There, in exile, they began to despair that God would ever deliver them from the hand of their hated captors.

It was to those despairing, grieving captives that a letter came from the prophet Jeremiah. And his advice to those exiles is a word we need to hear as we seek to be God's faithful people in our time and place. That letter—and its advice—now appears in Jeremiah 29:4–11.

> Thus says the LORD of hosts, the God of Israel, to all the exiles whom
> I have sent into exile from Jerusalem to Babylon: Build houses and
> live in them; plant gardens and eat what they produce. Take wives
> and have sons and daughters; take wives for your sons, and give
> your daughters in marriage, that they may bear sons and daughters;

multiply there, and do not decrease. But seek the [*shalom*] of the city where I have sent you into exile, and pray to the LORD on its behalf, for in its [*shalom*] you will find your [*shalom*]. . . . For thus says the LORD: Only when Babylon's seventy years are completed will I visit you, and I will fulfill to you my promise and bring you back to this place. For surely I know the plans I have for you, says the LORD, plans for your [*shalom*] and not for harm, to give you a future with hope.

SEEKING THE SHALOM OF THE CITY

"Only when Babylon's seventy years are completed will I . . . bring you back to [Jerusalem]." Yahweh's initial promise to the Israelite political, economic, and religious leaders in Babylonian exile seems a harsh promise. Through Jeremiah, God tells them that they will remain in exile for seventy years[2]—or in other words, a lifetime! They will not be restored to their precious city of Jerusalem. Likely, neither will their children. Only in their grandchildren lies the hope that Israel will once again be restored to its land.

One might ask why Judah had to be in exile seventy years. Could not the Jews negotiate this sentence with God, as Abraham negotiated the sentence of death God had made upon the people of Sodom (Genesis 18:22–33)? No, they could not negotiate. That was because of the rationale for the sentence of seventy years.

The reason for such a heavy sentence is presented in 2 Chronicles 36:20–21:

> [Nebuchadnezzar] took into exile in Babylon those who had escaped
> from the sword, and they became servants to him and to his sons
> until the establishment of the kingdom of Persia, to fulfill the word
> of the LORD by the mouth of Jeremiah, *until the land had made up for
> its sabbaths.* All the days that it lay desolate it kept sabbath, to fulfill
> seventy years (author's emphasis).

The reason Israel had to be in exile seventy years was that it had failed to keep the sabbatical year seventy times—or, in other words, for 490 years. Therefore, one way or another, God would require of the nation that sabbatical rest and redistribution of wealth—if not voluntarily, then by force. But one way or another, Israel *would* keep Sabbath.

So it was that the Israelite captives were condemned to a seventy-year exile. What depressing news this must have been to them. How is it, then, that God could say to them, "I know the plans I have for you, plans for your [*shalom*] and not for harm, to give you a future with hope" (Jeremiah 29:11)? What kind of future is he giving to them if they must live and die in captivity? How is such a life in slavery "a future with hope" and free of harm? Is not such a promise a cruel hoax on the part of God?

No, it is not a cruel hoax. Though they will remain a lifetime and die in Babylonian exile, God's plan for these captive Israelite leaders is meant for their good. It was as if God were saying to those Israelite captives, "I know what I am doing. It is my plan that you be here. And I promise you that I will bless you in this place—this foreign city. I will make you a rich blessing to all around you. For the promise I give to you is realized as you live out the plan I have for you here in this city of your exile."

Here, then, is God's promise for us called to be the church today: "I have good plans for you." What is God's plan that we are called to carry out in order to access God's promise? Here according to Jeremiah, is the good news in the midst of dark news. That good news is found in the double meaning of a word Jeremiah uses in what is the pivotal verse of that letter —verse 7.

> Work for the [*shalom*] of the city where I have sent you into exile,
> and pray to the LORD on its behalf, for in its [*shalom*] you will find
> your [*shalom*]. (Jeremial 29:7)

In the City by Circumstance or Call?

"Work for the [shalom] of the city where I have *sent you into* exile." The English words "*sent you into exile*" are actually the attempt by English translators to translate a single Hebrew word. The Hebrew word that is here translated "sent you into exile" has a double meaning.[3] It can rightfully be translated "exile." And it can also be translated "sent." Thus, it is reasonable to assume that in the use of this one Hebrew word, Jeremiah is seeking to communicate two distinct ideas to his Hebrew brothers and sisters in Babylon. He is in essence saying to the Israelites, "You are in captivity because your nation was defeated, your army destroyed, your city burned, and you were clapped into chains and marched across the desert into Babylonian exile. That is your *circumstance*. But you are also in captivity because I, the Lord your God, sent you there. You are in Babylon because I need my people in this wicked city. That is your *call from God!*"

Here, then, is God's promise—not only for Israelite captives, but also for all of us called to be the church wherever we are. We are not in our community simply because of our circumstances—because we were born here, or moved here to take a job or get an education or simply accompanied our spouse here. We are in this community because the Lord our God has called us here—sent us here—needs us here. We are in the city or town or university or mission station by the intentional will of God, acted out through the particularity of our circumstances.

Therefore, what are we called—as God's sent people—to be and do in the place where God has planted us? We are called to the very same task, as were those Israelite captives in the city of Babylon 2600 years ago. "[You are to] seek the [*shalom*] of the city where I have sent you into exile, . . . for in its [*shalom*] you will find your [*shalom*]." Our calling as God's people into whatever situation which God might call us is to seek that city's shalom—its peace, prosperity, well-being, wholeness, fullness, reconciliation.

Where Shalom Is to Be Sought

Note where we are to seek the peace. It is not in Jerusalem—the city of God. It is in Babylon! This statement was profoundly, even revolutionarily shocking to the Israelites—beyond anything they could imagine or dare to speak. The Israelites are called to seek God's shalom in the midst of Babylon. They would not experience either personal or corporate shalom as long as Babylon was not a city at peace within itself.

What made this statement such a revolutionary statement was that Babylon was the ultimate symbol of evil to Israel. In the Israelite culture, Babylon was a virtual synonym for depravity. This attitude toward Babylon is reflected throughout Scripture. Thus, in Genesis 11:1–9, the Tower of Babel (the Hebrew form of the name Babylon) is the symbolic place of the "confusion of language" where the unity of the world (symbolized by one tongue) is shattered. Throughout the Bible's historical books and the prophets (e.g., 2 Kings 20:12–19; 24:10–25:30; Jeremiah 25:8–14; Isaiah 13, 14, 47, 48; Amos 5:27; Acts 7:43), Babylon is pictured as evil. And in Revelation 17–18, the elder John gives the name "Babylon" to human civilization lived in defiance of God, practicing a politics of oppression and an economics of greed and exploitation.

To Israel, Babylon is the epitome of the wicked and darkest of cities. It is precisely in the midst of such wickedness and darkness, Jeremiah is saying, that we are to work for shalom. Shalom is not to be sought among God's people, but among those who most reject God. And why? Because God loves Babylon, and can only transform it by sending God's people there (even against their will).

In fact, Jeremiah takes it a step further. He states in verse 7, "for it is in its [shalom] you will find your [shalom]." Even one who is in relationship with God and within the embrace of a relational culture can never fully know peace for his own life, his family or his people, if his city does not experience peace. So God sends his people into precisely the darkest areas of human society to be ambassadors for peace there.

What Is the Shalom We Are to Seek?

But what does it mean to seek the city's peace? In chapter one, we explored the nature of shalom, recognizing that it is a key Hebrew word and concept for describing God's vision for human society. Let's now explore even more deeply the concept of shalom as it applies to the church's mission in the world.

As we pointed out in chapter one, the English word *peace* doesn't begin to capture the rich nuances of the Hebrew word, *shalom*. The English word *peace* is primarily negative in connotation. That is, it simply denotes the absence of something—conflict, violence, or war.

But the Hebrew word *shalom* means much, much more than the simple cessation of hostilities. Shalom is an exceedingly rich concept, a comprehensive word dealing with and covering all the relationships of daily life, expressing the ideal state of life in Israel and, indeed, the entire world. The concept of shalom essentially has to do with what the Israelites saw as being foundational to life—being in a sustained and sustaining community with each other. Therefore, the only words in English today that would capture the reality of shalom might be the words *holism* or *holistic transformation*. But such words are flat and dull next to the concept of shalom.

As we developed in chapter two, Jesus built his theology around the concept of the "kingdom of God." It takes very little reading of the Gospel accounts to recognize that what Jesus meant by the kingdom of God was simply the full living-out of shalom upon the earth. The kingdom of God was shalom personified and particularized in the life of God's people.

The supreme gift of Jesus to his followers was to be shalom, which was to be lifted above the commonplace and the everyday to its highest level—living in unbroken union with God in the midst of the adversities of life—and manifested in our union as brothers and sisters in Christ (John 14:27). This comes about as the result of each of us, and all of us together, embracing the life, death, and resurrection of Jesus as our own and in our stead (Acts 10:36; Ephesians 6:15, 2:17). Full shalom, therefore, is not something we can manufacture or earn, but comes as God's free gift to us—a gift of *amazing* grace (Colossians 1:2, Romans 1:7; 1 Corinthians 1:3; 2 Corinthians 1:2; Galatians 1:3; Philippians 1:2; 2 Thessalonians 1:2).

Finally, shalom is the ultimate hallmark, the identifying mark of the authentic church. Christ has broken down the wall of estrangement between all human dichotomies that separate and alienate us from each other (male versus female, slave versus free, parents versus children, race versus race, systems versus the people). Instead, God's free gift of shalom, continually provided to us as individuals and as a community, draws us into one body (Ephesians 2:14–17; Hebrews 7:2). This is God's continuing act of redemption, its intended scope being the restoration of the whole creation to its proper harmony (Colossians 1:19–22).

When God commands us in Jeremiah 29:7 to "work for the [shalom] of the city to which I have sent you," he is calling us, as God's people, to the universal ministry of shalom-making (Matthew 5:9). The scope of such a ministry is captured in the varied English words used in Jeremiah 29:7 for the Hebrew *shalom*; that word is variously translated as "peace," "prosperity," "welfare," "good."[4] Each translation seeks to capture the rich implications of this command—for, in a profound sense, our task is to be working for the peace *and* the prosperity *and* the welfare *and* the good of all the people, the systems and structures, and even the principalities and powers of our city. It means that nothing is outside the purview, concern, or commitment of the church, whether it is political, economic, religious, social, cultural, environmental, or spiritual, whether it is in the public domain or in the private. To work for the full and total transformation of all the people, forces, and structures of the city with the love of God is the call and responsibility and joyful task of God's people in the city.

Living Out Shalom

When I think of one who truly lived out shalom in his city, I think of a pastor I knew named Ron. Ron became the associate pastor of a Lutheran Church in Detroit in 1968, when that church's neighborhood was going through a painful transition. A major factory, employing a majority of the community's residents, had closed the year before, forcing many into unemployment. In a matter of just a few years, the community had gone from being a white, working-class community with high homeownership to a dominant African-American population with high unemployment. By the time I met Ron in 1978, the community was suffering from 74 percent unemployment and only 2 percent homeowner occupancy.

The membership of Ron's church plummeted overnight, as its constituency fled the neighborhood. But Ron continued on, faithfully serving both that church and the surrounding community, first as its associate pastor, and then after the retirement of its head-of-staff in 1969, as the senior pastor. There he ministered until his own retirement, 30 years later—this being the only church Ron ever served.

It always intrigued me that Ron had stayed his entire ministry in this one church, as its membership severely declined and it changed complexion and character. He never considered a call to any other congregation. One day, I asked him why he had stayed his entire career in this one congregation. I will never forget his response.

"When I accepted the call to become associate pastor of this church," he replied, "I was given the manse in this neighborhood where I was to live. I moved all my furniture into the house on April 4, 1968.

"That was the day Martin Luther King Jr. was killed," Ron continued. "The street that night was full of the neighbors talking in little circles—the whites in their own groups, the blacks in theirs. The pain of the blacks and the jubilance of the whites were obvious. I knew I couldn't just go about the task of moving in. So I left all my boxes and furniture on the porch and began going from group to group, introducing myself as the new pastor, listening to their conversations, and both seeking to minister to the pain of the blacks and trying to get the whites to reflect on the tragedy that had just come upon our nation.

"Then, two evenings later," Ron reflected, "Detroit began to burn. I climbed to the roof of my house, and watched columns of smoke rise from all over Detroit—one fire after the other. Soon the fires grew closer—within a few blocks of my house and church. I stood on the porch all night, weeping and praying for this great city as police and roving bands of both blacks and whites ran up and down my street.

"My immediate instinct was to ask 'What have I gotten myself into?' and to just run away and abandon my job. But then I realized I couldn't. As far as I knew, I was the only sane voice on the street that night. I knew I was being called by God to never abandon this community no matter how bad it got. I realized that night that I was being called to be a peacemaker here for the remainder of my ministry. With God helping me, that is what I have sought to do."

This is the work to which every Christian in the city is called and the church as a corporate body is called. That was what Pastor Ron was called to do. And that is essentially what we are to be about. To carry on ministry and to call and equip people to work effectively for shalom at both systemic and individual levels is what authentic ministry is all about. And when we as the church and as Christians

consistently, continually, and faithfully do that, then we will discover the fulfillment of God's profound promise to us:

> I know the plans I have for you, says the LORD; plans for your peace
> and not for your harm, to give you a future with hope.

WORKING FOR THE SHALOM OF YOUR CITY

How are we to work for the shalom of our city? As God's ambassadors to
Babylon, how are the Jewish leaders to seek the shalom of that evil city? Jeremiah
suggests for us three elements that need to be in our ministry in order to seek our
city's peace—and the New Testament record would add a fourth element. Let's
look at those elements together.

Become God's Presence

First, Jeremiah instructs us, become God's presence in your city. "Build
houses and live in them; plant gardens and eat what they produce. Take wives
and have sons and daughters; take wives for your sons, and give your daughters
in marriage, that they may bear sons and daughters; multiply there and do not
decrease" (Jeremiah 29:5–6). In other words, what Jeremiah is telling the Jewish exiles in Babylon is, "Don't isolate yourself from the rest of the Babylonian
community and create a Jewish ghetto. Enter fully into the life of that city. Get
a job and enter into its economy. Buy a house or rent an apartment. Become a
Yahweh-lover who loves your city's people and who commits himself or herself
to its life and being. Weep with those who weep. Laugh with those who laugh.
Live and move and have your being in the city as people who are transformed by
the magnetic love of Jesus Christ. And by so doing, become God's presence in the
city to which I have called you."

Pray for the City

Second, pray for your city. "Pray to the Lord on [your city's] behalf," Jeremiah instructs the Israelite captives (29:7). Pray for each other, St. Paul instructs
us, both as individual Christians and as the church, "that your love may overflow
more and more with knowledge and full insight, . . . so that in the day of Christ
you may be pure and blameless, having produced the harvest of righteousness that
comes through Jesus Christ" (Philippians 1:10–11).

But prayer for the people you know and love and for the community of faith
does not fulfill the ministry of prayer to which we are called in our society. We are
also to pray for the political, economic, and value-producing systems of our city

and the world, and for the people who are in the service of and provide leadership to those systems—*by name*.

There are many means by which one may pray for the city. There is, of course, individual prayer. But it is far more important to pray collectively for your city. Such praying might take the form of prayer-walks, civic prayer vigils to combat violence, numbers of congregations bathing the city in 24-hour long prayer, concerts of prayer, prayers for spiritual deliverance and intercession for the city, prayer confronting the powers—or it might even be congregations simply remembering to pray for the systems of their city and their representatives each Sunday in their prayers of the people. But whatever mode they take, it is crucial that God's people be praying regularly and systematically for the economic, political, and values-creating leaders of their city, the systems they represent, and the principalities and powers that lie behind those systems.

Practice Your Faith Through Action

Third, we are called by God to practice our faith by working for social justice and shalom. "*Work* for the shalom of your city," Jeremiah instructs the Israelites in Babylonian exile (29:7). And how are we to work for the transformation of the city?

First, we are to undertake *ministries of mercy* and seek to serve the needs of the poor. Matthew would call us to feed the hungry, give drink to the thirsty, welcome the stranger, clothe the naked, care for the sick, visit the prisoner, for "when you do it to one of the least of these who are *also* members of my family, you do it to me" (Matthew 25:31–40). The way that ministries of mercy are carried out today is through the provision of *social services*.

But there is a second way we are to practice our faith besides deeds of mercy. We are to be *advocates* for the powerless. It is the job of God's people to "stand in the breach" and defend the cause of the poor, the powerless, and the marginalized before the "principalities and powers" of the city and state. An excellent example of that ministry of advocacy was done by Jeremiah, when he confronted the king for his lavish lifestyle in the face of such intense poverty on the part of his people. "Woe to him who builds his house by unrighteousness and his upper rooms by injustice; who makes his neighbors work for nothing, and does not give them their wages" (Jeremiah 22:13). *That* is advocacy!

But there is still a further ministry of practice to which God's people are called. This is the ministry of *community development*—that is, working with and mobilizing the poor to provide needed community services for them. Isaiah states it quite clearly when he calls God's people to work with all of society to pressure for health care that would guarantee long life and the elimination of infant mortality, for adequate and affordable housing for everyone in the city, to create fulfilling work for everyone, to eliminate unemployment, and to work for all ethnic, racial, and national groups that have lived at enmity with each other so that they would live in harmony (Isaiah 65:19–25).

Proclaim the Good News

Fourth, although Jeremiah didn't suggest it, our New Testament roots would insist that an essential role of the church in its work of shalom would be that of proclamation. St. Paul puts the task quite directly: "Everyone who calls on the name of the Lord shall be saved. But how are they to call on one in whom they have not believed? And how are they to believe in one of whom they have never heard? And how are they to hear without someone to proclaim Christ?" (Romans 10:13–14). An essential task of the church in the city is to proclaim Christ to any who will listen, for only in that way will they believe.

But proclamation is to be made to more than people. Paul tells us in Ephesians, "through the church the wisdom of God in its rich variety might now be made known to the rulers and authorities in the [highest] places" (3:10). And Paul, in his practice of his faith, had no problem in proclaiming Christ to high priest, Roman governor, king, or even the Roman emperor. It is the responsibility of the church in the city to proclaim God's prophetic and reconciling word to the political, economic, and value-producing systems of the city and to the people who provide leadership to those structures.

Presence, prayer, practice, proclamation—these are the biblical ministries of the church in the city. They are not optional. We do not have the right to choose between them. All of them together make up the substance of the work of God's people for the transformation and shalom of the city. These four ministries make up the *essential* work of the church. They are the *strategic* work of the church. But, very frankly, neither in the global urban world of today nor in the biblical world are these four ministries *sufficient*.

Why are they not sufficient? Simply because none of these four by themselves nor all of them together are powerful enough to pressure the giant political, economic, educational, media/entertainment, religious, or social and health provider institutions and their massive bureaucracies to practice shalom. If presence, prayer, practice, and proclamation are essential and strategic but are not sufficient, what more must the church do in order to truly make a difference?

ACTION THAT IS SUFFICIENT FOR CHANGING SYSTEMS

What more must the church do in order to truly make a difference in today's world? The answer is found in one of the most disturbing statements ever made by Jesus.

> "I came to bring fire to the earth, and how I wish it were already
> kindled! I have a baptism with which to be baptized, and what stress
> I am under until it is completed! Do you think that I have come to
> bring peace to the earth? No, I tell you, [I have not come to bring
> peace] but rather division! (Luke 12:49–51)

What does Jesus mean when he tells us that he, the prince of peace, has come not to bring peace but rather division? I think the best way of getting at this disturbing statement is by sharing with you an event in my ministry when I had to learn what it meant to really follow Jesus.

We were about to begin a meeting of the governing board of the church I served in Chicago, and I was waiting for the last elders to assemble. Suddenly, the door opened with a bang and one of our elders—John—stalked into the room, obviously deeply agitated. "I can't believe it," he said. "I have just been turned down by our community banks for a housing-renovation loan." He then told us his frustrating tale. He had applied to bank after bank for a home-remodeling loan, and had been rejected by each one.

We were as shocked as was John. John was a top executive in his corporation, a man with considerable income and equity, as well as thirty years of longevity in the community and a reputation for involvement in community affairs. On what grounds could he possibly be rejected for a home loan?

"That's strange," spoke up another elder who lived in the community. "I was turned down for a home-renovation loan only the other day."

A third elder and then a fourth spoke up. They too had been turned down for home-purchase or remodeling loans over the past three years. What was going on?

I was suspicious. So at the next meeting of our ministerial association, I shared with the other clergy the strange discovery at that meeting of my church elders. The other clergy all promised to check with their respective church lay leaders, as well.

At the next meeting a month hence, the results were gathered. Every lay leader of each religious institution who had requested a home loan or home improvement loan for property they owned in our neighborhood had been rejected for that loan, no matter how good their credit rating might be. With that news, we spread out into the community, and soon discovered that we could not find a single homeowner requesting a home-improvement or home-purchase loan over the past three years who had actually been granted one.

We began investigating the reason—and it soon surfaced. The banks and fiduciary institutions in this declining neighborhood, a major insurance company, several major contractors and the city government were involved in a conspiracy to "red-line"[5] the community so that property values would plummet, the community would rapidly decline, buildings could be purchased at basement prices and the area could then be condemned and eventually rebuilt with luxury condominiums and apartment houses at great profit to the banks and developers.

The pastors, and church and community leaders gathered from the 23 churches. The very future of our neighborhood was at stake. What were the churches going to do?

Well, what could the churches do? We considered together possible alternatives. One alternative that was suggested was to simply seek to preserve and sustain our congregations as loving fellowships of believers. "You can't fight City Hall," declared one pastor. In other words, we would continue to be a *presence* in the community until the city claimed eminent domain and purchased the church sites. If we did that, we might sustain our churches for the interim. But we would not stop this intentional pillaging of our community.

A second suggestion was that we might hold prayer meetings throughout our churches to pray in a non-specific way for our community. By doing this, we would be carrying on a ministry of *prayer*. But we concluded that prayer without action would be insufficient to stop this willful destruction of the community.

A third alternative we considered was that we could evangelize in the community. In other words, we could all participate jointly in a ministry of *proclamation*. That might bring a number of individuals in the community to Christ, but that would not stop the community-destroying policy of those red-lining political and economic systems.

A fourth possibility would be to provide community services to the people of our neighborhood who became victims of the systems' intentional war of attrition on our community. That is, we could carry on a ministry of *practice* through *social services*. But such an approach, we realized, would not stop the systems from raping this community. In fact, it would actually encourage them, because our provision of social services would make less apparent to the rest of the city the results of the exploitive action the government and businesses were taking in red-lining our community.

Rather than a ministry of community services, we debated, we could enter into a ministry of *practice* through *advocacy*. We preachers could appear before city council and advocate the cause of the community. But we quickly realized that this kind of action would be insufficient. We 23 pastors were "too small" to make city council listen to us, if we didn't have thousands of our parishioners behind us.

Still another way we could carry out a ministry of *practice* was through *community development.* We could mobilize the community to take care of itself. Clean up the streets the city's sanitation department was neglecting; pick up the garbage and trash the city wasn't picking up. Police the streets ourselves. But once again, we quickly realized that mobilizing the people to develop our community, while an important task, would not stop the efforts of the city and fiduciary institutions to destroy our community so they could rebuild it at considerable profit to themselves. In fact, taking on the work the city was legally responsible for providing (like garbage removal, sanitation, policing, infrastructure maintenance) was just allowing the city to avoid its legal responsibility to our neighborhood.

We finally came to the inevitable alternative. We realized we had to directly confront those greedy political and economic leaders with sufficient people-power. Then, they would *have* to listen. Thus, if we were to save our community and our churches from literal destruction, we would have to learn to use *power.*

Now that filled all of us with dread, because we had always been taught as good Christians to obey the systems, not to confront them. And for some of us, it went against our understanding of what the church was called to be and do. But we were also faced with the certain destruction of our neighborhood and, eventually, of our churches if we did nothing.

So we went to our local community-based organization to which many of our churches (including mine) belonged—ONE (the Organization of the North East)—and shared our tale of woe with its lead organizer, Bob (we called him "Bob the organizer" in order to differentiate him from me [Pastor Bob] and several other "Bob's" in the organization). So Bob the organizer began to work with us to organize our churches to substantively address this issue of red-lining.

Whereas prayer, presence, proclamation, and the practices of social services, advocacy, and community development are essential and strategic elements of the church's ministry in today's society, they are not sufficient. There has to be a better way—and that way is a clearly biblical way that is often ignored—the discerning use of power by God's people.

Biblical use of power? Where and how is power used in the Bible? Well, what do you call it when Moses appears before Pharaoh and cries, "Our God says, 'Let my people go'"? What is it that David demonstrates against Goliath and the Philistines—and even against an ineffective Saul? What is it that Elijah was using against Ahab or Daniel against Nebuchadnezzar or Nehemiah as he organized the people to rebuild both their walls and their life together, even against the political and economic power of the Persian governor Sanballat and the economic power-house Tobiah? What was it that Jesus was using in his miracles, in his continuing confrontations of the Pharisees, Sadducees, priests, and scribes, and in his death and resurrection? What was it that Paul was doing when he defeated the Jewish leaders who sought to persecute the church, convinced the Christian leadership to aggressively seek the evangelization of the Gentiles, and who taught passive resistance to Rome? All of these people understood power. And all of these people were not afraid to use power.

The Nature of Power

What is power? Power is the *capacity, ability, and willingness* to act. Every word in that definition is important for an adequate understanding of power.[6]

First, power is the *capacity to act.* "Capacity" means, "the facility to produce, perform or deploy." For a group to have the *capacity* to act means that they have developed or gathered the resources together in order to exercise power. A military illustration makes the concept of capacity clear. If a military unit has been issued rifles, but hasn't been given any ammunition, then they don't have the capacity to act. Even though they might want to attack the enemy and are expert marksmen, the absence of ammunition means that they don't have the resources at their disposal that enables them to act.

Second, power is the *ability* to act. Ability consists of having the skill, aptitude and/or competence to carry out the action one wishes to undertake. Thus, to use our military illustration once again, if one has adequate rifles and ammunition in abundance, but no one in the unit knows how to fire the rifles or can't "hit the side of a barn," they don't have the ability to act. Capacity without ability still creates a powerless state.

Finally, power is the *willingness* to act. There must be a resolve and a commitment on the part of the group to act, even if that means taking the risks necessary to act. Thus, if one has sufficient ordinances (capacity) and the skill to use them (ability), but they do not have the resolve or motivation to go into battle, then you would still have a powerless situation.

It takes capacity plus ability plus willingness to act powerfully. And this is as true of individuals or of a community of people as it is true of an organized basketball team or college students or army or even a nation.

Change cannot occur in a city, a neighborhood, a church, a tribe, or a nation unless the people and their institutions have developed their capacity, ability, and willingness to act. Then—and only then—do they have power.

Now I particularly want you to note that power, as I've described it above, is neutral. It is neither good nor evil. What makes power either good or evil is the intent and commitments of those who exercise that power. The motivation and intentions of the person or people holding power determines whether that power will move in evil or transformative directions. Thus, Hitler had the capacity, ability, and willingness to act—and he used that capacity, ability, and willingness to drag an entire world into war. But, in a profound sense, Jesus also had the capacity, ability, and willingness to act, but exercised that power towards individuals, towards his community of disciples, and towards the religious-political powers of Israelite society and began a movement that has transformed society and millions of lives for more than two thousand years.

The Two Kinds of Power

There are two essential types of power. One type of power is called *unilateral*. The other type of power is *relational*. Both types of power are built by honing the capacity, ability, and willingness of its people and institutions to act. Either type of power can be used for good or used for evil—but most often is a mixture of both. But unilateral power primarily organizes institutions and those institutions' capacity to create and adjudicate laws, use military power, control wealth, or act symbolically. Relational power, on the other hand, organizes people and the institutions of people (e.g., churches, clubs, community groups, unions, etc.) to act as one. Thus, one can say that unilateral power is essentially institutional while relational power is built upon the people. Let's look more thoroughly at these two exercises of power.

Unilateral power is the kind of power used by the banks, fiduciary institutions, government and contractors in the illustration I presented earlier in this chapter about suspected red-lining in my community. Unilateral power is basically "power over" a people. There are two types of unilateral power. *Dominating power* is the lowest form of power. That is the power exercised by a government or group through the force of guns and physical intimidation. It is the tyrannical use of power—colonial, plantation, paternalistic power. It was dominating unilateral power against which most of the prophets protested.

A second form of unilateral power is *constitutional power*. This is a "higher" or more "sophisticated" form of power than dominating power. But it is still essentially unilateral in nature. Constitutional power is power over people as defined by the law rather than defined by force. It tends to be highly structured and hierarchical, with responsibility being delegated by the people to those who hold power. That was the kind of power being exercised by Pilate in his trial of Jesus as presented in the Gospel of John in chapter two of this book.

Under constitutional power, those in power theoretically rule by the consent of the governed and thus are responsible for representing the governed. But, in reality, the governed play little role in the operation or influence of the government. Thus, in the United States, the people's responsibility is to vote upon their selection of representatives and to write letters of protest or telephone their protest. That is what people assume is the limits of participation by the people in the decision-making process.

The other essential type of power is *relational power*. Whereas unilateral power is "power over" a constituency, relational power is "power with." Therefore, it is a higher form of participatory power than is either dominating or constitutional power. There are two types of relational power, the first being *mutual power*. Mutual power exists when two people or groups hold fairly equal power. Rather than trying to enhance their own power at the expense of the other party, however, mutual power will respect each other's power and position, working together for common objectives. It is therefore a negotiating exercise of power. A biblical example of mutual relational power was the power exercised by David and Jonathan toward each other. Jonathan had power as the son of the king; David's power was based upon his military acumen and popularity. Both men could have acted destructively toward each other, and Israel would have suffered. Instead, because they loved each other, they used their mutual power to both strengthen and secure Israel.

The second type of relational power is *reciprocal power*. This is the deepest form of relational power. It is one in which the people understand that both parties or forces can benefit from power decisions if they authentically share decisions. Therefore, reciprocal power is truly shared power, in which each party is of equal strength, is equally participative in the decision-making process, and each commits itself not to its private or exclusive good but to the common good. This was the type of power being presented in Deuteronomy as the base for a relational culture that resulted in justice, an equitable distribution of goods and the elimination of poverty. If power is the ability to get things done, relational power is the capacity to organize people around common values, relationships, and issues so that they can bring about the change they desire.

The stark difference between unilateral and relational power is very clearly articulated by Jesus in Mark 10:32–45. We looked at this passage in chapter two, but I now want us to revisit the passage from the vantage point of the understanding we now have of unilateral and relational power. It is a magnificent statement of the stark difference between the two.

In this story, Jesus shares with the disciples what the systems are going to do to him. He says, "The chief priests and the scribes will condemn me to death, then they will hand me over to the Gentiles; they will mock me, spit upon me, flog me and kill me" (Mark 10:33–34, adapted).

After receiving this bad news, two of Jesus' disciples (James and John) ask for special status in Jesus' kingdom and are denied (10:35–40). The ten disciples, hearing of James and John's request, take umbrage at it and complain to Jesus. Jesus' response to their anger lays out the standards for the use of power by the Christian community (10:36–45).

Jesus contrasts the exercise of leadership by "Gentile rulers" (i.e., their Roman colonial administrators) and Jesus' style of leadership. How do they differ? Jesus says, "Among the Gentiles those whom they recognize as their rulers lord it over them, and their great ones are tyrants over them" (10:42). The Gentile rulers and their Jewish counterparts rule by dominance. Whether that leadership is political, economic, or religious, it is all built upon the premise that "might makes right." They are "tyrants"—exercising power unilaterally that results in a selected few having authority and domination over all others.

That's why the alternative of revolution that is being pursued by the Jewish rebels that have driven out the Roman army is no alternative at all. Like the Romans, revolutionaries also operate on the premise that "might makes right." The Jewish revolutions may amass sufficient power to throw off the shackles of Rome and the Jewish priesthood (they actually didn't, but nobody knew that at the time of the writing of the Gospel of Mark). But even if the revolutionaries win, what will they have won? With what will they replace Roman oppression and priestly dominance? The oppressed, rising up to overthrow the oppressors, always become the new oppressors. Different people, same scenario, same results—the people are still oppressed. That is why revolution is not a radical response, but a reactionary response. And that is why revolution is always bound to fail—even when it succeeds.

So what will work to liberate the people of Israel? Mark would insist that it would be the third way of Jesus.

What is the third way of Jesus? Return to this story. Jesus taught his disciples, "Whoever wishes to become great among you must be your servant, and whoever wishes to be first among you must be slave of all. For the Son of Man came not to be served but to serve, and to give his life as a ransom for many" (Mark 10:43–45).

The root of the problem, Jesus is teaching, is our understanding of power. Both Roman governor and Jewish revolutionary, both Jewish priest and Jewish peasant understand power as unilateral, as domination. But what if Godly power is something entirely different? What if true power is relational?

In this radical statement by Jesus, he is teaching that *the image of a servant captures the essence of true power!* The "one who gives his life as a ransom for many" captures the essence of true power.

In other words, what Jesus is teaching his disciples in this Scripture is the power of relationships. Rather than "power over," relational power is "power with," shared power, mutual power, reciprocal power. It is not the power of weakness, of acquiescence, of apathy. It is direct, specific, realistic, flexible, accountable, and negotiable. It is a power that is built upon the relationships one has carefully built with others and that seeks the good of the other as well as one's self. Therefore, by definition, it is a power that seeks "not to be served but to serve," even if that means giving one's life as "a ransom for many." This is Jesus' "third way"—the radical solution that, if embraced, will keep the Jewish and Roman worlds from destroying each other.

Relational Power and the Holy Spirit

At this point in our analysis, a Christian might be tempted to say, "But are unilateral power and relational power truly the only kinds of power in the world? What about spiritual power? Is there not the ongoing work of the Holy Spirit in the lives and actions of Christians which manifests itself in words, deeds, or signs of power?" My response to that would be, "Yes, there are Spirit-filled words, deeds, and signs of power throughout the Bible. But they are not acts of power distinct from unilateral or relational power. Rather, those acts of Spirit-led or demonic uses of power are either relational or unilateral in nature."

Essentially, Yahweh is described in Scripture as a relational God; he yearns for relationship both with the people and society he has created. Even the words used for God are relational in nature—Father, Mother, Son, Spirit—and his work in and through us is described in relational terms—*chesedh* (grace-filled love), *agape* (selfless love), *phileo* (brotherly love), grace, truth, covenant. Evil, on the other hand is described unilaterally—whether it is the evil of people, society, the demonic, or the Evil One. The work of Satan is seen as a work of domination, of "power over" people and nations, with evil as its primary intent.

Now this is not to say that all relational power is good and all unilateral power is evil. Relational power, when carried out by humanity, can become manipulative and destructive; that is why the biggest danger of the oppressed, once gaining power, is to become the new oppressors. But relational power is never evil or destructive when in the hands of God. It is our responsibility, as children of God, to use relational power in a way that will be both pleasing to God and transforming with each other.

Jesus and Power

There is in the Gospel of Matthew a string of confrontations Jesus had with the leaders of Israel (Matthew 21:23–22:46) that presents us with an intriguing study of Jesus' use of power. The stories of these confrontations (called a "pericope") are introduced with the words, "When Jesus entered the temple, the chief priests and the elders of the people came to him as he was teaching and said, "By what authority are you doing these things, and who gave you this authority?" (21:23). The sequence of stories end with Matthew's commentary, "No one was able to give him an answer, nor from that day did anyone dare to ask him any more questions" (22:46).

This pericope includes stories of Jesus in verbal combat with the chief priests and elders, other stories of Jesus arguing with the Pharisees, and one story of verbal combat with the Sadducees. In the first story on the question of authority, Jesus outsmarts the priests and elders by asking, "Did the baptism of John come from heaven, or was it of human origin" (Matthew 21:25)? They rightfully deduce, "If we say, 'From heaven,' he will say to us, 'Why then did you not believe him?' But if we say, 'Of human origin,' we are afraid of the crowd" (21:26). So they refuse to answer Jesus' question. Jesus, in turn, refuses to answer their question.

In the next story (Matthew 21:28–32), Jesus confronts these religious leaders with the truth that "the tax collectors and the prostitutes are going into the kingdom of God ahead of you" (21:31). In the third story (21:33–46), Jesus tells the parable of the wicked tenants and declares, "The kingdom of God will be taken away from you and given to a people that produces the fruits of the kingdom" (21:43). In the fourth confrontation with the priests and elders (22:1–14), Jesus tells the parable of the wedding banquet and describes those who have been chosen (cf. these leaders of Israel) as being bound "hand and foot, and throw[n] into the outer darkness, where there will be weeping and gnashing of teeth" (22:13). He then concludes, "Many are called, but few are chosen" (22:14), implying, of course, that it is these primary political and religious leaders of Israel who, though called to their positions of authority, are rejected by God for their self-serving exercise of their office.

With the priests and elders defeated, it is now the Pharisees (a religious system) and Herodians (the political system) who "take Jesus on" (Matthew 21:15–22). They attempt to trap Jesus with the question, "Is it lawful to pay taxes to the emperor, or not?" Their trap is subtle, because if Jesus answers "You shouldn't pay taxes" he has broken Roman law and can be prosecuted. If, on the other hand he says "You should pay taxes," he will lose the support of the people who are groaning under Rome. But Jesus outsmarts these Pharisees and Herodians by responding, "Give to the emperor the things that are the emperor's, and to God the things that are God's" (21:21). Matthew then tells us, "When they heard this, they were amazed; and they left him and went away" (21:22).

The Sadducees (the economic system) are next. They seek to trick him in a question about the resurrection (Matthew 22:23–33). But again Jesus outsmarts them. Finally, the Pharisees regroup and confront Jesus once more (22:34–40) by seeking to catch him on a hotly contested theological issue of the day ("What is the greatest commandment of the Jewish law?"). But Jesus brilliantly deals with the issue by combining both commandments into one. Finally, Jesus goes onto the offensive (22:41–45) and proves to them from Scripture that the Messiah is the ruler even over the king (and therefore the systems).

Those are the stories. But how is power being used in this pericope? Well, consider the power of the priests, elders, Pharisees, Herodians, and Sadducees. The power they are exercising is unilateral power. They are using the authority of their office, their wealth, their political and religious clout, and the military authority of Rome to seek either to defeat Jesus or to discredit him. They are exercising unilateral power, and the type of unilateral power they are exercising is dominating power.

Jesus, on the other hand, is using relational power. But how can we argue that Jesus is using relational power? After all, he is not being very "relational" with these Israelite leaders. Rather, in these stories, he is being brutal. So how is he using relational power?

There is a very intriguing refrain that occurs throughout this pericope. "The chief priests and the Pharisees . . . wanted to arrest (Jesus), but they feared the crowds, because the crowds regarded Jesus as a prophet" (Matthew 21:45–46). And again, the priests and elders say "We are afraid of the crowd, for they regard John as a prophet" (21:26). And again, "When the crowd heard (how Jesus had outsmarted the Sadducees), they were astounded at his teaching" (22:33).

The political, economic, and religious leaders of Israel saw Jesus as a threat to their domination of the people and they wanted to publicly arrest him. But they didn't dare, because they were afraid that the crowd would rebel, a riot would ensue, and Rome would remove these leaders from their privileged positions. Jesus had built such a profound and deep relationship with the crowd *that the people had become the protectors of Jesus.* (Incidentally, this explains why the Israelite leaders arrested Jesus at night, while he was virtually alone in a garden and during the Feast of the Passover when everyone else would be in their homes celebrating.)

What the Jewish leaders want out of the people is compliance. In essence, all of the arguments they pose to Jesus can be summarized around their question of him, "By what authority are you doing these things?" Their plan was to expose Jesus as a charlatan and disgrace him before the people. By doing so, the Israelite elite hoped to communicate to the people that the only reasonable and rational course of action was for the people to continue to accept the restraints of living under the present leadership ("God has designed fundamental laws for society to operate as it does, and this man keeps defying those laws. So don't be fools and follow him, particularly when we can demonstrate to you how foolish his thinking is. Instead, accept the inevitable because it is God-ordained").

Of course, they hadn't planned on being bested in each argument by Jesus. It was they who were made to look foolish. And the systems of Israelite society, rather than looking like fundamental laws ordained by God, were exposed by Jesus as the power-grabbing, politically compromising, and greed-dominated systems they actually were.

Jesus, through his use of reciprocal relational power ("You people protect me from the elite, and I'll expose the elite for what they truly are"), had defeated the Israelite elite in debate. By doing so, Jesus had de-stabilized the power equation. The people were no longer willing to remain in compliance with the systems. So what would now happen? What would the people do? And how would the systems react?

At this point, the people are called by Jesus to move beyond compliance to a higher level of power. Jesus calls his followers to embrace the power of commitment to him (Matthew 23:34–35; 24:36–44; 25:1–46) and to the building of God's shalom kingdom. But he fears—in fact he *knows*—that a majority of them will settle for indifference, apathy, or conformity to custom as the systems reassert their authority (23:37–39; 24:32–51).

And what will the systems do? The situation has been destabilized by Jesus, and the people are no longer willing to be compliant. The intent of the systems, therefore, will be to move down to the lowest level—acquiescence. Their fear in doing this is that the opposite will happen—that the people, rather than accepting the new imposition of priestly authority will riot instead (Matthew 21:26, 45–46). Therefore, they decide that Jesus must be eliminated as quietly and as quickly as possible (23:29–36; 26:1–5), for only in this way can the Israelite elite re-establish their authority, receive the acquiescence of the people and once again stabilize the situation.

Jesus, of course, can see where all this will lead—to the betrayal of the people by Israel's political, economic, and religious elite (Matthew 23:1–36), inevitable retaliation by Rome in the destruction of the temple, the persecution and profound suffering of the people, and the destruction and even elimination of the nation of Israel (24:1–28). Once again, the people will be the victims. And all because the Israelite elite will not recognize what God is doing in their midst, repent, and embrace the shalom community that God would freely give to them (Matthew 23:37–39).

Relational Power in Action

People who act together with relational power operate in significantly different ways to people who don't know how to use power. The very way you respond to the system in a mutual encounter with them informs them whether or not you and the people possess power (and, therefore, whether they need to pay attention to you or can dismiss you).

For example, people who have built strong relational power with each other will be direct with the leaders of the system they have targeted for action; they will be confrontive in their statement of the issues (but not necessarily nasty) and specific in what they demand of the systems. People who don't feel powerful, on the other hand, will be vague and abstract, and will preach lofty principles but not specific concrete action. People with power will seek to negotiate; people without power will polarize. Thus, people with power will seek a win-win resolution of the issue (precisely because they negotiate from a powerful position); people without power will seek to destroy the opposition ("win-lose"). People with power, when meeting with the systems, will set the agenda for the discussion; people without power will let the systems set the agenda for them.

In essence, people with power will be extremely realistic in what they are seeking to accomplish, willing to build on little victory after little victory after little victory. People without power, on the other hand, will be idealists who will demand "the whole loaf or none of it." People with power are always able to accept "half a loaf" (because they have enough power to know that they can be back tomorrow with greater negotiating force to get the other half), and are therefore free to compromise, settle, and deal. People without power will feel the necessity to fight "to the death" or surrender. Thus, people with power are flexible while people without power are rigid. Finally, people with power will always be accountable for their actions, while those without power will refuse to be accountable to anyone other than themselves.

If the church is called to make a difference in its city, seeking to build a relational culture of justice, stewardship of the earth's resources, and equitable distribution of wealth, it will not accomplish this by pontificating on the same from lofty pulpits or by passing resolutions at denominational gatherings. It will make a difference—and will be respected by the political, economic, and values-creating systems and leaders of a city—only as the church uses power intelligently. And what does it mean to use power? It means a willingness to work together in a city as one single disciplined body, rather than each church "doing its own thing" and seeking to grab all the credit. It means being direct, confrontive, and specific in its demands upon the systems. It means a willingness to set the agenda rather than reacting to the city's agenda, being proactive in working for the city's social righteousness.

It means that it must set and execute its agenda out of its own perceived highest common self-interest in which it also understands both the articulated and unarticulated objectives of the systems. And out of that understanding, the church must seek a "win-win" resolution in which both the church / people *and* the systems benefit by the decision made. To accomplish that win, the entire organized body of God in that city must be willing to negotiate, settle, deal, compromise, work on details, negotiate, and negotiate some more while remaining flexible in the midst of the struggle. It must be realistic in regards to the decisions made and the toll of the struggle. Each church must be willing to be accountable to the full, organized body for both its actions and its delivery of the commitments it has made. In other words, to be powerful, the whole church in the whole city must be disciplined. And, finally, for power to be authentically and successfully exercised in order to build our city's shalom, we pastors and church leaders must *trust each other*, for that is the very essence of relational power.

Relational Power and the Discipline of Community Organizing

The exercise of relational power by the church or any other relationally based organization is difficult for it to undertake by itself. The reason why is because we have such little experience in actually exercising it in the world as it is. Consequently, to effectively exercise relational power in public life, a church needs to be in relationship with a professional community organizer—someone who has been trained and is deeply experienced in the mobilizing of relational power to enable churches to work for significant systemic change in its city or community. That relationship is best lived out in an organization of organizations—an organization of like-minded people and institutions that want to build and use relational power together as their base for impacting the political, economic, educational, and social systems of their city and thereby work towards the transformation of their city.

The way that such an "organization of organizations" refers to itself helps us to understand what the primary focus of that organization is for the building of power. If the organization refers to itself as a *church-based community organization*, then it is an organization of organizations involved in public life that builds its constituency of member institutions entirely upon churches (normally both Protestant and Catholic churches, but all the churches being Christian). If it is a *faith-based community organization,* then its constituency is made up of religious institutions that include religious groups beyond those that are solely Christian (e.g., Jewish synagogues, Islamic mosques, Buddhist temples, etc.). If the organization refers to itself as a *people's organization* that means it builds its constituency upon the membership of individuals rather than of institutions (e.g., the ACORN organizations). If the organization calls itself simply a *community-based organization*, that means that it is an organizing effort that is concentrated upon a given neighborhood or community, normally within a larger city. Usually a community-based organization is relatively small—15 to 30 member institutions.

If an organization is a *broad-based organization*, that means two things. First, the constituency of the organization is broad-based—that is, it includes all kinds of institutions that build their power primarily upon relationships: churches, synagogues, mosques, temples, unions, schools, not-for-profit organizations, civic organizations, local neighborhood clubs, etc. Second, the reach of the organization is also broad-based—that is, it might include not only the entirety of a city but the entire metropolitan area, and its membership may be immense—100 or even 200 or 300 such institutions that represent not only the poor and working-class but middle class and even upper class, as well. Thus, United Power for Action and Justice in the Chicago metropolis spans two counties as well as the city of Chicago, has 330 member institutions, rallies with 10,000 to 20,000 people present, and works cooperatively on issues of health care, family care, housing development, and homelessness. Finally, the term *community organization* is most often used as a generic term referring to any organizing effort, whether it is church-based, faith-based, community-based, or broad-based.

Whether church-based, faith-based, a people's organization, or a community- or broad-based organization, all such organizing efforts operate around the Iron Rule ("Never do for others what they can do for themselves") and concentrate upon equipping the people and their institutions to act powerfully together to bring about systemic change in their societies. The specific marks of an authentic community organization will be presented in chapter six. But for now, suffice it to say that unless a church joins with other relational institutions and is adequately equipped to use its relational power, it will have an exceedingly hard time being effective in bringing about significant systemic transformation in its parish area, community, or city. One must *know* how to use relational power to be able to exercise it effectively.

The End of the Story

This examination of power brings us back to the story I shared earlier about the discovery that churches made of the "red-lining" in the urban neighborhood in which I served as a pastor. We discovered that the community's banks and fiduciary institutions, the city government, and contractors were involved in a major conspiracy to "red-line" our community as the first step to destroying it—razing its housing, moving out its people, and building housing and an infrastructure for the very wealthy. So what did we do? We pastors began working with our local community-based organization, ONE, to mobilize the latent people-power of our churches to stop the red-lining and to get the banks to start making home loans once again.

Our action plan was to confront those systems. We began with a power analysis of all the institutions participating in the red-lining. We quickly realized that the most vulnerable of these institutions was also the most pivotal, because without its participation in refusing loans, the community would not rapidly decline. The largest community bank and the bank's president became our target, because that bank was most dependent on maintaining a positive neighborhood image and keeping the goodwill of its customers.

Once having selected that bank as our target, we then planned out a strategy to convince the bank to stop the red-lining, and planned the tactics to carry out that strategy. The strategy was essentially a "divide-and-conquer" strategy. We then began our campaign to implement that strategy, working behind the scenes for many months to recruit the church and community cooperation necessary to make our confrontation of the bank a success.

Finally, the day came for that confrontation to occur. A carefully selected team of well-known and influential neighborhood, religious, and business leaders met with the president of that bank. We presented to him the red-lining we had uncovered and the bank's involvement in it. He, of course, denied everything, but when we showed him our evidence—even the architectural drawings of the proposed apartment and condominium complex and the shopping mall—he stopped his denial.

We then got to the point of the meeting. "We understand," we said, "that the bank has a committee of five that makes the decision on each proposed home purchase or renovation loan that comes before you."

"That is correct," he confirmed.

Then came our proposal. "We demand," we said, "that six community representatives be appointed to serve on this committee, that the bank not increase its representation of five, and that we select those six community representatives."

"I can't agree to that," the president replied. "That would give the community control over the granting of loans. That would be an abdication of the bank's fiscal responsibility."

"We realize that," we said. "But we are unwilling to have our community destroyed before our eyes."

"Well, I won't do it," the president stated categorically.

"That decision is within your prerogative as bank president," we replied. "But before you make your final decision, it is important that you recognize the full consequences of that decision."

We then spread upon his desk legally-binding and notarized papers in which each of our twenty-three churches had agreed to withdraw all our funds and close our respective accounts, twenty-one of the churches had agreed to withdraw major investments in the bank worth millions, and many of the businesses and thousands of the bank's customers (most of whom were parishioners of our churches) had all agreed to withdraw all their funds and close their accounts—and all of these withdrawals would occur on a single day.

Threatened with a potential financial collapse of his bank, the president agreed to our demands. He signed a binding agreement between the bank and the community organization we had already drawn up, we named the six to the committee, and house purchase and renovation loans began flowing into that community. Faced with the effective withdrawal of that bank from the red-lining plot, the other parties gave up and the conspiracy collapsed. Our community had been saved by the willingness of all that neighborhood's twenty-three churches to confront those who intended to destroy that neighborhood for their own profit. And today, it is one of the healthiest, safest, and financially stable communities in that city.

The leaders of the religious institutions in that community learned a valuable lesson through their willingness to confront the "principalities and powers." They learned the profound limitations of the church's traditional response to the world through its ministries of presence, prayer, proclamation, and practice. They learned that such ministries are all essential and strategic. But they are not sufficient to deal with the political and economic institutions of the city when those institutions become caught up in greed and unilateral power that both drive those institutions and corrupt their leaders. Only learning how to use relational power is sufficient to bring about the changing of the systems that in turn brings long-term change to the city.

In the final analysis, the ultimate problem is not the people or the churches or the poor themselves. We are most often either the victims of the problem or we are seduced by the problem. The problem lies with the way the political and economic systems organize themselves to amass and maintain power. Such misuse of unilateral power is, at its root, a spiritual problem.

Therefore, if the problem is not dealt with at its root—the amassing and maintaining of power by the systems—it will continue to grow in its exploitation of the people, no matter what the community might do. Therefore to simply work at the level of providing services, advocating for change, preaching the gospel, or working to make changes in the community rather than in the structures is finally to be addressing the *symptoms* rather than the true *cause* of the problem. Any such effort will not bring about permanent resolution of the system's oppression and exploitation of the people. Only organizing the people to amass and use their relational power to confront and hold accountable the systems will bring about substantive change. This is not to say that services, community development, and advocacy are wrong. It is simply to say that all three are insufficient and inadequate against massed systemic evil.

There is a sequel to this red-lining story. Several weeks after the confrontation of this bank president, the churches and their community organization held a public accountability meeting. A sizeable gathering from the churches and neighborhood attended. The community organization announced the agreement with the bank. Selected clergy, business, and neighborhood leaders spoke to the wisdom of the agreement. And then the bank president was called upon to respond.

He magnificently rose to the occasion. Rather than being a "dog in the manger," the president talked about how the bank had been reminded of its community responsibilities by the churches. The bank had decided to embrace this new partnership with the community and join with the churches in working for neighborhood restoration. The people at the meeting rose to their feet, cheering the president.

The result of that accountability meeting was that the bank president no longer remained a reluctant participant in this process. Rather, he embraced the new role he had declared for himself and became one of the most enthusiastic, hard-working, and influential leaders committed to the rebirth of that community. In a profound sense, that president had acted his way into a new way of thinking. And that bank president had been transformed through the willingness of a large number of people and their institutions to organize together to act powerfully.

Now, I hope in my telling of this story that you have gotten the picture of how people-power can work to change the intent and directions of the systems. But I also hope you noticed the apparent contradiction between this story and what I presented earlier about the nature of unilateral and relational power.

Earlier, I developed the idea that unilateral power is "power over"; it is most used by the institutions of the political, economic, and values-building systems, and seeks to dominate, intimidate, and control. Also, I indicated that relational power is "power with," is most exercised by people and people's institutions (churches, community groups, unions, schools), and seeks to be mutual and reciprocal in its effect.

Well, obviously, when we were in the bank president's office and presented him with the alternative of either agreeing to our demand or seriously jeopardizing the future of his bank, we weren't acting relationally. We were using the tactics of unilateral power.

But for what purpose were we using the tactics of unilateral power? *It was not to close down that bank, but to begin a relationship!* We did not want that bank to go out of business. We wanted the bank to do what we believe God's intent is for a neighborhood bank—that is, to not only make a reasonable profit for its investors, but to be a service to its customers and to redistribute money in that community through loans and other financial services. Neither the community nor we would have been better served with the bank going out of business. So our confrontation was for the purpose of shocking the bank president into a true appraisal of what he was doing and to change his ways.

The first step we wanted was public accountability by that bank and its president. We got it! But for Christians, there is something more: we wanted conversion. We hoped to convince our adversaries to embrace the God-intended purpose for their systems and for their own lives both as individuals and as institutional leaders.

Our organizing objective is to build our "people-power." As that "people-power" increases, we can make proposals to leaders in institutions "gone awry"—and because we have demonstrated in our past actions how effectively we can wield that people-power, we will have built respect and credibility with those institutional leaders. Consequently, we will be listened to, taken seriously, and will, as Christians, influence the behavior and decisions of those institutional leaders. In this way, we will bring them closer to God's intentions for them.

The future of the church lies in our capacity to move out of the comfortable ways we have learned to be "church" in order to embrace "church" as that community which is in mission to the world. We exist, like Jesus, to "bring good news to the poor, to proclaim release to the captives, to recover the sight of the blind, to enable the oppressed to go free and to [work for the coming of God's kingdom of peace and justice]" (Luke 4:18–19). The only way for the church to bring the Shalom Community to the city or nation is for those who wish to pursue God's intended values and organize together across the lines of denomination, tradition, theology, and liturgy so that they can develop the power to address the causes of that society's corporate pain. It is only by using the power of a relational culture that the church can work for the shalom of the city and thus become, in their deeds as well as in their words, the people of God!

SUMMARY

"Blessed are the shalom-makers, for they will be called children of God" (Matthew 5:9).

It is intriguing to note Jesus' careful choice of words in this beatitude. He does *not* say, "Blessed are the peace-*keepers*." That role was being performed by the Jewish religious community of his day. They were "keeping" the ancient Israelite vision of the shalom community (while adapting it for their own agenda) through their Torah, traditions, and teachings. They were keeping alive for posterity Israel's understanding of God's intentions for humanity.

What Jesus called the church to be about, however, was to be peace-*makers*—a profoundly different role. A shalom-maker would be someone intentionally and proactively working to bring the vision of the shalom community to reality in our world today. Jesus was calling the church to actively work to "make" shalom, not simply maintain a remembrance of it.

The church is to work for shalom through its being an example of a shalom community before the world ("presence"), praying that God's shalom kingdom would come, proclaiming the gospel of the shalom kingdom to the world, and actively working for shalom through acts of mercy, advocacy, and community and economic development. But most of all, the church is to work for the world's shalom by using its power to bring about justice in the world.

Power is the capacity, ability, and willingness to act. Unilateral power is the power of the world and of the institutions of the world; it is "top-down," dominating and controlling power. But Jesus' power is relational power, the power that is built in people when they are called forth to work together for the transformation of the world into "the kingdom of our Lord and of his Christ." It is that relational power that we are called to exercise as the church as we work for the shalom vision of just political systems, an economics of equitable distribution that eliminates poverty, and people living in relationship with each other and with their God. And when we do, we will discover that we have become "shalom-makers."

QUESTIONS

1. If the essential mission of the church is to work for the shalom of the city (understanding the full biblical meaning of the word "shalom"), how do you respond or react to this insight? Why is it crucial to see the work of the church to be primarily shalom-making?

2. If shalom-making is the essential task of the church, what role does the proclamation of the gospel have in making shalom? What role does being God's presence play in it? What about prayer and practice (social services, advocacy, community development)?

3. If the building of relational power is the only work of the church that is capable of addressing the causes rather than the symptoms of the problems of the city, how do you react to that insight? How have you seen people power make a difference in the Bible? How have you seen it make a difference in your city or in other cities?

Chapter Five

RELATIONAL POWER'S MOST RADICAL ACT:
INDIVIDUAL MEETINGS!

How do we build relational power? The answer is obvious, but it is also quite radical. We build relational power relationally. We build relational power by intentionally building relationships that engage people in public life. This is the initiating and continuing radical action that lies at the heart of community and broad-based organizing—and it ought to lie at the very heart of the church, as well.

The word "radical" is from the Latin word, *radix*—which means, "getting to the heart of the matter." Individual meetings, people engaging one on one in intentional conversations about one's own life as it relates to public life, are at the very core of building a people of power.

But what is so radical about holding such relational meetings with others? It is radical because we don't perceive *talking with one another* as the primary means for building power. This is not how we have been taught by the world.

How does the world build unilateral power? The military builds power by the continual building of its stockpile of arms and its technology of creating ever-more sophisticated and powerful weaponry. Politicians build power by law and by hype, by eliminating foes and advancing their position through negotiation, compromise, and force. Business leaders build power by growing their corporations and by seeking to increase market share. Unilateral power builds itself by building its political or economic capital.

That's how we're taught to build power. To seek to build power by building relationships between people and between institutions as they engage in public life seems out of touch with the world as it is. Therefore, to build power relationally is the most radical of acts.

A biblical person who thoroughly understood this and placed that understanding into action was Nehemiah. His story is told in the book that bears his name. And it is a powerful story of how godly people can use relational power in public life to transform the life of a city and of a nation.

BUILDING POWER RELATIONALLY:
LESSONS FROM NEHEMIAH

Who was Nehemiah? He was a Jew. But the text also tells us that he "was cupbearer to the king" of Persia (Nehemiah 1:11). Those few words, so casually mentioned, belie his actual position. Nehemiah was one of the highest government officials in the largest empire of its time—an empire that had its origins in present-day Iran but which stretched, in Nehemiah's time, from the western border of India through the Turkish peninsula to the Mediterranean Sea, from the Caspian and Black Seas in the north to the northeast border of Egypt. As cupbearer to the king, Nehemiah was the personal servant of the Persian emperor Artaxerxes. He both tested and served the great king his wine each day, met daily with the king regarding affairs of state, and in essence, played the role of the prime minister of the Persian Empire. He was well rewarded for this service, having both wealth and influence in the empire.

Nehemiah understood power and the exercise of power—whether unilateral or relational. When he learned of the plight of the Jews in Jerusalem, his objective became that of enabling those Jews to develop the capacity, ability, and willingness to act to change their situation.

After a brief introduction, the story of Nehemiah and his mission begin with these words:

> In the month of Chislev, in the twentieth year [of King Artaxerxes], while I was in Susa the capital, one of my brothers, Hanani, came with certain men from Judah; and I asked them about the Jews that survived, those who had escaped the captivity, and about Jerusalem. They replied, "The survivors there in the province who escaped captivity are in great trouble and shame; the wall of Jerusalem is broken down, and its gates have been destroyed by fire." When I heard these words I sat down and wept and mourned for days, fasting and praying before the God of heaven. (Nehemiah 1:1–4)

Begin by Building Relationships

The first step Nehemiah took to empower Israel in this time of great vulnerability and apparent helplessness was to *build relationships*. And he did this by *asking questions* and *listening*. He began by asking his brother and "certain men from Judah" who had come to visit him in the Persian capital, "How is it going with the Jews that survived the Babylonian captivity, and how is it in Jerusalem?" (Nehemiah 1:2) What Nehemiah heard, in response, was an earful.

When the great Persian king, Cyrus, conquered the Babylonian empire in 539 BC, he reversed the Babylonian policy regarding political captives. In order to maintain its control over conquered nations, Babylonia brought to its capital city the political, economic, and religious leadership of each nation it conquered; it did this with Israel and its "Babylonian captivity" (see the previous chapter). When Cyrus overthrew the Babylonian empire, he allowed those of the captive elite to return to their countries on the condition that they would provide leadership to those countries under the authority of the Persian crown. A significant number of Israelite captives thus returned home to Judah and its capital city, Jerusalem. These people and their descendants were whom Nehemiah was asking about, together with all those who had remained behind in Jerusalem.

What Nehemiah heard was that the people were in trouble. As he talked with Hanani and many others, the grave situation Israel faced clearly emerged. Both the Jewish leadership and the people were in profound despair. Those in Babylonian exile had returned to see that Jerusalem was only a shadow of its former self. It was essentially a razed city, with the people making do as best they could among its ruins. The city's walls were broken down, leaving its citizens vulnerable to the lightning raids of tribal peoples who would come sweeping in from the Arabian desert to loot, pillage, and rape. The economy was a shambles, and the primary political authority was being exercised by Gentiles who were economically exploiting the people. The nation was in a vast, corporate depression as all that had made them uniquely Jewish had been taken from them, and they no longer had either a national or a spiritual identity as a people.

What is significant is what Nehemiah does about all this bad news. He simply keeps asking questions, probing, and listening to the stories people have to tell. But he doesn't seem to do anything other than ask questions and listen. He appears to be doing nothing. But, in reality, Nehemiah is doing a great deal.

The Iron Rule is "Never do for others what they can do for themselves." If you want people to take charge of their own situation and to solve their own problems, the way to do that is not for you to determine the solution to their problems and implement it. All that will do is to create dependency. The way that you get them to do for themselves is to get them to publicly articulate with each other their problem so that they get angry enough to do something about it. And the way you get them to articulate these problems is to ask questions and listen to their responses. Relational power can only be built upon relationships between people, and listening to and sharing with each other builds such relationships. That was what Nehemiah was doing.

But he was doing more than that.

Internalize the Pain

The text tells us that Nehemiah not only asked questions and listened to the people. He also "sat down and wept, and mourned for days" (Nehemiah 1:4). Nehemiah allowed his heart to be broken by the things that were breaking the hearts of his people.

It is not enough for the organizer, community worker, or the pastor to listen and learn from the people. In order to build the depth of relationships upon which relational power is based, they must allow the people's pain to become their pain. And that means allowing the anger and frustration of the people to connect with their anger.

Christians have trouble with anger. We tend to think of anger as inappropriate for the Christian life and witness because we believe that we ought to be loving, caring, and "happy all the time." But anger is absolutely essential for bringing about any change.

To understand the nature of anger, we need to recognize that the word anger comes from the Norse word for grief. Authentic anger is the process of grieving over the injustice our people are facing, and connecting that injustice with the pain we have experienced in our own lives. All of us have experienced injustice in our lives, when we were dominated, oppressed, or exploited in ways that diminished our sense of our own worth and self-respect. Those incidents may be overwhelming (such as Israel's oppression under Egyptian slavery) or may seem trivial to someone else (like being made to clean up someone else's mess at summer camp)—but it was still injustice to us that made us feel less of a human being. Our response may have been rage or tears or frustration or grief—but all of these are simply manifestations of anger. Anger is an essential part of human life, and to deny it is for us to deny our humanity.

Organizers are fond of differentiating between "hot anger" and "cold anger." Hot anger is the immediate response of anger one feels to an unjust situation—it is literally a flush of heat! If you respond to that flush of hot anger, your response will tend to be immediate, visceral, unconscious, and not thought through. It will, therefore, likely be destructive. Cold anger, on the other hand, is anger that is nurtured, that is allowed to ferment inside of us as we lay our emotions aside and begin to examine the injustice in a cognitive, reasoned way. In that greater reflection, we will decide what would be the most productive way of responding that will accomplish the greatest benefit. When we say after we have responded out of hot anger, "I wish I would have thought of saying . . . ," we are actually saying, "I wish I had allowed my anger to cool down so that I could have acted in a way that would have gotten the results I wanted to get."

When Nehemiah first heard of the plight of his brother and sister Jews thousands of miles away in Jerusalem, he likely felt hot anger. But he gave himself time to reflect upon it while continuing to talk to other Jews coming to Susa, so that, gradually, the problem shifted from being the Jew's problem to becoming Nehemiah's problem, as well.

Pray for the People

But Nehemiah did more than weep and mourn. The text tells us that he "fasted and prayed before the God of heaven" (1:4), and then presents a sample of his prayers (1:5–11). Prayer was a strategic part of the process by which Nehemiah prepared both himself and the Jewish people (although they did not know it) for the great work of liberation God would do through them.

It is instructive to examine Nehemiah's model prayer for Israel (1:5–11) for insights about the role of prayer in the building of relational power. The opening of Nehemiah's prayer is a prayer of intercession, simply bringing the plight of the people before God. And why? Was it that God needed to be convinced that his people were in trouble? Hardly! God was well aware of "the trouble we are in" (Nehemiah 2:17). But God wanted Nehemiah to be aware of that trouble, and to incarnate that trouble into the very pores of his being. Thus, just as is grief, anger, and reflection, prayer is often for the purpose of awakening within us the pain of the injustice others are facing so that we are willing to join them in working for change.

Second, Nehemiah offers to God prayers of confession. It is significant to note that he includes himself and his family in that confession. "[H]ear the prayer of your servant that I now pray . . . for your servants, the people of Israel, confessing the sins of the people of Israel which we have sinned before you. Both I and my family have sinned" (1:6). Nehemiah doesn't try to "white-wash" the culpability of Israel in contributing to their sorry state. Rather he is very open that "we have offended you deeply, failing to keep the commandments, the statutes, and the ordinances that you commanded your servant Moses" (1:7), (i.e., they have not practiced the Deuteronomic model of the shalom community, cf. Nehemiah 8–10). As God leads Nehemiah to include himself as part of the problem, this accomplishes two things. First, it is causing Nehemiah to identify with the injustice and pain of his people. Second, it enables him to identify with his people—even in their sin—and thus carry out an incarnational ministry among them.

Third, through his prayers, Nehemiah is coming to perceive the depth of the task that lies before him in building a people of power in Israel (1:9). The problem the Israelites have identified as their primary issue is their broken-down walls. That is their most immediate problem and that is where Nehemiah will organize them to start. But in this prayer, Nehemiah reveals for the first time that he is beginning to realize that the essential problem of Israel is far greater than broken down walls. It is their broken down corporate life, because they are no longer being faithful to what it means to be a Jew—a builder of the shalom community. These are prayers of reflection, and it reveals to us how God uses our praying to speak to us, enabling us to see the scope of the mission to which he is calling us.

Finally, Nehemiah prays prayers of supplication (1:10–11). He asks God to give the Jews and him clarity about what they need to do as they act in "cold anger" with carefully thought-through plans to rebuild walls and common life—and even to take the next immediate steps that must be taken to convince a king to cooperate with the will of the people.

This sample prayer of Nehemiah's is significant in that it gives us insight into the process through which he was going. It enables us to see the internal work God is doing in him in order to prepare him to organize this people to rebuild their walls and their life together. For it is in his praying that Nehemiah realizes that Israel's problem is essentially a spiritual problem, because the nation has abandoned its birthright of the shalom community.

Consider Your Resources

Chapter one ends with a peculiar sentence, "At the time, I was cupbearer to the king" (Nehemiah 1:11). Why is this sentence at the close of this chapter presenting God's formation of both Nehemiah and the leaders of Israel for the "great work" that he and they are about to undertake together? It is simply because, besides listening to the people, allowing their pain to become his pain, praying for them, and building relational power together with them as they listen to and learn from each other, Nehemiah must also reflect on the resources that he brings to deal with Israel's broken-down walls. Nehemiah does not yet have the trust or commitment of the people for his leadership. He does not yet have access to the material resources he needs if the people are to rebuild the walls. He does not yet have the permission of the king. But he does have one thing—he is cupbearer to the king. And how he now uses that office will decide whether or not he will be able to organize the people of Israel to rebuild their city and their life together.

Understand the Value of Timing

Perhaps one of the most important traits in Nehemiah's leadership of this organizing effort was his consummate sense of timing. Here, in chapter one, we see it clearly at work.

The text tells us that Nehemiah first became aware of the terrible situation in Israel "in the month of Chislev in the twentieth year (of King Artaxerxes)" (1:1). The text further tells us that Nehemiah took his first step of action "in the month of Nisan in the twentieth year" (2:1). So the period between the months of Chislev and Nisan was the period of incubation—of meeting with the people, listening to their stories, reflecting on their pain, praying over the situation, considering the available resources, and building the relationships. It was not until the month of Nisan that Nehemiah finally acted. So the question must be asked, how long was this period of preparation?

The month of Chislev is a portion of what is, in our calendars, the latter part of October and the earliest part of November. The month of Nisan is the end of April and the early part of May. It is a six-month time-period. So Nehemiah didn't rush into action. Instead, Nehemiah willingly took the time needed to build sufficient power to act. He did not allow himself to be rushed.

I am privileged to be a part of an enormous organizing effort throughout the entire Los Angeles metropolitan area. It is difficult for anyone who does not live in the Los Angeles metropolis to appreciate the immensity—both geographically and demographically—of organizing here. Geographically, the Los Angeles metropolis is wider than the state of Indiana, consumes more acreage than Massachusetts, Rhode Island, and Connecticut combined, and consists of over 130 cities and all or portions of 5 counties. Demographically, LA is the second largest Mexican, Guatemalan, Salvadorian, Nicaraguan, Columbian, Canadian, Cambodian, Korean, Vietnamese, Laotian city in the world and the largest Chinese city outside Asia. There are more Spanish, Korean, and Chinese speakers in the LA metropolis than there are English speakers! Now how do you organize a metropolitan area that geographically enormous and demographically diverse?

It takes time—enormous time to build the relationships across ethnic, religious, racial, economic, and geographic lines around which power can be built. We have been working at it since 1997. There has been complaining about how long building those relationships of power has taken. There have been people who have dropped out of the organizing effort, saying it is taking too long to build that base of power.

But that power is being built. The relationships are being created. And the people are moving ahead in the tens of thousands and in the hundreds of relational institutions to address together both local and metropolitan-wide issues in education, jobs, housing and homelessness, immigration and health care. I have been amazed at the unbelievable patience of the organizers who can work at building relational power month after month after month, year after year after year until that power is built and ordinary people can act with authority, and the "principalities and powers" of LA will pay attention and cooperate with the wishes of the people.[1]

Faced with the overwhelming task of building Israel into a people of power capable of not only rebuilding their walls and city, but also rebuilding their life and spirituality as a nation, Nehemiah began with individual meetings. He began by asking questions of individuals, listening to their responses, and allowing himself as well as them to be changed by the conversations he was having with them about the deepest challenge and pain in their lives and in their nation. He began to build the power of Israel by building it relationally!

BUILDING POWER THROUGH BUILDING RELATIONSHIPS

Whether you call them "individual meetings," "relational meetings," or "one-on-ones," the purpose of such meetings is to initiate the process by which relational power is built. Individual meetings are the intentional and systematic visiting of the people in a community by the community organizer, by pastors, and by church members in order to begin building public relationships, to identify potential leaders, and to help discern that community's most-felt issues in order to enable that community to organize itself to cope with its most substantive problems.

In an individual meeting, the person being visited is the proactive subject of the visit—one with whom you will interact, change, and be changed. Like Nehemiah, that implies that the person conducting the individual meeting can and will be impacted by that visit. The story that person tells should affect the way you respond, pray, and find your heart broken. Doing such a one-on-one changes the organizer as well as the person being visited. That is because this is an authentic encounter between two human beings—not just gathering data from that information. That makes it profoundly different from the conducting of a survey or interview.

The purpose of an individual meeting is to identify potential leaders and to build a public relationship with them. One may gather information from that visit. In fact, it is inevitable that information will be gathered. But the purpose of the visit is to build a relationship. And therefore, whatever information is gathered simply provides data that will help deepen that relationship and / or will enable the caller to connect that person to other people within the organizing effort who have similar pain, can be of support to each other, and can enable both each other and the community being organized to address the issues lying behind that pain.

Underlying the conduct of individual meetings is the essential assumption that all human beings, however uneducated, exploited, or beaten down by life, have a greater capacity to understand and act upon their situation than the most highly informed or sympathetic outsider. Every human being, no matter how deprived, is created in the image of God and as such is no less innately capable of determining his future than the most highly educated and self-determined individual.

If there is anything I want to communicate in this book, it is this: *You can't bring about significant change for justice and equality without building intentional relationships.* All truly transforming change—whether in a neighborhood or a city or your congregation—must be built upon the building and maintaining of strong relationships. But relationships that change people and systems are not superficial, uncommitted relationships. Nor are they "warm, fuzzy, gentle" relationships. We will discover in the next chapter how demanding Nehemiah's relationships with the people of Jerusalem really were. Jesus' words to his disciples, "If any want to become my followers, let them deny themselves and take up their cross and follow me" (Mark 8:34) are not sweet, gentle, undemanding expectations. Relationships that change society or even a church must require intentional, deep, and demanding commitments. And such relationships can only be built by selecting the people with whom we intend to build such intentional relationships and then investing time in them for the purpose of encouraging and equipping them to be powerfully engaged with each other in public life.

There are many benefits to visiting people in your community and church in this intentional way. Such individual meetings can greatly enhance the effectiveness of your church and (if you are a pastor) your credibility in the community. It can greatly inform your preaching, because you will have a strong sense of the major concerns of your people—and you can bring biblical insights to those concerns. It can increase your visibility and credibility in the community. It can identify community leaders with whom it is strategic to foster relationships. It can influence church plans and programming, so that such are far more oriented toward community issues. It can identify possible prospects for later evangelization. It can create a community awareness within your church.

But these are not the primary reasons for visiting people in your community and church. The primary purpose of individual meetings is to build the people that will enable that community to act powerfully. No slum or squatter settlement can be organized without building relationships through individual meetings. And no church, neighborhood, community, or city can be transformed without such an investment in people. It is the first step and the continuing means for building a people of power.

GOD IS IN THE DETAILS

How does one conduct an individual meeting? First, we must determine who should do such calling. I have suggested above that the caller could be a community organizer, a pastor, or a church member. In reality, everyone who might be involved in building a community organization needs to be involved in conducting one-on-ones. When the people of a people's organization are all committed to building relationships of power with those around them, the impact is profound. For example, I follow the discipline of trying to hold two meetings weekly with people with whom I want to build a public relationship. Most times, I visit with people I've never met before but whom I think it would be interesting to get to know. There are many people with whom the first visit was so valuable that I end up visiting them over and over and over again, deepening the relationship and moving it inexorably toward engagement in public life. For some people, it becomes a long-term investment in them—meeting regularly with them once a month as I seek to mentor and encourage them. I am a rather quiet, introverted person, and yet conducting these visits over decades of time has enabled me to become outgoing and concerned about others in a way that was never true when I was fixated on my introversion.

Who Should Be Visited?

Practically everybody! You begin by casting a wide net, calling on anyone you think might have potential and interest in being engaged in public life. But there are some particularly important people for you to call upon.

Visit the religious leaders of your community. Don't contact them because they agree with your theology. Instead call on them because they are the leaders of an organized religious body that, if it became committed to being engaged in public life, could become a pivotal force in your community organization and in your city. The point is not that they believe what you believe, but that they have the capability of bringing people together for action. In Chicago, within four days, our churches could mobilize up to 2,000 people for an action. No other institution in the city could do that. Because of their built-in constituencies, the churches and religious institutions can influence and use significant people power.

Visit political leaders, business leaders, educational leaders, and those who provide health and social services to the community. But most of all, visit ordinary folk.

The process I follow in order to hold intentional relational meetings with both leaders and ordinary folk has been to make an appointment with them and then keep the appointment. Only once in doing such calling over the past 35 years have I ever been turned down. Usually the opposite happens. People are delighted that the church is coming to them asking them to tell the church about the community instead of the church telling them how to live their lives. They are thrilled that the church cares and is demonstrating that caring by wanting to talk with them.

But I have used other means for having conversations with folk besides that of making a formal appointment. One of the churches I served was on a major arterial street of its city. We estimated that between three and five thousand people walked past the church every day! So we put out several benches flanking the entrance into the church. Passersby would come by, sit on the benches, rest, and chat; it became a gathering place for our community. I would go out and casually join them. I learned so much about that community through those informal conversations, and built relationships with hundreds of people I would otherwise never meet.

An associate pastor of our church had an even more creative strategy for conducting individual meetings. He would go to one of the local taverns (there were a number of them in the neighborhood). He'd sit down, have a drink, and start to talk with the people. In no time, all the people would be ringed around him, talking about the community. And they would tell him all sorts of things about the community that nobody else would share with us. Eventually, some of the best leaders of our community organization came from that pastor's tavern visits.

The point is this. You may know more about the Bible or about the gospel than the people in your community. You may even know more about the theoretical working of the political and social forces of your city. But the people know themselves. They know more about their own community than you do. They know its joys. They know its problems. They know its history and its struggles. Therefore, the first task of any urban worker is to learn from the people of the community and to build relationships with those people. They are the experts. We are the novices. They are the teachers and we need to become their students.

What Are We Seeking to Learn?

From our calling, we are seeking not only to build relationships, but also to learn three things.

Who Has A "Fire In Their Belly"? The first thing in importance that we are seeking to learn (but this is normally discovered later in the visit with a person, not as the first order of business) is, *does the person we are visiting have a "fire in his belly"?* We are seeking to discover those people who deeply care about what is happening to them, to their families, to their neighbors, to their community, to their people. Therefore, we are seeking to determine whether this person has sufficient passion, anger, and moxie to want to really make a difference in that community or city. Is she deeply concerned about one or more problems of the community? Does he care about what's happening to kids, senior citizens, or the homeless? Is she really committed to her community and its issues? And is he willing to work to bring about change—not just up-front where all the attention is focused, but behind the scenes and in thankless jobs. Do they have enough "fire in their belly" to be willing to take a risk and make waves?

What Do the People See Are the Issues? Second, *what do the people see are the issues?* Usually, when a church decides to work for the transformation of its community, it will ask, "What do we think are the issues of this community? What should we do to solve this community's problems?" The church thinks it knows what is best for the community and assumes it can do a better job dealing with those issues than the people can who live there. In the church's mind, the people of the community are objects to be ministered to, and the church is the one who will do the ministering.

When a church takes that approach to ministry, it is creating helplessness on the part of the people. People are taught by the church to be recipients and beneficiaries of the church's charity. The church may feel good providing food or clothing or social services. But the people feel demeaned—and they resent the church deeply for making them feel so helpless.

One of the essential tasks of individual meetings is to break this negative cycle of ministry. In conducting one-on-ones, the goal is to learn from the community what the people believe the issues are they face, and what they can do together to address those issues. The only way to find out what the people identify as their problems and issues is to *ask* them.

Who Are the Real Leaders? The third thing you are seeking to learn is *who are the real leaders of this community.* Rarely are the elected or appointed "leaders" of a community its true leaders. They only perceive themselves as being the leaders. And they do exercise a certain kind of negative leadership. That is, they have the ability to stop things from happening. They can block, harass, and cause trouble. Therefore, they must have their egos stroked by being made to think they are important. If such attention is paid to them, they will not get in the way.

But there are real leaders in every community. These are the people who make any community function. There are technical names for these people: gate-keepers, caretakers, flak-catchers, or brokers. Every community has them. In fact, if a community does not have them, then it is not a community but only a dysfunctional and unrelated amalgam of people. In the next section, we will explore how to identify these people and to build a relationship with them.

How Should I Conduct an Individual Meeting?

We will explore in this section how one actually conducts an individual meeting.

Keep Clear What You Are Seeking to Do: It is crucial in an individual meeting to always keep before yourself the purpose of this meeting. If you do not, the tendency of the visit to get diverted into something other than what it is supposed to accomplish is exceedingly great. Because the visit is done in an informal and casual way, it is very easy for the call to get diverted into a chatty visit or simply concentrated on getting to know each other in a personal rather than in a public way. Likewise, if you have a prior relationship or acquaintance with this person, it is easy for the visit to be sidetracked into talking about matters surrounding that prior relationship. So remaining centered on keeping the main thing the main thing is truly crucial.

In conducting individual meetings, you are seeking to discover those in your community who exhibit the capacity or potential to lead. It is that leadership capability (even if it is only potential rather than realized) that makes it worthwhile to build a public relationship with them (that is, a relationship that has to do with your shared commitment to work for the transformation of the political, economic, social, and religious environment of your community and city). Your task is not to build a warm personal friendship with that person (although that may result—but that's not your objective). Nor is your task to set down your agenda on the person with whom you are visiting. You are there to learn from that person and to understand their agenda—their issues, problems, needs, and their joys, hopes, and aspirations. You may thoroughly disagree with their agenda. That doesn't matter. Your task is to learn from them their agenda, how burning that agenda is to them, and whether they are committed to investing themselves in an organizing process that can address both their agenda and the agendas of the other people and institutions that are participants in this organizing effort.

There are six tools to bring to these one-on-ones. They are as follows:

- **Listening:** You are there to listen, and to listen actively and attentively to the person with whom you are visiting. You are paying them the supreme compliment that, in your opinion, what they have to say is of infinite worth to you. So you ask penetrating questions that encourage them to share, and you listen to that sharing with full attention.

- **Sharing:** You need to be willing to share from your own life and work for justice as well as to listen. Yet this must be carefully done in order not to dominate or even steer the conversation. The purpose of sharing a little with them is to make yourself as vulnerable toward that person as you are asking her or him to be with you, and to guarantee that what is occurring is a conversation and not an interview.

- **Affirming:** The affirmative way you respond to the person is crucial to getting them to share at a deeper level. You need not agree with the person to affirm what they are saying. Your countenance, your demeanor, your response to them, even the expression on your face, communicates to them whether or not you are genuinely interested in what they are saying. And your frequent nod, smile, or saying "great" or "OK" or "yes" is saying that you are taking them with utmost seriousness and are affirming their contribution to the conversation.

- **Challenging:** Along with affirmation, an essential task in conducting an individual meeting is to challenge the person. Challenging may be a small part of an early visit, but if you continue to meet with this person and begin building a solid public relationship, the task of challenging becomes increasingly strategic. Challenging may come in the form of asking clarifying questions or of placing a challenge before the person in a way that encourages the person to reflect on the implications of what he is saying. But it is an integral part of an individual meeting, and should not be avoided.

- **Thinking Through:** Getting a person to think through the implications of the way he is analyzing a problem or cutting an issue or typifying a group arena is crucial. Thinking through both implications and processes for action is part of the honing process one goes through when one shares in a relational meeting.

- **Teaching/Training:** Particularly if one holds a number of individual meetings with the same individual, teaching/training becomes important. That may include mentoring, engaging in Socratic dialogue, or direct teaching. But later individual meetings will tend to be much more strongly focused on learning than simply on exploratory conversation.

Creating a Record/Retrieval System: Doing an occasional individual meeting can be personally enriching. But what I am suggesting is that the conducting of individual meetings is the most strategic action in which you will be involved as you seek to build a people of power. If you are doing individual meetings on a regular basis (organizers normally do 20–30 a week and clergy, I believe, should do at least two to four meetings every week), you need to have at your disposal some means for keeping a record of each call and the capability of retrieving information from those calls.

This type of calling, to be effective, must be done systematically. That means keeping records and regularly collating the information gathered. Obviously, when you complete a call, what you have learned will stay with you for only a very short period of time. But, on the other hand, I discovered in my visits that if I wrote anything down during the visit, that would have a dampening impact upon the conversation. Instead, I talked with people in a casual, chatty way, honed my skill at remembering what they said, and then wrote down the salient points immediately after the visit. How to do that will be presented later in this chapter. But I soon learned that if I didn't store that information in a record-keeping system, I could not retrieve it at a later date for taking next steps in the organizing process (see next chapter). I have created a form on standard size paper that works well for me. A sample of that form is on the next page. Entering that information later into a computer's memory provides for me a way to store and retrieve that information when I need it in the organizing process.

Sample Form for Individual Meeting

Name of Interviewer:_____

Date:_____

Name of Person Being Interviewed:_____

Address:_____

Telephone:_____   Email Address:_____

Joys, Hopes, Likes:

Issues, Concerns, Worries:

Good Stories

How will this person be followed up?

Preparing for Your Individual Meeting: In order to begin an individual meeting, you need to first initiate a dedicated conversation with the person with whom you wish to visit. The process you use *must* be consistent with the standards and mores of the culture in which you are operating. In Anglo or Asian American cultures, I would never dream of conducting a formal individual meeting with someone without making an appointment first. I select the person whom I want to engage in conversation. If I know the person, I will directly contact them to make an appointment. If I do not know the person or I suspect I would lack the credibility to have my request to meet taken seriously, I will ask someone who is highly respected or trusted by that person to "credential" me before I contact them for my appointment (later on in this chapter we'll look at the tasks of referring and credentialing). It is my policy, when calling on Anglos, to do no cold calls (intriguingly, this was not the case thirty or even twenty years ago—consider my story of engaging people in conversation who were sitting on our church bench; but it is certainly the case with tightly-scheduled and pressured people today). When I make an appointment to meet with someone, I go to them; I never ask them to come to me. If it is a man, I normally meet with him in his office or place of business. However, with women, I am always careful to meet with them in a public place (I use so many Starbucks Coffee Shops in my region as my informal "offices" that I carry a Starbucks debit card with me to pay for all the coffee I purchase for my guest and myself).

There are other communities that, if I were to use the above approach, it would be an insult. In Africa, you walk door-to-door and use the marketplace for conversation. In Hispanic communities, you meet casually. In Arabic communities, you connect with people through family gatherings. But in Asian, European, or North American communities, you meet with people only through appointments.

When you make the appointment with the person with whom you wish to visit, be sure to state the length of time you wish for this appointment (normally a half-hour or a full hour). Make sure you arrive *exactly* on time—neither late nor early. And be sure to keep your visit to the time it was allotted. It is fine to end the individual meeting early—but never end it past the time to which you committed. This demonstrates you are trustworthy and true to your word.

When you go to visit the person with whom you have scheduled an individual meeting, bring along your form for gathering information. But leave it in your car or in your briefcase to be filled out *after* the visit.

Starting the Visit: As you greet the person at his door, tell him who you are and the name of your church or organization. Remind him of the appointment you have made with him, and ask if you can come in. If you have been referred to him or have been credentialed by someone, be sure to mention that fact. Perhaps this introduction could be something like this: "Hi, I'm Bob Linthicum, and I'm one of the pastors at First Presbyterian Church. I called you a few days ago for an appointment, and you said this would be a good time for us to visit. Jane Fitzsimmons suggested that I visit with you, and I think she contacted you about me." (The person being visited here acknowledges your and Jane's contact and invites you in).[2]

After you have been seated, explain the purpose of your visit. This is best done by sharing how you became involved in making visits like this one and why building relationships through individual meetings are important to you. If you can do this by telling a story, so much the better. It may go something like this: "As I mentioned, I'm a pastor at First Presbyterian Church, and we have been in this neighborhood for seventy-five years now. But we've come to realize that we as a church haven't been very good neighbors. We have kept to ourselves and nurtured our own members, but we haven't gotten involved in the neighborhood problems that seem to be getting worse. A month ago one of our church leaders got accosted in our parking lot and robbed, and we decided something had to be done about the growing problems of our neighborhood—including crime. So we decided that the first thing we needed to do was to start talking to our neighbors. And Jane Fitzsimmons, who's a member of First Church, said she thought you were a really key person for us to visit. So that's why I'm here—to get to know you better and to see whether we have some common concerns."

Obviously, almost all of the above only has to be presented on the first visit. After that, the person will know you, and when you visit again, you can simply get down to business.

Discovering a Person's Concerns, Issues and Hopes: The body of the visit is, of course, different for each call. What is contained below is important material to cover in an early call. Please take careful note that *there is no intention that you complete all the following topics in your first call or in any single call.* They all need to be covered, but in their own good time. It may take two or three visits to deal with all of them. But they are presented below as if in one visit in order to make sure everything is covered.

Further, it is quite possible that something of such urgency may arise in your conversation that you must temporarily lay aside these topics and concentrate upon that urgent matter. Or your conversation might take a different tack that you feel you need to pursue. What I am essentially urging, therefore, is flexibility—not a rigid commitment to a fixed agenda.

The first portion of the body of the visit (and this may be all you do in the first visit) is simply get to know the person and to discover what he or she really cares about. The way you do this is to ask open-ended questions, listen, and probe gently. You should ask questions around people's concerns, issues, and worries and around their interests, joys, and passions. You can ask questions to help them share their vision for the community or city, to articulate their primary values or to share where they perceive themselves as having gifts or skills. The best way for them to do this is by telling a story (that is, they will have the easiest time articulating concerns, passions, or convictions by telling a story rather than abstractly articulating it).

The best way you can get people to tell stories rather than articulating concepts is to tell stories yourself. When you tell a story, you help model story-telling rather than model conceptualizing. You build rapport with the person with whom you're visiting, because they will identify with your story. You make the visit more of a conversation than a visit. And you have demonstrated your willingness to take a risk in the context of inviting them to risk with you. It is therefore good for you to have thought through some possible stories you can tell that personalize your questions and have those stories up your sleeve for appropriate use.

On an initial visit, I have found that one of the easiest ways to get people to share is to ask them the question, "How long have you lived in this community?" (or, if it is a church visit, "How long have you been a member of our church?"). There are really only two ways that one can answer that question: "a long time" or "a short time."

If they answer the question with a "long time" answer (like, "I've lived here 20 years"), I then ask them, "How have you seen this community (or church) change over those (20) years?" With a question like that, the likelihood is that they will be off and running as they talk about the community's or church's changes. The very concerns they choose to mention will tell you a great deal about their priorities, values, and desires.

If, on the other hand, they answer the question with "a short time," I then ask, "What caused you to select this neighborhood (church) to move into? There are 138 neighborhoods (churches) in our city. Why did you choose this one?" When they give their answer (for example, "I moved here because I heard the schools were far better than they are in other parts of our city, and I wanted the best education for my children"), then ask them "Have you found that to be true? Are you pleased with the quality of education your children are receiving?" Again, they likely will be off and running as they talk about the community. And from what they say, you will have a good idea what their priorities, values, and desires are.

As I stated above, the best way to get people sharing their joys and concerns is through stories. Yet that is amazingly hard for some people to do, because they want to intellectualize and conceptualize, rather than to reveal their emotions by telling a story. The way you ask questions and what you say will either point people toward or away from the telling of stories.

In the illustration given above regarding the parent moving to a neighborhood because of the high reputation of the schools, you could get the person to share some stories by first sharing a story yourself, like: "I moved to my neighborhood fifteen years ago because it was close to my work. But the public elementary school that I had to send our children to was a disaster. Now my spouse and I are very committed to supporting public education and to work to make it quality education. But we ran into a situation that completely undermined our commitment. Our daughter's teacher hollered and screamed at the children, hit their hands if they weren't paying attention, and refused to let them go to the bathroom, so that my daughter soiled her pants and came home in tears. And my son tested a grade below the norm in reading, and yet tested above all the other children in his class. We decided we had a real problem on our hands, and began organizing to do something about that school." Then you can follow up your story by asking, "Would you share an incident when you felt your children were treated badly in school?"

The person's responses to these initial questions and stories could lead to further questions and stories from you. For example, you can ask them directly what they like or dislike about living in this community, what brings them joy or what causes them anger, what most bothers them about living in this neighborhood or what most bothers them about raising their children here. As you ask these questions, you seek to identify the issues they feel most strongly about, and you look for clues as to how passionately the person feels about these concerns. Seek to find out where people's passions lie and how deeply they feel about them.

Identifying Leaders: As I pointed out earlier, the elected and appointed leaders of a community are rarely perceived by the people as their real leaders. Grass-roots people who set the directions and priorities of the community are the gatekeepers, caretakers, flak-catchers, and brokers. And they are the real leaders the community recognizes as their leaders.

What is a *gatekeeper*? A community's gatekeeper is the person who decides whether someone "gets through the gates" (is acceptable to the people) of the community. He is the official permission-giver who decides what will get done and not get done in the community. He is the "chief," the "boss," the "mayor," the informal leader of that community.

When you were a child in school, did you desperately want to be accepted by a certain group in the school—but try as you might, you could never get in? If so, you had run into the blocking power of the gatekeeper—the child who exercised the power to exclude you. The work of the gatekeeper is a very powerful function in a neighborhood or in a church. If you are going to significantly impact a community, you must identify the gatekeeper and get him on your side.

The *caretaker* is also crucial. I was walking through a squatter settlement in Chennai (Madras), India with that community's organizer who was a part of World Vision India's organizing effort. We turned a corner to see all the children in that block playing together out in the dirt in front of one of the huts. I turned to the organizer and said, "I bet that's the house of this community's caretaker." And she responded, "That's exactly right!"

The caretaker is the person who is the "Mama," the "shepherd" of that community, the one who cares. He or she is the one who listens to people when they have problems, comforts them, encourages them, sometimes berates them and holds them accountable—whatever is the appropriate response to the given situation. Every community has its caretakers, and they can be both men and women.

The *flak-catcher* is the person who gathers and disseminates the issues and the news of a community. They gather the community's "flak." One of the best flak-catchers I ever knew was a member of one of my churches—Ruby. She knew everything going on in the church. And nothing delighted her more than being able to inform me of a church member who was in the hospital who I didn't know was in the hospital.

One day, I was visiting Ann in the hospital, a member of our congregation who was dying, when she breathed her last in front of me. After I prayed over her body and made sure the hospital staff had been informed and everything taken care of, I thought of Ruby. "There's no way she can know about this yet," I thought. So I gave her a telephone call. When Ruby answered the phone and learned who was calling her, she said, "Pastor Bob, I hope you're at the hospital with Ann. She just passed away, you know." I still can't figure out how Ruby knew. But that's the power of a flak-catcher.

The final natural leader of a neighborhood or church is the *broker*. A broker is a person who is the personal friend of a personal friend of a personal friend of a very influential person in the government or a business or multi-national corporation who can get something done for the community. The broker is the person who, because of his connections, can get a problem solved which, to be solved, needs outside help.

How can you identify who are the gatekeepers, caretakers, flak-catchers, and brokers in your community or church (and there can be more than one each)? You do it by asking a series of questions when you conduct individual meetings with people.

To identify the gatekeeper, you can ask three sets of questions. The first set of questions would be like these: "If a group of people from this community, including you, wanted to change something here (like clean the trash from the roadway or alley or install some sewage pipes), with whom in this community would you need to talk over the idea? Who needs to agree in this neighborhood before you begin making changes?"

Another set of questions helpful for identifying the gatekeeper are these: "Who can make things happen in this community? If the city government or the police or the school system is not doing right by this community, who can go to them and be listened to?" (If the person named is a government official, ask, "Who can go to that official and get him to listen?")

A third set of questions might be as follows: "Who has moved recently into the neighborhood? How do the people of the community feel about him? Why do you think he is . . . (whatever is the evaluation of the new arrival: "strange," "a loner," "very friendly," etc.)? Who decided he is (…)?"

When the same name occurs in two or more of these sets, you may be discovering the gatekeeper. And if the same name keeps coming up in many of your interviews, you have surely identified the gatekeeper. When you discover the person who gives permission on all important community decisions, who has credibility with outside leadership, who determines who is accepted and who is rejected in the community—you have found the community's gatekeeper.

It is equally important to identify the caretaker of the community—the one who brings heart to the community, who is loved and trusted by almost all the residents. To discover him or her, a questioning scenario like this may be helpful: "If you had a major crisis at two o'clock in the morning and none of your family was around to help, whom would you feel free to turn to for help?" When the same name keeps cropping up in interview after interview, this means you are identifying the community's caretaker.

To discover the flak-catcher, you might ask questions like these: "If you see a home go up for sale in your neighborhood, who is the person who will best know the plans of the owners, where they are moving to and why, and who is the likely buyer of the property?" If the same name keeps coming up, this is the community's flak-catcher.

To identify the broker can be a little more difficult, and usually requires a series of questions, like these: "Suppose there is a broken street light on the block, and it has been broken for months, and the city just has not come out and gotten it fixed, to whom would you go to get it fixed?" To that question, you might get the name of the broker or of the gatekeeper. So you need to push on. "If direct contact (which is what the gatekeeper will do) does not get results, is there anybody in this community who knows someone well enough in city hall—or who knows someone who knows someone—to get results?" If that name keeps appearing in your interviews, you have found the community's broker.

Why is it so important to find these four characters? These are the people necessary to have in your community-organizing effort if it is going to succeed. If they are not involved with it, it will not likely work, no matter how much you organize. The people in the community will look to see if the most respected people of the community are participating or boycotting. And on that observation, they will determine their own participation.

Discovering Those With "Fire In Their Belly": You need to determine if the person you are talking with is a person with "fire in her belly"—a person who really and deeply cares about their community. It is fairly easy to discover these people. Just pay attention to the person you are visiting with. Pay attention to the enthusiasm or boredom with which he tells you about the community. Observe whether she is excited or uninterested in the potentials of the community, whether she seems deeply concerned or is indifferent about the community's problems. If his approach seems to be nonchalant, he is most likely not a person who truly cares. But if you suspect that there is significant commitment on his part, ask him the question that will clearly reveal it: "When you look at this community (or church, or neighborhood), what really makes you weep over it? What breaks your heart about this community?" Then, get her to elaborate her answer. If you are able to observe the pain, you may assume that you have begun to discover a person with a fire for justice. And as you work with that person over the days and months ahead, you will have it confirmed to you by their enthusiasm, determination, and actions.

The power of individual meetings is exhibited in the earliest stage of the organizing work that World Vision did in the barrio Valle de los Reyes in Mexico City. The community organizer made 150 visits to 78 families in the first three months of this organizing effort. Although this was only about five percent of the total number of families in Valle de los Reyes, these calls revealed the primary issues and pivotal leaders of that barrio. Future calling uncovered additional leadership, but the seven most pivotal leaders were discovered in that initial round of calling. The primary issues never changed; additional calling only confirmed the accuracy of the initial one-on-ones.

An intriguing and unanticipated result of these relational meetings was the spontaneous movement of community leaders to address together issues that surfaced as a result of the visiting. While continuing his individual meetings, the organizer worked with these spontaneous organizing activities.

A number of parents got together and organized a family development program, including childcare, adult literacy classes, family health care, non-denominational Bible education, and summertime activities for children. The people, once organized, got all six churches in the community to endorse them, and came to Vision Mundial de Mexico for funding (which they received).

Pastors indicated interest in congregational leadership development. The result was the first ecumenical lay-training program in the history of that barrio. Held in one of the churches, over 40 lay and clergy leaders gathered for two full days of Bible study, biblical social analysis, and reflection on the nature of effective urban ministry addressing community issues. I had the privilege of leading these training sessions. Representatives were there from every church in the community, and three pastors who had previously had nothing to do with each other were reconciled and began planning how they could work together for the good of Valle de los Reyes.

Thus, the organizing of the people and the churches of Valle de los Reyes began; primary issues of the poor and marginalized people of that barrio were identified, leaders emerged to negotiate with the authorities, and the people began setting the agenda.

Concluding Your Visit: As your visit is drawing to a close, you are going to have to make a judgment call. As you have visited with this person, you will have one of two distinct impressions. Either the person with whom you are visiting strikes you as having the kind of potential leadership you would like to see developed and therefore you would like to build a public relationship with this person. Or the person doesn't evidence any capacity, ability, or willingness to make a difference.

If the person is someone you think has leadership potential, you should end your visit with this person by doing three things (and the very way they choose to respond to these three actions will either confirm your conviction that this person is someone you want to work with or it will raise "red flags").

First, ask the person to make a commitment to a next step. That next step might be to have another meeting with you. It might be to ask the person to meet with another person who is participating in this organizing effort (so that you can compare impressions). It might be to attend a meeting at someone's house in the neighborhood. Or it might be simply to ask if they would be willing to attend a meeting if such a meeting was called. But ask the person for a commitment of some sort.

Second, ask the person for a referral of a person he or she feels you should visit. Get a specific name, address, and telephone number of the person he suggests you visit. This demonstrates both his willingness to work with you and his knowledge of the community.

Third, if the person recommended is someone you do not know or do not know well, ask her to "credential" you with that person—to contact that person, tell that person about the visit she had with you, and recommend to that person that he agree to visit with you when you call for an appointment. If she agrees to credential you, this will give you the opportunity to test her capacity to follow through.

Then take your leave, thanking her for her time.

If the person is someone whom you feel doesn't have leadership potential or won't contribute to the organizing effort, then simply take your leave without asking for any commitment. However, don't eliminate a person because his political, economic, or religious ideology is incompatible with the organizing effort. It is amazing how people change when the organization and its reflecting process begins opening up to them other sides of an issue. Then, take your leave, thanking him for his time.

Be very sure that you have not overstayed your welcome. When you made the appointment, you should have asked them for the time you wished to take with the interview—a half hour or a full hour. Be sure to honor that commitment, and leave on time!

After the Visit: After you have left your meeting with the person, get into your car (if you drove), drive around the block and park. If you walked, walk around the block. Then, fill out the meeting form immediately after you leave. DO NOT WAIT, thinking that you will remember it. You won't! You'll be amazed how quickly you'll forget the details of the meeting. Especially, never do a call on another person before recording the information from your previous call. No matter how you try to keep them separate, you'll get the two calls confused. Fill out the form, and then later feed the information into your computer so that you can retrieve and collate it.

Never, never take notes or fill out the form in front of the person with whom you are visiting. To do so will turn the visit from the building of a relationship into a survey, and will ruin both the visit and abort the birth of the relationship.

Also, during the visit, never seek to evangelize the person or even invite him to your church. To do so destroys the integrity of the call. Even if he asks you about your faith, make an appointment for another meeting to talk about your faith. Don't compromise this call. Otherwise, he will interpret the interest you expressed in him as a ploy to evangelize him, and he'll both resist that ploy and will resent you for it.

A single visit will be insufficient with a person whom you see as having leadership potential or an important contact for the organizing effort. If there seems to be interest and/or potential, go back for further visits, nurturing the relationship you initiated by continuing to call on that person and by maintaining a relationship with him/her.

The conducting of individual meetings is the foundation upon which relational power is built. Therefore, it is the single most important thing you do as an organizer, pastor, or church leader. To build relational power means a continuing nurturing of the people whom you are seeking to call forth. Therefore, about half of your organizing time needs to be spent in conducting one-on-ones.

This is the art of individual meetings—the first and most radical step in community organizing. Without relational meetings, you do not have a ghost of a chance in affecting your community. You will fail in any ministry you seek to undertake there, because your work will not be based upon the people's identification of their issues and leaders. But if you do one-on-ones, you will have done the research and will have built the relationships that undergird community organizing and thus build a people of power.

How Individual Meetings Changed One Church

When I was installed as the senior pastor of Edgewater Presbyterian Church in Chicago in 1969, I not only inherited a church in trouble, I found myself pastoring a church in the midst of a deep depression. Over the previous ten years, the church had declined from its high of 1500 members to a little over 500. Without its sizeable endowment, the congregation could no longer have occupied their own building. The former pastor had left them in disgust in less than a year. The result was a massive inferiority complex on the part of the church.

By 1975, the church had experienced a major transformation. Sunday worship attendance had doubled, the decline in membership had been reversed, including 47 percent of new members being converts to Christianity, income had increased by 56 percent, 30 percent of the congregation was involved in adult education, the church staff had increased from three to ten people, and the church was carrying out twenty-two community ministries. It was selected by the National Council of Churches as one of eighteen Protestant churches in the United States having "the most outstanding ministry in a rapidly changing community." What had happened?

When I began my pastorate at Edgewater Church, I committed myself to one day each week to conducting individual meetings with the people in the community and another day to calling on church members. I quickly realized that the church leaders were thoroughly out of touch with what was happening in that community. So I challenged the elders of our church to join me in holding individual meetings with the people of our congregation and community.

The elders hesitated, but they didn't want to disappoint their new pastor. So they said they would do it if the deacons would do it (thinking I would never get the deacons to agree). So I asked the deacons, and they said they'd do it if I got the leaders of the women's association. The ladies thought it was a terrific idea. So within about a month, four months after I had arrived at the church, we set up calling-teams of 52 people, each committed to making at least two visits weekly throughout our congregation and the community.

Within six months, these teams had called on over one thousand people in our inner-city community and upon almost all the members of our congregation. Twice a month, we callers all gathered together for dinner, to study Scripture regarding the nature and mission of the church, and to share and reflect about what we were learning as the result of our visiting within the congregation and community. Out of that visiting and our regular reflection together, our leaders created a mission design for our church that set the future for our ministry, both for my tenure there and for several decades afterward.

What had that calling done for my church leaders? By the end of our visiting and twice monthly reflection, those leaders *knew* both the congregation and its community. They knew the community's issues and problems. They knew its history and aspirations. My people knew the real leaders of that community, not simply by reputation but face-to-face, for they had met with each leader personally. And that knowledge informed our ministry together. It created the foundation for Edgewater Church's ministry in that community, its commitment to the self-determination of that slum's poor and powerless, and the development of the interior programming and life of that congregation. I never had to argue for the necessity of that church's involvement in community organizing—no matter how confrontational or controversial the organization's actions became—simply because the congregation had identified the community's issues for itself, and in the process became committed to the people. Edgewater Church had become a church of and for that community, working with the people on the people's issues. And their transformation had occurred solely because all the church's leadership had become involved in conducting individual meetings.

This is the power of individual meetings, and how such meetings change those who are doing the calling as well as those who are called upon.

SUMMARY

"You can't bring about significant change for justice and equality without building relationships!" Relational power can only be built relationally. It can only be built by people taking the time to sit down with each other, talk intentionally, and build a trust relationship with each other. How to do that is presented, step-by-step, in this chapter. Therefore, use this chapter as a training manual to equip both yourself and leaders in your congregation to visit intentionally with members of your church and residents, business owners, educators, politicians, and other pastors in your community. *Your church's effectiveness in building the shalom of your community will be directly proportional to the amount of time you and your church's leaders invest in building relationships.*

QUESTIONS

1. Most churches today concentrate upon the development of programs—
   church school for kids, worship for adults, boards to make decisions,
   committees to develop programs, fellowship groups, mission-oriented

groups, institutional maintenance groups. What do you think would happen to the church if it placed a priority on people rather than programming?

2. What do you think would happen to your church if your church's leadership committed themselves to the nurturing of trust relationships with the congregation and with their community as the Edgewater Church did?

3. The way to begin the building of the relational power of your church is not to put together a program for building that power, but for yourself to simply start calling on people. Who are the two people you will call upon this week? Who will you call upon next week?

Chapter Six

BUILDING PEOPLE OF POWER THROUGH THE IRON RULE

I was in my study one afternoon in my Chicago church (the same church that fought the bank red-lining) when there was a knock on my door. When I answered it, I found twenty elderly ladies wanting to speak with me. I was well acquainted with these women because they gathered at my church twice a week to sew bandages for a leprosarium and to enjoy each other's company. Obviously, something had motivated them to leave their work and come downstairs to meet with me. So I ushered them into my study and asked, "How can I help you ladies?" With such an invitation, these women began to spill out their tale of woe.

"Pastor Bob," their spokeswoman, Vivian, said, "we ladies have lived most of our lives in this community. We all raised our families here. This was a wonderful community in which to raise children. We saw them graduate from high school; many of them got married in our churches. We brought our grandchildren here to be baptized. Some of us have buried our husbands here. All our lives are bound up with this community."

I nodded sympathetically. But Vivian pressed on. "But now our community is being taken away from us. We are afraid of this neighborhood in which we have lived our lives."

"How's that?" I asked.

"Crime!" The answer came swiftly, even bitingly. "Crime. We just made a horrible discovery up in the sewing room. We just discovered that every one of us twenty ladies has been the personal victim of crime in the past six months. Some of us have had our purses snatched, some of us have been accosted, some of us have had our homes broken into, one of us was robbed at knifepoint in her very own home. The crime and purse-snatching and prostitution and harassment has gotten so bad that we are afraid to go out on the streets of our own neighborhood—even during the day. Pastor Bob, what are you going to do about it?"

What was I going to do about it? I didn't know what I could do about the crime, prostitution, and decay of this community. But there they stood—20 very determined women. And I had to come up with a response. I began thinking fast.

"Ladies," I replied, "I don't know what to do about crime here. But I know someone who does—Bob the organizer. Let's go to him and you can tell him the story you just told me."

They agreed. So I called Bob and warned him that 20 angry women and I were coming over to see him. Then we walked down the street to the office of the Organization of the North East (ONE).

Bob, the organizer, met us at the door and ushered us into the ONE meeting room. He got the women seated. And then he asked an entirely different question than I had asked.

"Ladies," he asked, "what's your problem?"

"What's our problem? I'll tell you our problem," Vivian replied. And then she began her recital of their concerns all over again. I waited in breathless anticipation for the punch line to come. And come it did!

"Mr. Bob, what are you going to do about it?"

The organizer's response hit me like a profound wake-up call. That response began a conversion experience within me—a conversion of understanding ministry, not as helping and serving people, but as equipping people to help themselves. This was the organizer's answer.

"I'm not going to do anything about it. It's not my problem. It's your problem. What are you going to do about it?"

"What are we going to do about it?" Vivian indignantly answered. "What can we do about it? We're nothing but little old ladies!"

"You may be little old ladies," Bob the organizer responded. "But you are not 'nothing but little old ladies.' You are very powerful little old ladies. And if you want to do something to stop crime in this community, you can."

"But we don't know what to do," Vivian answered.

"Of course you don't know what to do," Bob shot back, "because if you had known what to do, you would have already done it, and there wouldn't be the problem of crime in this neighborhood that you face today. But that's my job as an organizer—to help you to figure out what to do and to train you to do it. The point is, however, that if you want crime to disappear from this neighborhood, you have to make it stop yourself."

Then Bob the organizer drove his message home to the women. "It comes down to a simple choice, ladies. Do you really want to stop crime in this neighborhood? Or do you simply want to stand around and complain about how bad it is? Will you or won't you take charge of stopping crime in this neighborhood. That's what I want to know from you."

The women looked at each other. And then Vivian answered for them all. "We want to stop it!"

"Okay," responded the organizer. "Let's get to work!"[1]

And to work they got! Trained by Bob the organizer how to recognize, accept, and use the power at their disposal, those "little old ladies" organized all the little old ladies and all the little old men of that community—hundreds upon hundreds of them—to confront the precinct captain and eventually to negotiate directly with the chief of police to get the Chicago Police Department to increase the number of police patrols in that neighborhood, to organize "Neighborhood Watches" on each block, and to get cops walking beats for the first time in 37 years. Crime plummeted overnight, and those little old ladies won back their community and safety once again.

As I look back on this incident, I realize that those "little old ladies" felt powerless—not because they were powerless, but because they perceived themselves as powerless. They didn't discern the relationships they had built over the years as a base of power. Therefore they viewed themselves as victims rather than the victors they had the potential to be.

But also, in a profound sense, I was powerless as well. As a pastor, I felt helpless to help them with their problem. I felt helpless because: (1) I didn't have a sufficient understanding or experience in using power to help them deal with their exploitation; (2) I didn't really understand the Iron Rule.

How did Bob the organizer work with these little old ladies to equip them to build their power and rid that neighborhood of crime? He did it by getting these women to embrace in their actions and reflections the Iron Rule: "Never do for others what they can do for themselves." Rather than "doing" for these women, Bob's job was to get them to assume responsibility for solving their issue themselves, using their own capacity, ability and willingness to do so.

STRATEGIES FOR BUILDING THE POWER OF THE PEOPLE

What Bob the organizer later explained to me was that, since power is the capacity, ability, and willingness to act, the problem of the ladies was that they perceived themselves as having neither the capacity nor the ability to rid that neighborhood of crime. And because they believed they didn't have the capacity or ability to act, they lacked the willingness to act, as well. This is the essential problem that keeps most people from bringing about the significant change they have the capacity to bring about.

The women didn't know how to deal with the unilateral power of city hall or of the Chicago Police Department. They lacked the skills and abilities to confront, negotiate with, or hold accountable such power. Instead, they were intimidated by it. So one of the tasks that Bob the organizer had was to teach the women how to develop their ability to act.

But the more serious problem was that the women didn't recognize their capacity to act. They understood power only in terms of force, dominance, and control. And they certainly didn't have that kind of capacity in public life. But, in reality, they had great social capital at their disposal because between the twenty of them, they had built relationships over the years with hundreds upon hundreds of people in their neighborhood and throughout Chicago. Because they had always perceived those relationships as private—that is, as personal, friendly, and supportive, they had never attempted to use those relationships in public life. Now it was time for them to call upon those investments in people and use those relationships to build power.

What would Bob the organizer do to build the capacity and ability of these little old ladies? How would Bob organize them to become people of power?

Begin with Individual Meetings

His first step was to train these women to do individual meetings. And then he sent them out to visit every one of their friends. This they did in very short time, talking with them about their concern about crime in our community as well as listening to their friends regarding their concerns as well. To their surprise, they discovered that almost everyone with whom they visited was as concerned about crime as our women were—and many of them had also been personal victims of crime.

As we developed in the previous chapter, individual meetings are the first step for any empowerment strategy. But they are also a constant and continuing step.

Like love, individual meetings never cease (1 Corinthians 13). They are the life-blood of any organizing effort, both the way you keep the empowering process fresh and exciting, and the way you stay grounded in the people's issues and concerns. The organizing effort with the little old ladies was grounded in individual meetings—what eventually resulted in over a thousand individual meetings.

Hold House Meetings

In essence, a house meeting is an expanded individual meeting. It is seeking to accomplish the very same task as an individual meeting—identifying, motivating, and calling out those people who want to make a difference in their environment and are willing to risk doing something about it. But it is done in a group rather than one on one. It is done in a group to give people the opportunity to hear each other's stories, to share in the moans about the problems and concerns facing that community, to break people's sense of isolation ("I am the only one who really cares about this"), to identify others who are also concerned about these issues, and to begin to form action plans to do something about their common concerns.

The basic emphasis of a house meeting is to get people to tell their stories to each other in ways that address their common pain. Speaking about their pain publicly, listening to other people's pain, awakening curiosity, compassion, and anger are all essential to the success of a house meeting. The primary objective of a house meeting is to build solidarity and community, and thus enable people to trust each other. It is therefore a strategic step in the empowering process. For it prepares people to take the next step—action!

A Biblical Example: House meetings were an integral part of the organizing strategy of Jesus. There are frequent references in the four gospels of Jesus meeting with his disciples, often in a home, to share very frankly with each other and for Jesus to teach them in the light of actions taken earlier. In fact, such meetings compose the majority of his ministry.

One such house meeting is recorded in Mark 8:27–38. The disciple band is traveling with Jesus, and they are resting together. Jesus asks them, "Who do people say that I am?" It is an objective question, a research question. "What are you hearing as you move among the crowds? What are people saying about me?" They report back what they have heard, "John the Baptist; and others [say you are] Elijah; and still others, one of the prophets." Their answers are noncommittal, objective, demanding no choice on their part.

Then Jesus cuts to the quick. "But you, who do you say that I am?" The question has radically changed—from objective to subjective, from noncommittal to convictional, from simply gathering data to making a decision. How would they answer? Peter answers for them all, "You are the Messiah." And everyone agrees with that verdict. Thus, Jesus is asking agitating questions and demanding a response.

But now he presses them toward next steps. And he does so by sharing a true story (not a parable) with them. "The Son of Man must undergo great suffering, and be rejected by the elders, the chief priests, and the scribes, and be killed, and after three days rise again." He states this very matter-of-factly, very openly.

Peter can't stand it (and, likely, neither can the other disciples). This was simply too much agitation. It threatens everything *Messiah* means to Peter, for he embraces the popular Jewish teaching that Messiah would be a conquering hero, not a suffering savior. The Big Fisherman takes Jesus aside and begins to "rebuke Jesus"—to attack what Jesus is saying. It is intriguing that, at this point, Mark writes, "But turning and looking at his disciples, Jesus rebuked Peter." Peter sought to deal with Jesus privately. Jesus admonishes Peter publicly, in front of the disciples. It is a rebuke that is meant, not only for Peter, but also for all the disciples, because they were all silently feeling and reacting the same way that Peter felt and reacted. Jesus responds, "Get behind me, Satan! For you are setting your mind not on divine things but on human things." This is agitation and confrontation, *par excellence*.

Then Jesus uses the occasion to teach the larger lesson that has been behind the exaltation and the confrontation of this house meeting between Jesus and the disciples. Mark tells us that Jesus "called the crowd" in on what was up to now a private conversation with Peter and his disciples. And Jesus presents as an essential principle of God's kingdom what the disciples had earlier so desperately tried to avoid. "[Those who] want to become my followers, let them deny themselves and take up their cross and follow me. For those who want to save their life will lose it, and those who lose their life . . . for the sake of the gospel, will save it" (Mark 8:34–35).

The lesson is not lost on Jesus' disciples—or on Peter.

Building Capacity and Ability in Little Old Ladies: The next step for the little old ladies was house meetings. They had conducted more than a thousand one-on-ones over the course of several months. Out of these individual meetings, the women had selected people who had "a fire in their belly" about community crime. They gathered these people into house meetings that met literally in the homes of people all over the community. Bob the organizer trained our "little old ladies" as well as others to lead these house meetings. Then they all got together in groups of twelve to twenty in each other's homes to play the game, "Ain't It Awful!"

The purpose of each house meeting was to have a gripe session—but not simply any old gripe session. Each leader provided firm, clear leadership to her group. The main objective in these meetings was to get people sharing with each other, both about their mutual concern about crime but also about other issues in the community. In essence, people had shared quite openly with the ladies in the individual meetings. But nobody besides the caller had ever heard any of these stories. The purpose of the house meetings was to give opportunity for everyone to share his or her story, listen to the stories of the others, understand that she or he was not alone, and thus decide to act together to solve the issue underlying each of the stories.

In order to get the people to share, Bob the organizer had trained these ladies to be firm in their leadership of the house meeting (firm but not autocratic leadership creates a sense of security), to monitor the meeting so that everyone would get the opportunity to talk, and to make sure that no one person would dominate the group's time. Their primary effort was to get people to share stories, not discuss concepts. As Bob the organizer put it in his training of the ladies, others, and myself, "People connect to stories that are vivid, not to concepts that are profound."

In order to spur discussion, each leader asked agitating questions. Agitation is not irritation, nor is it attack, sarcasm, or blatant confrontation. Agitation is asking the hard questions that make people think and grow. In their training, the ladies and others leading the house meetings practiced asking agitational questions, and forming certain "pat" questions ahead of time so that they didn't need to think of them all on the spot.

Finally, the leaders of the house meetings were trained to press toward next steps. Although having a gripe session in a house meeting might be therapeutic, it wasn't going to be enough to solve the actual problem of crime in our community. So our objective was to get people thinking about what they wanted to *do* about it. Many great ideas surfaced this way. But it became quite clear that the energy created by these house meetings needed to be channeled into action teams that could do both research and build actions that would compel the police department to provide the protection against crime the community so badly needed.

The house meetings went extremely well. More than 40 of them were held throughout the community within a month. Most groups had between 10 and 20 people in them, all of whom had been found through the individual meetings.

People just plain enjoyed getting together and visiting. Sharing was deep, including not simply sharing incidents but emotions of fear and helplessness. And the very sharing of those emotions somehow began to lessen them as we began to plan to bring safety to our community. But, most important of all, the sharing prepared the participants in the house groups and the little old ladies for the next step—the forming of an action team.

Form Action Teams

The next step of organizing is to move toward the formation of action teams. Once house meetings are being held and people are getting motivated to assume responsibility for exercising the Iron Rule (i.e., they are becoming increasingly agitated to assume responsibility themselves for solving the problem), an action team provides the planning and implementing body for acting upon the issue at hand. Whereas house meetings work at stirring up people and institutions to take responsibility for an issue, problem, or concern, and then mobilizing those people for action at the appropriate time, the responsibility of the action team is to move the community organization toward action. Typically, an action team does this in two ways: by conducting research actions and by planning actions.

Research actions are done for the purpose of gathering sufficient information to determine where are the points of vulnerability of the target and to discern the most effective actions to get the response out of the targets that you desire. An *action* is the activity done by the community organization to get out of the target the decision you want from them. Normally, a community organization will have a great number of action teams simultaneously working and planning on a wide spectrum of issues and concerns.

The work of the little old ladies now moved to the action team phase. The issue of this action team was community crime. It joined other action teams in ONE—an action team on red-lining, another team on jobs, another on education, and still another on political voice (i.e., we weren't being listened to by "the powers that be"). Each action team had one representative (usually its chairperson) who served on the ONE Leadership Team, along with one representative from each Protestant and Roman Catholic church, synagogue, mission organization (a settlement house and a neighborhood organization), and businesses that were dues-paying members of ONE. The Community Crime Action Team was made up of thirteen of the twenty little old ladies (seven only wanted to be involved in actions, and not in the planning) plus a representative from the house meetings. So it had close to fifty people on it.

The job of the action team was to determine the research they needed to undertake in order to wisely plan actions, to recruit from both the action team and the house meetings the appropriate people to undertake each research action, to keep the house meetings informed and motivated at their meetings, to plan the actions the team wanted to undertake to reduce crime in the community, and then to mobilize the constituency of the house meetings, the ONE member institutions and the other action teams to take those actions. Bob the organizer had the job of training the little old ladies and their action team how to do successful research actions. The ladies were now well on their way to stopping crime in the community, because they had now built a sizeable committed constituency of angry people and had created a structure to organize them for action. Now they were ready for the next step.

Undertaking Research Actions

When we hear the word *research*, the first thing that comes to our minds is the gathering of data. But that is not the primary purpose of a research action. A community organization is primarily concerned with researching strategic people, not gathering data. The only data it will gather is for the purpose of corroborating the research done on people and to support their case.

The primary purpose of the research of a community organization is to determine who are the people they want to target for action and what will be the most effective actions they will want to undertake. They do this through a power analysis. The action team seeks to determine how power actually flows in the institution they are concentrating upon and who are the main players. Out of that analysis, they seek to ascertain who is the person who has the final authority for making a decision the community organization wants him to make, what is the likelihood that this person will be cooperative, and what is the action that needs to be taken in order to get the desired response.

Thus, for example, in the red-lining story in chapter four, the research conducted by the churches and ONE uncovered the information that the community banks, the city government, and various business interests had conspired together to destroy the community through red-lining and the withholding of city services so that the community could be razed and luxurious high-rise apartments and condominiums could be built, with their accompanying infrastructure. That conspiracy was uncovered through a "mole" in the city government—an angry and discontented government employee who felt unjustly treated. Out of this knowledge, the red-lining action team did a power analysis of all the key players in the organizations involved in the conspiracy, and decided that it was the president of the largest bank who would be the most vulnerable to the demands of the churches, businesses, and the community people. That president therefore became the target of the action that would get the bank to begin making home loans once again, and thus break the conspiracy.

A word needs to be said about the word "target." Community organizations call the recipient of their action a "target." The word is very intentionally chosen. He or she is not an enemy—that is, a continuing opponent. He or she is a "target"—that person who, for the issue being considered, is the one who has the greatest authority to make the decision the community organization wants made. Once the decision is made, that person is no longer the target. In fact, the task often then becomes to build a more positive relationship with that person (as was done with the bank president in the red-lining story).

A Biblical Example: One of the best biblical examples of research actions is that undertaken by Nehemiah, as he prepared for his action of getting the Israelites to rebuild both their walls and their life together as God's people. In doing this research, Nehemiah conducts five research actions in which he both learns a great deal about the decision makers with whom he must deal but also gets some important decisions made that enable the Israelites to rebuild their walls. These research actions are found in Nehemiah 2:1–16.

Nehemiah's *first research action* is on the most powerful king of his day, the emperor of the Persian Empire, Artaxerxes (2:1–8). As cupbearer, Nehemiah had the relationship with Artaxerxes that would enable him to take this action.

Protocol demanded that one did not make a direct request of the king. Therefore, Nehemiah put on a sad face and moped around in order to get the king to ask, "Why is your face sad, since you are not sick. This can only be sadness of the heart" (2:2). The king's question was an invitation to Nehemiah to share his concern, which he did.

Nehemiah tells Artaxerxes of the news he has received from his brother and others (see chapter five of this book) of the poverty, helplessness, and vulnerability of his people. Then, he makes several requests of the king. Nehemiah asks (1) that he be permitted to go to Jerusalem to assess the situation; (2) if the situation is as the people have shared it is with him, that he be authorized to organize the people to rebuild their walls; (3) that the king guarantee safe passage for Nehemiah to Jerusalem; (4) that the king be willing to have the Persian empire supply the materials (timber, rocks, etc.) at no charge for the rebuilding of the walls; and (5) that the king write personal letters to the appropriate government officials authorizing Nehemiah's requests of them. The king agrees to all of Nehemiah's requests.

This is a classic research action because the primary purpose of Nehemiah's action was to see whether or not the king would be receptive to acting through Nehemiah to address the plight of the Jews. Not only does Nehemiah's research action demonstrate that the king would be positive, but it got specific commitments out of the king that would enable Nehemiah to begin the reconstruction of Jerusalem's walls.

The *second research action* is with the queen (2:6). Nehemiah informs her of his plans, as well. This is likely done in order to guarantee that the king will not renege on any of the agreements made.

The *third research action* is with governors and officials of the Persian Empire whose cooperation is strategic to the successful implementation of Nehemiah's quest. He begins his journey to Jerusalem, but diverts from that journey to visit with the "governors of the province Beyond the River" (2:9) and with Asaph, keeper of the king's forest (2:8) in order to get their cooperation. He receives it, including the promise of all the material he needs to rebuild the walls.

A *fourth research action* may have occurred in a meeting with Sanballat, the governor of the Persian province in which Judea and Jerusalem lay, and with Tobiah the Ammonite official, the most wealthy person in that province and a colleague of Sanballat's (2:10).[2] Here he gets a very icy reception.

The *final research action* occurs in Jerusalem itself after Nehemiah's arrival (2:11–16). It is a clear example of data-collection as the final research action in order to corroborate and confirm the people research done earlier. At night, Nehemiah "inspected the walls of Jerusalem that had been broken down and its gates that had been destroyed by fire" (2:13). His collected data supported the conclusions he had made regarding the rebuilding of the walls. Thus Nehemiah had completed his research actions. And now, it is time to act.

In essence, we see Nehemiah doing two things in terms of research actions. First, he is *initiating action on the organizing effort* by discerning which government officials will cooperate with him and then testing that cooperation by getting agreements from them. He builds that action upon previous relationships with the king and perhaps with others who provide him with credibility. Thus, his first approach is not to confront, but rather to negotiate with them and to seek their cooperation because of his relationship with the king. This approach works with the queen, governors, and Asaph; it fails with Sanballat and Tobiah.

Second, Nehemiah is *conducting a power analysis*. He is determining the relative power of each of the key government and business leaders with whom he will have to deal if the walls of Jerusalem are to be rebuilt. He is seeking to determine each person's sphere of power, his relative strength vis-à-vis the others, and his influence upon others in power. From his actions later, it is clear that Nehemiah decides that Sanballat and Tobiah, although opposed to the organizing Nehemiah will be doing, are relatively isolated and are not key players in the Persian power structure. Therefore, he can confront them with impunity if they don't cooperate (which they won't).[3]

Building Capacity and Ability in Little Old Ladies: How did undertaking research actions contribute to the little old ladies' exercise of the Iron Rule, and consequently, their empowering of themselves? The Crime Action Team (with 13 of the 20 little old ladies aboard) began the research they needed to do in order to be able to determine the campaign they wanted to put together to radically reduce crime in our community. By this time, the Red-lining Action Team had uncovered the extent of the red-lining conspiracy our community was suffering, including the degree of involvement of the city in its execution. Of course, as fellow action-teams of the same community organization, the Red-lining Action Team immediately shared its findings with the Crime Action Team.

Soon after their meeting with the Red-lining Action Team, one of the ladies said to me, "Now we understand why there is such a problem with crime in our community. We couldn't figure out why crime had accelerated so quickly within just a few years—how the community seemed to go overnight from a peaceful, safe community to what it is today. Now we understand. As part of the city's plot against us, they are reducing the amount of police protection this community is receiving. Now we understand why it takes 45 minutes for the police to answer an emergency call, even though the precinct station is just a few blocks down the street. Now we know why you can never find a cop when you need one. Now we understand why you rarely see patrol cars cruising the street. This is all part of the plot to guarantee more rapid devaluation of property." The ladies had begun to engage in rather sophisticated social analysis.

Taking as a given the city's abandonment of the community for fiscal profit, the Crime Action Team began a series of meetings with key government officials, bank and insurance officers, and businesspeople. They were trained how to do these interviews by Bob the organizer, and they would role-play over and over again until they could anticipate every possible response an official might give—and know exactly how to remain in charge of the interview and not let the official control the conversation.

Out of the dozens of visits made by the little old ladies and others on the action team, two were particularly strategic. The first was to our community's precinct commander. They found him to be polite and respectful. But they also found him uncompromising and inflexible. Consequently, they determined that it would be a waste of time to try to negotiate with him; what it would take would be an order from the chief of police to get compliance on the precinct commander's part.

Another informative meeting was one the ladies had with the city council person of the 48th Ward (which included Edgewater). She was an independent councilwoman, belonging neither to the Republican or Regular Democratic Organization (RDO). The RDO was the true power in town, tightly controlled by the mayor. The little old ladies realized, in talking with our councilwoman, that because she was outside the RDO, she had been shut out of all the inner workings of the city council. And because she didn't have the limited but still real clout of the Republican Party behind her, she wouldn't even be consulted on decisions made in "smoke-filled rooms." Consequently, our ladies realized that the councilwoman could be of no help to us in getting better police protection.

The ladies learned one other extremely strategic piece of information. In examining the nature and extent of crime in our community, the Action Team uncovered a police report that stated that the crime was not haphazard, but was organized. A crime syndicate (like the Mafia, but much less powerful) had targeted our community over a year earlier for development as a center for crime. So although there might be occasional spontaneous crime, most of the crime was part of a larger effort to bring the community under the control of this syndicate. They further discovered that the front for the syndicate was a local bookstore that traded in pornography; the gang's headquarters was literally in the back room of the store.

It was in the light of all this research that the little old ladies and the Crime Action Team put together their strategy for stopping crime in our community. They decided that it would take action on the part of the mayor and the chief of police to bring about any reversal in the prosecution of crime in our neighborhood (particularly in the light of the conspiracy, which we weren't supposed to know about). But how would we get the mayor and the chief of police to decide that it would be in their self-interest to change their policy? The little old ladies, guided by Bob the organizer, began to hatch a plan that would get their attention. And it was built around an action that would focus publicity on the operation of the gang.

Take Action

An action is a public meeting between representatives of a community organization and the target that results in an exchange of power. It may be one or two or three representatives. Or it may be hundreds or even thousands of representatives. It may be a confrontive demonstration. Or it may be a quiet and intimate negotiation. But the objective of the action is to bring about an exchange of power.

What is meant by "an exchange of power"? Put simply, those holding unilateral power at the meeting have something the people exercising relational power want. And the objective is to get it. That is the exchange. It is a redistribution of power because those holding the power recognize that it is in their self-interest to allow such redistribution. Obviously, the objective of the negotiation is to make it worth the while of the power holder to share some of that power.

A community organizing mantra is the phrase, *"The action is in the reaction."* That means when an action is taking place, the concern of the community organization is the reaction by the holder of unilateral power. In its planning for an action, the organization constructs the action in such a way that a reaction from the target is expected. *How* the target responds is all-important. Will she accept the demand the organization places? Or will she reject it? The objective is to get a reaction. And it is out of that reaction that the next action of the community organization will be determined.

There are three possible positive reactions that a target can have to each action. And there are three possible negative reactions. The choice in positive reactions are:

- Agreement and concurrence with the community organization's proposal. The second action of the community organization to the target's positive reaction is then to celebrate the victory.

- A modification of the proposal in a way that is acceptable to the community organization. The second action of the community organization is to study the proposed modification, publicly accept it, and then celebrate.

- Present a new proposal that accomplishes the same objectives as the community organization's proposal. The second action of the community organization is to study the new proposal, publicly accept it, and then celebrate.

The positive reaction of the target brings about a clear exchange of power that brings resolution to the issue that has brought about the use of relational power by the community organization.

There are also three ways the target can say "no." They are:

- The target refuses to accept the demand. The second action of the community organization is to thank her for attending the meeting, dismiss her, and then plan the organization's next step to turn up the pressure on the target.

- The target receives the document, but does not accept or approve it. Instead, she says that it needs to be studied. Since the target is the person who has the sole authority to approve the demand, promising to study the proposal is most often a delaying tactic. The second action of the community organization is to demand that a date be set for the target to return with a final answer on the proposal. If the target reacts again by refusing to set a date, that is a signal of a clear delay. The organization then publicly states that it interprets the decision to study the document as a clear "no," dismisses the target, and plans its next action.

- The target makes a counter proposal or a modification of the proposal he/she knows will be unacceptable to the community organization, but does it in such a way that she appears cooperative. The second action of the community organization is to expose that subterfuge, dismiss the target, and plan the next action.

The negative reaction of the target prevents an exchange of power, guarantees that the issue is not resolved, and increases the tension between the target and the community organization. How the organization then plans its next action is crucial. Most people who use unilateral power are used to opposition either crumbling at this point or going ballistic. If it crumbles, that ends the matter. If the organization goes ballistic, then the holder of unilateral power can portray the group as being unreasonable, ruled by their emotions and can likely bring moderate to conservative citizens behind them. Thus, they have won. But "the action is in the reaction," and the task of the community organization is to respond with cold anger, not hot anger. It should neither crumble nor go ballistic. Instead, it should quietly dismiss the target with the words, "You will hear from us later," and then in its own good time, determine what it is going to do, how and where to press the issue to the next stage.

There are different kinds of actions. We are most familiar with public confrontation. But there are many others, as well. There is the conducting of team negotiation, as well as team confrontation, and personal negotiation or confrontation. Just consider the wide spectrum of actions Nehemiah took in order to get Jerusalem's walls rebuilt.

A Biblical Example: In his effort to organize the Jewish people to rebuild their walls, Nehemiah undertook three clear and distinct actions.

The first action was toward his people: According to Nehemiah 2:17–20, the cupbearer calls a public meeting of the Jewish residents of Jerusalem. He climbs onto a platform so all can see and hear him speak, and makes one of the most compelling speeches in Israel's history.

> Then I said to them, "You see the trouble we are in, how Jerusalem lies in ruins with its gates burned. Come, let us rebuild the wall of Jerusalem, so that we may no longer suffer disgrace." I told them that the hand of my God had been gracious upon me, and also the words that the king had spoken to me. Then they said, "Let us start building!" So they committed themselves to the common good. (Nehemiah 2:17–18)

Virtually every sentence of this remarkable speech is packed with meaning. But the first thing we need to note is that Nehemiah gathers everyone in Israel to listen to it. No one is excluded. Noble and commoner alike, male and female, adult and children, business owners and workers, priest and peasant—all are invited to participate in this action. This is a clear signal that the rebuilding of the walls and corporate life of Israel is going to be a people's action, not an action of the elite. The work is not going to be done for the people but by the people who must assume the ownership of it if it is going to succeed.

Second, note how Nehemiah opens his speech. "You see the trouble we are in." He begins by identifying himself with the people. He included himself in their deepest concerns. That inclusion wasn't lost on the crowd.

Nehemiah publicly states the problem in the presence of all the people. "You see the trouble we are in, how Jerusalem lies in ruins with its gates burned" (2:17). By publicly declaring the problem, Nehemiah is taking several strategic steps in organizing the people to act powerfully about their situation.

First, by stating the problem, he is making that problem the immediate concern they need to deal with. Earlier, I stated that Nehemiah knew the primary problem facing Israel was not their broken-down walls but their broken-down life together (1:7). Until they reclaimed for their lives the shalom community, they would never know peace and well-being as a nation, no matter how tall their walls.[4] The Israelites had attributed the vulnerability they so desperately felt to their broken-down walls. But that vulnerability was actually a manifestation of their deepest problem—a profound spiritual problem.

What was significant, however, is that the people didn't discern that. Only Nehemiah did. But Nehemiah didn't try to force his insight upon them. He knew what they were concerned about because he had talked with so many of them: their broken-down walls. So, like any good organizer, Nehemiah began where the people were—organizing around their perceived issues, and biding his time until, through the continuing process of action and reflection the people would themselves come to the conclusion that their problem was a spiritual problem. Once they perceived their problem as spiritual, they would undertake solutions so radical that not even Nehemiah could have convinced them to carry out.

Second, by publicly articulating this problem, Nehemiah is making the rebuilding of the walls the exclusive issue the people should deal with. By stating it before the people and getting their concurrence, he eliminated all other problems from consideration. This focused the attention of the people on addressing this single problem at this specific time.

Third, by publicly articulating this problem, Nehemiah gains public ownership of the problem and thus makes it possible for the people to do something about it. Most people own their problems privately. Because they have kept the problem to themselves, they think they are the only persons facing this problem. Consequently, they begin blaming themselves for having the problem. When the problem is articulated publicly, they perceive that many are having the same problem and begin to feel support ("misery loves company"). They stop blaming themselves for the problem, and begin to act together to solve the problem.

For example, a single mother may be having trouble with her son in school. No matter what she does, her son seems to be falling further and further behind in his schoolwork. She begins to think that her son is not very bright and she is a rotten parent. She has had private conferences with the teacher and the school counselor who suggest all sorts of things she could do to improve her son's learning capacity (some of which are very expensive and that she can't afford). With everything they say, the conviction is reinforced for that mother that she is a rotten parent and her son is not very bright.

Then she visits with another parent in the community and hears that the other parent is also having trouble with her children in the same school. That parent invites her to a meeting of other parents, and in that larger meeting, she hears many parents share how poorly their children are doing, and how the school keeps suggesting courses of action that are financially unfeasible for any of the parents to implement. Suddenly the problem changes. Not all these children can be stupid. Not all these parents could be so bad. Perhaps the problem lies, not so much with these parents and children, but with the school and how it is seeking to teach these children. By publicly articulating the problem, the problem has moved from being a private problem to a public concern, and from one of self-blame to the shortfall of the educational system. That was what Nehemiah was accomplishing by publicly articulating the problem of broken-down walls.

Nehemiah Turns the Problem into an Issue: "Come, let us rebuild the wall of Jerusalem, so that we may no longer suffer disgrace" (2:17). At first glance, it appears that Nehemiah is turning the problem into a solution (i.e., the problem is broken-down walls; the solution is to rebuild the walls). But that is not what he is doing at all. Rather, what he is doing is turning the problem into an issue.

A problem is a complex situation that is, because of its immensity, so amorphous that it is difficult to determine a simple plan of action to resolve that situation. Thus, the problem facing Israel ("Jerusalem lies in ruins with its gates burned"), while appearing simple, is really quite complex. What do you need to do to reverse Jerusalem lying in ruins? Well, obviously, the walls need to be rebuilt. But so do the streets and the homes. The market square needs to be reopened and business needs to be able to be conducted there. Provision needs to be made for handling street traffic, providing drinking water to the populace, removing body waste and trash. And a palace needs to be built for the governor. The problem of rebuilding Jerusalem is so complex that it is difficult to determine a simple plan of action to resolve that situation.

But "How do you eat an elephant?" the old African proverb asks. "One bite at a time." The purpose of an issue is to reduce the problem to "bite-size." It is to remove all the possible tasks that are capturing your attention and select a single task to do. And then, it is to require a response, "Will you or won't you undertake this action?"

This is what Nehemiah was doing when he challenged the people, "Come, let us rebuild the wall of Jerusalem." He was, in essence, asking them, "Will you or won't you rebuild the wall?" Forget about the streets, the houses, the public buildings, water access, and waste removal. Will you or won't you rebuild the walls? There are only two ways to answer that challenge. Either the people will do it. Or they won't. What are they going to do?

The People Determine the Solution: Up until this point, the people are essentially being organized by Nehemiah, with him as the organizer playing the pivotal role. Now the role begins radically changing, as the people assume the full leadership of the organizing process and Nehemiah moves into a supportive role.

"Then they said, 'Let us start building!' So they committed themselves to the common good" (2:18). The people decide that what they are going to do is to organize themselves to rebuild the walls of Jerusalem. Nehemiah isn't going to do it. The Persian government isn't going to do it (the government would supply the building materials but they won't do the actual construction—cf. 2:1–8). The people will take charge of their own situation, and solve their own problem. They will take on that issue and rebuild the walls.

The People Create Their Own Strategy to Rebuild the Walls on Self-Interest: Chapter three lays out the plans for the rebuilding of the walls. It is a deceptively simple strategy.

The strategy was, in essence, to assign each extended Jewish family (usually fifteen to fifty men and women who shared in the construction, cf. 3:12) the task of rebuilding a designated portion of the wall. The strategy was that each family would build in concert with the families to their right and left, so that the entire wall would be raised evenly over its entirety (3:1–32). This would, in turn, provide significant stability to the wall as it moved upward.

What is particularly significant was that, whenever possible, families were assigned to build "in front of their houses" (e.g., 3:28–29). Thus, those creating the building plan intentionally used the self-interest of the people to accomplish the building—because, obviously, one would build his portion of the wall very securely if it were guarding access to his own home.

The People Carry Out the Action: The book of Nehemiah now moves to a report on the people's implementation of their strategy (Nehemiah 3–5). The people simply set to work, each family constructing their portion of the wall, using the materials provided by the Persian government. And the wall slowly grew upward. Thus, Nehemiah has completed his first action on the people, moving them from helplessness to beginning the task of rebuilding the walls of Jerusalem.

The second action was an action on the systems of the province:

> But when Sanballat and Tobiah and the Arabs and the Ammonites and the Ashdodites heard that the repairing of the walls of Jerusalem was going forward and the gaps were beginning to be closed, they were very angry, and all plotted together to come and fight against Jerusalem and to cause confusion in it. (Nehemiah 4:7–8)

The success of the Israelites in their effort to rebuild the walls created opposition by the political systems (symbolized by Sanballat, the governor of Palestine), the economic system (symbolized by Tobiah, the Ammonite "official") and those people who were not Jews (who were obviously intimidated by the renewed energy of Israel). That opposition took three forms.

First, the political and economic systems and the people mocked the efforts of the Jews, making light of their accomplishment (Nehemiah 4:1–5). When that didn't work, they threatened Israel with violence (4:7–14). Finally, when that reaction failed, these opposing systems and people-groups attempted an assassination of Nehemiah (6:1–9).

It is intriguing to note how Nehemiah and the Jews responded to these three attempts by outside interests to block their rebuilding effort. When mocked, the Israelites chose simply to ignore the taunts; they didn't take the mockery seriously and just went right on building (4:6). When threatened with violence, however, the Israelites took that threat quite seriously. They divided the Hebrew work force in half with one group doing the construction for a period of time and the other group standing guard; then, at a prearranged time, they traded roles and the builders became the guards while the guards became the builders (Nehemiah 4:15–23). As they worked, the builders kept their swords with them, so that both groups were armed for battle at any time. The preparedness of the people stopped Sanballat's implementation of this plan (4:23).

The third attempt by Sanballat, Tobiah, and the Gentiles to block the rebuilding effort was an attempt at assassination. In this action, Nehemiah was clearly in charge. The coup leaders sought to lure Nehemiah into a trap by asking him to attend negotiating sessions with Sanballat on two separate occasions. Nehemiah simply refused to attend (Nehemiah 6:1–13). Intriguingly, when Sanballat threatened to report Nehemiah's action to Artaxerxes (interpreting his actions as an effort to rebel against Persia), Nehemiah, in essence replied, "Go right ahead. Report me to the king. See what trouble it will get you into" (6:6–9). Nehemiah was confident in the trust relationship he had spent years building with Artaxerxes that he need not fear any such threat.

It would be expected that the systems and people whose power would be threatened by Israel's action would oppose the rebuilding of Jerusalem's walls. What came as a particularly bitter pill for Nehemiah to swallow, however, was betrayal by the wealthy and powerful Jews. But the action Nehemiah brought against those Jews is a classic example of how to effectively confront.

The third action was against the principalities and powers of Israel: A number of the Jews working on the wall came to Nehemiah with "a great outcry." They reported to him that a number of wealthy and powerful Jewish leaders were taking advantage of the circumstances created by the rebuilding of the walls to make significant money and gain power at the expense of the people (Nehemiah 5:1–5).

Because the people were spending so much of their time in rebuilding the walls, they could not continue to work their fields sufficient to generate adequate income. Therefore, they had to turn to rich Jewish leaders for short-term loans. Those leaders were requiring the people to commit their fields, vineyards, and houses as collateral for those loans, and they were being charged exorbitant interest—both activities forbidden by the Deuteronomic law code. These leaders were now foreclosing on those loans, taking away the people's "birthright" and even taking their sons and daughters as payment—turning the sons into slaves and the daughters into prostitutes (once again, against the law). "We are powerless," the people complained to Nehemiah, "and our fields and vineyards now belong to others" (Nehemiah 5:5).

It is instructive to note what Nehemiah did, when he learned of this injustice occurring "inside the camp." He begins by telling us, "I was very angry when I heard their outcry and [their] complaints. [But] after thinking it over . . ." (5:6), and then he describes his first action steps. Nehemiah's first reaction was to be angry. But then he thought it over. The Hebrew actually says, "But I took counsel with myself." He had a conversation with himself and reflected on what he should do. In other words, he changed his anger from "hot anger" into "cold anger" and calmly and calculatedly developed a plan of action. Now consider that plan of action.

First, Nehemiah met with "the nobles and the officials" (the Jewish political and economic elite) who were making profit off the financial straits of their brother and sister Jews (5:6–7). He confronted them privately about what they were doing, making it clear to them that they were breaking the law. The text is unclear whether he asked for a response from them at that time, but it is clear that they are "put on notice" that they are going to be held accountable for their actions.

Second, Nehemiah "called a great assembly" of all the people (5:7–13). That assembly was a classic example of how to bring powerful leaders to accountability for their actions.

At the assembly, Nehemiah placed the economic and political leaders on trial, literally facing their accusers—the people. Presumably, he had the people tell their stories of the exploitation and oppression they and their children were experiencing from these leaders. Nehemiah then confronted the leaders, summarizing the crime of which they were accused (5:8), and then presenting the people's demands to stop the charging of interest and to return their collateral to them (5:9–11).

The Jewish political and economic leaders, overwhelmed at such public confrontation, replied, "We will restore everything and demand nothing more from them. We will do as you say" (5:12). But Nehemiah wouldn't accept their verbal agreement. He made them commit to a binding contract by having them take an oath before the Israelite priests and the people (5:12). He then concluded by declaring that they would be banned from Israel if they did not conform to this agreement (5:13). The assembly supported him in these demands. And the confrontation ended with the word "And the people (i.e., the political and economic leaders) did as they had promised" (5:13).[5]

Building Capacity and Ability in Little Old Ladies: As a result of their research actions, the little old ladies and the rest of the Crime Action Team came to the following conclusions: (1) the only way to significantly reduce crime in our community was through the intentional efforts of the Chicago Police Department to reduce crime; (2) that would not happen unless it came as an express order of the chief of police; (3) the parent community organization, ONE, had to convincingly demonstrate its capacity, ability, and willingness to act so that the chief of police would decide that it was in his self-interest to reduce crime in our community. With the help of Bob the organizer, the ladies and the Action Team put together a campaign to accomplish the above three objectives and to train the little old ladies and other members of the action team to implement that campaign.

The little old ladies and the action team decided that the first part of the campaign had to be an action against the crime syndicate that would, in reality, target the Chicago Police Department. The plan they devised was extremely creative. And its execution was flawless. This is what these formerly powerless little old ladies did:

The strategy of our little old ladies was to picket the pornographic bookstore where the crime syndicate had its headquarters. So the ladies got in touch with the television stations and newspaper reporters, informing them about an upcoming public demonstration. The action team recruited all the senior community residents they could from the house groups of the Crime Action Team and from the remainder of ONE. Their advertising said, "Only those with white hair, blue hair or no hair should come to picket."

Now in the United States at that time, there was a very popular and unique advertising campaign undertaken by the Burma Shave Company. The company introduced a succession of small signs along a given stretch of highway, each sign with just a few words on it—but all of the signs, considered together, conveying a message. The aim was to tantalize people driving by to keep reading all of the signs until they got the full message.

At the same time, there was a popular song being played on the radio about little old ladies in tennis shoes from Evanston, Illinois, who were trying to get everyone to stop drinking whiskey (Evanston was the site of the Women's Christian Temperance Union). Both of these American phenomena became the base for this creative action.

On the day of the action, over 300 senior citizens (all associated with ONE) assembled in front of the pornographic bookstore. All of them had on tennis shoes. They produced a bunch of placards, each in the Burma Shave format. The television cameras stationed themselves at both ends of the picket line in order to catch the signs just before they made the turn. And the picketing began.

As they marched, everybody chanted, "This place' got to go; this place' got to go!" Then the little old ladies made the first turn of the picket line (where the TV cameras were). And suddenly, up came each sign. The first placard said, "We may be little old ladies." The cameras went to their faces; sure enough, they *were* little old ladies. The second sign declared, "We may be wearing tennis shoes." The cameras went down to their feet, and sure enough, they *were all* wearing tennis shoes. The third: "But we don't live in Evanston." The fourth: "We live in the Edgewater community of Chicago." The fifth: "And we don't like this bookstore, because . . . " The sixth: "It's a pornographic bookstore." And on and on the signs came.

Then came the *coup de grace*. Suddenly, a little old lady whom the action team had carefully selected came roaring up to the television cameras on a Harley-Davidson "hog" motorcycle. She was dressed in the tightest blue jeans, a black leather motorcycle jacket and black motorcycle cap (the most popular motion picture playing in America at the time was "The Wild Ones" about an outlaw motorcycle gang). She kept roaring around the marching protestors on her Harley-Davidson and would periodically stick her face into a television camera, ranting and raving about "these dirty old men trying to corrupt us lovely young ladies with their evil intentions."

As you can imagine, the reporters and television crews just loved all of it. It was *hot* copy. On the news that night, our little old lady picketers and motorcyclist were not only picked up by every Chicago television station—it was shown nationally on every network news.

As we noted earlier, "the action is in the reaction." Well, you can imagine the reaction—not simply of the crime syndicate, but of the mayor and the Chicago police chief. Before the network news had gone off the air, the mayor had telephoned the chief and commanded him, "Meet with those ladies and get this matter settled." Our little old ladies had demonstrated how truly powerful they really were.

Monday morning, bright and early, the spokeswomen of the Crime Action Team received a telephone call from the secretary of the chief of police. Within a week, the little old ladies were sitting at a conference room at police headquarters with the chief of police, his senior staff, and the commander of our precinct. But the ladies were not alone. They had brought with them over 200 people who were standing in the courtyard below.

The ladies presented their demands: a serious effort of the precinct to stop crime in our community, organizing a "Neighborhood Watch" program, an ongoing dialogue between ONE and the precinct including monthly crime reports to ONE, driving out the crime syndicate, and cops walking beats. The police balked at the proposal that cops should walk beats; "They haven't walked beats in 37 years," the commander stated. "Too bad," the little old ladies responded. "We want them walking beats now." The police chief intervened, ordered the commander to have all officers walking beats in five days, acceded to all the demands, and ended by saying to the commander, "Not only are you to produce monthly crime reports for ONE; I want to see those reports each month as well—and I will be watching your performance."

So it was that the syndicate was driven out of Edgewater, crime plummeted overnight, a dialogue had begun between citizens and police, cops walked beats, and the little old ladies had discovered how truly powerful they actually were.

"You may be little old ladies. But you are not 'nothing but little old ladies.' You are very powerful little old ladies. And if you want to stop crime in this neighborhood, you can."

What I had learned from this entire organizing effort and from these little old ladies was the Iron Rule of organizing—and what ought to be the Iron Rule of all ministries: "Never do for others what they can do for themselves." That Iron Rule was profoundly expressed in an understanding of ministry, not as helping and serving people ("Ladies, how can I help you?") but as enabling people to help themselves ("Ladies, what's your problem?").

PRINCIPLES FOR BUILDING THE POWER OF THE PEOPLE

We have now examined some of the most pivotal strategies for building people power. We have looked at each strategy from a conceptual perspective, from the study of biblical examples and from the examination of one organizing effort ("the little old ladies"). In this section, we now want to broaden our perspective to articulate the essential principles of building people power upon which these strategies are built.

The Task of Organizing Is to Build Power

The chief objective is for people without power to build and demonstrate their power in such a way that they will be taken seriously by the political, economic, and cultural controllers of power who will choose to enter into good faith negotiations with the people out of their own enlightened self-interest.

People Power Is Built on Relationships

Unless confronted to change, users of economic, political, and cultural/religious power will exercise power unilaterally (that is, "power over") that is backed up by laws, force exercised through police and the military, economic pressures, and cultural norms that were created by those unilateral power-actors to maintain themselves and their heirs in power. The only kind of power that can oppose unilateral power without creating warfare, oppression, or revolution is relational power, painstakingly built upon the trust created over years of sharing together in the struggle to make life just.

All Organizing Is Reorganizing

The world is already clearly organized by those in power for their own advantage. The organizing task of the people through the exercise of relational power is to reorganize the way power is exercised. Such "reorganizing" goes on constantly, because every organizing effort will inevitably seek to serve its own ends to the exclusion of other claims. Therefore, those exercising power must do "actions" not only upon the establishment but also upon themselves.

The Objective Is an Exchange of Power

Any action that is designed to reorganize the status quo results in an exchange of power. That is, those holding unilateral power have something the people exercising relational power want. The objective is to get it. That is the exchange. It is redistribution of power because those holding the power recognize that it is in their self-interest to share some of that power.

The Action Is in the Reaction

The objective of any action conducted by the people is to get a reaction from the systems or people they are dealing with. It is to place a demand before the systems, each other, or one's self that requires a response. How that person, group, or system reacts and responds determines the next step the organizing effort will take.

Negotiation and Confrontations

The primary tactic of community organizing is negotiation—the art of people and targets reaching a settlement together that achieves the objectives of both and in which an exchange of power has occurred. However, most business and government targets will not negotiate with the people until they have witnessed a display of power that will motivate their desire to negotiate. Confrontation is a primary tactic for bringing a target to the negotiating table; so are the tactics of agitation, civil disobedience, and demanding accountability.

The Pedagogy of Action and Reflection

The vehicle for learning and for building relational power is the interaction of action and reflection. No action is ever undertaken without considerable reflection beforehand. No action, once undertaken, is complete until a full evaluation of it has occurred so that success can be celebrated and mistakes can be identified and corrected. When a spiral of action and reflection takes place in the organizing effort, every action will become more substantive than the action before it, and every reflection will become more penetrating than the reflection before it.

The Task Is Building Leaders

An essential task of organizing is to build leaders who have developed the capacity, ability, and willingness to act and to lead their communities in acting powerfully to bring about the kind of change that will both strengthen the people and serve their development as a human community. All the organizing steps and theories of building relational power is the means by which the leadership capability of the community's people is developed and is lived out as a people who practice the Iron Rule.

Building Community Is the Ultimate Objective

Community is a group of people with a continuing experience, tradition, and history who support and challenge each other to act powerfully, both individually and collectively, to affirm, defend, and advance their values and self-interest. This is the primary purpose of community organizing—to create out of a victimized, marginalized, destructive collection of people a community where the quality of life is such that people find fulfillment and joy in living there. The power of the oppressor must be replaced by a quality of corporate life that is of such superiority to either that of the formerly oppressed or their oppressors that it brings purpose, direction, joy, and fulfillment to all who experience it. That is the chief end for building a people of power.

SUMMARY

Nehemiah 6:15 tells us that it took fifty-two days to rebuild the walls of Jerusalem—once the people put their mind to "this great work." The reconstruction of those walls was completed by October 2, 445 BC. But in the midst of the joy of a work well done, it is easy for us to overlook the fact that those walls had been demolished for 141 years (they were demolished in 586 BC by the Babylonian army, according to 2 Kings 25:10).

For 141 years, the Jewish people had tolerated the demolition of their walls. For 141 years, they had put up with the loss of protection against marching armies, the looting and pillaging by marauding bands, the raping of their wives and daughters, the burning and demolition of their homes and public buildings, the leveling of their temple so that they had no place to worship God. For 141 years, they accepted the critique of the rest of the world that they were a nation of nobodies, a people oppressed first by the Babylonians and then the Persians and even by the local tribes whom Sanballat represented, a people exploited by both those who controlled Palestine's economy and even their own Jewish elite, a people marginalized by their religion and by their belief in an apparently dormant God. Because their city's walls were broken down, the Jewish people accepted the abuse of the rest of the world, making them into second-class citizens for 141 years. Yet, as Nehemiah demonstrated to them in 445 BC, the power to radically change their situation had lain for all 141 years in their own hands. At any time during those 141 years, they could have chosen to rebuild those walls.

The question that must therefore be asked is this: why did the Jews not say, sometime during those 141 years, "We're not going to take this anymore?" Why did they take such abuse from the tribes around them, the desert people pillaging them, the nations oppressing them? Why did they choose to remain in such bondage?

The answer is simple. They lacked a Nehemiah. They lacked a person who would ask questions, who would listen to their pain, who would learn from the people, who would build relationships with them, who would allow his heart to be broken with that pain, who would pray to God for his people, who would assess the resources at hand, who would not be afraid of stepping out into public life and confronting even an emperor, and who would gather the people and declare to them, "You see the trouble we are in, how Jerusalem lies in ruins with its gates burned. Come, let us rebuild the wall of Jerusalem, so that we may no longer suffer disgrace."

The Jews lacked a person sufficiently committed to the empowerment of his people that he would dedicate his life to enabling them to determine the issues of their society they would address, teach them both by relationships and by example how to act powerfully for the common good, and trust them with the responsibility to rebuild their own nation rather than depend upon emperor, priest, or business leader.

But once they found a person who both believed in and personified the Iron Rule of Power—"Never do for others what they can do for themselves"—and carried it out in his ministry with them, Israel was reborn.[6]

QUESTIONS

1. This chapter presented the building and using of relational power through the steps of individual meetings, house meetings, research actions, and actions; it used both the story of "Little Old Ladies" and of the biblical account of Nehemiah to illustrate each of these steps. What was similar in this strategy to the approach churches tend to use today to work for community change?

2. What is significantly different in Nehemiah's and the Little Old Ladies' strategies to the approach churches tend to use today both within their own interior life as a congregation and in their engagement with their neighborhood or city?

3. How is the health, well-being, and effectiveness of the Church affected by our not taking seriously the Nehemiah model for ministry?

Chapter Seven

CALLING OUT AND BUILDING LEADERS

One of the most strategic tasks in building a people of power is the identification, calling out, and building of leaders. In both chapters five and six, we have dealt with the importance of developing leaders and the strategic roles the organizer and the present leaders of a community organization play in identifying and calling out leaders. But how are people shaped into becoming leaders? How do you build leaders?[1]

When I was a seminarian interning in a local congregation, the pastor said to me, "The primary indicator of the success of your ministry will be revealed six months after you have left that ministry." That pastor's insights equally apply to any organization. How our organization fares six to twelve months after we have left is the clearest indicator of how effective a job we have done in building leaders within that organization. The greatest compliment we can receive is for that organization, six months after we leave, to be running along so smoothly and effectively it was as if we were never there.

The leadership myth under which we all tend to operate is the myth of the charismatic leader who "rides into town on a white stallion" and sets things right. But that's the myth of the leader as Messiah, as conquering hero. In reality, being a leader is much more simple and much more profound than that.

What is a leader? A leader is a person with followers. That is, a leader is someone who influences other people and can organize them for a given purpose. Such a definition of leader makes clear that the image of leader as charismatic or dynamic personality is a myth, because all of us can be leaders if we choose to build a constituency that follows our lead.

The pastor's, organizer's, or leader's task is primarily to nurture and call out potential leaders, to encourage their growth, to guide them in discovering their own authentic call in life, to evoke their gifts and to sharpen their skills, and in all of that effort, to create a generation of leaders who can lead that church, mission agency, or community organization into the future. Our task is not so much to be a dynamic, "take-charge," inspirational personality as it is to raise up people who can lead. And that is particularly true in the building of a people of power.

How does one carry out this all-important responsibility of leadership development? Examining the leadership-building practices of some of the most recognized leaders in the Bible can provide us with valuable insights in answering that question.

We will explore the leadership style of Jesus Christ as a template for team building, then compare and contrast the styles of Moses, Elijah, Paul, and Barnabas to that of Jesus. We have chosen these people for three reasons. First, these five are some of the most strategic players in the Scripture, responsible for the continuing of Israel or the Church after their deaths. Second, three of the five (Moses, Jesus, and Paul) founded movements upon which Judaism and Christianity were built. Third, each of these leaders had a distinct style, yet they shared many things in common, which can become informative for us as we seek to build leaders in our organization.

BIBLICAL LEADERS

Jesus of Nazareth

All four gospels are full of insights on Jesus' leadership style. In fact, it can be argued that there is more attention paid to Jesus' leadership training and team-building practices in Scripture than is given to any other biblical personality.

Integral to Jesus' leadership style was his essential personality—the personality of a commanding leader. He was, first of all, a visionary—one who perceived his ministry in terms of a clear-cut mission: to proclaim the coming of the kingdom of God, and to live out that kingdom in his very life and death (Mark 1:14–15). He was the one both proclaiming and living out that kingdom, so that this kingdom—both in formation and at the end of the age—would long outlast his bodily presence on earth.

Second, Jesus was a man of passion, often of anger and always of power. The coming of the kingdom of God was not an intellectual exercise for Jesus, but something he felt passionately. This included significant grief over those who were blind to the good news he was bringing, but who chose to ignore and to even work against the coming of his kingdom (Matthew 23:1–36).

Third, Jesus was a risk-taker, one who believed so thoroughly in the mission upon which he had been sent that he took significant risks. His ministry was essentially one of confrontation—confrontation of religious, political, and economic leaders. But Jesus was also willing to confront his disciples. He was not afraid to make enemies, and he was not one to duck an issue. In fact, his enemies acknowledged that fact when one of them, seeking to set him up to break Roman law, said to him, "Teacher, we know that you are right in what you say and teach, and you show deference to no one, but teach the way of God in accordance with truth" (Luke 20:21).

Finally, Jesus was a man of deep interior self-validation. He had profound compassion for those who were the poor, marginalized, sick, or deformed of the world. But he was not a "soft" man. Rather, he was a man of deep conviction who could not be diverted from his mission, even by his mother and his brothers (Matthew 12:46–48).

There is a clear strategy repeatedly used by Jesus in the four Gospels to build a team of leaders for his kingdom (examples in one gospel account, Mark, are found in 4:1–20, 8:1–21, and 8:27—9:9). First, Jesus presents a parable or teaching to the general populace. Second, this popular teaching is followed by taking his disciples aside to reflect at further depth on what he publicly taught. Third, in the light of this more intensive reflection, Jesus calls his disciples to a specific and concrete action that places what they have learned to the test. Fourth, he then follows up that action with a time of evaluation or further reflection to learn from the action they have just completed. Thus, he holds them accountable for their performance and their perceptions.

A clear example of this methodology was the feeding of the five thousand (Luke 9:10–17). That story took place in the context of a chapter given over to the teaching of the disciples and Jesus' continued formation of them into a team capable both of doing ministry and of teaching the gospel. This and an entire grouping of leadership-formation stories are "book-ended" by the two incidents of Jesus sending out disciples into mission (9:1–6; 10:1–12).

The story began with Jesus' teaching of five thousand men (so, presumably, there were actually seven to ten thousand people, including women and children). The disciples came to him near the close of the day, urging him to send away the crowd so that they might find lodging and provision on their own. Jesus instead challenged the disciples, "*You* give them something to eat." They demonstrated how ridiculous a request that was because they had only five loaves and two fish—scarcely enough to feed a few people, never mind seven to ten thousand people. The Scripture then states,

> And taking the five loaves and the two fish, [Jesus] looked up to heaven, and blessed and broke them, and gave them to the disciples to set before the crowd. And all ate and were filled. What was left over was gathered up, twelve baskets of broken pieces. (Luke 9:16–17)

The important point about this miracle is that it was performed for the benefit of the disciples and not the crowd. We know that was so because there was no significant reaction of the people upon being fed by Jesus. They were not aware that a miracle was taking place. Only the disciples knew that there were only five loaves and two fish. The people in Luke's story simply think they are being fed.

It was the disciples who saw Jesus "take," "bless," "break," and "give" the broken loaves and torn fish to them for distribution (the formula for the sacrament of holy communion and the church's understanding of Christ's life as being taken, blessed, broken, and given comes from this miracle). It was each disciple who received only a small portion of one loaf and a piece of fish. It was each disciple who was then instructed by Jesus to feed the multitude with such scarce fare. What was each disciple to do? Would he obey Jesus and make a fool of himself? Or would he refuse to do as he was called by Jesus to do and preserve his dignity?

To their credit, the disciples decided to be obedient to the Master's command. Thus, as the disciples distributed the little they had received, the loaves and fish multiplied *in their very hands*, and the people were fed. And thus they learned that Jesus was all-sufficient for them as they carried out ministry.

We see this teaching pattern followed repeatedly as Jesus molded the disciples into a ministry team destined to reach the world. Out of reflection with the crowd, Jesus grasped a "teachable moment" provided by the concern of the disciples for the crowd, got them to reflect on the situation, and had them then act on that reflection.

The next story then leads into the inevitable evaluation that Jesus would use to mold his disciples. "Who do the crowds say that I am" (Luke 9:18)? The disciples answered, "John the Baptist, others Elijah; others say that one of the ancient prophets has arisen." "But who do *you* say that I am?"—you who know better, you who have seen the miracle of the loaves and the fish—who do you say that I am? "And Peter answered, 'The Messiah of God'" (9:20).

This is just one of a countless number of stories—of miracles and parables and stories—told in all four gospel accounts that trace Jesus' profound building of the disciples into the strongest of leadership teams spiritually, intellectually, and in practice. A measurement of the use of Jesus' time in the four gospels reveals that it was in reality a comparatively brief amount of time the Master spent in healings, miracles, teaching, and preaching. About two-thirds of the "teachable moments" were spent on the disciple band and others he was molding into leaders.

Perhaps the most significant time of "teachable moments" in Jesus' ministry was the time surrounding his crucifixion. We normally study Jesus' death, concentrating either on the events or what Jesus was doing that has brought about our salvation. But we rarely look at that event in terms of the hell through which the disciples and the women were taken.

It was not that Jesus orchestrated his death in order to "teach his followers a lesson." Rather, as he lived into the experience (and died within it), Jesus had both the clarity of his discipling mission and the profound love for his followers that caused him to use the events as he experienced them to work for profound change in their lives.

It began with Judas, and Jesus' announcement at the Last Supper, "The one who has dipped his hand into the bowl with me will betray me." Judas, rapidly withdrawing his hand, "innocently" asked, "Surely not I, Rabbi?" And Jesus replied, "You have said so" (or, in other words, "You've got it right!") (Matthew 26:23–25). Follow this with Jesus' statement to Judas at the betrayal scene, upon receiving Judas' kiss, "Judas, is it with a kiss that you are betraying the Son of Man?" (Luke 22:48). The impact these two events had on Judas must have been overwhelming when he realized he had been used by the religious/political system to betray the Son of Glory. Jesus, of course, would have longed for Judas' conversion at this point, but he accurately predicated that the implications of what he had done and its utter irreversibility would weigh so heavily upon Judas that he would condemn himself (Matthew 26:24). Suicide was the inevitable outcome of such a momentous deed (Matthew 27:3–10).

Second, Jesus used this historic occasion as a way to reach into the soul of each disciple. He warned them at the Last Supper, "You will all become deserters because of me this night; for it is written, 'I will strike the shepherd, and the sheep of the flock will be scattered.' But after I am raised up, I will go ahead of you to Galilee" (Matthew 26:31). Desertion was exactly what they did do. Upon his arrest, the disciples fled, with only John and the women who followed Jesus having the courage to come to the foot of the cross (John 19:25–27).

The disciples, of course, had to be devastated not only at Jesus' death but also at their own cowardly complicity. What is significant, therefore, is that Jesus did "go ahead of them into Galilee." It is to these very disciples, as well as to the women who remained faithful to him, that Jesus first appeared. His wishing of *shalom* to them ("Peace be with you" Luke 24:36), his solicitation for them, and his efforts to convince them he was truly alive (Luke 24:38–43), his teaching of them (Luke 24:46–49), his gift of the Holy Spirit to them (John 20:22), and his commission of them (Matthew 28:18–20; John 20:23) all assured them that they were forgiven, accepted, loved, and called to minister in spite of their desertion and abandonment of him in his greatest hour of need.

Finally, the most profound spiritual formation of a disciple was Jesus' interaction with Simon Peter. Upon Jesus' assertion that his disciples would desert him, Peter indignantly responded, "Though all become deserters of you, I will never deny you" (Matthew 26:33). Jesus replied, "I tell you, Peter, the cock will not crow this day, until you have denied three times that you know me" (Luke 22:34). And with the shock of his prediction assaulting Peter, Jesus further declared, "Simon, Simon, listen! Satan has demanded to sift all of you like wheat, but I have prayed for you that your own faith may not fail; and you, when once you have turned back, strengthen your brothers" (Luke 22:31).

Of course, Peter—against all his intentions and resolve to the contrary—did deny Jesus three times, and when the cock crowed and Peter came to his senses about what he had just done, "went out and wept bitterly" (Luke 22:54–62). The terrible prediction had come true. And Peter was devastated, destroyed, and driven to despair over it.

Notice, then, how the resurrected Jesus ministered to Peter, restored his self-confidence, and dedicated him to ministry. Peter, of course, must have considered himself eliminated from the disciple company—a total failure before his Master, before God, and before the other disciples. The first glimmer of hope must have come for him when the excited women returned from the empty tomb, saying that the angel who had announced Jesus' resurrection also was careful to command, "Go, tell his disciples *and Peter* that he is going ahead of you into Galilee!" (Mark 16:7) What hope must have sprung into Peter's heart at his intentional inclusion in the disciple band!

And then, in Galilee, came the most poignant scene of restoration and commissioning between the risen Christ and the now-humbled Simon Peter. Jesus met with Peter on the shore of the Sea of Galilee, and there he asked him three times, "Simon, son of John, do you love me?" The now humbled and chastened Peter responded, "Lord, you know everything; you know that I love you." It was as if he were saying, "Lord, you can see into my heart. You know what is there. You know my weaknesses and my shortcomings as well as my strengths and potentials. And you know—even beneath the denials, the desertion, the cowardice—you *know* I love you!" And Jesus simply replied, "Feed my sheep" (John 21:15–17).

Three times Jesus was denied. Three times Jesus reclaimed Peter. And Peter knew that he was accepted, was loved, was believed in by Jesus, and was invested with the responsibility of being the rock of the Rock upon which the Church was to be built.

It was Jesus' capacity to build profound spiritual and missional leaders out of apparently ordinary people that constituted his most significant ministry achievement. And the profound job he did in Peter, in the women followers, and in all the disciples revealed itself in only fifty days after his death and resurrection: at the Feast of Pentecost, a once intimidated Peter openly declared Christ before the whole world (Acts 2:1–36); the disciples who once deserted Jesus now converted three thousand in one day with the gospel (2:37–42); the Christians formed themselves into the most just of communities (2:43–47), and the church was born.

Using Jesus as a measurement of effective leadership in the building of leaders, let us now turn to two of the most pivotal people in the Hebrew Bible, followed by two of the most influential Christian leaders in the New Testament.

Moses and Elijah

Moses would be considered the dominant leader of the Hebrew Bible—the liberator of the children of Israel from Egyptian oppression, the founder of Israelite law and the nation of Israel, and the one who brought to Israel its sense of mission and destiny. Elijah would be considered among the greatest of Israel's prophets, at one of the most profound periods of crisis in Israel when it appeared that the nation would reject Yahweh, adopt the worship of Baal, and embrace the political practices of all the nations around them. Both men had the most profound impact upon Israel's future yet were significantly different in leadership style and vision. Therefore, they provide a profound contrast in leadership style and in their effectiveness in building leaders to follow after them.

Moses. If we were to characterize Moses as a leader, we would have to stress that he was both a man of vision and of anger, a significant risk-taker and a person of deep interior self-validation. All of these characteristics were centered in a deep, personal faith in Yahweh, the God of his ancestors but also his God with whom he was in a vital relationship. This resulted in a strong vision of the nation of Israel as it should be, a commitment to create the shalom community (Deuteronomy 10:12–21).

Moses not only embraced a vision of a nation, under God, on mission to the world. He was also pictured as a man of anger—"hot" anger when, as a young man, he slew the Egyptian, beating a Hebrew slave; "cold" anger when, matured by years of exile as a shepherd in the desert, he met God at the burning bush and was called to liberate Israel. That "cold" anger would serve Moses well, for it would become for him an overwhelming grief (the root meaning of the world *anger*) at seeing his people enslaved by Egypt and then later enslaved by their own lust for wealth, exploitation, and control.

Moses is represented in the Pentateuch as a considerable risk-taker—particularly when he saw injustice, the weak being exploited, or God being ignored. We need to only begin recounting his life to recall numerous illustrations of risk-taking: the slaying of the Egyptian master, the attacking of the shepherds seeking to take advantage of Jethro's daughters, the confrontation of Pharaoh, the initiation of the plagues, and the parting of the Red Sea.

Moses could be this kind of risk-taker because of two factors. The first was his immutable faith in Yahweh. He had proven God's commitment to Israel and to himself over and over again. Even when Moses first met God at the burning bush, God reminded him that He was "the God of Abraham, Isaac and Jacob" (Exodus 3:6)—the God who had been faithful to all Moses' ancestors and would therefore prove faithful to him.

That bedrock faith in God's faithfulness brought out in Moses the second factor that enabled him to become a risk-taker as well as a man of vision and of anger. That second factor was his increasing sense of the value of his own judgment, an internal conviction that following in the ways of Yahweh—whether for an individual or for a nation—was the way humans were meant to live, and therefore, he could embrace with surety the path on which he was leading the children of Israel.

It is in the light of these leadership characteristics that we can examine Moses as a builder of leaders. Who are the leadership team Moses called that set the future of Israel?

The first person on that team was Aaron, the brother of Moses. Upon hearing God's call at the burning bush, Moses demurred leadership by saying, "I am a poor speaker" (Exodus 6:30). God gave him Aaron to be his spokesperson both to Pharaoh and to Israel. Later, Aaron was made the high priest of Israel's worship of God and filled that role to his death. But Aaron was also a disappointment to Moses, for he did not have the internal self-validation Moses had. Instead, he wavered against the demands of the crowd (Exodus 32:1–2), and gave way to their creation of a golden calf to substitute for the worship of Yahweh. He also publicly criticized Moses (Numbers 12:1–15).

Moses also turned to his sister, Miriam (Exodus 15:20–21), who led the worship of Yahweh and created the first choir. Later in the desert, she joined resistance to Moses and was struck with leprosy as a result (Numbers 12:1–15) but was healed and restored to Israel again. The stories of Aaron and Miriam remind us that those who are built into a leadership team don't always turn out well. Like us, they have faults, will fall short and disappoint, and in fact will sometimes betray, desert, or deny. What is beautiful about Aaron and Miriam, however, is that they are teachable—able to see their own sin and shortcomings, repent, and become effective leaders once again.

The third effort in leadership development was Moses' decision to create the office of elder for adjudication and decision-making in the nation of Israel (Exodus 18:1–27). The creation of this office was not Moses' idea (he simply felt overwhelmed with the work), but the idea of his father-in-law, Jethro, who saw Moses' dilemma and came up with that solution. "So Moses listened to his father-in-law and did all that he had said. Moses chose able men from all Israel and appointed them as heads over the people, as officers over thousands, hundreds, fifties, and tens. And they judged the people at all times; hard cases they brought to Moses, but any minor case they decided themselves" (Exodus 18:24–26). These "officers" became the foundation for the formation of Israel's system of rulership by elders, which provided the form and structure for the adjudication of Israel both for the remainder of its existence as a nation and its transition into Judaism, even to today.

Finally, perhaps Moses' most successful development of a leader was with Joshua—the man who eventually succeeded Moses as leader of Israel. Over a significant period of time, the Scriptures reveal Moses including Joshua in assigned responsibilities of leadership, leading worship and dealing with personal formation, so that he was being created as a leader. In these encounters, it was clear that Moses was the leader and Joshua the student as he learned from Moses how to guide that great nation (Exodus 33:7–11). In specific instances, Moses gave major responsibility to Joshua (e.g., scouting out the Promised Land) which then, in turn, placed Joshua into significant danger and conflict. Thus, Moses was not trying to protect Joshua, but rather letting him face difficult and dangerous leadership situations that put him "out there" on the "front-line," to see how well he could handle the situation (e.g., Numbers 13:17—14:9). In essence, by reflecting with Joshua, giving him exceedingly difficult tasks, and trying him "with fire," Moses was seeking to mold Joshua into a man of vision, of anger, a risk-taker, and a person sure of his own convictions—qualities his brother, Aaron, his sister, Miriam, and not even the elders could attain. Finally, after Joshua had so clearly proven himself, Moses publicly chose and anointed Joshua for leadership in front of all Israel, so that Moses' credibility passed to Joshua. This, therefore, was a public "passing of the baton" to Joshua (Deuteronomy 31:1–8, 14–23).

Elijah. One of Israel's greatest prophets, Elijah's had many similarities to Moses, and yet marked contrasts. Like Moses, he was a man of great vision who deeply loved Yahweh and was committed to God's covenant with Israel. Who can forget his dramatic prayer to God, "I have been very zealous for the LORD, the God of hosts; for the Israelites have forsaken your covenant, thrown down your altars, and killed your prophets with the sword. I alone am left, and they are seeking my life, to take it away" (1 Kings 19:14). He was a man of great conviction, driven by the contradictions between an Israel as he knew it should be under the Mosaic Covenant and an Israel under the rule of a despotic king committed to making his nation a worshiper of Baal (1 King 18–21).

Elijah was certainly a risk-taker, confronting politically, economically, and religiously the king of Israel (cf. 1 Kings 18:17–19; 20:13–22; 21:1–24) and contesting with the four hundred priests of Baal on Mount Carmel for the spiritual loyalty of Israel (1 Kings 18:20–40). "How long will you go limping between two different opinions?" Elijah challenged Israel. "If Yahweh is God, follow him; but if Baal, then follow him" (1 Kings 18:21). He was, of all Israelites next to Moses, the most confrontive and agitating of prophets. "When [King] Ahab saw Elijah, Ahab said to him, 'Is it you, you troubler of Israel?' He answered, 'I have not troubled Israel; but you have, and your father's house, because you have forsaken the commandments of the Lord and followed the Baals'" (1 Kings 18:17–18).

Finally, Elijah was a person of deep interior self-validation. If anything stood out about the man, it was his absolute resolve and his certainty that he was right. Even when he thought he was the only person left in Israel faithful to Yahweh (19:10), he remained steadfast to what he perceived as his call from God. The only self-doubt Elijah demonstrated was not in his call or in the Mosaic Covenant, but in wondering why he must receive such persecution when he was busy being faithful to God (19:1–4). So, in these four ways, Elijah compares with Moses.

But there are two significant differences between the men. And those two differences may be the decisive factor why one built Israel's future while the other acted only as a temporary restraint upon its decline into unfaithfulness.

First, Moses was building for the future; Elijah was seeking to conserve the past. In the dichotomy between Israel, as it was under Egyptian despotism, and Israel as Moses believed it could become under the Ten Commandments and the covenant, Moses was thoroughly committed to moving Israel into God's future. He was always planning for a nation that would someday enter the Promised Land and leave its wilderness wanderings behind it. So in the desert, he led the nation in building for itself its vision, priorities, laws, and structures. And this, in turn, informed Moses' building of leadership. In the implementation of the office of elder and in preparing his successor and others, Moses invested in people the work that was needed to guarantee for Israel "a future and a hope."

Elijah, on the other hand, was a conservator of the past. His vision of Israel was to a glory that had now departed. He saw his task as calling Israel back to what it once was. But Israel was now living in a different era of history, with its own demands, peculiarities, and priorities. Simply calling it back to its historic covenant would be insufficient to give it direction for a new age. Others who were as intensely committed to Yahweh and to the Sinai Covenant understood that adaptation needed to take place. Thus, King David led Israel into a future in a world becoming increasingly monarchal. Jeremiah the prophet promised Israel a new covenant for a defeated nation heading into captivity. Nehemiah saw the inevitable end of nationhood and led Israel into changing from being a nation centered on royalty to a people centered on the Torah that would travel with them wherever they might be dispersed. Elijah was unable to create a vision that would lead Israel into the future and that, in turn, led to the second significant difference between Moses and Elijah.

Second, Moses was able to build a significant core of leadership and a strong leadership team to lead Israel into the Promised Land and to continue to duplicate itself. Elijah—because he was concerned with conserving the past—saw no real need for this, and had no team of people working with him. Rather, for years he saw himself as standing alone for truth, justice, and for God. God, instead, showed Elijah that was not the case—that there were seven thousand people in Israel whose "knees have not bowed to Baal, and [whose] mouths have not kissed him" (1 Kings 19:18). Surprisingly, there is no indication in the text that Elijah ever made any attempt to identify those seven thousand people or to enlist them in his cause. Instead, he selected only one man who would work with him, and did so only because God commanded him to do so (19:16–17). That man was Elisha, son of Shaphat.

God promised Elijah one to share in his ministry, and so he was led by the Spirit to the young Elisha (1 Kings 19:11–18). Placing his cloak around him, Elijah challenged this young man to join him in the ministry of calling the king to covenant accountability. He gave Elisha free rein to commit or not commit to following Elijah and Yahweh. But once that commitment was made, the older prophet both mentored Elisha and called out his leadership skills and his prophetic imagination. Finally, in his home going, Elijah brought Elisha to the place where the young man asked for a double portion of the prophet's spirit and thus committed himself irreversibly to the demanding, thankless, and dangerous job of proclaiming "Thus says the Lord" to the kings of Israel (2 Kings 2:1–15). This conserving effort continued for the remainder of Elisha's life and ministry. But that prophetic effort ceased once the younger man died, for following the example of his mentor, Elisha stood in solitude before the kings and called them back to covenant responsibility.

Paul and Barnabas

When one considers the great leaders of the New Testament, Paul would be in the forefront. This man took a Christianity centered in the men and women who surrounded Jesus and turned it from a Jewish sect into an empire-wide religion that would shape the future of the world. Paul was the dominant Christian of the first century. He brought the Gospel to much of Asia Minor, Macedonia, Greece and Italy, and likely, Spain. He founded an amazing number of churches throughout the Roman Empire. He wrote at least nine theological works, and probably several others, since lost. His was the outstanding theological mind of the first century; he would even now be listed among Christianity's most influential theologians. Probably no one in the history of Christendom has impacted the church as profoundly as has Paul.

Next to Paul, Barnabas is a virtual unknown. Even among first-century Christians, he would not be considered in the same position as Simon Peter, James the brother of Jesus, or the apostle John. Why, then, would we have chosen him? That will become evident when we examine both his remarkable ministry and his leadership style later in this chapter. But first, to Paul.

Paul. St. Paul was a man of extraordinary vision. His experience of Christ, who accepted and redeemed him even though he least deserved it, as one who "persecuted the church of God" (1 Corinthians 15:9), was an experience of God's love as being totally unexpected, unconditional grace—so that we "are now justi-fied by his grace as a gift, through the redemption that is in Christ Jesus" (Romans 3:24).

The profound vision of Paul was the grace of God—that one is not made right with God because of his obedience to the law, or by persecuting heretics, or by doing good works, but solely on the unmerited, freely-given love of God coming to us through the sacrificial death of Jesus Christ (Philippians 3:3–9). Others before Paul had perceived God as a graceful God—both in the Hebrew Bible and in the Early Church. And clearly, Jesus stressed both in his words and in his actions (especially his healings) the unmerited love and the giving nature of God. But no one had articulated a theology of grace as clearly as Paul had. And no one had shaped his ministry, perceived mission, and purpose of the Church around the doctrine of grace with such clarity as had Paul.

As one with such clarity of vision, Paul also was one who burned with the passion to see others receive the grace of God, for "I am again in the pain of child-birth until Christ is formed in you" (Galatians 4:19). Because of such a passion for the world to receive this good news of God's forgiving love through Jesus Christ, Paul took unbelievable risks (2 Corinthians 11:24–28).

Finally, because of his clarity of vision and of his passion to see everyone experience the same freedom he had found in Christ, Paul was a man of deep interior self-validation. One would not often win an argument with Paul. And one would never win an argument when it came to Paul's belief in the redeeming grace of God through Christ and the church as the inevitable outpouring of that grace through a community of grace.

Along with his clarity of vision, Paul added the dimension of clarity of com-munication. He was able to clearly articulate and to act out a theology of grace in his ministry. And this he did both through the spoken word and the written word. That clarity of spoken word allowed him to become chief of the apostles, spreading the good news of God's acceptance and founding churches built upon that grace all over the known world. The clarity of his written word provided him the means to spread that message of the amazing grace of Jesus to generations and millennia of Christians after him; it is his writings that provide, even to today, the foundation upon which all later Christian theologies would be built.

Finally, Paul was able to build a church and a growing core of leaders who embraced his good news and built together a movement that would shape the course of Christianity and of the western world for thousands of years after their deaths. Paul's writings are sprinkled throughout with the names of people whom he mentored and helped to form into outstanding church leaders—Silas (Acts 15:40), Priscilla and Aquila (Romans 16:3; 1 Corinthians 16:19), the deaconess Phoebe (Romans 16:1), Epaenetus "who was the first convert in Asia for Christ" (Romans 16:5), Mary "who has worked very hard among you" (Romans 16:6), Stephanas, Fortunatus, and Achaicus, who have "devoted themselves to the service of the Christians" (1 Corinthians 16:16–17), Epaphroditus, "my brother and co-worker and fellow soldier, your messenger and minister to my need" (Philippians 2:25), Timothy (Philippians 2:19–24, 1 and 2 Timothy), the author of the second gospel, Mark (Colossians 4:10), and Luke, the author of the third gospel and the Acts of the Apostles (Acts 16:10–28:31; Colossians 4:14), Onesimus (the entirety of Philemon; Colossians 4:9), Titus (the book of Titus), and on and on. In fact, a total of fifty-eight people are named in Paul's writings as people whom he mentored toward church leadership.

The leadership methodology of Paul is particularly apparent in his building of ministry teams with Timothy, Titus, Epaphroditus, Silas, and with Priscilla and Aquila. With Timothy, for example, Paul identified with the struggles and the potentials of the young man. He concentrated on developing Timothy's self-esteem, and yet at the same time, called for commitment, responsibility, and perseverance (2 Timothy 1:3–14; 2:1–15). Here we see Paul mentoring and discipling Timothy, preparing him to become a leader and, eventually, an outstanding bishop of the church.

Titus, who spent considerable time traveling with Paul, was eventually placed by Paul to be in charge of building the church in Crete (Titus 1:5). He was instructed by Paul how to develop leaders himself, how to work with rebellious people, women, young men needing to learn the discipline of self-control, and with slaves (Titus 1–2). In due time, Titus became the first bishop of Crete (according to tradition) following Paul's death.

Onesimus is a particular example of how a person can be nurtured into strong leadership. Onesimus was a slave, working in the household of a Christian, Philemon, who was a personal friend of Paul's. Onesimus escaped from his master and fled to Rome, where he surrendered himself to Paul. There, Paul led him to Christ and nurtured him in the faith. Finally, Paul required Onesimus to return to Philemon, "no longer as a slave but more than a slave, a beloved brother" as Paul writes in a cover letter to Philemon which Onesiums bore to his owner (Philemon 16). "Formerly," Paul wrote, "Onesimus was useless to you, but now he is indeed useful both to you and me" (Philemon 11; this is a play on words because the name "Onesimus" means "useful"). Apparently, Philemon received Onesimus back into his household, and did so not as a slave but as a brother. With further mentoring from Paul and from others, Onesimus became an outstanding Christian and eventually, according to church tradition, bishop of the most important Christian church outside Jerusalem, the church in Ephesus.

Barnabas. Barnabas provides us with a stark contrast to Paul. From a conceptual perspective, Barnabas was neither visionary nor a person of deep theological distinction. He was not a recognized Christian leader of the caliber of Paul, Peter, James the brother of Jesus, or John the apostle. But Barnabas is one of the most creative and inspirational leaders in Scripture, giving us significant insight into the nature of true leadership. Therefore, it is appropriate that we study him and his ministry as the final person we will examine in this chapter.

Barnabas' name was not Barnabas. It was Joseph the Levite (Acts 4:36). As a Levite, therefore, his occupation was that of being a priest. But his vocation or calling was to a ministry of encouragement. This was acknowledged by the early Christians who gave to Joseph the Levite the name of "Barnabas"—which means "Son of Encouragement" (4:36).

Barnabas perceived the newly converted Saul of Tarsus as being a man with great leadership potential for the Church (Acts 9:26–31). But other Christian leaders feared this former persecutor of the Church, and therefore shunned him. It was Barnabas who became Saul's advocate, who defended him before the Jerusalem leadership, and who called the tentmaker forth to a mission outreach to Gentiles. Saul, to indicate his new mission focus, changed his Jewish name to the Greek name, Paul. But it was Barnabas who truly made Saul Paul (11:19–30).

Thus we see Barnabas reaching out into new areas of ministry (the gospel to the Gentiles), identifying one who had the capacity to become a significant leader in such a ministry (Paul), connecting him with established church leadership and gaining their reluctant support, and then organizing both Paul and himself for missionary action—first in the city of Antioch and then in missionary journeys to Greek and Gentile cities (Acts 13:1—14:28).

In the earlier chapters of Acts, it was clear that Barnabas was taking the lead. He was Paul's mentor. But as Paul's skills were honed, his vision grew, and his knowledge and capability of communicating the Christian faith developed, the two men increasingly moved into a collegial relationship until finally, Barnabas yielded first place to Paul (Acts 13:2; 14:1).

Barnabas is a particularly significant model of leadership because he had the capacity to perceive new ways in which the Spirit was moving and then had the faith to step out into *new ministries and new mission challenges.* He was unbelievably innovative in ministry. Barnabas was the first person who was able to act out one's relationship of faith in Christ in one's attitude and action regarding his money. He gave away his personal fortune to the Church (Acts 4:37). He was the first person who was proactive in inaugurating ministry to the Gentile world, perceiving that the gospel was intended for Gentiles as well as Jews (11:19–26).

Perhaps one of Barnabas' greatest capacities was his ability to reach out to *new people* who were otherwise shunned and marginalized by the church. He connected them to church leadership, organized them for action, called them out and trained them for leadership, and then was willing to take second place to them.

Thus it was Barnabas who was the first person to discern that the young Saul was a leader chosen by God and, in the face of significant opposition from the other Christian leaders, mentored him in ministry, and called him out to join him in an outreach to the Gentiles that would revolutionize Christianity (Acts 11:19–26). Likewise, Barnabas was the first person to see potential in a young Hellenistic Jew, John Mark, whom Paul rejected because of his undependability. Barnabas shaped that young man into the kind of Christian leader who could eventually author the Gospel of Mark (Acts 15:36–39). Eventually, Barnabas had the satisfaction of seeing Paul admit that the man he once rejected as being undependable was, in reality, one who had become of significant value not only to the Church but to the great apostle, as well (2 Timothy 4:11).

Barnabas was always stepping out into the new. He perceived a new mission advance or a new person to call out. But perhaps the most profound reality about Barnabas and his leadership style was his capacity to put the common good before his personal status and position. This was seen most profoundly in his relationship with Paul when he purposely allowed Paul to develop his leadership talents to such a degree that Paul took over the leadership of their shared mission to the Gentiles, and Barnabas voluntarily took second place. How rarely do we see Christian leaders recognize the superior gifts or leadership of their protégés, nurture them to mature leadership, then voluntarily turn over that leadership to them, assuming a secondary role until God calls them into some other ministry? Yet that was the leadership style Barnabas models for us.

BIBLICAL PRINCIPLES THAT BUILD LEADERS

Many of the great leaders in the Bible saw the building of leadership as one of the most pivotal tasks they did. Ministry not only included the work to which they were called (redemption, liberation of a people, holding leaders of the systems to accountability, ministering to the poor or the lost, evangelizing the city or nation, etc.). It also included the spiritual and strategic formation of those who would replace them or would carry forward their tradition. It is intriguing that both Old and New Testament leaders who did not commit themselves to the building of leaders (e.g., Isaac, Jacob, David, Solomon, many of the kings of the divided kingdoms, Nehemiah, disciples such as Philip, Bartholomew, James, Simon Zealot, and Matthias) either had a collapse in their ministry or revolt at the end or they slipped into obscurity. Only those biblical characters who built a strong leadership to succeed them finished strong. There could be a direct correlation between finishing weak and one's inability or unwillingness to "make disciples."

As we consider together how to build a people of power through community organizing or any other strategy, it is important that we embrace the recognition that one cannot build a people of power without building leaders of power. Any organizing effort is only as good as the leaders who guide it. Therefore, our primary responsibility as pastors, organizers, or urban workers is to commit ourselves to the shaping and building of strong leaders.

The Bible thus provides for us a two thousand year-long record on leadership building. What are essential principles regarding leadership development that we learn from Jesus, Moses, Elijah, Paul, and Barnabas?

Leaders Must be People of Vision, Passion, Risk, and Personal Validation.

A strong leader is one who has a clear vision that informs all she does and is; she may or may not have clear-cut objectives or a plan of action, but without the vision, there is nothing to capture people's imagination or to mobilize their commitment. As well, a leader must be a person of passion—deeply convictional about the vision she is seeking to bring to reality. That passion may express itself in deep grief over injustice in the human condition or anger at personal injustice that fires that passion. But a good leader must intensely care about the vision she is seeking to fulfill, and must communicate that passion to her followers and leadership team.

An effective leader must also be willing to take risks. It is the taking of risks that validates the commitment to her vision and passion—putting her body where her mouth and head are. As well, the leader must have a deep sense of personal validation. She must so believe in the vision that she does not doubt herself. She may take very seriously other people's difficulties with that vision and may respectfully listen to opposing perspectives. She may be persuaded away from

certain strategies and objectives to realize that vision. But she will have a strong
sense of ego, of self-validation.

A Christian Leader Must Have a Capacity to Trust.

It has often been said that you can lead a person only as far as you yourself have gone. It is only because these great biblical leaders were themselves
profoundly and deeply committed people, in love with God and with God's call
upon their lives, that they could become ones who profoundly formed, taught, and
influenced others. Their capacity as great leaders was because of their capacity to
trust—to trust God, to trust God's call to the mission and ministry to which they
had been called, to trust the vision, and to trust the people they were developing to
have integrity, be dedicated, and be committed followers of God who would also
be obedient to the heavenly vision.

And trusting the people whom you are developing as a leader means a willingness to let them fail. Initially, they aren't going to do the job as well as you do.
But they will never do it as well if they are not given the opportunity to fail. So a
builder of leaders must trust in the people he is molding into a team.

A Primary Task of a Leader is To Discern Potentials in People and Call Them Out.

It is crucial that a leader perceive the potentials in people and call out those
potentials. This is critical because most people cannot see their potentials with
the clarity that other discerning eyes can. Jesus could look at Peter the first time
they met and say, "You are Simon, son of John. You are to be called Peter [which
means Rock]" (John 1:42). Jesus could see in this bumbling, earthy, well-meaning, naïve, and unsophisticated fisherman a person upon whom a church could be
strongly and firmly built (Matthew 16:18). The unique characteristic of a Jesus, a
Barnabas, an Elijah, a Paul, and a Moses was their respective capacity to perceive
potentials in people, to call out those potentials, and in so doing, to call out each of
those people into a depth and purpose and fulfillment of life (along with pain and
suffering) that none of them would have ever perceived in themselves.

A Leader Must Foster a Close Relationship between Himself and the Student.

The relationship is a mentoring relationship. The two are not equal when one
is being discipled by the other. But they are very close to each other, and both
care immensely about the other. That caring is important—particularly on the

part of the disciple toward the leader, because such caring is what the student can contribute to the bonding and mutual satisfaction of that relationship.

A Leader Uses Every Informal Situation as a Vehicle for Teaching.

As we look at Jesus, Moses, Elijah, Paul, and Barnabas, none of them gave formal instruction to their disciples nor taught in a classroom. And that is an important observation. Rather, these leaders took advantage of every situation in which they found themselves to get their people reflecting. Every situation, to these leaders, was a teachable moment. That meant that developing specific people into leaders had to be "front-and-center" in their minds. Otherwise, they would not see the opportunity each moment provided for being a teachable moment. The desire to develop leadership has to be of such a high priority that such leadership-building will become a filter for every activity in which the mentor is involved with his disciples.

I remember fondly the way Bob the organizer discipled me. Whether I was chairing an action team, leading a research action, or guiding a team in planning an action, Bob the organizer was always in the background, letting me lead while he listened and inserted himself only when it was strategic. But after the meeting was over, the research action completed, or the action planned, Bob would say to me, "Bob, let's go have a cup of coffee." We would go to our favorite restaurant across the street from my church (the owner was actively involved in ONE so we always gave him our business), sit in a booth, and enjoy a cup of coffee together. Then Bob would question me about the activity I had just led, getting me to evaluate it, complimenting me when I had done well, urging me to consider how I could have done it better (no matter how well it was done, there was always room for improvement), helping me to think through next steps of the organizing effort and directly teaching me. It was always an informal time for my learning, was always done in a non-judgmental but affirming way, and always led to significant growth in me. I now look back to those informal times of learning as the process that essentially formed me in community organizing theory and practice.

Action and Reflection Is the Primary Pedagogy for Leadership Development.

The essential pedagogy for shaping either individuals or a team into effective leaders is the pedagogy of action and reflection. Learning that is only study will result in a theoretical and conceptually-oriented knowledge. Learning that is solely action will lack any conceptual or spiritual framework. Learning occurs only through action and reflection intentionally coming in rapid and close encounter with each other—over and over again. Only in a rapid succession of actions and reflections will each action become more substantive than that which preceded it, and each reflection more profound than that which came before.

Leaders Work alongside Their Students and Use That Work to Reflect.

Leaders do not lead from afar. They do not assign to their disciples a task they themselves would not do. Rather, they roll up their sleeves and work alongside those whom they are developing. A leader develops fresh leaders by leading them into shared action and reflection.

A basic rule of effective ministry is "Never ask of members of your congregation what you are not willing to do yourself." If you ask your followers to call upon people to build relationships, to ask for commitments, or to raise money, the leader should be willing to visit for the same purposes. It is a far more effective teachable moment when a leader asks his students, disciples, or team to accompany him in the sharing of a ministry of healing, teaching, caring, challenging, or confrontation than it is to assign them to do it by themselves.

A Leader Must Be Willing to Confront and To Speak the Truth in Love.

When we think of confrontation, we think of being "at-foreheads" (the literal meaning of the word "confront") with our enemies. However, an amazing amount of confrontation in Scripture occurs between a leader and his disciples. Although we see this plainly in such leaders as Paul and Moses, the person Scripture portrays as most consistently and constantly confronting or agitating his disciples was Jesus. Unlike the Pharisees, Sadducees, and priests whom he confronted because they were the enemies of the people and were committed to values of building their own power, Jesus confronted the disciples as friends. He confronted them in order to prepare them for leadership of the church and for ministry with the poor. Confronting in love is therefore an essential element in building leadership teams, both spiritually and strategically.

A Leader Must Lead People from the Known to the Unknown.

An essential way of teaching and mentoring people is to move them from the known to the unknown. Each of the biblical leaders we studied did just that. A number of tactics can be used to accomplish this: relating to those elements of life they understood or with which they felt comfortable, sharing in hands-on work, reflecting on or evaluating the activity in which they have just participated and its implications, encouragement, confrontation, suggestions, demonstration, etc. But the essential learning strategy, no matter what the tactic that is used, is to lead the potential leader from what she knows to that which is at the edges of her consciousness.

Those Being Mentored Should Be Pushed to Their Limit.

Learning occurs by the one being mentored being pushed to the limits of his capacity. Growth and teachable moments do not occur by staying in safe zones but only by moving out to our margins.

Present Your Disciples as Credentialed Leaders.

If the people you are developing for leadership are to effectively lead, they must be presented to the people as authentic and skilled leaders in their own right—and not as a student or aide. The team players must be fully credentialed and given credibility before the people; otherwise the people will not trust them and will not transfer allegiance from you to them.

Let the New Leaders Go!

Once the emerging leader is ready to assume leadership, it is crucial that the leader "let them go." When you work closely with people and shape them, you love and care intensely about them. The real sign of such love is your willingness to let them go. And that means they may end up not imitating you or may disagree with you. To become authentic leaders means that they are capable of standing and thinking on their own. And the directions in which they may choose to move may be much different than the directions in which you would choose to move. In such an eventuality, the depth of your commitment to them is revealed by your willingness to let them move in directions that are not immediately appropriate to you. The new leader does not need to imitate you. Rather, you must be willing to let him go!

SUMMARY

You cannot build a people of power unless you are building leaders. Unless you are finding the people in the community, the village, the mission agency, or the church who are the natural leaders of that group, discerning the gifts of those people, and then discipling them, you are not doing the work of ministry. This is one of the most important ministries any Christian can do—to disciple potential leaders and to build leadership teams. Your effectiveness in the work in which you are involved will be directly proportional to the depth of leadership and the number of leaders you develop. That is why, at the beginning of this chapter, I stated that the real test of how good a job you have done is demonstrated six months after you have left that job.

You are being called to be a leader in the work you are doing. Leadership doesn't mean being in the spotlight. Leadership means providing direction and purpose to an organization. The most important task of leadership, I believe, is the creation of a strong, committed leadership team and thus, the mentoring of the next generation of leaders of that community organization or of the church.

How effective you are as a leader will be shown after you leave the job—not while you're there. If the organization is in chaos and falling apart after you have left, that is a clear witness to the ineffectiveness of your leadership—no matter what accolades you received or ministry that was accomplished while you were at its helm. You created a dependent organization—and when you were no longer there, that organization sank into chaos. On the other hand, if you have taught others to work together as a leadership team, they will take over and they will provide firm and sure leadership and direction. And that is the greatest testimony to you as a leader.

There is a "Christian midrash" that is reputed to have been told often by the church of the first several centuries. When Jesus returned to glory after his victorious resurrection and ascension, the angels received him back into heaven with joy and celebration.

During the celebration, however, the archangel Michael said to Jesus, "Lord, you have selected a handful of men and women to whom you entrusted the building of the church and the advancement of the kingdom. But they are such weak, simple, and inadequate folk. What if they fail? What if they fail to win humanity to your Father and do not become transformers of society? What will happen then? What is your plan if those who follow you fail to do the job?"

Jesus looked at Michael and replied, "Michael, Michael, do you not understand? Whether God's kingdom manifests itself on earth and whether my church is built from generation to generation depends solely upon those weak, simple, inadequate folk. *I have no other plan.*"

QUESTIONS

1. This chapter laid out eleven principles of building leaders, as follows:

   - Leaders must be people of vision, passion, risk, and personal validation;

   - A Christian leader must have a capacity to trust;

   - A primary task of a leader is to discern potential in people and call it forth;

   - A leader must foster a close relationship between one's self and the student;

   - A leader uses every informal situation as a vehicle for teaching;

   - Action and reflection is the primary pedagogy for leadership development;

   - A leader must be willing to confront and to speak the truth in love;

   - A leader must lead people from the known to the unknown;

   - Those being mentored should be pushed to their limit;

   - A leader must present one's disciples as credentialed leaders;

   - Let the new leaders go!

   Do these principles "ring true" to you? Why or why not?

2. Which of these leadership principles do you feel you need to work on? How will you do that work?

Chapter Eight

WHAT IS IT ABOUT ORGANIZING THAT EMPOWERS PEOPLE?

What is it about community or broad-based organizing that empowers people? Is it the individual meetings? Is it the house meetings? Is it the action research? What is it in organizing that turns "little old ladies" from "nothing but little old ladies" to "very powerful little old ladies"? That dynamic is the pedagogy of action and reflection.

What is the pedagogy of action and reflection? It was best described by Dom Helder Camara, the late archbishop of Recife, Brazil. Dom Helder was the bishop to the poor who introduced the structure of base ecclesial communities into Brazilian church practice and theology. For the Latin American Christian, these base communities were the equivalent of community and broad-based organizing, in empowering the peasants to work for the transformation of their favellas and squatter settlements. In an interview in which the archbishop was explaining the concept of the base communities, Dom Helder said:

> We highly educated priests made the magnificent discovery that
> even illiterate people still know how to think. They might not be
> able to read—but they can think, and think most profoundly! So
> we discovered that it is impossible to work with the people without
> learning from them. You teach and you learn; you teach and you
> learn.[1]

What Dom Helder and his priests had discovered was the pedagogy of action and reflection. Once they discovered it, the building of a people of power was not far behind.

"Pedagogy" can be defined as "the art and science of teaching."[2] Pedagogy is simply the study of how human beings learn.

The pedagogy used by community and broad-based organizing, as well as the base ecclesial communities, is the pedagogy of action and reflection. That pedagogy is a very pivotal teaching-learning approach that frees people from the control of old ways of thinking and of acting, and enables them to take charge of their own future.

What is that pedagogy? It is simply the recognition that when people act, their action then affects the way they think. Likewise, reflecting "outside the box" creates receptivity for further and more adventurous action. Thus, action and reflection feed upon each other, with each action leading to a deeper and more insightful reflection that, in turn, leads to a more courageous action. A spiral of learning is created, with action pushing toward reflection which results in a more decisive action which in turn causes deeper and more analytical reflection which leads to further action, and thus to reflection. Thus, people act their way into a new way of thinking. And they think their way into a more substantive action. Thus this cycle repeats itself, over and over again, spiraling to ever-deeper reflection and to more substantive action.

In the life and work of the church, we tend to separate reflection and action. We are action-oriented in the implementation of church programs and community projects, but rarely stop to reflect on their effectiveness or rationale. How often would we think of evaluating a committee meeting once it is ended? It would never occur to us to have a congregation evaluate their worship.

Our theologizing as Christians, on the other hand, tends to be highly reflective without much application to everyday life. Theology ought to be the process by which the church thinks through and articulates its faith as it seeks to live out that faith in everyday life. But, in reality, we have isolated it into an academic discipline undertaken in seminaries and theological schools that remove the budding theologian from everyday life to consider theology in a cloistered setting. The church has separated its actions from its reflection so that each cannot influence, strengthen, and evaluate the other.

This is not how human beings learn, however. We do not primarily learn by being removed from life and dedicated to learning in an academic setting. Most of our learning is actually accomplished in our moving back and forth between action and reflection. We learn by doing, and that doing then informs our thinking. Life-changing learning occurs only when reflection and action are related.

George Merck, the former president of the pharmaceutical company that bears his name, was recently named as the fourth most effective CEO of all time by Fortune magazine.[3] He received that honor by turning the corporate world upside down. Most CEOs become fixated on maximizing profit for their shareholders, seeing this as their primary, and sometimes exclusive, objective. Merck, on the other hand, did not.

Under his leadership, Merck and Company became known for giving medication away to the poorest and most unfortunate in the world. They dispensed free streptomycin to Japanese children following World War II, and having researched a new compound to battle parasites in animals, Merck and Company distributed Mectizan free each year to thirty million people in Third World tropical countries to combat blindness and skin diseases.

To give away so much medication to the world's poor seems like no way to run a business—if your primary objective is making a profit. But Merck said in a *TIME* article, "Medicine is for people, not for the profits. And if we remember that, we discover the profits have never failed to appear. The better we remember and operate on that principle, the larger our profits have been."

What had happened to bring about this amazing commitment on the part of an American pharmaceutical? George Merck had acted his way into a new way of thinking. The pedagogy of action and reflection was at work. And a major corporation taught the corporate industry, against all logic, that the way to make a profit was not to think about making a profit but to authentically serve people.

Let us examine more closely this pedagogy that actually empowers people and groups.

THE CYCLE OF ACTION AND REFLECTION

If the disciplines of action and reflection are systematically executed, one upon the other, in a community or broad-based organization, a cycle of learning will develop that progressively deepens the peoples' empowerment. That cycle is as follows:

- Each action will lead to a reflection that is more *profound* than the reflection before it, and a more intense analysis of the systems or the human condition will result.

- Likewise, each reflection will lead into an action that is more *substantive* than the one before it, and will have greater capacity to change the system with which it is dealing.

The cycle of action and reflection can be described as a spiral, as illustrated below: Let's interpret the chart.

Individual and House Meetings

The empowering cycle of the organizing of people begins, not with reflection but with action. Like George Merck, we must *act ourselves into a new way of thinking*. In community organizing, that action begins with the most radical activity of organizing—the individual meeting.

We begin the process of building our relational power one on one—sitting down with the people of our church, neighborhood, community, or city to talk about the public things that really matter to them—the joys they take in their community, the concerns that worry them, the issues that start a fire in their belly, their desire and willingness to contribute leadership to the rebuilding of their community or city, and the people they perceive to be leaders, as well. A relationship is built with each one of them. Once a sufficient foundation of relational meetings has been laid, house meetings begin to form where people can share with each

The Action-Reflection Spiral

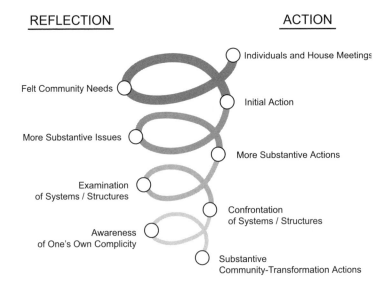

REFLECTION   ACTION

Individuals and House Meetings

Felt Community Needs

Initial Action

More Substantive Issues

More Substantive Actions

Examination
of Systems / Structures

Confrontation
of Systems / Structures

Awareness
of One's Own Complicity

Substantive
Community-Transformation Actions

other the pain they feel and can take courage from each other that something significant can be done about these community-destroying issues.

After I had pastored Edgewater Church in Chicago and had played a role in the organizing of ONE, I was called to a large Presbyterian church in a suburb of Detroit, next door to the poorest neighborhood in Detroit. I accepted a call to that church to be its senior pastor because that church's leadership was committed to seeing that church become engaged in working for the transformation and restoration of that poor neighborhood.[4] They rightly concluded that if they were to reach that objective, they needed to have a senior pastor who would both understand and have experience in organizing in difficult communities. So they called me in 1975 to be their pastor—and I continued as pastor at Grosse Pointe Woods Presbyterian Church for the next ten years.

That Detroit neighborhood had no name; it was only known by its census tract number—5130. It had been named in 1975 by the US Census Bureau as the poorest urban census tract in the United States, with well over 76 percent unemployment and only 2 percent owner occupancy of housing. The story about Pastor Ron in the fourth chapter dealt with one of the clergy and churches in the 5130 neighborhood.

In my first year at the Grosse Pointe Woods Church, I held either individual meetings or house meetings with over nine hundred of the twelve hundred members of the congregation. In those meetings, I discovered the biggest concern of my parishioners was with the senior citizens living in the Grosse Pointe. Therefore, our church spent my second year organizing around their concerns. But during that same time, I began holding individual meetings with all the pastors (including Pastor Ron) in 5130.

The following year, several of the Protestant and Roman Catholic churches in 5130 decided to begin organizing in that community, and because of the relationships I had built with them all, they invited me and the members of Grosse Pointe Woods Church to join with them. I pulled together a team of members from my church, and we began our work.

Our first task was to build relationships with the people living in 5130. About 30 of us from all those churches (including Grosse Pointe Woods) began visiting the people. As we began building relationships with the residents, they began to share with us their fears, frustrations, and difficulties—especially in the light of widespread unemployment and deteriorating living conditions.

Eventually, the thirty had done enough individual meetings that we felt it was time to begin holding house meetings, made up both of selected residents and members of our congregations. We decided to have these four new groups hold their first house meetings in the neighborhood on the same evening. We purposely selected a fifth Tuesday of that month, because we decided no organization would have a meeting on a fifth Tuesday. I led one of these first house meeting, and I wasn't prepared for what happened.

Felt Community Needs

The action-reflection spiral, initiated by individual and house meetings, will quickly uncover felt community needs; in doing so, the spiral will begin to operate. After conducting the initial individual meetings, those doing the organizing will draw the people into house meetings where they have the opportunity to listen to each other as they share together their outstanding community concerns and issues. The objective of the organizer or group leader is to get the group to settle upon a felt need—perhaps not their deepest, most substantive need, but a need that these people feel strongly about and would be motivated to do something about. It will be out of that house group's articulation of their felt need that the empowerment of that community will take place.

After we had convened our house meetings in Detroit's 5130 and got acquainted with each other, I asked people to share what worried them the most about living in this neighborhood. I expected them to name crime, lack of jobs, poor police protection, or issues like that. But an elderly widow, who was probably old enough that she no longer cared what people would think, was the first to speak. Her words were simple but horrifying. "I am so hungry," she said.

I thought she meant that in some sort of general way. But she made it very clear that she was hungry—right here, right now! "I haven't eaten for the past two days," she said.

The ice broken, others quickly chimed in. And I realized we had eight people in that room that had had little or nothing to eat over the last several days. So I immediately sent one of the church members out for pizza, and she soon returned with her bounty that was rapidly wolfed down.

While we were waiting for her to return with the pizza, I began asking them to tell us why they hadn't eaten for several days. They told us they were all subsisting on welfare, and the amount they received each month was not nearly enough to feed and clothe their families, to pay rent for their apartments, and to care for life's necessities. Invariably, no matter how carefully they managed their money, they would run out of cash before the end of the month—especially when it was a five-week month. As one of them put it, "The money always ends before the month ends."

This, then, was their primary issue. They wanted to be able to live life without starving at the end of each month. And when I compared notes with the leaders of the other three house groups, we discovered that their house meetings had come to the very same conclusion. We had found our "felt community need."

The People's Initial Action

The empowerment process begins with an action—individual and house meetings. Out of that action, each house group meets and reflects together. Such reflection usually results in one or two felt community needs surfacing in the discussion. After sufficient sharing has occurred so that people are increasingly motivated to act, the organizer or the leader of the house meeting asks the magical question, "What are we going to do about it?" And out of the wrestling that the group does in response to that question, a plan of action is usually created, and an initial action is developed to respond to that felt need.

In our organizing of 5130, the next meeting was not in our house meetings but in a combined meeting of all the groups—what was in reality the beginning of an action team. Since we had all come to the conclusion that the immediate problem was, "I am hungry," then that was what we needed to move upon. As we sat around and debated what to do, one community resident articulated what we needed to do more clearly than anyone else. She said, "Why should we sit around and wait for the city government to do something about our hunger? If we wait for them to act, we'll starve to death. Let's start a soup kitchen of our own to provide at least one good meal each day of the last week of the month, for us and our neighbors." So that was exactly what the action team decided to do.

Over the next several weeks (the deadline being the last week of that month), the community people took charge of creating their own soup kitchen. A small delegation of them talked with Pastor Ron at the Lutheran Church (who was a part of the organizing effort) and requested the daily use of the church's large kitchen and accompanying dining hall. They got it for free on the condition they would clean it after each use. They decided to urge each diner to contribute 50 cents for lunch (if they had it), but no one would be refused service. Some went to the Day-Old Bakery for bread each day, others visited the Detroit Farmers Market early each morning to get inexpensive vegetables and fruits, others made hearty soups and salads, still others baked cookies, one got a local dairy to donate milk each day, and still others set tables and cleaned the kitchen and hall afterward. It was a total community project, initiated and implemented by the people themselves. It continued on for years, with between seventy-five and two hundred neighborhood people attending each day.

More Substantive Issues

As the action continues, those doing the organizing bring the action team, house meetings, and community organization itself together regularly to reflect on their action. What are they learning about the issue they are addressing? What are they learning about themselves, about the community, about those who originally opposed them? The intention of the leaders and / or organizer is to get the people to reflect about their situation, using as the incentive for that reflection the success of that action. Thus, by reflecting and action, the people have begun to act their way into a new way of thinking.

During this early stage of reflection, a subtle change will take place in the organizing group. Instead of thinking only of their felt need, they will begin to examine and reflect on the real issues. That was exactly what happened in our organizing effort in 5130.

Of course, we pastors and organizers didn't let a good opportunity for organizing pass us by. We would lunch with the people and then have discussions around the tables—and sometimes even with the entire group assembled together. With people getting at least one hearty meal a day, the tenor of the people's reflection began to change. We asked them to reflect on what had caused them to be hungry. Soon the people were saying, "Well, the reason why we were hungry was because we had lost our jobs and we had no income except for welfare. And that was so limited that we would run short of cash before the month ran out of days. So, to save money for rent and medicine, we just wouldn't eat."

Through our table conversations, people began to realize that it was not hunger that was their problem (although it had certainly felt that way). It was the reality that they were the ones last hired and first fired in Detroit. It was an economic issue, not a physical issue. They recognized that they were extremely vulnerable in the hourly-rate jobs they occasionally held. They needed more employment certainty than was their option at that time. So what should they do?

More Substantive Action

Out of the discussions emerging from this more intense and perceptive reflection, the people will decide upon a new, more intense and substantive action. That action will be one that will be designed to address the new (and more profound) issue that has emerged from the discussion. Thus, the forthcoming action will address not only the felt need but also the more substantive issue that lies behind the felt need.

Since the reflection had demonstrated to them that the people needed to have a source of employment that was more secure, and since most of the unemployed people had automotive experience (remember, Detroit is an automobile-manufacturing city), they decided to start up their own automotive repair service. After all, they couldn't be the first fired from a business in which they were part owners.

Their plan was to operate out of their respective garages and in a corner of the parking lot of the local Episcopalian Church. The local community organization that my church, the community churches, and these community residents were forming (named PIFU or "People In Faith United") was able to get some small grants through our tax-exempt status and began advertising in our respective churches this repair service, urging people to take their cars to these businesses for repair work. So the car repair service got started.

But then, something unexpected happened. Chrysler Corporation made the announcement that they were going to build a new Dodge truck factory, and the tentative site was a far-out suburb. Well, this enraged the community members of PIFU because the primary reason for the economic depression, as a result of such high unemployment, was that Chrysler had closed a Dodge truck factory in 5130 only a few years earlier. Now here they were announcing the opening of a new Dodge truck factory in a suburb that economically didn't need it. There was a lot of "hot anger" in the PIFU meeting room the night that Chrysler made that announcement.

But this was an opportunity from heaven. Our research uncovered that the actual site hadn't been determined yet. The announcement was a "trial balloon" to see how that suburb and the larger Detroit community would react to the proposed site. So we pastors got the people thinking about whether they could change Chrysler's mind.

Examination of the Systems and Structure

The reflection of the community organization now becomes intense and penetrating. It thoroughly researches the issue it has identified and the institution it has determined is its target, seeking to understand it, how it actually makes decisions (as opposed to its theoretical decision-making process), and how the issue can be cut in a way that empowers the people and at the same time can appeal to the enlightened self-interest of the institution.

But reflection deepens in another way, as well. There is not simply the necessity of understanding the target and how to best engage it for the results we want. There is also the necessity of understanding the nature and exercise of power at this operational level of the political, social, or economic system. They begin to understand that the way they have been forced to live is not because of the lack of material goods or money, nor even of a few bad people or companies. Rather, it is primarily caused by the deeply interwoven systems of the world which exist to gain and maintain economic and political power on behalf of a few at the expense of the weak. Such growing knowledge *conscientizes* (see definition on page 216) the people and institutions of the community organization, and they begin to formulate actions that will confront the systems of their city and pressure them into making significant changes and concessions, thus more equitably sharing power and wealth.

How did this happen in the PIFU organizing effort? The research done by our people soon revealed that Chrysler was actually considering a number of sites for the Dodge truck factory—and one of those sites was its old site in 5130. It was wrestling with whether to raze the old factory on that site and to build the new Dodge Truck factory in its stead. With this knowledge, we realized that the issue had changed. It was no longer how could we get Chrysler to change its mind, abandoning the suburban proposal. The issue now was how to so reinforce the arguments in favor of the 5130 site that the leadership of Chrysler would choose that alternative rather than any of the others.

Through our research, we were quickly able to determine who the pivotal person was at Chrysler in the making of this decision. The people from PIFU would have to get a meeting with him and present our claims for the new factory to be built on the site of Chrysler's old abandoned factory in 5130. But in order to strengthen our argument, we had to be able to demonstrate the proposal's economic viability as well as its social impact. So the people organized to do their homework.

The site of the soup kitchen became a research center of senior citizens, men greasy from working on cars, women, and even teens becoming involved in studying both the economic viability of the project and the actual decision-making structure of Chrysler. Gradually, a pattern in our research emerged. We discovered the dollars made sense for building the factory in the city, primarily because Chrysler wouldn't have to purchase the land and the city would give some significant tax breaks the suburbs wouldn't. We knew Chrysler knew all this, but it was important that they knew we knew it. Finally, if Chrysler committed itself to employing 5130 residents first, as well as building the factory in our community, that would play a significant role in the rebirth of the community (for which Chrysler could justifiably take some credit).

But how would we ever get a meeting with the key officer of Chrysler who had the final authority to make the decision? Our research uncovered a close and trusted friend of his who was a member of one of our churches, and he agreed to intervene. Soon he was back in contact, telling us the meeting had been arranged.

Confrontation of the Systems

The next step in the reflection-action cycle is the confrontation of the systems at substantive levels. Actions against the systems may have been going on in the organizing process for a while. Even the initial action and earlier subsequent actions may have been actions that were directed not simply at the people themselves (as they were in the PIFU illustration), but on actions with the local police precinct (as they were with the "little old ladies") or with the banks (as they were with the "red-lining story"). But this is confrontation at a much more substantive level, for it is taking on the powers at the very heart of the systems and motivating them to change the very way they go about doing business. And that can happen only through a mature community organization that has really come to understand the exercise of relational power, is highly experienced in using it, and wants to marshal its capacity, ability, and willingness to bring about systemic change.

The meeting with the Chrysler senior officer and his senior staff was set. The people of PIFU gathered together to prepare for that meeting. The decision was made that whereas some pastors would come along for moral support, it would be the people themselves who would do the talking. The documentation we would give to the senior officer and his staff was written up and assembled. The speakers who were selected prepared their presentations. And then, we rehearsed and rehearsed and rehearsed again. Finally the day came, and our delegation went in to meet with this senior executive of Chrysler Corporation and his senior staff.

The officer listened carefully, asked pointed questions, and carefully examined our documentation. I was impressed with how seriously he considered our case. Intriguingly, his staff said nothing. As our team approached the end of the presentation, our spokesperson presented our demands: (1) that the factory be built in 5130, using the old Chrysler factory site; (2) that Chrysler accept only construction contractors who would hire primarily from the PIFU neighborhood; (3) that once the factory opened, the first to be hired would be people from 5130, and (4) that they be trained at company expense for their new jobs. The senior officer complimented us on a proposal that was well done, told us that many of our conclusions were conclusions Chrysler had arrived at as well (which gave us some hope), and said he would be back in touch with us.

The team was exhilarated at the reception they had received and how well the presentation had gone. But everyone was even more thrilled when word came several weeks later from Chrysler that the factory would be built in 5130 and that the company would concur with all of our demands. But what thrilled us the most was the officer's comment to us: that it was the community's intervention that proved to be the action that tipped the Chrysler debate to 5130. Our intervention had been the decisive factor in convincing Chrysler to invest in our community.

Awareness of One's Own Complicity

The spiral of action-reflection is not yet finished, however. It is about to move to its most profound levels. On the final cycle, the people and institutions of the community organization look honestly at their own culpability. They publicly acknowledge that they themselves have contributed to the formation of the problems. It is a recognition, in the words of the cartoon character Pogo the Possum, "We have met the enemy, and he is us!"

At the beginning of the action-reflection-action cycle, to look at the community's own culpability would have been disastrous. They already felt badly about themselves, and looking at their faults would have crushed them. But there comes a point in the cycle when the people can afford to be brutally honest with each other. It is at this point in the cycle of action-reflection that they have developed the self-esteem needed to take an honest look at themselves.

It is crucial, in the building of a people of power, for the people to recognize that they have contributed to the creation of the injustice against which they are now organizing. That contribution might simply have been due to the people's acquiescence over the years and even centuries that allowed unilateral power to build in the hands of a few. But the fact is that all participated, even unwillingly or unknowingly, in the creation of the imbalance of power. If we do not perceive that in the organizing effort, then we will have turned the world into "good guys" and "bad guys," rather than recognizing that the very same potentials for oppression, exploitation, and dominance lie in us all.

At PIFU, we recognized the necessity of reflecting at the level of our own complicity. So after our celebration, we began reflecting at the soup kitchen, in our house meetings, action team meetings, and in our body as a whole about our own participation in the severe problems 5130 faced. We cut that analysis in two ways.

First, most of our churches and most of our people acknowledged that we had avoided being engaged in public life, leaving the fate of our city to its economic and political machines. We had not stood up for our rights, so we allowed ourselves to be exploited. We realized that before our victory with Chrysler we could not have shouldered some of the blame for the decaying of our community. We were too beaten for that. But now that we were victors, we could acknowledge how our own avoidance of engagement in public life had contributed to the creation of the problem.

Second, some of our churches and some of our volunteers were from wealthy churches in Grosse Pointe (like my church). We had contributed to the problem in another way. Each of our churches and each of us, personally, had benefited from cooperating with the powers that be. Those political and economic structures employed us and paid us well, and we had used that wealth to "buy into" a highly consumer-oriented world. Our churches had benefited directly from this so that we lived well while our brother and sister churches in 5130 (sometimes of the same denomination) suffered. We both had some repenting to do and some need to be terribly honest with ourselves and our priorities in life. It was a devastating experience to go through—but a very necessary experience, as well.

Substantive Community-Transforming Actions

Now the community is ready to conceptualize, act upon, and take charge of its own community transformation. That, in turn, will lead to the spiritual transformation of the community.

But confession must precede assurance of pardon and the building of a life together. That is why the complicity stage cannot be eliminated. As a result of such confession, the people and their institutions can then take action under the redeeming grace of God to correct such potentials for evil within themselves and each other that have contributed to their vulnerability.

Out of the action and reflection of confession of sin, the community can then move toward its own transformation. A sense of oneness with each other, the identification of and commitment to commonly developed values, and a celebration of their life together will occur. People will begin talking both publicly and privately about relationship with and thanksgiving to God—and will do so naturally and without being urged. Thus, those who began their common journey with the words, "we are hungry" conclude it by declaring, "we will increasingly advocate the values and celebrate the life of our community, so that we will remember and rejoice at who we are and will refuse to ever be exploited or marginalized again."

The action-reflection spiral brings about a funneling process in the community or region being organized. The people and their institutions have moved from discussing superficial problems to addressing the deep issues within themselves and their community, bringing them to spiritual transformation. They have done this through the pedagogy of action and reflection.

The commitment the Chrysler Corporation had made to 5130 became the fulcrum for negotiating a plethora of community-transforming commitments by government and business. With the employment of community members in the construction of the Dodge truck factory, with its opening and subsequent employment of hundreds of residents of 5130 and the consequent radical economic reversal of the community from 76 percent unemployment to over 80 percent employment, the people, churches, and PIFU concentrated on the rebuilding of the housing, infrastructure, values, and spiritual life of that community.

In short order, actions run by PIFU got the State of Michigan to guarantee the payment of all house-purchase loans, recruited a number of banks to provide high-risk housing loans to community residents at 2 percent below prime, and got agreements from the City of Detroit to rebuild the infrastructure of the community. The PIFU Housing Corporation was created, well over a hundred new homes were built while hundreds of others were renovated, and the residents of the community became home owners through a "sweat-equity" program that allowed people to make their down payment on their homes by contributing work hours. The city rebuilt the entire infrastructure of the community: paving roads, rebuilding the antiquated water and electric power systems, and lighting the streets, adding new side streets and constructing a new vest-pocket park. The Detroit School System built a new state-of-the-art vocational high school in the community and renovated its elementary school. The federal government constructed a new post office.

But besides the real estate changes, the truly important change was in the people's self-perception. Through the venue of our house meetings and our public meetings, PIFU led the community in reflecting upon and naming the values around which they wanted to build their neighborhood. Our times of area-wide shared worship reflected our increasing perception of ourselves as children of God who refused to be exploited and marginalized ever again.

But the crowning achievement was the people's decision to give census tract 5130 a name. Today, the PIFU community is no longer known as 5130. Taking the name of a small river that ran through the neighborhood before it was covered over in the early twentieth century, the community now calls itself "Fox Creek." We are now a community with a name!

ELEMENTS OF REFLECTION

In chapters five and six, we examined the essential elements of action: individual meetings, house meetings, action teams, research action, and action. These are the primary strategies for equipping a people to act powerfully. But as we learned from this chapter, building a people of action without building them into a people of reflection will only result in creating a people who, once given the opportunity, will prove themselves as oppressive, exploitive, and controlling as those who have formerly acted unilaterally toward them.

In the introduction to this book, I introduced the word praxis. As you recall, praxis is the junction between action and reflection. Therefore, the entire topic of this chapter has been on the learning praxis of broad-based and community organizing! It is at the junction of action and reflection that true learning—true pedagogy occurs. Without reflection, action has no meaning or purpose; it degenerates into activism. Without action, reflection is nothing more than a mental exercise; it degenerates into verbalism. The church is guilty of both.

If individual meetings, house meetings, action teams, research actions, and actions make up the elements of action, what are the elements of reflection? That is what we will now examine.

Evaluation

Arnie Graf is one of the outstanding broad-based organizers in the United States today. He loves to tell a story on himself in which Saul Alinsky, the man who first developed the praxis of community organization, said to him over thirty years ago, "You young men—you're nothing but a bunch of undigested actions!"[5]

Alinsky said this to Graf because Arnie was deeply involved in the civil rights movement and was only concerned about the next action. What Alinsky feared was that young activists like Graf never took time to evaluate what they were doing, and therefore they were in danger of making the same mistake over and over again. Action without reflection becomes nothing more than sheer activism.

The first element in reflection, and perhaps its very foundation, is evaluation. Evaluation is both the lifeblood of community organizing and of any effort to build a people of power. It is a primary strategy to teach to anyone seeking to transform her world.

No action or no meeting should ever conclude unevaluated. Whether the evaluation is done one on one over a cup of coffee as Bob the organizer did with me or whether the entire group participates in a formal evaluation, no organizing activity should conclude without evaluation.

There are four types of evaluation. One is to simply reflect together on *what you have learned* as a body and/or as individuals through that meeting or action. Such an evaluation is an open-ended sharing of insights that have come as a result of one's participation.

A second type of evaluation is examining the *process* of the action or meeting. How well did it accomplish its objectives, and how did the very way it was structured contribute to or detract from the accomplishing of those objectives? The emphasis in that type of evaluation is on the structure and process rather than its content.

A third type is to evaluate the *content* of the event. Again, the measuring rod for the evaluation is the event's objectives. But the emphasis is on the content of the meeting or action rather than its structure or process. Did the content and the way the content was developed and presented engage people, and did it move the event and its people toward the understanding and embracing (or intentional rejection) of that content?

A fourth type of evaluation is the *performance* of an individual or a group. What did a person or the group do to contribute to the reaching of that event's objectives? What could have been done better? What actions do we simply celebrate, done as well as it could be done in these circumstances? What did the absence of a particular person or several people do to the accomplishing or the shortcoming of that event?

A fifth type of evaluation is drawing the *relationships* between the implementation of that event and the accomplishing of the primary mission of the organizing effort. Here, the evaluation has moved onto the macro level rather than dealing with the particularities of that meeting or action. It is looking at the accomplishment or shortcoming of that event in the light of the overall objective of the organizing effort. Did it contribute to the realization of that mission, did it work against it, or was the holding of that event of no impact upon the organizing mission (in other words, a "non-event")? How, specifically, did it contribute, work against, or make no difference? What can we do in the future to guarantee a more intentional movement toward the addressing of that mission?

Evaluation can be as short or as complex as the group wants to make it. Sometimes, simply going around the room and have each person share one word about how they feel about that meeting is sufficient. Sometimes, the evaluation needs to be in detail, going through the action step-by-step and being very honest, direct, and penetrating in the analysis.

The point is, you and your work will remain "undigested actions" if you do not invest the time to reflect upon and learn from those actions. What would it do to the quality of the work and life of the church if every meeting, every event, every committee, every Sunday School class, and perhaps even every worship service were honestly evaluated by those who were most committed to the success of that work? The difference it would make would be startling.

Planning

The second element of reflection is that of planning. If measuring the effectiveness of an event after it is over is essential to reflection, so is the very way the event was planned in the first place.

Planning is an integral part of reflection. The people in the house meetings, action teams, and in the organization itself need to be engaged in planning together the actions, research actions, meetings, and one-on-ones they will be conducting. That planning should always be done both in the light of the objectives toward which the community organization is working and in the light of the evaluations that suggest what work is going well and what is not.

An essential part of the planning of any organizing activity is the inclusion of all the stakeholders in that planning. It is important that everyone have the opportunity to share his or her input into the planning process. Ownership of the plans will not occur if the decision-making process hasn't created ownership.

But it is also crucial that the decision not be made by vote. Although voting might work in a large assembly, it does not work well in building a community organization, because voting always results in winners and losers. One can accept losing from time-to-time, but if one always loses, then resentments build and it becomes increasingly easy for the loser to opt out of the decision-making process.

The building of consensus should always be the primary strategy for making decisions in a community organization. An issue or a strategy should be discussed until the group has arrived at consensus. If consensus can't be achieved, then the action should not be taken or the plan implemented.

Planning should also be done in the light of what the group is learning from its wider reflection—its reading, its discussions together about the nature of relational and unilateral power, its study of Scripture, its continuing analysis of the social, political, economic, and religious "principalities and powers" with which the organization is contending. But most of all, planning should be seen as an integral part of that organization's work of reflection and not simply its pragmatic strategizing divorced from its reflection.

Conscientization

The concept of conscientization was first developed by the radical Christian educator Paulo Friere as the English translation of the Portuguese word *conscientizacao*. He defined *conscientizacao* as "learning to perceive social, political, and economic contradictions, and to take action against the oppressive elements of reality."[6]

To conscientize one requires both a participation in reflection and in action. One cannot be conscientized if one simply acts (Alinsky's concern about the young Graf) nor if one solely reflects. It only occurs if one is intentionally integrating what he is learning and thinking and studying with what he is actually doing as he seeks to be obedient to the mission of building a people of power.

This means that such reflection must move beyond evaluation and planning to thinking—to consider the new, to allow oneself to learn, and to use that reflection as a means for both expanding one's understanding of reality and of allowing one's self to be informed by what he is learning. The purpose of this kind of reflection is to move beyond an evaluation of technique and the planning of next steps to a new "*Aha!*" that brings one's empowering actions into a synthesis with one's reflection on the world as it is and the world as it should be.

What kind of reflection moves beyond the evaluation of technique and the planning of next steps into a new awareness of reality—into conscientization? Let me share with you one instance of how such liberating reflection is being done.

The church in which I currently serve is a member of ONE LA, the broad-based organizing effort of the Industrial Areas Foundation throughout Los Angeles County. ONE LA is an exciting organization to be a part of as it successfully seeks to remold the political, economic, and social environment of Los Angeles, particularly in regards to immigrants, the poor, and the middle class. But what I like most about ONE LA is the depth and constancy of the reflection that is designed (along with our continued actions) to bring about conscientization.

For example, ONE LA's director and lead organizer is Ernesto Cortes, Jr. Ernie is a prolific reader, particularly of theological, political, and sociological thought as it has to do with public life. But Ernie wants for everyone involved in the organizing effort to be reading as widely as he does. Every wall in the ONE LA office—a considerable suite housing the 13 organizers, support staff, and conference facilities—is lined with bookshelves. The books filling those shelves are there for our reading. Whenever he sees you, Ernie's first question is "What are you reading?" And you better have a substantive answer.

Another example is the training that both ONE LA and its parent network, the Industrial Areas Foundation, conduct continually. That training can vary from a 45-minute session in the middle of a planning meeting to IAF's famed ten-day training which teaches you more about relational and unilateral power than you ever knew was possible. Some of that training is skill-enhancement. But most of it is conceptual in nature, designed to get you to think through not only what to do in building power but what kind of a society it is you are seeking to form through your organizing.

A third way ONE LA seeks to stimulate profound reflection is through its frequent seminars and workshops. Through the Interfaith Education Fund, Sr. Christine Stephens and Ernie Cortes bring to ONE LA and other IAF organizations throughout the southwest United States as many as three to five workshops a year that feature such seminal thinkers as Walter Brueggemann (Old Testament scholar on public life), Ron White (American historian and Lincoln expert), Johnny Ray Youngblood (perhaps America's premier African-American pastor-community organizer), William Julius Wilson (Harvard sociologist), Cornel West (theologian and author of *Race Matters*), Glenn Loury and Ron Ferguson (economists) and James Cone (theologian and sociologist). If sitting under two or three days of the teaching of any of the above doesn't get the little gray cells in your skull agitating, I don't know what will!

My personal favorite mode of reflection is ONE LA's leadership retreats. Several times each year, the entire leadership of ONE LA (about sixty people) goes away on retreat for several days. Although some business is always conducted at these retreats, the primary emphasis is to engage all of us in substantive and very stimulating reflection. Normally, a book or a series of provocative think-pieces on some aspect of public life or social analysis will be assigned, which we read beforehand. And then, when we come together, our task is to tear that material apart and to reconstruct it for our situation. These pieces enable us to look at reality in new ways, evaluate together those insights, and apply them both to the work of ONE LA but more often to our own ways of acting out our faith as people and institutions in the world. Through such reflection, combined with our organizing actions, conscientization is occurring in each of us.

Imagination

The result of evaluation, planning, and conscientization is the acute awakening of our imagination. One cannot organize to bring about change without first imagining it. It is out of a growing and articulated understanding of the world as it is and of the mission that stands before us (working towards God's intentions for a shalom-filled world) that we can begin to imagine creative new ways to work towards that world. A good example of the use of imagination for empowerment was the picket line and motorcycle woman of the "little old ladies"—a very creative approach that got the attention of absolutely everyone.

Actions are successful to the degree that they are imaginatively developed. It is out of substantive reflection that people may become conscientized and may perceive more clearly the issues before them. But if they don't develop their action strategies in creative ways—if they don't learn to use their imagination—they will make winning so much harder. So the strengthening of a community organization's capacity to imagine must be an integral part of its reflection, as well.

Devotion

The final element in reflection—and perhaps its most important—is devotion. Reflection reaches its apex in a spiritual response, not in an intellectual response or in action.

Conscientization has brought about an understanding of the way society operates to create systemic injustice and permanent poverty and powerlessness; it has also brought about an understanding of how to act to confront the systems and bring about substantive change. The planning and evaluation learned through reflection provides means to undertake and appraise the intentional systems-transforming actions by the people. Imagination has provided the means to creatively determine how to act in ways that will gain the desired results. But none of these elements of reflection will transform the reflection and action from pragmatic strategies to a life-transforming effort. Only the spirituality of devotion will do that.

Devotion is built in two ways in a community organizing process. For those who are Christians, devotion is built through biblical reflection. Working with Scripture enables the Christian to perceive that the principles of community organizing are not foreign to the Bible but are of its very warp-and-woof as God's servants seek to build a people of power and praise. What the Bible is primarily about is the liberation and salvation of humanity—the transformation of each human being, all society, and even the environment itself into the image of God. To clearly perceive God's intentions for our world, the sinful forces that drive our political, economic, and religious systems and their people toward domination, the salvific work God has done and is doing through Christ to set the world free, and how we can join him in this personal and society-transforming work is the primary purpose for our doing biblical reflection. That is why this book has been written. And that is why many other biblical theologians[7] have taken on this responsibility as well.

The second way devotion is undertaken is shared by both Christians and those who are not Christians but who either embrace another religious faith or embrace the radical principles of democracy. That is a devotion that shares our respective heritages with each other so that we can gain a greater appreciation for the richness of that tradition, identify common or connecting insights or principles between that tradition and our Christian faith, and celebrate our oneness in a commitment to justice. As one evangelical has so wisely put it, "We don't have to put another person's religion down in order to put ours up."

In community organizing, this is done by honestly acknowledging our differences, not ignoring them. Thus, every meeting and every action opens with prayer. Biblical reflection is a regular part of meetings, and asking people to share out of their respective traditions in the light of the teaching of a biblical passage is common. It is in doing such sharing that we begin to encourage the devotions of each person and institution and connect those devotions to public life. And this is as true for a secular organization that would embrace democratic principles as it is for any church.

Early in my organizing experience, I had been asked to open a large public assembly with prayer. As I prepared that prayer, I telephoned a good friend of mine, the local Jewish rabbi. "Herman," I asked him, "you know that Christians always pray in the name of Jesus. Would you or the members of your temple present at this assembly be offended if I prayed in Jesus' name?" His answer spoke volumes to me about embracing our differences. He replied, "No, Bob, I would not be offended. But I would be offended if you didn't pray in Jesus' name."

Building a culture of devotion, building together the spirituality of a community organization, of its people, of its member institutions, and of that community is the ultimate task of reflection.

SUMMARY

Action and reflection are the twin dynamics of organizing that actually empower people. As we act our way into new ways of thinking and think our way into new ways of acting, we become changed people and change our institutions. Action-reflection is the pedagogy by which people free themselves and each other from the control of old ways of thinking and of acting, and enables them to take charge of their own future. It is the dynamic upon which a people of power are built.

We have demonstrated in the action-reflection spiral that each action is more substantive than the one that preceded it and each reflection more profound than the one before it. That spiral is the process that brings about the transformation of any structure, system, or value of a society.

People acting and reflecting together cause change in a community. The needs of the people cause them to take a look at their values, which moves them out to new behavior. They begin to accept those new values as being true for themselves. Subtly, their belief system begins to change. This drives them to look at the next level of needs.

When we talk about community transformation, we are talking about a *conversion* process in an entire community. It is most often not a sudden conversion. It is a slow, driving process causing an entire community to change its way of understanding itself. But it is truly a *conversion*, and not simply an improvement.

In the third century AD, the pagan Celsus and the Christian Origen engaged in a debate on the legitimacy of Christianity. In the course of the debate, Celsus mocked,

> When most teachers go forth to teach, they cry, "Come to me, you
> who are clean and worthy," and they are followed by the highest
> caliber of people available. But your silly master, when he goes forth
> to teach, cries, "Come to me, you who are down and beaten by life,"
> and so he accumulates around himself the rag, tag and bobtail of
> humanity.

Origen's response to Celsus' attack ranks as one of the most profound statements ever made about the power of Christianity. He replied,

Yes, Celsus, they are the rag, tag and bobtail of humanity. But Jesus does not leave them that way. Out of material you would have thrown away as useless, he fashions [people of strength], giving them back their self-respect, enabling them to stand on their feet and look God in the eye. They were cowed, cringing, broken things. But the Son has set them free.[8]

This is the work to which the church is called in the cities of the developed, developing, and undeveloped worlds. This is the ministry it needs to have to the broken, the poor, and the lost in the slums and squatter settlements of our giant cities. To enable people to free themselves from being cowed, cringing, broken things. To enable the poor to regain their self-respect. To support people as they fashion themselves into people of power and dignity out of material exploiters would use and then throw away. In the name of Christ, to unbind them and to let them go free. This is the work of the church in the cities of the world. It is accomplished by engaging the people in the powerful pedagogy of action and reflection.

QUESTIONS

1. People do not primarily learn by moving into an academic environment, but learn in the midst of life as we move back-and-forth between action and reflection. Recall a significant time of learning for you. How did it occur? How did that learning interact with life? How did life interact with that learning?

2. This chapter described an ever-deepening spiral of learning in which each action leads to more profound reflection and each reflection eventuates in more substantive action. When you consider your own faith journey, how have you seen that spiral working in and through you?

3. What do you see as the implications of the pedagogy of action and reflection upon the ways the church both does ministry and reflects theologically? What would it mean for your local congregation to intentionally operate out of this pedagogy?

Chapter Nine

CONFRONTATION, NEGOTIATION, AND USING POWER:

LESSONS FROM JESUS, PAUL, AND MOSES

In the film, "Cry Freedom," the South African revolutionary Stephen Biko was witnessing at the trial of a fellow activist. The prosecuting attorney asked, "Mr. Biko, do you advocate violence against the state?"

"No, I do not," Biko replied.

"But your writings speak a great deal about the need for confrontation," the attorney pressed.

"Yes, they do," Biko countered, "but confrontation and violence are not the same."

"How are they different, Mr. Biko?" the attorney responded, with a slight sneer.

"Well, your lordship," Steve Biko retorted, "you and I are confronting each other most directly right now, and I don't see either of us becoming violent."

There is much confusion about the nature of confrontation and that of violence. Confrontation is simply an activity between human beings in which they are disagreeing, and because of that disagreement, are challenging one another. The word literally means "at foreheads"—that is, foreheads physically placed against one another. It is direct face-to-face encounter, seeking resolution.

Violence, on the other hand, is the exercise of physical force to gain one's way. Whereas confrontation is verbal, violence is normally physical. In a profound sense, these words are not synonyms but antonyms for, by its very nature, an act of violence is the indication that confrontation has failed. Good and effective confrontation ought never to lead to violence, but should instead lead to resolution of the issue.

Confrontation is an inevitable part of effective community organizing. Violence is the prime indicator that confrontation has failed.

Christians have traditionally had trouble with confrontation. Our theology teaches us to be loving toward one another, always thinking of the other rather than of ourself. Because we perceive ourselves as brothers and sisters to each other, we feel that confrontation is inappropriate (thus avoiding the element of confrontation which is part of the makeup of a healthy family).

Intriguingly, Christians are actually among the most confrontive people I know. The reason we are confrontive is that we are a convictional people, and therefore easily divide the world into "us" and "them."

There is nothing wrong with Christians being confrontive. The problem is when confrontation is unacknowledged and is covered over with religious pietism. When confrontation is unacknowledged, it goes underground. Because we believe it inappropriate to our faith, we avoid talking about it. But confrontation is inevitable in human relationships. It is actually the process that enables humans to function in relation to each other when there are pronounced differences of opinion. So when we pretend it doesn't exist among us, confrontation goes underground into the individual and collective unconscious of an organization or Christian ministry. It becomes unacknowledged and consequently much more vicious. That is why, in my opinion, "loving" Christians are among the dirtiest fighters in the world.

If we are to enter into the building of a people of power, we must learn to be comfortable with confrontation. Without becoming at ease with confrontation, no conditions will change and empowerment will not be embraced by the city's "rag, tag and bobtail."

LEARNING FROM CONFRONTIVE BIBLICAL LEADERS

Confrontation is found throughout the warp and woof of the Bible. All truly formative leaders in the Bible, whether Christian or Jewish, used confrontation as one of their foremost strategies. But the three who most frequently and most skillfully used confrontation were Jesus, Paul, and Moses.

The Confrontive Jesus

Perhaps the most confrontational person in the Bible was Jesus.[1] How confrontational was he? Well, simply consider the number of incidents in the ministry of Jesus that appear in just one of the Gospels—Luke. There are 133 stories or incidents recorded in Luke in which the adult Jesus figures. Of those 133 stories, 116 are confrontational in nature. The remainders are primarily miracles or commentary (for example, Jesus went from point A to point B).

Of the 116 incidents in which Jesus acted confrontationally, 66 were confrontations of representatives of the religious, political, or economic systems of either Israel or Rome, 45 were confrontations by Jesus of his disciples or followers and 10 were confrontation of demons. One would have expected Jesus to confront the systems and demons. But given the significant number of confrontations by Jesus of his disciples and friends, we would have to say that Jesus was an equal opportunity agitator.

Only one action by Jesus in Luke is clearly violent. That was the cleansing of the temple when he "began to drive out those who were selling things there" (Luke 19:45–48). One can argue that it was the cleansing of the temple—Jesus' single resort to physical violence—that got Jesus killed, and not his many confrontations of the leaders of Israel. His confrontations made the leaders exceedingly angry, but their decision to get Jesus crucified in Luke was not made until after Jesus escalated the stakes through his cleansing of the temple (Luke 20:2; 22:1–6). Violence begot violence—and that was Jesus' intention.

Jesus confronted the leaders of Israel and Rome's political, economic, and religious systems. Why did he do that? Why did he choose to make enemies out of the most powerful people in both the temple and the state?

That question is perhaps most profoundly answered in Matthew 23, the story of Jesus' final confrontation of the Pharisees. Throughout his ministry, Jesus had been calling on these religious leaders to acknowledge how they've misused the law by building up the power and wealth of the Jewish elite of which they were a part, while covering it all with a pious veneer. He had repeatedly called upon them to embrace the full jubilee, to redistribute wealth so that poverty would be eliminated, and to proclaim both spiritual and physical liberty throughout the land. But they had refused, preferring to maintain themselves in positions of power and wealth rather than to seek the shalom of their people. Now their resistance to his message has built to a crescendo, and Jesus bursts forth in what can only be called a diatribe against them. (Read Matthew 23:1–39 out loud and with conviction, and you will realize that Jesus was certainly not being "nice.")

His final attack begins with these biting words: "The scribes and the Pharisees sit on Moses' seat; therefore, do whatever they teach you and follow it; but *do not do what they do*, for they do not practice what they teach" (Matthew 23:2–3, emphasis mine). That sets the theme for the remainder of the attack, as Jesus proclaims seven "woes" against those religious leaders. But Jesus' intention in confronting the Pharisees comes out most clearly and poignantly in the closing lines of his argument against them:

> Woe to you, scribes and Pharisees, hypocrites! For you tithe mint, dill and cummin, and have neglected the weightier matters of the law: justice and mercy and faith. It is these you ought to have practiced without neglecting the others. You blind guides! You strain out a gnat but swallow a camel!
> (Matthew 23:23–24)

The English word *anger* is actually from the Norse language, where its root is the word *grief*. What was at the heart of Jesus' anger? It was profound grief. Jesus confronted the religious leaders of Israel, its economic system, and both Jewish and Roman political systems. He confronted them because they were the enemies of the people and were committed to building their own power rather than building the shalom community of Israel.

But Jesus also confronted inside the community of faith. Jesus' confrontation was not reserved for those in high places. He also confronted those whom he loved the most—in particular, his disciples. And why did he confront them so mercilessly? He confronted them in order to prepare them for leadership of the church and for ministry with the poor and powerless. He confronted them to understand and articulate the values and vision of the shalom community. The only people Jesus rarely confronted were the poor, marginalized, or weak. They already had enough dumped on them.

What drove Jesus to so relentlessly confront friend and foe alike? It was love. Jesus confronted out of love for those powerful Pharisees and scribes who could not see that their policies of greed and lust for power would bring about the destruction of their nation. He confronted them out of love for the people who would eventually become the victims of the system's lust for unilateral power that would lead to the destruction of Jerusalem. He confronted out of love for his disciples, who were responsible for building the vision of the shalom community, the kingdom of God, out of the destruction those Pharisees and scribes would bring upon their people.

One could argue that the difference between the Jewish leaders and Jesus' community was that the leaders held to a different set of values than did those of Israel's poor and powerless and of Jesus' disciples. The leaders' values were centered on preserving economic, religious, and political privilege in the hands of a select few while exploiting those who were that society's "underclass." That was why they came under such attack from Jesus—because they would undermine and even destroy the weak and defenseless to strengthen their own position. When Jesus looked at the physically and spiritually poor, however, he saw the potential for the calling out of a different set of values—values that would enhance relationship with God and humanity, values that would be committed to justice and mercy. Jesus perceived his disciples as being the bridge between himself and these poor, who could organize them to create a shalom community together that would sustain and minister to each and every one. Thus, it was among the receptive and "blessed" poor that Jesus perceived that he could best build his church.

Because he loved the people and his disciples and the nation's leaders so much, Jesus was both agitated and agitational. He was seeking to agitate because only out of extreme discomfort and agitation would (1) people be sufficiently motivated to change and (2) systems be forced to change or face themselves. The first did happen to some degree—some people profoundly changed and became the rock upon which Christ would build his church, seeking the transformation of Roman and Jewish society. Other people refused to change and thus missed the greatest revolution in human history. The systems would not change at all; they would not face themselves, but blindly sped on in their greed and lust for unilateral power. Thus, their destruction at the hands of Rome became inevitable. Therefore Jesus cried out, "Jerusalem, Jerusalem, the city that kills the prophets and stones those who are sent to it. How often have I desired to gather your children together as a hen gathers her brood under her wings, and you were not willing. See, your house is left to you, desolate" (Matthew 23:37).

The Confrontive Paul

Jesus was not the only New Testament person practicing confrontation. St. Paul was an expert at it. His letters are full of confrontation. He not only regularly confronted the heretics and those who would stand in the way of a strong church—his enemies. He even confronted his friends (Galatians 2:11–14).

Both of Paul's letters to the Corinthian church were written to a warring church. In 1 Corinthians 1:10–17, Paul described that struggle for dominance between four factions: those who were loyal to himself—the one who planted that church; those who were disciples of its current pastor, Apollos; those who belonged to the party of the Judaizers and who named Peter as their patron; and those loyal to none of these leaders, but rather named Jesus as their leader. Each party was seeking to be the controlling influence in the church.

Paul masterfully used his position as the founder of the church to exercise influence and power in this situation. He reminded the Corinthian Christians that, in a profound way, he was father to all of them (1 Corinthians 4:15). As their parent in Christ, Paul stated that he was going to visit them, and when he did, he will take to task "these arrogant people" who are tearing this church apart. When he comes, he said, he would test the power of those who are creating dissension, "I will find out not the talk of these arrogant people but their power. For the kingdom of God depends not on talk but on power. What would you prefer? Am I to come to you with a stick, or with love in a spirit of gentleness?" (4:19–21).

Paul understood confrontation. And he was not the least bit bashful about exercising it. His letters, which make up the bulk of the New Testament, are full of his use of confrontation through argument, influence, authority, and logic. And the book of Acts is replete with Paul's use of power to defeat the enemies of Christ, to help shape the course of the church, and to strengthen the spreading of the gospel throughout the Roman empire. Let's look at a few examples from Acts.

Paul before Temple Leadership
Paul decided to go to Jerusalem (Acts 19:21) to report on his missionary work, to handle affairs of the church, and to worship in the temple as a way of demonstrating his continued commitment to Jewish custom and faith. However, his presence instigated a riot. Soon, Paul found himself arrested by the Roman tribune, Lysius (21:32–22:21). His arrest by the Romans, as opposed to the temple police, was fortuitous, because Paul was now under (and would remain under) Roman protection by being in their custody.[2] Lysius, wanting to more clearly understand the charges brought against Paul, had him make a hearing before the Jewish Sanhedrin (22:30). But before he entered the Council Chambers, Paul took action to protect himself (22:25).

In this first confrontive action by Paul, he informed the Roman arresting officer and through him, the Roman magistrate, that he was a Roman citizen. Why would Paul do this? Because this would change the condition of his imprisonment and trial.

Roman citizens were accorded a different level of jurisprudence than were others. In essence, a person who was not a Roman citizen was *arrested by the state*, which had the objective of disposing of the case as quickly and quietly as possible. On the other hand, a Roman citizen was *protected by the state* from violence against his person, and guaranteed due process. He could not be beaten or punished without first being found guilty by an approved court, he was accorded rights of safety and decent living conditions, and he was to be fully accorded due process under Roman law.[3]

In this case, the magistrate had assumed that Paul was not a Roman citizen and was therefore about to deny him full protection and due process—and Paul would have none of it! Through the centurion, Paul informed the magistrate of his status—and this changed the entire way Paul would be both treated and tried. For the remainder of Paul's conflict with Jewish leadership, it became Rome's obligation to protect Paul both from the wrath of the mob and the machinations of the Jewish priests and religious leaders—all of whom wanted Paul dead.

Having claimed his citizenship and having received the full protection of the Roman state, Paul now came before the Jewish Sanhedrin (Council) for a hearing on his supposed crime. What Paul did in this second confrontive action demonstrates his profound knowledge of power.

In order both to manage the situation and to take away from the Sanhedrin control of the trial, Paul used the tactic of divide-and-conquer. He perceived that the Sanhedrin was about evenly divided between Sadducees (who denied the resurrection of the body) and Pharisees (who believed in the resurrection). So he declared himself a Pharisee (immediately gaining their sympathy) and raised the issue of resurrection, knowing the dissent it would cause.

But Paul did more than use the tactic of divide-and-conquer. He then did something that was extraordinary. He redefined the issue. His presence and persuasiveness was powerful enough that, given the political volatility of the situation, he literally tricked the Sanhedrin into changing the crime of which he was accused.

The crime for which Paul was standing trial was his teaching that Jesus was the Messiah and his taking of that gospel to the Gentiles (Acts 21:28; 22:14)—a crime punishable by death in the Jewish court (except for the protection Paul was receiving from Rome). The "crime" Paul told the Sanhedrin of which he was accused was "the hope of the resurrection of the dead." And because the issue of resurrection was such a combustible issue for the Jewish religious elite, it so thoroughly diverted them from the true purpose of the trial that, in their righteous indignation, they didn't even realize they had been thoroughly manipulated by Paul. The trial therefore ended in chaos and Rome had to assert its authority once again, rescuing Paul from potential harm.

Paul before the Roman Magistracy

The apostle uncovered a Jewish plot to assassinate him (Acts 23:12–19) and reported it through his nephew to the Roman tribune. This becomes the third confrontive action by Paul. The tribune then acted to protect Paul, moving him in secret to be under the Roman governor's protection, and giving him a sizeable military escort. This tribune was taking no chances.

At first glance, our reaction to this Scripture is to think, "How fair the Roman government is, and how committed they are to protect Roman citizens." That may be true, but that is not fairly stating the case. Paul was protected because Paul demanded protection. The tribune was already painfully aware of how well Paul knew Roman law. Now, by exposing this plot to the tribune, Paul was exercising powerfully his legal rights for protection and a fair trial, and the tribune had no alternative but to provide those rights. This is evidenced in the pains that the tribune took to give Paul a military escort (200 soldiers, 70 horsemen, 200 spearmen protecting one prisoner—Acts 23:23) and how careful he was to word the letter to the Roman governor of Palestine, Felix, indicating how assiduously he had protected Paul and thus fulfilled Roman law (23:26–30).

So the text of Acts tells us, "When they came to Caesarea [the Roman capital of Palestine] and delivered the letter to the governor, they presented Paul also before him . . . . Then [Felix] ordered that he be kept under guard in Herod's headquarters" (Acts 23:33, 35). Paul was not placed in prison but under house arrest in the luxurious palace Herod the Great had built for his own enjoyment, which was now being used by Rome as the chief residence and administration building of the Roman governor. And Paul was accorded a guard—not to keep Paul under arrest, but to protect Paul from attack.[4]

Paul Before Caesar

Felix found himself with a dilemma. He knew that he could not find Paul guilty because Paul had broken no Roman law. On the other hand, Paul was a Roman citizen. As such, Felix was responsible for the protection and safety of his prisoner. He knew of the plot to assassinate Paul upon his release, so he could not release him. If he released Paul, and then Paul was killed and it was exposed that Felix knew of the plot, his career as a Roman magistrate would be over.

So Felix was faced with an apparently irresolvable dilemma. What would he do? He did exactly what any government bureaucrat would do. He passed the problem on to his successor, Porcius Festus.

This is the fourth confrontive action of Paul. With his knowledge of Roman law, Paul recognized the dilemma the new governor was in. Paul realized that the only strategy Festus could follow was to keep Paul under permanent house arrest in the governor's palace. Therefore, Paul acted to break the stalemate. He appealed his case to Caesar. This was an intentional, deliberate power action of the apostle.

What did it mean to appeal one's case to Caesar? Any Roman citizen accused of a crime, no matter how poor he might be nor how distant he might live from Rome, had the right to have his case heard directly by Caesar. The case had to be heard by the emperor, as Caesar would sit as the highest court of Rome, acting as both judge and jury.[5]

From my perspective, there were five clear benefits to Paul deciding to appeal his case to Caesar. First, it would resolve the stalemate in which he might otherwise remain for the rest of his life. Second, it would mean that his case would be heard directly by Caesar who had little patience with Jewish religious arguments. Third, it would be held in Rome, which would physically distance Paul from both his accusers and those who would seek his assassination (they would likely not travel to Rome to kill him because if they were caught, they could not be protected by the Sanhedrin and would face certain execution). Fourth, he would be tried exclusively under Roman law, with no concern for sensibility to the Jewish religious establishment; therefore, the case would likely be dismissed.[6] And finally, appealing to Caesar meant that the emperor himself was going to hear a proclamation of the gospel by Paul.

It is important to realize that Paul's decision to appeal his case to Caesar was not a sudden whim on his part. It was a carefully calculated and highly intentional act in which Paul was exercising the power vested in him as a Roman citizen. It was therefore a very deliberate act of power.

"You have appealed to the emperor; to the emperor you will go," Festus replied (Acts 25:12).

Did Paul know how to use power to protect himself, advance the gospel, and position the church to profoundly impact both the present and the future of Rome? Oh, yes![7]

The Confrontive Moses

Another giant in Scripture who was extremely confrontational is Moses. Christians who want to avoid the confrontational are fond of quoting Numbers

12:3, "Now the man Moses was very humble, more so than anyone else on the face of the earth." But what does the writer mean in declaring Moses "humble" or "meek"?[8] He does not mean that Moses offered no resistance to wrongs suffered; if anything, he was the exact opposite. Meek in Scripture doesn't mean "weak." It means that Moses did not fight for his own status in either Egyptian or Hebrew society (the true meaning of the word "humble"). Rather, consistently in Scripture, he fights for the status of others—whether it was the Israelite being beaten by the overseer (Exodus 2:11–15), the daughters of Jethro, who were trying to draw water from a well when attacked by shepherds (2:16–22), or whether he was confronting Pharaoh with the words, "Let my people go" (5:1 ff). Moses was authentically a humble (that is, not self-serving) man and thus he was a very confrontational man.

The dynamic of organizing relational power as developed thus far in this book is as follows:

- Build power relationships through individual meetings;
- Hold house meetings to get people to identify and address the problems;
- Move from identifying problems to determining the issues;
- Determine the objective and build a strategy to act powerfully upon the issue;
- Organize and carry out the plan of action;
- Reflect on how the action is going;
- Complete the action;
- Celebrate and evaluate;
- Set next objectives and organize to accomplish that new objective.

Let's consider the organizing effort that resulted in the liberation of Israel from Egyptian slavery and how Moses used confrontation as his essential tactic for bringing about that liberation.

Build Power Relationships through Individual Meetings
Even before Moses is aware of God's call to him to free the Israelites from bondage, Moses was already building the primary relationships with the people who would be strategic to Israel's liberation (e.g., Jethro in Exodus 2:15–22, Aaron in 4:27–31, Miriam in 2:1–10). Most intriguingly, Jewish tradition emphasizes that as a youth, Moses built a strong relationship with his Egyptian "brother" who would later become the pharaoh by the time of Moses' action against him.

Building those relationships enabled Moses to identify potential leaders both for the liberation of Israel from Egypt and the sustenance of Israel while in its 40 years in the wilderness. These people with whom Moses built power relationships who eventually became leaders of Israel included Aaron (4:14–17), Jethro (4:18; 18:1–27), Miriam (15:20–21), Joshua (17:8–13; Numbers 14:26–30) and Caleb (Numbers 14:26–30).

Hold House Meetings To Get People To Identify and Address the Problems

Exodus 2:23–25 reports how the Israelites "groaned under their slavery and cried out," and God heard their groans, "remembered his covenant with Abraham, Isaac and Jacob," and "took notice of them." Likewise, Exodus 4:27–31 tells us of the "house meeting" Moses and Aaron had together in the desert, where "Moses told Aaron all the words of the Lord with which he had sent him." It then describes how Moses and Aaron both went to the leaders of Israel, gathered them together into groups to talk together about their corporate pain, to weep together, and to now recognize that Yahweh "had seen their misery" and was about to act through them. Later, the Israelites meet with Moses to complain about the way he was handling the confrontation of Pharaoh (5:19–21).

The greatest use of house meetings in the Exodus story, however, is the first celebration of Passover. Each family gathered in its own home, spread a lamb's blood on the doorposts and lintels of their home, huddled inside, prayed, recited God's deliverances in the past, and heard the angel of death come by to "pass over" their homes while taking the first-born of all the Egyptian households in death (Exodus 12:1–28). These stories communicate to us, as we seek to understand how Israel built its relational power to free it from Egyptian tyranny, that an integral part of its organizing strategy was for families, leaders, and small groups to meet together many times to identify the problems and "rub raw" their anger and resolve to do something about it.

Move from Identifying Problems to Determining the Issues

The problems of Israel were manifold, for they were living in poverty, in forced labor, physically weak, beaten, and forced to watch the execution of their own children. But the issue underlying this wide spectrum of problems was that they were in slavery. All these problems would eventually be dealt with if the issue of slavery were resolved. In God's confrontation of Moses at the burning bush (Exodus 3:1–4:23), it is intriguing to note how God moved Moses from naming the problems to determining the primary issue. God describes the problems to Moses: "misery of my people," "their cry on account of their taskmasters," "I know their sufferings," "their cry has come to me," "I see how the Egyptians op-press them" (3:7, 9). Obviously, Moses agreed with everything God was saying.

But then, in one lightening stroke, God changes the matter from an examination of the problems (an intellectual discussion) to the issue (a matter of the heart). "I have come down to deliver Israel from the Egyptians, and I will bring them up out of that land to a good and broad land, a land flowing with milk and honey, to the country of the Canaanites, the Hittites, the Amorites, the Perizzites, the Hivites and the Jebusites" (Exodus 3:8). The problems are manifold, even as described by God. The issue is simple, single, and solitary: "Let my people go!" The issue is to set the Israelites free from slavery.

But how will God set Israel free from Egyptian tyranny? Moses would have asked himself that question. God's answer is stunning. "The cry of the Israelites has now come to me; I have also seen how the Egyptians oppress them. So come, I will send YOU to Pharaoh to bring my people, the Israelites, out of Egypt" (Exodus 3:9–10, author emphasis). That is the real indication that this is the essential issue. The issue is not so much whether God will free the Israelites as it is whether Moses will be the one to make it happen. Suddenly, the discussion has moved from an intellectual examination of the plight of Israel to a truly existential moment. "Moses, you are the man! Will you assume this responsibility, and Israel will be freed? Or will you refuse to do it, and Israel will remain in bondage? That is the issue. Moses, will you or won't you?"

Moses, of course, is dumfounded. He never expected this turn of events. Still incredulous, he asks, "If I come to the Israelites and say to them, 'The God of your ancestors has sent me to you,' and they ask me, 'What is his name?', what shall I say to them?" (Exodus 3:13).

This was no idle question. In the ancient Near East, knowing the name of a person was to know the essence of that person. His name captured the depth of his spirituality. So to know and share God's name was to have immense power at one's disposal. God's answer to Moses' inquiry gives to Moses the assurance that it will be God and not Pharaoh who will win this confrontation.

Against the might of Egypt, the reigning power of the time, God's simple statement to Moses that he plans to set the Israelites free seems absurd. How can that happen? Moses himself wonders about that (3:13–15) and, by asking God his name, raises that question with God. In essence, Moses is asking, "Who are you, God, that you think you can come up against the most powerful man in the world—the incarnation of the Egyptian chief deity, Amon-Re—in the country where Amon-Re, in his incarnation in Pharaoh, reigns supreme and win? What makes you think that I, nobody but a shepherd, can set Israel free?"

God answers, "I am who I am. Tell the Israelites, I am has sent me to you!" (3:14). It is at this point that the name "Yahweh" is given to God. "Tell them YHWH (Yahweh) has sent me to you!"

Yahweh is God's name. The word can't be translated into English. "I am who I am" is the closest approximation. But it is not an accurate approximation, because in English, it implies a state of being. The actual Hebrew word has more of a causal sense to it: "I become what I become" or "I cause to be what I will cause to be" or "I am what I will be." Thus, rather than God's name being a noun, it is an early form of the Hebrew verb "to be."

By telling Moses his name, God is identifying his essential nature. By using this name, God proclaimed that he was not a regional deity, like the chief Egyptian God, Amon-Re. Amon-Re's power was confined to Egypt; God's power is everywhere. Nor is God a nature deity, controlling the cycles of nature (as was Amon-Re). Rather, Yahweh told Moses and tells us that this God—by the very fact that he is named "Yahweh"—was sovereign over all of history and of life. The name Yahweh reveals God as the one who causes to be everything that exists or will ever exist—the God who is creator and controller of history.[9]

God told Moses to return to the Israelite slaves with the message that the God who created the world and who created history was also their God—the God of Abraham, Isaac, and Jacob. Their God is the God who controls history—and thus, controls the Egyptians. Their God is the God who creates the future—and therefore can defeat a pharaoh and can create a new people out of a fugitive bunch of slaves. By revealing his name, God told Moses to return to the Israelite slaves with the news that the sovereign king of the whole universe is about to rescue them from their slavery.

Now the only question is whether Moses will take on this responsibility. He has been given the power to defeat Pharaoh. The issue before him is whether he will assume that responsibility or not. Moses accepts!

Determine the Objective and Build a Strategy To Act Powerfully upon the Issue

Yahweh now builds with Moses the strategy that Moses is to follow (Exodus 3:13—4:17). The target will be Pharaoh. The objective is to get Pharaoh to set free the Israelites, and then get them out of Egypt. A secondary objective is that they are to be formed into a nation while in the desert so that they can then take the land of Palestine as their own. The action chosen to win Israel's freedom is confrontation of Pharaoh with the demand, "Let my people go," followed by one plague for each demand. Each plague will inflict damage on Egypt's economy, society, and people. These twin actions of confrontation and plague will continue until Pharaoh acquiesces and sets the Israelite slaves free. It will be Moses' responsibility to confront; it will be Yahweh's responsibility to visit Egypt with each plague (but they are to be either initiated or announced beforehand by Moses). The desired response both God and Moses want from Pharaoh is acquiescence. There is no room for negotiation or compromise here. Moses' confrontation of Pharaoh is to lead to acquiescence, and if Pharaoh resists instead, the king will simply bring more disaster upon Egypt.

Organize and Carry Out the Plan of Action

Yahweh and Moses have now planned their action. They must now act out their plan. That action occurs from Exodus 5:1 through 12:32.

Moses returns to the Jewish slave quarters in Egypt, recruits Aaron as his spokesperson, convinces Israel's leadership to cooperate with the planned action, and then holds his first meeting with his boyhood companion, the pharaoh of Egypt.

Moses confronts Pharaoh with the words, "Thus says [Yahweh], the God of Israel, 'Let my people go, so that they may celebrate a festival to me in the wilderness'." (5:1). Pharaoh refuses. So Moses seeks to demonstrate the power Yahweh has invested in him, and a contest breaks out between Pharaoh's magicians and Yahweh (through Moses). God (and Moses) win each contest. But Pharaoh refuses to yield. Instead he increases the production expectations for the Israelite slaves, hoping to get them to get Moses to abandon this confrontation (5:1–7:13). The contest intensifies as the stakes steadily rise.

Pharaoh's heart is hardened against the Israelites. He means to win this contest! Thus Pharaoh refuses Moses' demand once again, and the plagues begin (7:14–25). There will be six such plagues, each one preceded by a confrontation between Moses and Pharaoh and each one followed by a confrontation between the two men. Each plague, begun and ended and controlled by Yahweh, was a decisive defeat of Egyptian minor deities, as well as Amon-Re. Each plague discredited a particular Egyptian god (the frog, the sun, the Nile, etc.). In the plagues, therefore, the Egyptians' own gods are turned against them and those gods are proven powerless before the might of the God of history and creation, Yahweh.

Reflect On How the Action Is Going

One of the amazing elements of the entire Exodus story is the degree to which reflection on action is recorded. For virtually every action of confrontation and plague, there is a subsequent reflection that occurs (e.g., Exodus 7:1–5, 14–19; 8:1–5; 16; 11:1–2, etc.). Each reflection includes an honest evaluation of how the action is going. But each reflection also includes an emphasis on what God is doing through this action, what he is teaching Israel, and what they are learning about acting powerfully. Thus, in reality, the book of Exodus is telling us that Moses, Aaron, Israel's leaders, and even Israel itself were engaging in the pedagogy of action-reflection, with each action leading to a more significant action than the one that preceded it, and each reflection more profound than the one before it.

Complete the Action

Moses' confrontation of Pharaoh and God's action upon Egypt now reaches its denouement. Despite all the pressure placed upon him and the terrible economic and social calamities the Egyptian empire had sustained, Pharaoh still refused to release the Israelite slaves. So Moses proclaimed God's final and most awesome plague: Yahweh would kill the first-born child of every Egyptian and the first-born of every animal in Egypt. But to Israel, Moses declared, there would come no harm (Exodus 11:1—14:31).

Such a plague was unthinkable to Pharaoh. After all, he was the incarnation of Amon-Re. And his first-born son, the heir apparent, was also Amon-Re in the flesh. Even with all God's proven power, Pharaoh believed that Yahweh did not have the power to take the life of Amon-Re in Amon-Re's own land. Pharaoh dismissed Moses and Aaron, convinced that they had finally overextended themselves. But the Scriptures tell us,

> At midnight the LORD struck down all the firstborn in the land of Egypt, from the firstborn of Pharaoh who sat on his throne to the firstborn of the prisoner who was in the dungeon, and all the firstborn of the livestock. Pharaoh arose in the night, he and all his officials and all the Egyptians, and there was a loud cry in Egypt, for there was not a house without someone dead. Then he summoned Moses and Aaron in the night, and said, "Rise up, go away from my people, both you and the Israelites! Go, worship [Yahweh], as you said. Take your flocks and your herds, as you said, and be gone.
> (Exodus 12:29–32)

With this final action—the plague of the death of the firstborn—the Israelites were freed! Moses and the people of Israel had won. Pharaoh and the people of Egypt had lost. Pharaoh's unwillingness to yield to the proven superior relational power of Moses had brought a great devastation upon his nation. And with the end of this plague, Yahweh's defeat of Amon-Re was complete. The ability of Yahweh to take the lives of those protected by Amon-Re indicated that Yahweh was the God who controlled life, nature, and history. By defeating the god of the world's mightiest nation in the very land where that god supposedly ruled supreme, Yahweh proved himself the strongest God of the universe. In this act, the Israelites had broken the myth that each god ruled supreme in his own locality, and had established the foundation upon which a more adequate monotheism would later be developed. To this day, the Jewish people recall this momentous event in their national life by celebrating the Feast of the Passover, so named because the Israelites believed that when the "angel of death" sent by Yahweh entered Egypt, it "passed over" the homes of the Israelites.[10]

Celebrate and Evaluate

But the action wasn't over yet. After the Israelites had left, Pharaoh had a change of heart and attempted to attack Israel at the Red Sea. But God again miraculously intervened, parted the sea, and Israel crossed on dry ground to the safety of the Arabian Peninsula, while Egypt's army was drowned by the sea closing in upon them as they gave pursuit.

With this final defeat of the Egyptians, Israel began to celebrate. Led by Miriam, the people danced and celebrated their victory over Pharaoh (Exodus 15:1–21), because celebration needs to be an integral part of any great victory of the people.

Celebration was then followed by evaluation (12:22–27), as they looked at what had happened and began to reflect on what needed now to happen. Thus, they decided the immediate steps they would take next (to go to Mount Sinai where they would receive the Ten Commandments), and begin the process of being formed into a nation.

Set Next Objectives and Organize To Accomplish That New Objective

With the defeat of Pharaoh and of Amon-Re, and with Israel's release into the desert, the original organizing objective of Yahweh and of Moses had been met. Now Yahweh laid out for Moses the next major objective—to form this ragtag collection of former slaves into a nation. That would require the creation of the essential principles upon which this nation would live its life together (the Ten Commandments), the laws, statutes, and ordinances that would apply those commandments to the everyday life of the nation (the Mosaic Law), the creation of the means by which this nation could defend itself, and the building of the religious apparatus of the nation that would enable its essential values to be celebrated, implemented, and taught to ensuing generations. It would require Moses learning how to delegate responsibility rather than to shoulder it himself (Exodus 18:1–27) and, consequently, to build leadership for a new generation (Deuteronomy 31:1–29; 32:44–52). The remainder of the book of Exodus, as well as the entirety of Leviticus, Numbers, and Deuteronomy tell us that story of transition as the people implemented (sometimes reluctantly) their new objectives and over a 40-year wilderness wandering, formed themselves into the nation of Israel.

What is important for us to see in this study, however, is how Moses used the essential principles of organizing and of building relational power in order to bring about the freedom of Israel from Egyptian bondage. An integral part of that sophisticated use of relational power was both the understanding of and willingness to use confrontation as his essential tactic for bringing about the acquiescence of Pharaoh to a demand that would have profound economic, social, and spiritual implications for Egypt.

Incidentally, an important question to ask is, who was the organizer there? I would like to suggest that it was not Moses, but Yahweh. Moses was the person whom Yahweh saw had leadership potential, called out both the man and those potentials, shaped him into a fearless leader, an organizer in training, and the developer of the future leadership of Israel. And because Moses was a humble and "meek" man, he was both teachable and capable of being used by God to birth a nation out of defeated and beaten-down slaves.

NEGOTIATION AS THE USE OF POWER

This chapter is about the twin tactics of confrontation and negotiation. But we will not spend much time exploring negotiation because that is a skill most Christians have in abundance. Negotiation is an essential part of the "tool kit" of any Christian executive or leader. Therefore, we have concentrated upon that tactic that we tend to avoid and even fear—confrontation. And we have particularly explored biblical examples of confrontation to demythologize that tactic and help us to realize that it is an essential part of both building relational power and enabling a people's group to experience victory in public life.

There is one important point to be made about the tactic of negotiation. Negotiation can only be used effectively when the other party perceives you as powerful enough that he must take you seriously and therefore must negotiate in good faith.

Negotiation can't occur until the community organizing has demonstrated both its capacity and its willingness to confront and/or to use its power. To attempt to negotiate when the two sides in that negotiation are unequal is to guarantee a victory for the powerful side and defeat to the other.

It may seem obvious, but it needs to be said. Authentic negotiation can only occur between equals. Only if it is between equals will both parties enter into truly good faith negotiations. Confrontation is the tactic used by those holding relational power to build and demonstrate that power before those who hold the unilateral power in the situation.

Students do not have equal power with their professors who ultimately grade them. Employees don't hold equal power with their employers. Prisoners don't hold equal power with their judges. Church members don't hold equal power with bishops. Only when they organize their power around their relationships of trust with each other, and demonstrate that power by acting collectively will the people be taken seriously by the apparent holders of power at the table. There are only two kinds of power in this world: the power of money and the power of people. And if the people don't organize their relational power, then the power of the establishment will always win. That is why you can't have negotiation occur in good faith unless the capacity, ability, and willingness of the people to exercise their relational power are demonstrated beforehand. That organized relational power is demonstrated through successful confrontation.

SUMMARY

When you confront the systems of your city, there is no guarantee that violence will not occur. But be sure that violence never begins with you. If you or the community organization stoops to violence, then you have lost the high ground. You have lost the integrity of your position and the respect of your peers. But, though you completely eschew violence, you cannot guarantee that there will be no violence. The systems of a city, when confronted with relational power and truth, can become significantly violent. The question is whether we can have enough integrity to take such violence if and when it occurs. This was the power of the civil rights movement in the United States under Martin Luther King, Jr., a power that made their ultimate victory inevitable.

In chapter six, we shared the story of the Little Old Ladies and described how they built their relational power in order to confront the systems and to greatly reduce crime in our neighborhood. But I didn't tell you the remainder of the story.

After the little old ladies so publicly picketed the pornographic bookstore and gained the concessions they wanted from the police, the community organization continued to work with them to eliminate as much crime, prostitution, and gang activity as possible from our community. The primary gang was particularly furious at our constant pressure of them. And they returned that confrontation with the threat of violence.

A message was put out on the informal network of our community that the gang would demonstrate to the community how powerful they really were and why we should all be in fear of them. They announced that one of the community's leaders would be assassinated, killed in his performance of a public responsibility. And they even had the effrontery to name the leader they would kill. They named *me*.

Well, to say the least, I didn't take that threat lightly. The community organization's leadership met to decide what to do. We realized that we could not yield to this intimidation and maintain our credibility and our effectiveness as the community's organization. To yield to this threat would be for us to surrender to all the powers of darkness (both human and spiritual) in that community. The people would never stand up to intimidation and exploitation again. Our community would be doomed.

We decided we would not be intimidated. We would continue our attack upon the gang. And we—and I—would take our chances.

For the next twelve months, as I stepped into the pulpit of my church each Sunday, I did not know if I would live to finish that Sunday's sermon. As I would climb into my car, I never knew whether this would be the time that, upon the turn of my key in the ignition, my automobile would blow up. As I spoke at a public assembly, I never knew whether that would be my last speech. As I walked the streets of my community to conduct individual meetings with its people, I never knew if I might get gunned down from a speeding car. Every minute of every day for twelve long months, I—and the entire leadership of that community organization—lived in terror of my death.

But our community organization would not be intimidated. We continued our war against the prostitution and criminal forces of our community.

Those twelve months were hell for me. The spiritual warfare I went though is almost impossible to describe. To simply go through the tasks of each day—never mind battling the primary issues of our poor neighborhood—became an almost insurmountable obstacle for me. It brought me up against myself and my personal lack of spiritual resources. And that was the beginning of my own struggle to develop the spiritual foundation I needed in order to sustain myself in the warfare with my city's principalities and powers.

No attempt was ever made against my life. We do not know whether they ever intended to carry out the threat. We don't know whether they discovered we couldn't be scared away. We don't know whether they decided that carrying out the threat wasn't worth it. All we know is that about ten months later, the pimps and prostitutes and crime lords began moving out. And by the end of the year, they were all gone. And all because we would not be intimidated.

Confrontation—this is a primary means for bringing about the empowerment of the poor of a community—or even yourself. Such empowerment cannot happen without the use of confrontation. Therefore, as those who seek the empowerment of people and as Christians, we should not avoid the use of it. To choose not to confront is to guarantee that you will surrender your community to all the powers of human, systemic, and spiritual darkness arrayed against the poor and the people. Refusal to use it will guarantee that the people will never stand up to intimidation and exploitation again. And your community will be doomed.

But if you choose to follow the lead of Jesus, Paul, and Moses and confront for the sake of justice, you can change your world.

QUESTIONS

1. In this chapter, we examined the confrontive style of Jesus, Paul, and Moses. Each of those styles was unique. But what do you see that the three had in common in their confrontation both of the systems and their own people?

2. This chapter makes the point that authentic negotiation can only occur between equals, and that equality can't happen between the people and the powerful unless the people have demonstrated their command of relational power through confrontation. How do you respond to that insight? What evidence can you provide that either confirms or questions that assumption?

3. As you consider the necessity for you to be confrontive if you truly want to make a difference in society, what most intimidates you about assuming that role? What can you do to help yourself to embrace that task?

Chapter Ten

IT WASN'T ABOUT BUILDING A WALL:
WHAT NEHEMIAH WAS REALLY ABOUT

The task of the church in today's world, in the final analysis, is not simply to win souls to Christ, nor is it to plant or to build up the church, nor is it to organize around the issues of the people and to work for justice. All of these are strategic tasks in working to achieve the mission of the church. But the full and authentic mission of the church, as we discovered in chapter four, is to work for the building of the shalom community in our congregations, our communities, and our cities. As the prophet Jeremiah so astutely put it, "Seek the [shalom] of the city to which I have sent you, and pray to Yahweh on its behalf, for in its [shalom] you will find your [shalom!]" (Jeremiah 29:7).

Intriguingly, this biblical mission is also the primary task of community organizing. The ultimate purpose of community organization is not simply to enable the weak and vulnerable to successfully confront the issues that are destroying them. It is not to discover, call forth, and develop the leaders of the people. It is not even to enable a community to act powerfully by acting corporately.

The primary purpose of a community organization is to create a community—to create out of a victimized, marginalized, destructive conglomerate of people a community whose quality of life is such that people find fulfillment and joy in living there. It is to enable the people to build their society around their common articulated, intentionally pursued values. If such a community is not created, then all that we have accomplished through community organizing is the replacement of one oppressor by another in the tyranny of the now-powerful poor. The power of the oppressor must be replaced by a quality of corporate life that is of such superiority to either the formerly oppressed or their oppressors that it brings purpose, direction, joy, and fulfillment to all who experience it. That is the true objective of community organization.

But how is such community created? How are such life-giving values determined? And what does community organization contribute to the creation of a people who are committed to each other and their tradition? How are a defeated people spiritually transformed through Christian-based community organizing?

No significant transformation of a culture can occur if the cultural heritage of the people is ignored. People can make great sacrifices for the good of the community if they see that their action will affirm their cultural heritage.

How are we to bring about the birthing of God's community as we build a people who are taking charge of their public life? Surprisingly, the answer lies in that biblical book that first taught us how to build a people of power—the book of Nehemiah. It is intriguing that Nehemiah, which taught us how to build relational power in order to empower the people to address their immediate issues is also the book that most clearly sets forth principles for birthing God's community around common values. Let's now study the remainder of that book.

NEHEMIAH ON REBUILDING A NATION'S SPIRITUALITY

When one asks biblically literate Christians what the book of Nehemiah is about, they will most often answer, "Rebuilding the walls of Jerusalem." Yet in the book of Nehemiah, the rebuilding of the walls are completed by Nehemiah 6:15—which is not even the halfway point of the book. The book of Nehemiah continues for seven and a half more chapters before it ends in 13:31. Obviously, one must ask, "With what does the remainder of the book of Nehemiah—Nehemiah 6:15 to 13:31—deal?" The answer is that it deals with the rebuilding of the life—the values and spirituality of the Jewish people.

Throughout chapters one through five, it is clear that the Israelites believed that their real problem was their broken-down walls (1:2–3; 2:11–15; 2:17–20; 3:1–32; 4:21–23; 5:1–13; 6:15–16). But Nehemiah did not see it that way. As I suggested in chapter five, in his season of prayer for Israel (1:5–11), God revealed to Nehemiah that the Jewish people's problem was far greater than broken-down walls. Their real problem was their broken down spirituality—they were no longer being faithful to the Mosaic covenant (1:6–7) and were therefore no longer being faithful Jews. They had embraced the values of the Persian Empire and of the Gentile world and thus had lost their distinctive as followers of Yahweh.

What is intriguing is that Nehemiah was not the only person who recognized that Israel's real problem was a spiritual problem. A contemporary of his—the final writing prophet, Malachi, also realized the same thing.

Malachi

Most biblical scholars date the ministry of Malachi as being the decade 460 to 450 BC. Nehemiah served as governor of Jerusalem from 444 to 431 BC. So Malachi's final prophecies precede the start of Nehemiah's ministry by six years. This makes what Malachi wrote extremely valuable—because it is giving us an independent reading of what life was like and what the essential issues were in Jerusalem immediately before Nehemiah began his ministry there.

In the book bearing his name, Malachi tells us that life was very grim in the Israel of 450 BC. Palestine, of course, was living under the domination of Persia. It had just survived a series of natural disasters—a drought, a plague of locusts, and a blighting of all the vineyards (Malachi 3:10–11). Those natural disasters had brought severe economic depression, even economic collapse, upon the Jews to add to the shame and oppression of political domination by Persia.

The reaction of Judah to both political oppression and economic collapse was twofold. The first was that the people had concluded that they were powerless. That, in turn, had led to a deep resignation that manifested itself in a total breakdown of morality. Adultery, perjury, perverse sexual practices, and intermarriage with pagans all signaled the collapse of Israelite life. Added to that was the victimization of the poor and the marginalization of the lowest classes of Jewish society by more powerful Jews (Malachi 2:10–12; 3:5).

The second reaction of Judah to their political domination by Persia and their economic collapse was the belief of the people that they had been abandoned by God. Earlier, the temple had been rebuilt, and formal, orthodox Yahweh worship had been reintroduced to Israel. The restoration of the temple initially provided a wave of revival throughout the land. But that soon wore off as they faced their worsening political and economic situation. Therefore in resignation, the people had by and large abandoned their religious traditions and practices that had earlier made them distinct among all Eastern peoples (1:14; 2:13; 3:7–14). They believed God had abandoned them. And therefore, they abandoned God.

Adding to this was both the apostasy and profound betrayal of the people by Israel's religious leaders. Israel's priests also felt abandoned by God, but they wanted to maintain their status and influence among the people. Therefore, they continued to formally conduct orthodox worship (although very few Jews attended such worship), but they performed these liturgics in a perfunctory way while compromising their faith and practice. They were obviously very bored with Yahweh worship (1:7–8, 13).

This was the condition of the Jewish people in Palestine reported by Malachi only six years before Nehemiah arrived in Jerusalem. This was the condition of the people that Nehemiah inherited when he was made governor of Jerusalem and authorized by the Persian emperor to rebuild that city's walls. Therefore, Nehemiah's insightful prayer in Nehemiah 1:5–7 was a very accurate reading of the situation.

Rebuilding the Spirituality and Values of the Jewish People

The real task facing Nehemiah and Israel, therefore, was not to rebuild their walls. Nehemiah started there because he understood the dynamics of relational power. He understood that the people would be motivated only to rebuild their walls because that was what they perceived as their real need. The people had to solve what they perceived as the problem, rebuild their walls, and then discover that, in spite of the protection of the new walls, they still felt terribly vulnerable as a people. Only after dealing with their apparent issue would the people begin to realize that their problem was greater than broken-down walls. In essence, Nehemiah could take the people no farther than the people were willing to go. So he simply bided his time, worked hard with them in rebuilding the walls, and then let them continue to feel vulnerable. Once they recognized that the emptiness was still there, then Nehemiah could take them into the next step of their spiritual healing as a nation.

That is exactly what happened. Once the Jews were receptive, Nehemiah began to organize them to rebuild their corporate life and rediscover their unique spirituality as Yahweh-worshippers by getting them to determine and embrace the values by which they wanted to live together and to create a permanent organization that could maintain that corporate life. The last half of the book of Nehemiah tells us how he did that.

Recognize Your Power

In chapter eight, we examined the unique dynamic within community organizing that actually empowers people—the pedagogical spiral of action and reflection. It is significant to note that the spiral is a spiral, not a cycle. That is, it is not a process of reflection and action that goes around and around, over and over again, simply engaging in never-ceasing actions and reflections. Rather, it is a spiral that is going ever deeper. Thus, each action in the spiral eventually leads to an even more substantive action than the one that preceded it. And each reflection will be more profound, more insightful, and more analytical than the one that preceded it. Only in this way does a community grow, become intentionally reflective, and deliberately build its life together.

In the latter part of the empowering spiral, we noted that substantive confrontation of the systems and structures of a society (action) should then lead to an increasing *awareness of one's own complicity* or participation in the way the systems are formed in that society (reflection). That should then lead to *truly substantive actions that go beyond changing the systems to begin the actual transformation of one's community* (action). That is exactly what Nehemiah did in reformulating and reforming the spirituality of Israel.

The final action of Nehemiah's initial organizing effort (rebuilding the walls) is also the first action of the second organizing effort (rebuilding Israel's spirituality). Through their organizing to rebuild their walls (Nehemiah 2:17–6:16), the people had won. And they had won in a big way. The report in Nehemiah of the scope of the people's win dwells on how big that win actually was.

> So the wall was finished on the twenty-fifth day of the month Elul, in fifty-two days. And when all our enemies heard of it, all the nations around us were afraid and fell greatly in their own esteem; for they perceived that this work had been accomplished with the help of our God. (6:15–16)

This is not mere gloating. This is an acknowledgement of the impact the rebuilding of the wall had had upon "the nations around us." The peoples, cities, societies, and nations that surrounded Israel recognized the enormity of what had happened in Palestine—that the Jewish people had taken charge of their own situation, and in the face of significant opposition both from within their midst and from the governor and economic leaders of the Persian province of Palestine, had rebuilt their own walls. Through their organizing to rebuild their walls, the people of Israel had demonstrated their capacity, ability, and willingness to confront the systems, deal with their own situation, and win. The acknowledgement of "the nations around us" therefore became an acknowledgement to the people themselves of the enormity of what they had done. And the result was that the people acknowledged their own accomplishment. They recognized their considerable people-power.

This, of course, is the *closing action* of the initial organizing effort, as the people both acknowledged and celebrated their own power. But it is also the *open-

ing action of the second organizing effort, the continuation of the action-reflection spiral into ever deeper and more substantive response. The place to begin the next organizing effort was with the ending of the former organizing effort. "The action is in the reaction." So the people, now able to own and embrace their considerable people-power, are now in a position where they can take even more risky steps of faith and action.

Celebrate Your Past

The next step in the action-reflection spiral is a reflection in which the people celebrate not only their victory, but celebrate their past. But how they celebrate that past is most worthy of note.

Tell the Story of the People

The people gather in the city square for a major celebration (Nehemiah 7:1–4; 7:73–8:3). On seven successive days, Ezra, the high priest, read from "the book of the law of Moses" (since the reforms the Jews implemented that came from the reading of "the law of Moses" were all Deuteronomic reforms, it is reasonable to assume that the book from which Ezra read was Deuteronomy). Nehemiah tells us, "They read from the law of God, with interpretation. They gave the sense, so that the people understood the reading" (8:8). Thus, Ezra read Deuteronomy "from cover to cover"; he also explained it, so that everyone understood it. This he did each day "from early morning until midday, . . . and the ears of all the people were attentive to the book of the law" (8:3). Then, each of the seven days, once midday arrived, the following happened:

> And Nehemiah, who was the governor, and Ezra the priest and scribe, and the Levites who taught the people said to all the people, "This day is holy to the Lord your God; do not mourn or weep." For all the people wept[1] when they heard the words of the law. Then he said to them, "Go your way, eat the fat and drink sweet wine and send portions of them to those for whom nothing is prepared, for this day is holy to our Lord; and do not be grieved, for the joy of the Lord is your strength." . . . And all the people went their way to eat and drink and to send portions and to make great rejoicing, because they had understood the words that were declared to them. (Nehemiah 8:9–10, 12)

Thus, the people of Israel gathered in the morning each day for seven days to listen to the reading of the Law, and then spent their afternoon and evening feasting, sharing their bounty with each other, and rejoicing. And then, on the eighth day, they gathered for what Nehemiah called "a solemn assembly" (8:18).

Interpreting Their Story

> Now on the twenty-fourth day of this month the people of Israel
> were assembled with fasting and in sackcloth, and with earth on their
> heads. . . . Then the Levites . . . said, "Stand up and bless the LORD
> your God from everlasting to everlasting. Blessed be your glorious
> name, which is exalted above all blessing and praise. . . . And you
> saw the distress of our ancestors in Egypt and heard their cry at the
> Red Sea. You performed signs and wonders against Pharaoh and all
> his servants and all the people of his land, for you knew that they
> acted insolently against our ancestors.
> (Nehemiah 9:1, 5–6, 9–10)

Nehemiah 9:1–25 is a recital of Israel's history from creation through the
patriarchal period, the release of Israel from Egyptian bondage, their wilderness wanderings and their entrance into the Promised Land. The entire passage
(through 9:37) continues that recital to include the period of the Judges, life in
the united and divided kingdoms, the defeat of the northern kingdom by Assyria
and of the southern kingdom by Babylonia, the Exile in Babylonia, and Israel's
eventual return to Palestine under the Persian monarchy. In other words, it is a
recital of Israel's history from the beginning to the time of Nehemiah.

But it is more than a recital. It is an interpretation of that history. Crucial
elements of the story are left out; others are chosen to be included, and most of all,
it is not presented as an objective history, but rather one that is interpreted. That
becomes nowhere more apparent than in the next portion of this recited story.

Israel's Complicity in the Creation of Their Situation

The recital now substantively changes. "Nevertheless your people were dis-
obedient and rebelled against you and cast your law behind their backs and killed
your prophets, who had warned them in order to turn them back to you, and they
committed great blasphemies" (Nehemiah 9:26).

The message is clear. Israel is in a mess. But it is not in that mess simply
because of the greed and lust for power of other nations. It is because Israel has
essentially been unfaithful to God, to his Law, and to the poor. Nehemiah 9:27–28
presents the cycle that Israel went through over and over again: turning their backs
on God and not being committed to the poor; entering into suffering at the hands
of their enemies; crying to God for mercy; God showing them mercy and delivering them through a strong leader; a temporary commitment to the Sinai Covenant;
increasingly acting irresponsibly and irreverently, and being conquered by Israel's
enemies—and so on. The painful history of Israel was not due to God's abandon-

ment or punishment; it was due to Israel's own penchant for autonomy from God, lust for power, and greed (9:32–35). Thus, the writer states, "You (God) have been just in all that has come upon us, for you have dealt faithfully and we have acted wickedly; our kings, our officials, our priests, and our ancestors have not kept your law or heeded the commandments and the warnings that you gave them" (9:34).

The important point about this portion of the recital of Israel's history was the reminder to the Israelites that they have no one to blame but themselves for what happened to their nation. Their rejection of God, commitment to be "like all the other nations of the earth," and greed have been primary ingredients in the creation of their unhappy situation. "We have met the enemy, and he is us!"

Making an Accurate Social Analysis

It is out of the twin ingredients of perceiving how God has worked in Israel's history and how Israel has consistently undermined God's intent so they could serve their own purposes that Ezra now leads the people in their making a startling social analysis:

> Here we are, slaves to this day—slaves in the land that you gave to
> our ancestors to enjoy its fruit and its good gifts. Its rich yield goes to
> the kings whom you have set over us because of our sins; they have
> power also over our bodies and over our livestock at their pleasure,
> and we are in great distress. (Nehemiah 9:36–37)

The social analysis of their society is profound. The interpretation has painted a picture of a significant social history, the perfidy of the people in destroying that history, and now the final interpretation of what causes them to be in the present situation in which they find themselves. It is presenting the cruel reality that they are living today as slaves in the land that God had once given them as their possession. Others now rule their land. They are reduced to being slaves, and their masters "have power over our bodies and over our livestock, and we are in great distress."

The intriguing element to me in this analysis is that it is only at this point that such an analysis can be made. There is no effort at an earlier time on Nehemiah's part to try to convince the Israelites of their complicity—they could not have borne it. Earlier, they were only too convinced of their low estate and had only a negative evaluation of themselves. But the victory of the building of the wall had restored their confidence in themselves. Now it was necessary, if they were to be groomed into leadership, that they recognize their own duplicity and repent of it. Now was the time for truth. Only by sharing honestly out of their corporate social analysis would they be made whole.

Nehemiah 8–9 has provided us a profoundly insightful look into how Israel reflected upon the reality of their situation. It gives us eyes and ears into the process they followed to think through what they were learning about themselves, their targets, and their community. It demonstrates to us that celebration doesn't simply mean "partying" but can provide the opportunity for critical thinking about one's self and one's community in the light of the history they are claiming for themselves as a community. It is therefore the most profound of reflections.

Determine and Act upon Newly-Articulated Values

In the light of this celebration, social analysis, and new definition of who they are, Israel acted to rebuild their corporate lives by some very specific and drastic actions. They did this by entering into a covenant with each other:

> [We] enter into a curse and an oath to walk in God's law, which was given by Moses the servant of God, and to observe and do all the commandments of the LORD our LORD and his ordinances and his statutes (as follows):
>
> 1. We will not give our daughters to the peoples of the land or take their daughters for our sons;
>
> 2. If the peoples of the land bring in merchandise or any grain on the Sabbath day to sell, we will not buy it;
>
> 3. We will forego the crops of the seventh year;
>
> 4. We will forego the exaction of every debt;
>
> 5. We also lay on ourselves the obligation to charge ourselves yearly for the service of the house of our God;
>
> 6. We will cast lots so that we all share in the care of the temple;[2]
>
> 7. We obligate ourselves to bring the first fruits of all our produce and of our wealth to support the three major festivals at the temple and to redistribute wealth;[3]
>
> 8. We will tithe the firstborn of our sons and of our livestock in order to repopulate Jerusalem.[4] (Nehemiah 10:28–11:2, author summary)

This covenant assumes certain values—the values of the Deuteronomic code and, consequently, of pre-exilic Israel (see footnote 4). Those values include: (1) the centering of the entire life of the community and of each individual Israelite in a vital relationship with God that is acted out in the worship of God; (2) a politics of compensatory justice that is concerned with the protection of the vulnerable of that society; (3) an economics of stewardship of the wealth both of the community and of each family so that poverty might be eliminated and wealth be distributed equitably; (4) maintenance of racial and ethnic purity (see the third paragraph below).

But it is one thing to make a promise, and another to keep it. Once Israel determined the values upon which they would build this Jewish community and covenanted together to keep them, did they? The evidence is clear that they did.

For example, covenant stipulations 2 through 4 deal with the redistribution of wealth (especially the keeping both of the Sabbath and of the Sabbatical Year) and 5 through 7 with the maintenance of the temple and of liturgical activities (such as the obligatory festivals of First Fruits, Passover, and Booths). Nehemiah 12:44 and 13:12–14 report that they are observed. Nehemiah 13:15–22 indicates that during the period when Nehemiah returned to Susa, many in the nation grew lax regarding their liturgical and economic responsibilities. But when he returned, he set things right, (rather violently, it seems because he writes, "I contended with them and cursed them and beat some of them and pulled out their hair" 13:25). Soon, things were set to rights again.

Covenant stipulation 1 seems the most troublesome: "We will not give our daughters to the peoples of the land or take their daughters for our sons" (10:30). This, too, was obeyed. Nehemiah 13:3 tells us, "When the people heard the law, they separated from Israel all those of foreign descent." In other words, all marriages between Israelites and people of other ethnic groups were dissolved. That this actually happened is confirmed by Ezra 10:9–17, the report being introduced with the words,

> Then Ezra the priest stood up and said to them, "You have trespassed and married foreign women, and so increased the guilt of Israel. Now make confession to the LORD the God of your ancestors, and do his will; separate yourselves from the peoples of the land and from the foreign wives." [5]
> (Ezra 10:10–11)

On the face of it, this action on the part of Ezra and Israel to expel foreigners from the Jewish community and to maintain the ethnic purity of Israel seems both immoral and cruel. Presumably, many of the couples forced to divorce loved each other, and families were torn asunder by this action. This action would have created economic and personal misery for many. The decision by the people to appoint a special commission of laypeople to investigate each case (Ezra 9:14–19) indicated the desire by the people to find extenuating circumstances to prevent as many divorces as possible. But it is important to understand what this admittedly radical action was seeking to accomplish.

A persistent problem in Israel was the seductive nature of the gods of other nations who would woo Israel away from the far-more exacting nature of Yahweh, who demanded responsibility rather than license in public and private life. In Deuteronomy, for example, a clear differentiation was made between "aliens" or "foreigners" (Deuteronomy 14:21; 15:3; 23:20; 31:16) and "strangers" or "sojourners" (Deuteronomy 10:17–19; 14:28–29; 16:11–12; 26:4–15). The stranger or sojourner (also translated in the NRSV as "resident alien") was a non-Israelite who lived permanently in Israel and who embraced the worship of Yahweh. The alien or foreigner was a non-Jew who either resided temporarily or permanently in Israel but was a believer in another god than Yahweh. As a believer in one of the Baals, he was a profound threat to Israel because his values were totally different than were the values of an Israelite truly committed to Yahweh. Whereas the Israelite was to be committed to a relational God of love and justice and called by him to act justly and to equitably distribute wealth, the "alien" or "foreigner," precisely because he was committed to a Baal, was committed to a politics of power leading to the oppression of people and an economics of greed leading to the exploitation of people. The two sets of values could not exist side-by-side in Israel, because they would conflict with each other.

The issue that stood before Israel when its people considered the embracing of the Deuteronomic code as the foundation of their society was the question of what to do with married couples where one was an Israelite and the other was a foreigner. Presumably, the reason for the commission was to determine, case-by-case, whether the non-Israelite in the marriage was a "stranger" or a "foreigner," a "sojourner" or an "alien." Was that non-Israelite participating in the worship of Yahweh and therefore embracing the Mosaic covenant, or was this non-Israelite loyal to another god than Yahweh and therefore committed to a politics of domination and an economics of exploitation? The indication from the book of Ezra is that there were only 110 divorces while, presumably, there were many more mixed marriages (Ezra 10:13). The adjudication likely hinged on whether the non-Israelite spouse was a stranger or an alien.

What this shocking action dramatically illustrates to us is the primacy of the community over either the individual or the family. It was the preservation and integrity of the community that was primary—not the preservation of a marriage. Families would be born and would die—just like individuals, but the community would have to continue on. If a marriage in any way jeopardized the continuity or spiritual integrity of the community, it would have to be dissolved. That was the principal priority of post-exilic Israel.

The final commitment in this new covenant, "We will tithe the firstborn of our sons and of our livestock to repopulate Jerusalem," we will examine in the next section.

Create Symbols and Celebrations

It is inadequate simply to articulate values that come out of your history and to act upon those values. If your group simply does that, it will soon find itself disintegrating. The creation of symbols is essential for providing continuity to an organization. The decisions the body makes to rebuild their corporate lives are made real by participating in some very strategic acts. The Jews make their resolutions real by creating two crucial symbols.

The first symbol is found in Nehemiah 9:38. After the recital and interpretation of their history and the creation of a covenant between them, they take this step: "Because of all this, we make a firm agreement in writing, and on that sealed document are inscribed the names of our officials, our Levites, and our priests" (9:38). The symbol is a signed document. The covenant is reduced to writing, and the appropriate people sign it as an indication that all the people support it. Just as the British did with the Magna Carta and the Americans did with the Declaration of Independence, the signing of names indicates a level of commitment far beyond that of a verbal agreement.

The second symbol was even more intriguing.

> Now the leaders of the people lived in Jerusalem; and the rest of
> the people cast lots to bring one out of ten to live in the holy city
> Jerusalem, while nine-tenths remained in the other towns. And the
> people blessed all those who willingly offered to live in Jerusalem.
> (11:1–2)

The problem facing Israel was how to repopulate Jerusalem. The walls now provided for the first time in 141 years protection and safety for the residents of the city. But the city itself still lay essentially in ruins, and the vast majority of its populace had long since fled it when the walls were down and it was subject to lightning raids by the desert people. Now those people had settled into the towns, villages, and farmland of Judah, and didn't want to move back to the city. But unless Jerusalem became the economic, marketing, and political center of Judah, there would be little future for the Israelites. How, then, were they going to convince people to give up their homes, occupations, and status in the places where they had settled and migrate to Jerusalem? The solution that the Israelites came up with was ingenious.

The giving of the Israelites to the temple had two essential components to it. The first was that the giving was always done by family units, not by individuals, clans, or larger units. The second was that giving was always done in terms of a tithe—10 percent. Thus, for each of the festivals, each participating Israelite family would contribute 10 percent of its produce, its livestock, or its goods (according to what was appropriate). The leaders of Israel took these two components and solved the problem of repopulating Jerusalem.

The people covenanted together to tithe each of their families (a family being an extended family of cousins, uncles, grandparents, etc.), so that one out of every ten members of their family would move back to Jerusalem. Rather than tithing produce, livestock, or goods, they tithed people. To move to Jerusalem, therefore, became a spiritual act, an act in which the person designated as the tithe committed himself or herself to the mission of resettling Jerusalem and reclaiming it for Yahweh. Although he would now seek to make a life for himself, settle down and begin to develop a family, livelihood, and a public place in Jerusalem, he would still remain connected to the extended family back in his hometown, and thus would be connected to both worlds.

By using the symbol of the tithe, the Israelites were able to bring about a significant migration to the city and the building of its foundation to once again become a strong and pivotal city economically, politically, and religiously. Thus is the value of symbol.

Create a Permanent People's Organization

With the repopulation of Jerusalem (Nehemiah11:1–2), and the creation of a structure and assignment of people to manage the economy (12:44–47), the political decision-making process (13:4–9) and the religious system (12:1–43; 13:30–31), Nehemiah had begun the construction of an ongoing organization to make permanent the reforms he had brought. He had created a permanent organization to (1) hold the people accountable to the commitments they had made; (2) to administer the city, the temple, and the state; (3) to centralize authority in the temple; and (4) to guarantee the continuance of the Deuteronomic reform without his personal involvement. In that way, he could return to Susa or even eventually face death without worrying about the sustainability of Israel.

But the most brilliant action Nehemiah took was something that seemed insignificant in the time. That seemingly innocuous action would have the most long-term implications for both the sustenance of worldwide Jewry and the establishment of Christianity. In a passage describing how the towns and villages of Judah were organized around Jerusalem, there appears this most innocent line. "And certain divisions of the Levites in Judah were joined to Benjamin" (11:36).

What did that mean? The Levites were the Jewish tribe who had been responsible for the organizing and supervision of temple worship since the time of Moses. Benjamin, which had once been a tribe, was by this time the designation for the most outlying areas of Israel, at the very periphery of the nation.

This meant for the very first time in Israel's history, "certain divisions of the Levites" were being assigned—not to conduct temple worship in Jerusalem—but to go to the towns and villages throughout Israel to teach the Jewish faith there and to provide priestly services. The temple was being dispersed to the people, rather than the people coming to a centralized temple. This was a very significant reassignment of duty because, up to this time, all Jewish worship had occurred at the temple in Jerusalem with the Levites assigned solely to administer that worship.

This action on the part of Nehemiah became the base for a dispersed and localized religious system. It was, in fact, the initiation of the synagogue system. In turn, the synagogue became in less than 100 years the center of religious instruction, decision-making, and the maintaining of the values of the people of Israel. By the time of Jesus 300 years later, the synagogue system was rivaling the temple in importance. Jews went each Sabbath to their local synagogue, no matter where they lived (even in cities throughout the Roman Empire and hundreds or even thousands of miles from Jerusalem), to worship God, be instructed in the Torah, capture the vision of Israel's shalom community, learn the Law and the Prophets, and even learn to read. Meanwhile, their only obligation to the temple was to travel there three times a year to participate in the Feasts of the First Fruits, Passover, and Booths. A localized faith was winning out against a centralized institution.

More than 400 years after Nehemiah, when the temple was destroyed and Israel annihilated by Rome, the synagogue and its written law (Torah) went with the Jews in their dispersion throughout the world. Their faith had become portable. Wherever they went—to Russia, throughout Europe, to the United States, to Latin America, Africa, and Asia, their holy books and rabbi (Pharisee) went with them, and wherever there were three adult Jewish males, they could form yet another synagogue.

Likewise, it was the synagogue that became the model used by Christians for the formation of the local Christian church, so that synagogue became church, rabbi became priest or pastor, and the book of the Law became the Bible. In fact, it was the synagogue that built Judaism into the movement that would eventually give us Jesus. Nehemiah little realized the wonder he had created.

We have looked at the second organizing effort through which Nehemiah brought the Jews in Palestine. What he did in this second stage of organizing was to move from solving a single problem (broken-down walls) to building a permanent people's organization and articulating the values upon which that organization would be maintained. That is what gave power to the Jewish people for the next 2400 years—even into the present and into the future. That is why I like to say that Nehemiah was as important to the formation of Judaism as Moses was to the creation of the nation of Israel.

In the final analysis, it is not a single action or organizing effort or program or project that is important. It is the building of a permanent people's organization of the churches and people's institutions in a city that is the means by which the systems can be held accountable and the shalom community can begin to be realized. But that organization can become partisan, manipulative, and even demonic if it is not built upon commonly held values articulated by those churches and people. A truly permanent organization cannot be built without articulating or creating a common history, discerning the values upon which that history is based, embracing symbols that capture the essence of that vision, and creating the structure and organization that gives shape and direction to the organizing effort. And that can't occur except as a result of continuous action and reflection.

BIRTHING A GODLY POWER COMMUNITY IN THE CITY

The task of faith-based community organizing is not so much community development as it is community organizing. That is, the task of faith-based organizing is not, finally, to organize institutions to address their issues of public life, as it is to organize in order to create a community. A shalom community is birthed in the city by moving beyond the continuing addressing of the people's issues by continuing the action-reflection process that we have examined in the latter chapters of Nehemiah. It is done by the community intentionally taking three steps.

STEP ONE: Determine, Articulate, and Own the Values which That Community Chooses To Hold and Maintain in Common

Every collection of people functions with a set of values. Often those values are unarticulated, but they are still there. Those values either knit the people and their institutions into a community together, or those values make it unable to cope with the larger world.

Urban and suburban communities, in particular, often have few common values (particularly if the community is comprised of people from many cultural or ethnic groups). The individuals and the families, and sometimes even some of the institutions (such as churches) may hold to common values. But the neighborhood will not. Rather, it will reflect the values of each group, culture, or religious tradition that is there. This inevitably creates a conflict of values and no continuing focus around which the community can coalesce, except for a temporary emergency (such as a flood or someone getting shot). Most of the conflicts between neighbors are around the disparity between their respective values.

Because most urban and suburban communities don't operate out of common values, the commonality they accept is to "not make waves," to "keep to yourself" and to privatize all of life. People move in this direction in order to get along. But such movement is deadly because it withdraws people from dealing with each other and therefore not addressing the issues or concerns they may have in common. Often a pastor or church or community organizer living or working in that community may operate by values (usually unarticulated or even unformulated) that are in significant disparity or even disagreement with the values of the community. But even if this is the case, the tendency will be to go along with the unwritten rule to not make waves and to keep those values to one's self.

But a neighborhood, a region, a church, or a city can't discover purpose and direction for its life and can't build a functioning shalom community without identifying and owning common values. Simply organizing a community to build its relational power and to address its own issues will not create a continuing, self-sustaining community. That is because such organizing doesn't address the self-marginalization or lack of purpose or direction the people place upon themselves, or their temptation to use power to serve their own ends. If the people of a community operate out of the self-perception that they are unacceptable and can't truly compete (the mind-set of most urban and inner-city communities, slums, and squatter settlements), or if the people believe that they are acceptable only through their performance or through their status (the mind-set of most suburban and middle-class communities), they are unable to reformulate their existence into a corporate life that is meaningful and full of hope.

How, then, can a neighborhood, church, or a city call forth common values that will give them direction, meaning, and hope, and move them toward becoming a community? They can do so only through an intentional and continuing process of action and reflection. They can do so only by following the Nehemiah model for community building.

Recognize Your Power

The people must begin by organizing to address the issues they perceive as the issues most destroying their community. They must build and learn to use their relational power. And they must have victories—actions that substantively address their issues and begin to introduce hope to that community. Then they must reflect on their victories. They must recognize their proven capacity, ability, and willingness to identify and deal with their corporate problems by confronting the systems and winning. Acknowledging their power demonstrates to them that they are people of worth and ability.

Celebrate Your Past

Fresh and emboldened by their victories, they begin to remember and to celebrate their corporate past. That corporate past can come to them from a number of sources. If they are a neighborhood made up overwhelmingly of the same ethnic group or origin, they can begin to explore that origin. Thus, if the neighborhood is primarily an African-American community, they can begin to learn about their roots, moving beyond their fore-parents' experience of American slavery to their ancestors' origins in Africa. They can enrich their reflection together by celebrating such festivals as Kwanzaa together.

If they are a neighborhood that is made up of a number of ethnic groups, they may explore the origins of their neighborhood or city. Thus, as I shared in chapter eight, the diverse census tract 5130 in Detroit, which my church and I organized, reclaimed its nineteenth-century name, "Fox Creek," and then used that to create a turn-of-the-century motif in street names, street lights, cobble streets, and a park.

If they are a church together, they may examine their theological tradition or their historical derivation for clues to the values they want to claim for their heritage. For example, my Detroit church decided to take its Presbyterianism seriously. We held a highly attended course at our church on the confessional standards of the Presbyterian Church[6] that helped our congregation identify the core beliefs that our denomination is based on (including its historic commitment to continuing engagement in public life). Some of our members created a banner for each confessional standard, which, one by one, were then dedicated at Sunday worship that celebrated how the church that wrote that confession had sought the reformation of society. Each banner was then hung from the rafters of our cavernous Gothic sanctuary, adding much-needed color and ambience.

Perhaps the most fun we had was conducting a 1678 Puritan worship service (we spared them the full three-hour service with a ninety-minute sermon), with the order of worship as close to the original as we could get and most parishioners coming in costume for the occasion (including myself, as I preached in Genevan robe, ties, frill collar, knickers, and buckled shoes). Our big hit was our "beadle" whose job it was to keep the congregation awake by walking the aisles (in costume, of course) using a long pole with a knob on one end (to hit dozing men on the head) and a feather on the other (to tickle the noses of ladies who had nodded off). Of course, all this was fun! But its purpose was serious—to enable my congregation to embrace from its theological and historical origins an entire way of being church that has been, for nearly 500 years, centered on the transformation of society through public engagement.

As part of the process of discovering, remembering, and claiming our community's corporate past (whether that community is a church, a neighborhood, or an ethnic grouping), there must be the willingness to perceive how we have been unfaithful to that vision and thus, part of the problem. It includes doing a new social analysis of the culture we have discovered that includes admitting how we have contributed to our own powerlessness and marginalization. We need to perceive that it is not just "the systems and structures" but "we, ourselves" who have contributed to our church's, community's, or city's malaise. And then it must include the confession of our sin and complicity and the receiving of absolution.

Finally, out of the recapturing and claiming of our origins as a people, out of the social analysis and the confession of our complicity, we need to create an action plan for the next phase of our community by which we can rebuild our life together. Such an action plan must include our selecting and naming the values we intend to hold in common on which our new community will be built.

Determine and Act upon Newly-Articulated Values

If you want to see a shalom community birthed from your organizing efforts, the task at this stage of the action-reflection process is to enable the group, church, or community whom you are organizing to *determine* and *articulate* and then *embrace* and *act upon* the values that they want to see at the core of their community life. For both Christians and non-Christians involved in community organizing, I would think those values would be built upon the exercising of relational power, acting in politics for justice alone, the stewardship of wealth for the good of all with a particular intent to eliminate poverty, and a particular commitment to the Iron Rule: "Never do for others what they can do for themselves." For Christians, I would think another value would be that of embracing a personal relationship with God through Jesus Christ, the filling of the Holy Spirit, and the willingness to allow that Godly relationship to infect all of our life and our relationships.

The role of the organizer, the pastor, the mission worker, or the church within this process is to gently but firmly "walk" the community through this process by prodding and asking questions but not giving answers. For it is the community itself that must determine, articulate, and choose to act upon these values.

From 1985 through 1995, I was the director of the urban work of World Vision International in Africa, Asia, and Latin America. One of the World Vision entities with which I worked closely was World Vision India. World Vision India had embraced the strategy of community organizing for its urban work throughout that sub-continent. My work with them was similar to the services any community organizing network offers its "on-the-ground" organizations. I helped plan strategy, train organizers, supervise staff, participate in evaluation teams, and lead three- to ten-day workshops for key community leaders, volunteers, and religious leaders. But it was the work the local organizers and community leaders did that truly built this remarkable "people of power."

The organizing project that World Vision India initiated was named "Organizing People for Progress" (OPP). It has been focused for its entirety among the "poorest of the poor" in India's cities, especially the "untouchable" caste. The Untouchables or Dalits number more than three hundred million and are born at the bottom of Hinduism's caste system. As their name implies, they are considered by many other Hindus as "untouchables"—uneducated and impoverished people who are to be avoided. Since the ending of the British Raj, a few Dalits have achieved political power, and from time-to-time, the Dalits have shown themselves as capable of organizing considerable short-term power, but they have not been able to build ongoing permanent power that would free them from impoverishment and ignorance.

Organizing People for Progress began in 1988 in five of the worst slums and squatter settlements in Madras (now Chennai). By 1994, it had expanded to slums of four cities in southwest and southeast India. Today, Organizing People for Progress is working to organize the poor in nearly fifty slums in the thirteen largest cities of India with an organizing staff of well over a hundred.[7]

OPP has built its organizing on the traditional principles and strategies of community organizing. When its organizers come into a slum community, for example, they spend enormous amounts of time in individual meetings with residents. These one-on-ones then progress into house meetings where the people share their stories and groans and begin to define issues. Then the people organize around the unique Indian institutions of "women's associations," "youth associations," and "men's associations" as action teams that then organize research actions and mobilize the entire slum for actions. Negotiations are sought with power-structure decision-makers and direct action is taken against "targets" that refuse to negotiate in good faith.

Paralleling this action dimension of organizing, people engage in community-building activities aimed at strengthening relationships among each other and deepening the meaning of their work together. Victories are celebrated, with recognition given to local people who become heroes in their community. Through a reflection process, people learn to connect deeply-held beliefs and values to the action in which they are engaged—and these values are directly related to the Hindu, Muslim, and Christian religious convictions of the people. Throughout all aspects of the work, leaders and potential leaders are identified, encouraged, developed, and trained.

The use of reflection as an essential principle for equipping the untouchables for engagement in public life had to be done with a deep sensitivity to the multiplicity of religious traditions in the urban slums and squatter settlements in which World Vision India worked. In these slums, about 90 percent of the people were Hindu, about 8 percent were Muslim, and 2 percent were Christian. World Vision India had to learn that it could both be engaged in Christian mission and respect the faith perspectives of the people with whom it was working.

One of the OPP organizing efforts was in Shastri Nagar, one of the worst inner city slums of Madras. The center of the organizing effort was the women of that slum (the men proved almost unorganizable and defeated by life). Like most Indian communities, Shastri Nagar was religiously divided—consisting of Hindus (the majority), Muslims, Christians, and secularists.

Over about a two-year period, the women had successfully organized the slum to get government action on a number of infrastructure issues. They pressured the government to replace the three toilets that were to accommodate the five thousand residents of Shastri Nagar; the government built an adequate latrine system. The women convinced the city government to install street lighting, to bring electricity into each family's hut, and to replace the slum's muddy streets with asphalt roads. The result was that the women were feeling increasingly powerful and more in charge of their situation.

But now the problems with which the Women's Association began to deal were more substantive, dealing with the quality of their lives. To deal with these issues, there had to be some common convictions of what Shastri Nagar, as a community, ought to be. How would an organizer ever get Hindu, Muslim, Christian, and secularist women to embrace common values?

The way the organizer brought the women to commonality was around their twice-monthly meetings. They already knew that they were powerful because, by working together, they had gotten the city government to do far more for Shastri Nagar than any of them had dared hope. The organizer began by getting them to share stories about their victories and to articulate the power they were feeling.

Then she got them to begin talking about their common history as Dalits, and what it was like to grow up as untouchables. They talked about the traditions of the Dalit people and why those traditions were important and should be embraced. They recognized that they had contributed to the oppression of the Dalits by not standing up to authority. They confessed that together and participated in an action of mutual forgiveness of each other. They then determined what they thought were the best features of Dalit life that ought to be protected and nurtured.

At one of these meetings, the organizer asked each woman to reflect over the next two weeks on naming the value around which each wanted to build the life of Shastri Nagar, and to return to the next meeting with her answer. They did this, and the overwhelming value around which they wanted to build their community, they said, was sobriety.

"Why sobriety?" the organizer asked them. Then the women shared that their husbands, who worked as rickshaw drivers, day laborers, or at other menial jobs, would be paid daily. Many of them would spend most of their daily wages on alcohol before ever getting home. They would arrive home drunk and aggressive. The result was that many of the wives were being beaten and abused by drunken husbands. Therefore, they longed for the virtue of sobriety.

After spending some time in sharing their mutual stories of spousal abuse and drunkenness, the women were led by the organizer to discuss what they wanted to do about it. They decided on two parallel actions against their drunken spouses. The first action would be held on an upcoming national holiday. The women got their children to make placards and on that holiday (when their fathers would be home), the children staged a parade through the slum, calling for sobriety and displaying signs with slogans like "Fathers, stop beating our mothers" and "Fathers, stop drinking." They particularly singled out the houses of the worst offenders where they paraded and shouted their slogans.

That parade was only the opening volley of what now was going to become a more sustained action on the husbands. The women formed an intervention team. Then, whenever a man would come home drunk, a signal was sounded throughout Shastri Nagar, and the women would descend upon that man's house, pinning him against the wall and shouting at him to stop drinking until he would sink exhausted to the ground. Besieged, embarrassed, and overwhelmed, the men stopped coming home drunk, and sobriety became the accepted behavior in the slum. In essence, through these planned actions on their husbands, these women had changed the value structure of Shastri Nagar.[8]

STEP TWO: Seek Together the Spiritual Transformation of That Community

To complete the birth of authentic community in that urban or suburban neighborhood, there must be a spiritual transformation. But what do we mean by the word spiritual? What is spirituality?

Spirituality is that force which breathes life, form, and purpose into a unit of society (a family, a church, a group, a neighborhood, a region, a city, or a nation) that shapes that unit into a "community" rather than a "collection" of people. In one sense, all groupings of people have a "spirit" about them—an aura or essence that results from those people holding to the beliefs, principles, and convictions that govern their lives and society. Often, that "spirit" is negative, self-deprecating, or destructive—an "evil spirit." This is often true of a poor community where people feel powerless, marginalized, and abandoned. But it can also be true of a middle-class or upper class community where people feel competitive, measuring worth only according to performance or status.

The issue, then, is how the "spirit" of the community in which you are seeking to organize can become one which gives positive meaning, purpose, and empowerment to the people—one which is truly reflective of the common values the people are discovering and owning as a result of their participation in the building of a people of power through community organization. How can the people, through the organizing process, create a community in which the spirit is healthy, holistic, and good rather than self-deprecating, debilitating, and evil?

Create a Permanent Peoples Organization

The formation of a community's spirituality begins with reflection—especially in house meetings, action teams, and in small groupings. That reflection centers on the primary disparities in that grouping, seeking to discover the commonly held values within those disparities. For example, if the primary disparity were differing faith traditions, the group would look at the values they had identified that they hold (or want to hold) in common and then ask how those values appear in each of their faith traditions. That might lead to a study of the holy books of each tradition in order both to discern those common values and to see the unique nuance each tradition places upon those values. How (and in what ways) does each faith tradition support these community-determined values and how do the respective traditions fall short (in other words, what do we need to learn from each other)?

How is this done, practically? Let's return to our Shastri Nagar illustration. The primary diversity of that slum was not ethnic (they were all Dalits) nor geographic (they were all Tamils) nor national (there were all Indians). Their primary diversity was their religions—with about 78 percent being Hindu, 12 percent being Muslim, 8 percent being Christian, and 2 percent being secularists. The people of Shastri Nagar maintained peace in their religiously diverse slum by never talking about religion with each other. They simply avoided any discussion about or even public observance of their respective religions. So how did the women of Shastri Nagar (its only organized body) deal with this diversity in a way that would build them into a community?

In the twice-monthly meetings of the women's association, the organizer allotted time for evaluation on how the intervention campaign against their drunken husbands was progressing. The women reported with great glee how their interventions were making a difference, and that drunkenness and spousal abuse had almost stopped throughout the slum. Then the organizer did an almost unthinkable thing. She broke the informal agreement that religion should never be discussed and asked the women to be prepared to share at the next meeting how their respective religions and holy teachings taught the value of sobriety.

The next meeting came with great anticipation and was fully attended. Women shared with each other for the first time from their respective religious traditions about the value their religion placed upon sobriety. It was as if the "lid had blown off." For the first time, these slum residents had given each other permission to talk openly about their own and each other's faith. And talk they did—for meeting after meeting.

But it didn't stop there. Someone suggested they needed to read their sacred texts on sobriety. So that is what they did. They began with Hindu texts, then the Koran, and ended with the Holy Bible, with all the women gathered around to explore what both Old and New Testaments had to say about sobriety. Thus, women who had feared the Bible were now gathering around to study the Bible together. And it became acceptable in Shastri Nagar to talk about one's faith.[9]

The next step is particularly crucial. In ongoing reflection, they must compare and contrast the relationship of the commonly identified community values and the emerging articulated spirituality of that neighborhood with the political, social, economic, and religious systems and institutions of that city. This is done in order that the people can see the disparity between the newly-articulated values that are beginning to tie them together and the values of domination, unilateral power, greed, and control that bind those systems together and lead to the oppression, exploitation, and domination of the people.

From that comparison and its accompanying clarity, the group then moves to building a permanent organization of that community that can hold together the people and their institutions around the values they have determined are primary and the commonalities they would celebrate within their diversity. That organization would need to recognize and make space in that community both for those who find the community's values in the dominant tradition but also for those who find the same values in other traditions, so that respective traditions can be talked about, shared, and celebrated without fear of proselytization. If this final step is not taken, then the emerging spirituality of that community based upon such honest sharing will wane, and will eventually disintegrate. Only a permanent organization will continue to sustain that spirit of sharing.

Create Symbols and Celebrations

Finally, it is crucial to create ways to celebrate together the common spirituality of that community, including those elements of the respective traditions found there. Such celebrations should include the creation and use of symbols that appropriately capture those values and represent them to the body.

In Shastri Nagar, the women decided that they would celebrate selected "holy days" of each tradition. Rather than ignoring each other's religious observances or forcing such observances to be private, the Women's Association concluded that there would be value in the entire slum sharing in the celebration of each other's holy days. But they also recognized that many of the holy days of each tradition would be offensive or unacceptable to the other traditions. So how would they overcome that barrier so that participation could be an activity of the entire slum?

The women determined that they would carefully select the holy days that would be observed by the entire slum, and they came up with a highly creative way of selecting those days. The women who were not of that tradition would choose the days of that tradition they would observe together. By making the selection this way, holy days that were selected would be days deemed acceptable to those who were not of that tradition. For the Hindu faith, the Muslim and Christian ladies chose national holidays that celebrated former outstanding (Hindu) Indian leaders, including two pivotal Dalit leaders. For the Muslim faith, the Christians and Hindus chose the close of Ramadan.

Two Christian holidays were chosen by the Hindu and Muslims for the whole community to celebrate. They were the Christian holidays of Christmas and Easter. Why Christmas and Easter? Well, Christmas was well known throughout India and people liked the idea of celebrating the birth of a peasant child in a stable (not much different than their own births) who grew up to become the savior of his people. Easter and the celebration of the resurrection of Jesus was agreeable because Muslims believe in Christ's resurrection and Hindus consider Jesus a god. So all the people of Shastri Nagar gather at the river that flows past the slum for an Easter Sunrise Service.

By following this strategy, the community was able to discover, articulate and own common values that helped to build them into a truly relational community. This, in turn, began the process of faith sharing with each other.[10]

STEP THREE: Create the Space for the Freedom To Share Faith with One Another within the Context of the Growing Positive Spirituality of This Community

How does Christian witness occur within this context? Christians, obviously, participate in the entire action-reflection process, including suggesting values that are consistent with Christianity and sharing relevant insights about the faith as the community explores the varied "roots" for their values in their respective faith traditions. But faith sharing can be more than that.

By its very nature, the process of community organizing can build intense relationships of trust and commitment to one another. It can unite people in a commonly identified struggle, and through its process of action and reflection, it can create an atmosphere of open sharing with one another. So it is in those growing relationships that faith can be naturally shared, one on one.

One must first live out, in the community organization, his or her faith by how one chooses to act and the integrity in both one's action and reflection. In due time, people will want to know what it is that leads you to do what you do and nourishes your spirit. So it is within this context that one can very naturally share one's faith, when people give permission for that to occur.

The atmosphere had been created for faith sharing to occur in Shastri Nagar as a result of the local Christians and the community organizers (whom everyone knew were Christians) being an active part of the building of a relational culture, the success of common victories, and the articulation of values. That sharing occurred on the part of both the organizers and the Christian residents in Shastri Nagar.

Faith sharing by the organizers occurred in a context none of them could have anticipated would become an avenue for sharing. The more open faith atmosphere in Shastri Nagar and the capacity of the women to organize around common values allowed many of these ladies to come to the women organizers with their personal problems. Soon considerable time was being spent by organizers listening to the personal concerns of women, being an encouragement to them and, when appropriate, sharing Christ with them. The result was a number of women making decisions to receive Christ as their savior.

This growing trend provided the opportunity for the organizers to bring together a newly converted woman with other Christian women from Shastri Nagar. They would hold "Christian house meetings" together to be of support and encouragement to each other. That, in turn, emboldened some of the women to share their faith with others. This new openness then led to a wider sharing of the faith with young men and community leaders.

The result was, finally, the formation of a small house church within that slum, as Christ became increasingly alive to the people living there. But all this occurred, as one person put it, because "you don't have to put another religion down in order to put Christianity up." Rather, by creating the open faith sharing atmosphere based upon the claiming of common values, God could do his work through the relationships already built, and people would naturally come to Christ.[11]

SUMMARY

The book of Nehemiah ends with a prayer that is worth considering. This is the prayer: "Remember me, O my God, for good" (Nehemiah 13:31).

What is notable about this prayer is that the Hebrew is ambiguous. The New International Version, for example, translates it "Remember me with favor, O my

God," whereas the Jerusalem Bible translates it, "Remember me, my God, for my happiness." Either translation is equally valid. Either translation is right.

But think of the differences between these two translations. If one translates the prayer, "Remember me with favor, O my God," then this is essentially a prayer of self-interest. If this was Nehemiah's prayer, then he was essentially asking God to give him credit for his selfless, fifteen-year ministry to the Jews in Jerusalem.

But if he instead prayed, "Remember me, my God, for my happiness," this would essentially be a prayer of thanksgiving. It is a prayer in which Nehemiah in essence is saying to God, "Thank you, God, for giving me this great privilege of helping to rebuild the walls and the corporate life of your people."

Which is right? Which captures the intent of Nehemiah's prayer? It is intriguing that the NRSV translation of the prayer purposely tries to combine both ideas—self-interest and gratitude—in the more ambiguous translation, "Remember me, O my God, for good."

I would suggest that both ways of translating this prayer are correct—that Nehemiah was purposefully wording this prayer in an ambiguous manner in order to capture both nuances.

First, it is a prayer of self-interest. "Remember me with favor, O my God." Nehemiah is asking God to give him credit for the faithful work of building Israel into a people of power. What's wrong with that? It is reasonable to expect recognition for the hard work we have done. Self-interest is not evil; it is essential to the functioning of life. We eat, sleep, rest, even work out of self-interest. If we didn't eat, we would starve. If we didn't sleep or rest, we would destroy our bodies. If we didn't work, we wouldn't have meaning or a focus to our lives. Self-interest is a legitimate motivating power in our lives, while selfishness is not. Selfishness is concerned for one's self to the exclusion of everyone else while self-interest acts for the interest of the entire body, including one's self. In this prayer, Nehemiah is being as honest as ever, reminding us that all that we do is motivated, in part, by our self-interest—but that such motivation works for the strengthening of all those around us.

Second, it is a prayer of thanksgiving. "Remember me, O my God, for my happiness." Yet Nehemiah ruined his career as cupbearer to the king by staying fifteen years in Israel to complete the task of rebuilding both city wall and the nation's corporate life. He lost his position in the Persian court as a result of his commitment to Israel and was never restored to that position. He went from the second-highest person in the Persian government to being a nobody. He tells us, as well, that he was financially destroyed in his role as governor, for he had to subsidize the job from his own reserves until he could no longer afford it. So, why would he praise God for his happiness if his work as governor had cost him his political capital, his position, and his financial base?

Nehemiah could pray such a prayer because he had not only organized the Jewish people to rebuild their walls, but to rebuild their life together. He had enabled them to become a new and purposeful people, embracing for their nation and for their own lives the reality of the shalom community. Through building a people of power, Nehemiah had led his people to liberate themselves from all that had been destroying them. An entire people—individually, corporately, systemically, spiritually—had been both empowered and transformed. He had enabled the Jewish people to fulfill, for their national life, God's promise given through Jeremiah centuries before, "I know the plans I have for you, says the Lord, plans for your [shalom] and not for harm, to give you a future and a hope" (Jeremiah 29:10). And that realization that this is what he or she had done for the people would give to any person the most hilarious happiness!

So, dear reader, that is our task—to set free the society to which God has called us. To set our city free, for we have been set free by a Savior committed to the transformation of us as individuals, of the systems which would otherwise destroy and use us, and of all society—so that we might increasingly become the City of God—the shalom community that God intended for the human race. That is the great task of ministry. That is the great task of community organization. And that is the great ministry to which you and I are called.

QUESTIONS

1. Nehemiah follows a distinct strategy to rebuild the spirituality and values of his nation: getting them to recognize their power, to celebrate their past (including recognizing their complicity in creating their current situation), to name and act upon the values they wanted to embrace as a community, to create symbols and celebrations, and to create a permanent people's organization. What strikes you about this strategy? How would it articulate the values that community would hold dear? Why would it be necessary to move to this level of action/reflection in order to make reform permanent?

2. A continuing illustration of the Indian squatter settlement, Shastri Nagar, is used throughout this chapter to illustrate how a community can move from concrete change to a transformation of the values and spirituality of

that community. What struck you about this illustration? What did you find yourself questioning? What stimulated you to think?

3. The chapter ends with the suggestion that the primary task to which we are all called as Christians is to work to set our city free from the values and myths that besiege it in order to embrace the gospel through building its people into people of relational power. In what ways are you seeking to set your city free?

Chapter Eleven

WHAT KIND OF TRANSFORMATION ARE WE SEEKING?

What kind of transformation are we seeking to accomplish? As God's people working with the people of a neighborhood, community, or city, what is it that we are primarily trying to do? Are we seeking to evangelize them? Are we seeking to plant or build up the church there? Are we seeking to provide social services? Are we seeking to provide the formation of the infrastructure necessary for a functioning community? Are we seeking to build a people of power who can take charge of their situation and empower themselves? What, precisely, are God's people called to do? There is no more important task than wisely answering these questions.

THREE RESPONSES TO THE CITY

There are three distinct responses that any church or mission can make to its community. The response the church chooses to make will decide whether that church will play a significant role in the building of the power of the people, will provide social services, will concentrate upon evangelizing, or will simply ignore the people around it. What are those three responses that determine the kind of transformation that you are seeking to accomplish?

The Church *In* the Community

The first response of the church to its neighborhood or city is to see itself as being in but not of that community. In such a situation, that church does not feel any particular attachment to or responsibility for the neighborhood around it. It is simply physically present in that community. Where it is happens to be the place where its brick and mortar happen to meet the ground.

Most churches fall into this category. And they will tend to fall into that category for one of two reasons.

Some churches that fall into this category are there because of their theology. Their theology sees no connection between their existence as a congregation and the existence of the community around them. They have no significant outreach to the community around them (except, perhaps, in trying to woo people out of that community to Christ and into their church). Rather, they perceive the church as a boat on the ocean of life, rescuing people out of that ocean and into the safety of their ship. The members of that church drive furtively into the community, park in the church's parking lot, and scurry into the safety of their church building where they worship God, study Scripture, and fellowship together, and then hurry back out to their cars to drive out of the neighborhood and think of it no longer.

Other churches fall into this category because the community has changed around them. In earlier days, they may have been significantly engaged with that community. But the neighborhood began to change ethnically, economically, or religiously, and as that neighborhood began to change, the people who had lived in that neighborhood and who went to that church began to move out. So, increasingly, the church became a commuter congregation with people traveling into the city and into that neighborhood to attend that church, but whose lives are lived out in another community. Whenever, for example, you see a white church in a black community, it is a sure sign that this phenomenon has occurred.

Whether a church is only physically present but is unengaged in its community because of theological reasons (the first example) or for demographic and sociological reasons (the second example), the result is still the same. The result is that this church has no stake, no psychological ownership in, and no spiritual connection with its community. It is just the happenstance place where that church's bricks and mortar meet the pavement. It could just as easily be located elsewhere.

The Church *To* the Community

The second response of a church or mission organization is to be a church to its community. Only a minority of churches fall into this category, but most have gotten there through one of two ways.

Some churches are churches to their community because of their theology. That is, they belong to a denomination (e.g., Lutheran, Methodist, Presbyterian, Episcopal) or hold to a theology (e.g., Calvinist, Wesleyan, Lutheran) that stresses the church's engagement in public life. That denomination or that theological position has always taught that the local church bears a significant responsibility toward the community around it (e.g., perceiving the community as its parish). Out of its theological or ecclesiastical presuppositions, such a church will believe that it is their privilege and obligation, as the body of Christ, to be seeking the transformation of its community.

Other churches will embrace the response of the church to their community out of enlightened self-interest. Although that church in the past might have been isolated from its community and simply "minded its own business," it might come to the realization that as the community changes, if it doesn't begin to reach out to that neighborhood, it will eventually die. As the neighborhood around that church changes and the church's members move from the neighborhood to distant suburbs but continue to commute out of loyalty, the church begins to realize that such loyalty is only one generation deep; that generation's adult children are likely to attend churches near their homes and not commute back to the old congregation. If the church is to have any future at all, it is going to have to find some way of reaching out to its immediate neighborhood and bringing those new neighbors into the life of that church. So the church begins to become concerned about its city, its neighborhood, and its problems.

However a church arrives at becoming the church *to* the community—whether through its theology, its denominational mission perspective, or its self-interest—the church comes to such a conclusion. In doing so, it has adopted a more holistic approach because of the recognition that the church must be present to the people around it and must be concerned both with evangelism and social action. It is inadequate to be concerned with the souls of the people around the church (that is, rescuing them from hell and bringing them into the safety of the church-boat) unless the church is also going to be concerned about the social and economic needs of the people as well.

There is great potential in this kind of approach. But there is also a fatal flaw! The Achilles heel of this approach is the perception that the church knows what is best for that neighborhood. Those Christians look at their neighborhood and say, "Look at all these pagans here; what they need is to receive Christ. Let's hold a revival meeting or let's open a coffee house to get community residents under our roof, and then let's share the gospel with them." The church says, "Look at all these poor people here; what these people need is a youth program for their teenagers to get them off the streets." Or the church looks at the number of senior citizens sitting on their porches and says, "What our church needs to do is to develop a ministry to senior citizens."

Do you see the common element in all these diverse ministries? The common element is that *the church decides what is best for the community.* The church determines the ministry that will transform the lives of the people of that community.

But this flies directly in the face of the Iron Rule: "Never do for others what they can do for themselves." A primary assumption of ministries that empower is the recognition that the people who are best able to deal with a problem are the people most affected by that problem. The people best able to deal with teenagers running amok in their neighborhood, for example, are the people who live in that neighborhood.

Now, although that seems self-evident, I have discovered in more than 50 years of ministry that *this concept is the single most difficult insight for Christians to grasp and apply to their ministry.* We can understand it intellectually and we can affirm it, but it is extremely hard for Christians to implement that perspective in our own ministries. Instead, we want to do everything possible to do ministry *to* people.

Why do Christians have such a hard time applying the Iron Rule among the people to whom they minister? I believe it comes from our perception that, because we know the gospel—and we know it's good for people—we know what is best for the community in all things. And no insight could be further from biblical faith! So we undertake ministry *to* people out of our "definitive" understanding of the needs of the community. And that, in turn, robs the people of that community from the responsibility of identifying and dealing with their own corporate problems.

When I was doing organizing in the Detroit neighborhood that would one day become the formation of PIFU (see chapter 8), some of the women in a local church came to me to inform me that they were going to start an after-school program at their church for neighborhood children. "Have you talked with their parents about doing this?" I asked.

"No," they replied. "We don't need to. Those children are always playing in the streets, right in front of our church. It's obvious they don't have anywhere to go or anything to do. So they just chase each other in and around our parked cars. The need is obvious."

"Well, you should talk with their parents to see what they want," I replied. But I realized I was speaking to a brick wall.

Well, the program began, using that church's gym and dining hall. And it was a big success. It was set up to operate from 4:00 p.m. (when the children got out of school) until 7:00 p.m., Monday through Friday. The women wrote a grant to their denomination and got funding for it. They hired a director. And it was successful: nearly 100 children participated in the program.

But soon, things began to go wrong. Volunteers from the church were well intentioned, but after a few weeks of it, they began not to show up. The trustees started complaining about the wear-and-tear on the church building. A window got broken, and two gym lights—expensive to replace—got knocked out by a basketball (some felt, intentionally). The director quit in frustration.

Faced with the possible collapse of the program, the women called a meeting of all the parents of the children. "After all," they said to me, "it's their children who are receiving the benefit of this program. They should assume some responsibility for it."

The night of the meeting came. The women had fixed great refreshments and gathered to meet with the parents. I thought it would be wise for me to be present. So I was.

None of the parents came! The women were shocked. A half hour after the meeting was to begin, I led them in an evaluation of the failed meeting. "It just shows you," said one woman. "These people are irresponsible. They don't care about this community. And they don't care about their kids. All they want to do is to use the church and just take, take, take from us."

I asked if anyone agreed with this outspoken woman. Every lady in the room agreed. So I said to them, "First of all, these people do care about this community. And they do care about their kids. They care as much about their kids as you care about yours."

"Then why didn't they come tonight?" one person asked.

"Would you come to a meeting of a program you didn't want for your children?" I responded.

"Well, we're just going to shut this program down," the leader responded in frustration.

"Whether you should shut the program down or not, I wouldn't know," I responded. "But before you decide to act on this, I want to ask you to do something first—what I asked you to do in the first place. You owe it to yourself, to your church, and to the denomination that provided the funding for this program to go and talk to the parents. Will you do that?"

To my utter amazement, they agreed. We set a Saturday morning when they would all make these calls at the same time in teams of two. I agreed to train them for these calls. On the assigned date, they all showed up and went out on their assigned one-on-ones.

When we gathered again at one o'clock for lunch, I could tell they had learned the truth from the people because they all arrived at the end of their calls, looking despondent. I asked, "What did you learn?"

The leader spoke up. "I learned that they have never wanted the program our church was offering. They just acquiesced to it because their kids saw it as something interesting to do."

"Why didn't they want the program?" I replied (already knowing the answer, because I had heard it from my individual meetings with these parents).

"They don't want it because they *want* their children playing on the street."

"Well, why would they want that?" I countered, playing devil's advocate. "After all, think of all the danger those kids are in from passing cars, playing on the street like they do."

"They want their kids playing on the streets," the leader responded, "because when the kids play on the streets, the mothers gather on one of their porches to supervise their children. And when they're all gathered together, they talk over the problems of the neighborhood and figure out what they need to do to deal with them."

The church women had gotten the point; I was grateful to the parents for being honest in their answers. So I summarized this learning experience for the intended do-gooders of that congregation: "So in other words, what you are telling me is this: you perceived the children playing on the street as a problem. But in reality, that was the community's *solution* to a much bigger problem, which was how to come to decisions regarding the substantive issues of the community. And you would have found that out if you had taken the time to visit the parents to ask about their hopes and ambitions for their children. So you didn't solve a problem at all. What you did was to solve a solution, and as a result, you created a much bigger problem."

Thankfully, the women learned from this experience, and they eventually led that church into becoming one of the major players in the formation of PIFU and the transformation of Census Tract 5130 into Fox Creek.

This story, however, reveals clearly the problem of doing ministry *to* a community and its people. The fate of any such program or project developed under the assumption of ministering to people is inevitable. It will function successfully only as long as the church or mission agency is willing to commit its people, money, materials, and buildings to the program. But burn-out will eventually happen. And once programmatic exhaustion has set in, so that the well-intentioned pastor or mission executive can no longer raise sufficient money or resources or workers to maintain that program, it will die. And it will die because it has never been a project of the people. They never perceived it as their program, but rather a program of the church or mission agency. And because the people have no ownership in the program, they will always remain spectators and clients of it, never partners and goal-owners. Therefore, its death is inevitable.

It is not appropriate for the church—in fact, it is strategically a very bad thing—to look at its community and decide what it needs to *do to* that community to change that community. It is not appropriate because that approach is to perceive the community and its people as clients, as objects to be ministered to, and the church as the provider—the only viable change agent in that community. Such an attitude is actually colonialist in nature, and it reveals a paternalistic attitude toward people. The inevitable result of these attitudes will be rejection by the people of the community.

The Church *With* the Community

The third response of the church in the city is to be the church *with* its community. There is a profound difference between being a church *in* or *to* a neighborhood and being a church *with* its neighborhood. When a church takes this third approach, that church approaches its community with an entirely different mindset than when it is seeking to minister to people.

When a church seeks to minister *with* its community, it seeks to incarnate itself in that community. That church becomes flesh of the peoples' flesh and bone of the peoples' bone. It enters into the life of that community and becomes partners with the community in addressing that community's needs. That means the church allows the people of the community to instruct it as it identifies with the people. It respects those people and perceives them as being people of great wisdom and potential. Such a church joins with the people in dealing with the issues that the people have identified as their own. That is the approach in which the most authentic ministry is actually done.

The third response of the church—to be the church *with* the people of its neighborhood—is an approach that enables the church to join with the people in addressing the issues of that community, but to do so recognizing that the only people who have the capability to change that community and to deal with its problems are the people of that community. The church comes alongside them and supports them and works with them in that endeavor, sharing with those people the particular gifts and strengths the church has to contribute to that situation. It is that body of Christ that identifies with the people, casts its lot with the people, and works alongside the people. But it cannot and will not do the people's work for them. Only the people can assume responsibility for their own empowerment. "Never do for others what they can do for themselves."

I often get asked the question, "How can the church empower the poor?" I love that question because it affords me the opportunity for a "teachable moment." My response to that question is always as follows: "That is the wrong question. To ask that question that way is to tell me that you neither understand the nature of empowerment nor what are appropriate or inappropriate roles for the church to play." Invariably, the question-asker will ask me to clarify, and that will provide me with the "teachable moment."

The question, "How can the church empower the poor?" is the wrong question simply because *no one can empower another person.* The only person who can empower someone is the person himself. The only group that can empower a community is the community itself. Only you can take charge of your own situation. No one can take charge of it for you. The task of the church is not to empower its community. The task of the church is to join the empowerment of its community—to participate in it, to be an integral part of it, and perhaps even to participate in making it happen.

As we can see from this exploration, there are three essential responses of the church to its city:

- First, it can ignore the city and the needs of the people around it as it concentrates on preserving its own life. *It can view itself as a fortress.*

- Second, it can provide evangelism and social services and do good works for and to the people in the city. *It can view itself as the savior of the community.*

- Third, it can provide leadership for and participate in the community's struggle to determine for itself what kind of community it wants to become, a community with shalom and justice for all its people. *The church can view itself as a partner with the community.*

TAQUARIL AND DETERMINING
THE TRANSFORMATION YOU SEEK

World Vision Brazil (WVB) was one of the major national offices participating in the Urban Advance, the major community organizing effort I directed throughout Asia, Africa, and Latin America from 1985 through 1995. The primary organizing WVB did was in the cities of Belo Horizonte and Natal. Belo Horizante is a city of nearly 3 million people, the third-largest city of Brazil. It is about 210 miles northwest of Rio de Janeiro in the Serra do Espinhaco mountains, and has a principle economy based in the mining of gold, iron, and manganese.

One of the squatter settlements (called "favellas") in which WVB decided to do organizing was the community of Taquaril. Taquaril was obviously a community in distress. A town of canvas and cardboard shacks, ten thousand families of about fifty thousand residents had moved into this "invaded area" between 1987 and 1991. It had essentially been ignored by the two mayors and city administrations of Belo Horizonte during that period. Beginning in April 1991, Valdemar Gomes Silva began organizing in Taquaril. In just a few months, he conducted individual meetings with most of the adult and youth residents as well as with ten pastors of churches serving in or near Taquaril. As well, he held meetings with city administrators in the fields of housing, health care, schooling, and public transportation. Out of these meetings with the residents of Taquaril, Valdemar began conducting house meetings.

In their house meetings, the people determined that their greatest immediate concern was with creek drainage, rain, and landslides. They were also concerned, long term, with housing and unemployment. But their immediate concern was with the danger of the community simply being washed away in the torrential rains around Belo Horizonte.

The people organized to address these immediate needs. Within one year, they had won concessions from the Belo Horizonte government to provide bus service to the community, to install street paving in highly-trafficked areas, to get telephone lines and two public telephones installed. But the most substantive organizing focused on getting the city to deal with the drainage of the creek that could both cause the flooding of much of Taquaril and was filled with highly polluted water and human waste. Through a series of meetings with the appropriate government officials, the people of Taquaril were finally successful in getting the creek converted into an enclosed sewer, which both channeled the water and removed the waste without the risk of human contamination.

In 1993, Valedemar resigned to accept a professorial position in community organizing at the local Presbyterian seminary and he was replaced by two seasoned organizers, Maria Joana de Oliveria and James Andris Pinheiro. By this time, the now-mature and experienced Taquaril community organization had gotten the city to pave all the arterial and primary streets of the favellas and to partner with Habitat for Humanity in the replacing of the canvas shacks with adequate housing. But as Joana and James met with the people in their action teams and house groups, it became clear that the people still saw as their main problem the matter of water. Trucks were bringing water into the community to sell to the residents at high prices. And there still was no source of clean, plentiful, bacteria-free water for the residents. It was clear that the permanent solution would be the building of three large water reservoirs, one for each of the three sectors of Taquaril. But how were they to be built?[1]

There are four basic questions that need to be asked of any effort to bring transformation to a neighborhood, a community like Taquaril, or a city. Answering these four questions will expose the nature of the transformation being sought and accomplished. The four questions are as follows:

1. What is the action to be taken?

2. Whose idea is it to take this action?

3. How will the impacted community feel about itself as a result of this action?

4. Who would the government (or relevant decision-making force) perceive as the force with whom they have to deal?

Let's examine five primary means of working for community transformation by using the Taquaril issue of water, ask these four questions of each means, and understand whether the work being proposed is ministry "in," "to," or "with" a community like Taquaril. By doing so, we will think through the kind of transformation your church or organization would like to undertake.

Evangelism

The work of evangelism is, first of all, to win people to a saving knowledge of Jesus Christ, and secondly, to get them integrated into the life of a local church. The first objective is of the essence of the gospel—that is, enabling people to embrace Christ as Savior and Lord is, in the final analysis, what the Christian faith is about. The second objective is to get them integrated into the life of a local church, because they will likely not survive as a Christian unless they are in a church that can nurture, teach, care, and support them and in which they can join others in the frequent worship of God. As John Wesley so profoundly put it, "The Bible knows nothing of solitary religion."[2]

The work of evangelism is, by its very nature, transformational! In the account of my own conversion to Christ in chapter 3, it takes no imagination to see how that single event at age fourteen changed the entire course and direction of my life. And so it has done for millions of people over the past two thousand years

There is no question that conversion to Christ is totally transformational for anyone who has experienced it. Using those four questions that help us analyze transformational work in Taquaril, let us examine if the work of transformation under consideration is the work of evangelism—of winning people to Christ and getting them connected to a church.

What is the action to be taken? As Valdemar, and later Joana and James worked with the ten pastors of the churches in and around Taquaril, most of the pastors saw evangelism and winning converts to Christ and for their church as their highest priority. In fact, there was some competition among them, for none of them were interested in winning residents of Taquaril to Christ so that they might join someone else's church. Conversion and church membership were seen as of one cloth. There were two possible actions that commended themselves to these pastors: evangelistic meetings or personal witnessing.

Whose idea is it to take this action? It was exclusively the idea of the Protestant pastors of the churches in and around Taquaril. No one from the community ever suggested this action. In fact, one could argue that the desire of the pastors to win the residents of Taquaril to Christ and to their churches fell into the category of placing the pastors' agenda upon the community, not seeking to discover the community's agenda. The community wanted an adequate supply of water; the pastors wanted them to experience the Water of Life. Thus, the pastors, if they would push this agenda, would be guilty of breaking Nehemiah's rule, "Start where the people are, not where you would like them to be."

How will the impacted community feel about itself as a result of this action? First, it will feel that the issue they are concerned about—water—was not addressed at all. Second, those who receive Christ will be grateful. Those who reject Christ or don't choose to respond will feel resentful and perhaps even manipulated into filling the agenda of the pastors. And the issue most important to the people—water—will still not be addressed.

Who would the government (or relevant decision-making force) perceive as the force with whom they have to deal? The government would likely not even be aware of this evangelistic effort. They would not see either the pastors or the people as a force to be reckoned with in regards to water or any other issue.

Is this commitment solely to evangelism a ministry "in," "to," or "with" Taquaril? It is clearly a ministry "in" the community, one the community has not requested or wanted, but one that is placed on them through the convictions, commitment, and zeal of the pastors. The pastors are interested in the kind of transformation that is essentially personal transformation. They have no functioning social consciousness or commitment to the building of community beyond the community of their respective churches. Therefore, the church is perceived as a boat rescuing these Brazilian peasants from the storms of life in Belo Horizonte, and only sallying forth to rescue folk.

This, then, is an inadequate response of transformation. This response will bring about profound changes in individuals and, perhaps, even in some families, but it will not bring about any direct change in Taquaril in regards to water or any other issue of the people. It would likely be marginalized by the community as irrelevant to the formation and building up of their life together as a neighborhood.

Social Services

Mercy ministries or the provision of services are normally a very short-term solution for dealing with immediate community needs. The devastating tsunamis as a result of the 9.0 earthquake in the Indian Ocean on Christmas night, 2004, is the kind of catastrophe to which the only immediate appropriate response is to rush food, clothing, medicines, and temporary housing to the millions throughout southeast Asia and eastern Africa whose lives and communities have been devastated beyond recognition. Only later will longer-term social services be introduced to rebuild the destroyed infrastructures, to provide jobs, and to start to give people the capacity to survive on their own.

The point is that sometimes social services and mercy ministries are the only appropriate response. This is particularly true in a natural disaster, war, or terrorism. But whereas social services are, in grievous situations, strategic and essential, they are not sufficient for the long-term.

In terms of the Taquaril example, the expressed need of the people is for an adequate and sanitary water supply. They perceive that happening through three reservoirs, one in each sector of the community of nearly sixty thousand people.

If the agency working with the people of Taquaril for transformation of that community were a social service agency whose only mode of operation is to provide goods, they would take action to provide the three reservoirs. The aid agency would purchase the reservoirs, build the superstructure to hold them, install them, and get them working properly. They might even maintain them over the long term, not being willing to trust the people.

Whose idea, then, would it be to install the reservoirs? It would be the idea of the aid agency, not the people. The people would have nothing to do with the installation. In fact, there might be some likelihood that the people might not have even advocated for or desired this intervention, but only acquiesced to it because it met their need for water.

How will the community feel about itself as a result of this action? They would be grateful to the aid agency for making the reservoirs possible, but they will not feel any ownership toward those reservoirs. They would, in essence, feel powerless.

Who would the government perceive as the force with whom they would need to deal? Obviously, they would feel that the aid agency was the powerful party, not the people. If the government would like reservoirs or any other infrastructure work to be done in other favellas in the future, they would see the courting of the aid agency as being strategic.

The bottom line, therefore, is that through the provision of social services, the people's physical needs would be met (in this case, an adequate and sanitary water source), but it would be met at the price of the people's own dignity, sense of participation, and ownership of the project. Therefore, the people would likely do little or nothing to maintain those reservoirs and will not see the reservoirs as being theirs but rather as belonging to that aid agency—even if the aid agency gives them to the community. Therefore, the people will be made to feel powerless by the well-meaning social service agency, and there would be no community transformation resulting from this action. Doing social services is always doing ministry "to" a community; it is never doing ministry "with" a community.

Advocacy

Advocacy is essentially engagement in public life with the strong standing up for the weak. The work of advocacy is beautifully expressed by the prophet Isaiah who, as the outstanding prophet of his day and most likely a relative of the king, declares to King Jotham of Judah this word from Yahweh: "Listen to the LORD, you leader of Israel! 'I am sick of your sacrifices,' says the LORD. 'Don't bring me any more burnt offerings! . . . I hate all your festivals and sacrifices. Learn to do good. Seek justice. Help the oppressed. Defend the orphan. Fight for the rights of widows!' "[3]

This is a classic example of advocacy. Isaiah, both a prophet and a member of the king's own household—therefore a person of power and influence—stands up for the oppressed, the orphan, and the widow whom he feels is receiving short shrift from the nobility. The Mosaic laws called upon all Israel, but particularly its people of power and means, to protect those least able to defend themselves. Instead, King Jotham and his courtiers were accumulating wealth for themselves at the expense of the poor and then were covering over this inhumanity and violation of Mosaic Law by making a spectacle out of the worship of God. So Isaiah speaks passionately (and publicly) against such hypocrisy.

Advocacy is a crucial role the church needs to play in any society where it holds favor or leverage. It needs to be standing up for the poor. But in terms of our Taquaril example, what would the work of advocacy on the part of churches accomplish in working for the transformation of that squatter settlement?

If the agency working with the people of Taquaril for transformation of that community were an advocacy organization, what would they do regarding those three reservoirs needed to supply fresh water to the slum? They would advocate before the Belo Horizonte city council, mayor, and the appropriate administrators for the city to build those reservoirs. They would see the provision of reservoirs as an appropriate responsibility of the city toward its citizens, and therefore would pressure the city to assume that role.

Whose idea, then, would it be to get the city to install these reservoirs? It would be the idea of the advocacy organization, not the people. The people would obviously be grateful for the intervention of the advocacy organization, but they would not have been a part of the determination process to confront the city.

How will the community therefore feel about itself as a result of this action? They might be grateful for the organization's intervention. But they will also leave the experience clearly feeling powerless. In fact, in a profound sense, the intervention of the advocacy organization would be a continuing painful reminder to the people of their own powerlessness. They couldn't get the city to build the reservoirs. They had to depend upon the intervention of this outside advocacy organization, using its leverage to get the city to do what the people couldn't get them to do. So, if anything, the people would leave the situation actually feeling more powerless than they did before intervention began!

Finally, who would the city government perceive as the force with whom they would need to deal? Obviously, they would identify the advocacy organization as the powerful body that held them accountable. They would not consider the opinion of the people at all.

Through advocacy, therefore, the people's physical need for water would be met. But it would be met at a terrible price—their own sense of power and dignity. In a very real way, the intervention of the advocacy organization would be an insult to the people, because they would be reminded once again that they had such little power that they had to depend upon the good graces of this outside institution to come to their aid and advocate for them.

Consequently, the result would be obtaining sufficient healthy water for Taquaril, but at the price of the dignity and sense of worth of the people. Little authentic community transformation would occur. Doing advocacy is always doing ministry "to" a community, never "with" that community.

Community Development

If you really want to annoy me, use the terms "community organization" and "community development" interchangeably. Lots of people do it all the time, especially in Christian circles.

Why does this annoy me so? Because using the terms interchangeably says to me that the person doing this sees no difference between the two—that they are simply two terms for the same thing. That is simply not true.

Community organization and community development are two very distinct disciplines, each operating out of its own set of principles, objectives, and strategies. We do a disservice to both when we confuse them or are unable to see the distinctives between them.

Community organization and community development hold some very essential principles in common, but it is precisely because they are two distinct disciplines that it is important we do not allow their similarities to blind us both to their distinctives and the respective roles each plays in working for the transformation of a community.

Community development works for the transformation of a poor community by identifying the essential problems of that community and then mobilizing the people as well as resources from both inside and outside that community so that the community can solve those problems. For example, if the community development body perceives that the lack of affordable, available housing is an essential problem of a community, it will mobilize the people of that community to build the houses and will also mobilize suppliers, volunteers, churches, fraternal organizations, and financial institutions from outside the community to work with the people to get those homes built and then distributed to the people in an equitable manner. Habitat for Humanity would be an example of a well-known community development body that specializes in the building of affordable housing for the poor.

A majority of community development agencies also place a major emphasis on the participation of the community's people in the decision-making process. Sometimes it is superficial, such as taking polls of the people or doing door-to-door surveys. But in other community development groups, it is substantive, even including representatives elected by the people to sit on decision-making bodies, sharing in the determination of the directions of that agency.

An essential element of most community development efforts is that they are holistic in nature. That is, they rarely fall into the trap of seeing the debilitating problems of the community as being singular in focus. In that sense, they will not be oriented around a single issue. They will recognize that the dysfunctional nature of their community is due to a plethora of problems (e.g., lack of affordable housing, unemployment, lack of marketable job skills, poor education for children, the presence of drugs and chemical dependency, crime, etc.). Therefore, only a broad spectrum of response will be adequate to bring about any perceivable transformation of that community.

Some community development agencies are created by and/or are accountable to the local government. Others are independent and are accountable to their sponsors, the people, or themselves. Some community development agencies are Christian in focus; others are Christian in origin, while still others may be secular.

But what all community development agencies have in common is their locus of the essential problem. They perceive the community they are serving as in some way dysfunctional and unable to compete in the economic mainstream of national life. Therefore, the primary task of that community development effort is to "raise up people by their bootstraps" so that they develop the skills, capacities, and willingness both as individuals and as a community to compete in today's society.

How would the best community development effort work with the problem of supplying fresh, safe water to Taquaril? That agency might perceive water as a problem. But they would be careful to check out with the people whether the people saw it as a problem. If they did not, the agency would be unlikely to go ahead to build reservoirs. But if the people concurred in seeing this as a primary issue, they would go ahead with the project to build the reservoirs.

What would be the action to be taken to solve the water-supply problem? Once determination was made by the community development agency for the building of the reservoirs, the first step would be meetings with the people in small groups to plan together regarding the construction. The agency would mobilize the people of Taquaril to build the reservoirs. But they would also mobilize the resources of outside organizations—the churches and volunteers of Belo Horizonte, national non-governmental organizations in Brazil, and perhaps even international NGOs to provide primary funding and volunteer labor to the project. Then all the people together would build the three reservoirs.

Whose idea, then, would it be to install the reservoirs? Initially, it would have been the community development agency that discerned this as a primary need, but they would have worked at building community support and ownership of the project. Without a commitment to the project on the part of the community, the development agency would likely not go ahead.

How will the community feel about itself as a result of this action? Well, the people would have played a strategic role in achieving this objective and in physically sharing in building the reservoirs. Therefore, there would be a great deal of community ownership in the project, a sense of fulfillment and pride, and, consequently, the people would feel powerful.

Who would the government have perceived as the force with whom they would have to deal? No government is naïve about power. They would understand where the initiative for building the reservoirs came from and what the source would be for any further initiatives. At the same time, however, the government would know that the community development agency, precisely by mobilizing the people to build the reservoirs and outside groups to fund that building had, in fact, let the government "off the hook." In the final analysis, it is the government that needs to be responsible for the welfare of its people. The community development agency, by its mobilizing of inside people and outside funding, had assumed that responsibility for the building of the reservoirs and had made it possible for the government to resolve the situation without having to do anything about it (except give permission). This action had allowed the city government to abdicate its responsibility. Therefore, the government would know that if it finessed this community development agency effectively, it could get it to assume the responsibility, not just for the water in Taquaril, but also for its housing, education, policing, streets, and sanitation—and could perhaps get the agency to do that for many other of its favellas. The government had found a "sugar daddy."

Community development is clearly far superior to social service provision or advocacy in contributing to the empowering of people. Its two strengths lie in its capacity to mobilize a community to assume responsibility for addressing its problems and in assembling coalitions of outside institutions like churches, NGOs, governments, fiduciary institutions, and volunteers to invest their time and money in rebuilding a community. But its weakness lies in both the tendency to centralize the perceiving of problems and determination of solutions or actions in the hands of the professionals and its identification of the essential problem of the poor being the poor themselves (more on this later). A significant degree of community transformation will occur under community development, but it rarely results in government and business agencies developing a respect for the community that becomes transformational. Doing community development, therefore, is sometimes doing ministry "to" a community and sometimes "with" a community—according to the depth of the people's participation and leadership of the community development process.

Community Organizing

The primary objective of community organizing is not to solve a problem (like supplying fresh, clean water to Taquaril) but to build a people of power. It seeks to discover the people in a community who have the capacity to lead, to call them out and train them to lead, and to get them to organize their people to address the issues the people perceive as their issues, addressing those issues in ways that will require government, business, educational, religious, and social agencies to be truly responsive to the demands of the people. If you have gotten this far in this book, you have already studied the primary principles, objectives, and strategies of community organizing. So you know that it sees its task as teaching a community through the pedagogy of action and reflection how to act powerfully, training leaders, and enabling that community to articulate the values around which it wants to shape its corporate life.

How, then, would community organizing address the decision of the people of Taquaril, which was to obtain adequate, sanitary water for their community? What would be the action that would need to be taken?

The community, doing social analysis together, would come to the recognition that, according to the laws of Brazil, it is the responsibility of the local government (in this case, the city of Belo Horizonte) to supply clean, adequate water to all its citizens. The government has not assumed that responsibility in regards to the Taquaril favellas. It is the government's unwillingness to assume what the law requires them to assume that is the problem—not the people of Taquaril. Therefore, if the government has created the problem, the government should fix the problem! Anything else is not only allowing the government to abdicate its responsibility, but is teaching both the government and the people of Taquaril that the government doesn't have to assume such responsibility. Therefore, the action that needs to be taken is to make the government do what the law requires it to do—not to ignore that law. The government must assume responsibility for the building of the reservoirs.

Whose idea is it that this action against the city government needs to be taken? It is not the idea of the organizers. It is not the idea of outside agencies. It must be the idea of the people themselves. Through the process of action-reflection, they have done the social analysis that would have brought them to the place of decision—and this is the course of action they decide upon.

How will the community feel about itself as a result of this action? If in following their plan of action, they are successful in getting the government to assume responsibility for the reservoirs, they will feel victorious, elated, and very powerful. If they are not successful, they need not feel defeated—just ready to regroup and determine a different approach to getting the government to assume its rightful authority (for example, perhaps getting to the appropriate state or federal government official to order the city government to cooperate). The point is, win or lose, the people are going to feel themselves a people of power for having taken this action.

Who will the government perceive is the force with whom they have to deal? They will perceive that it is the people of Taquaril, organized together, with whom they must deal—not a social service agency or an advocacy organization or even a community development agency. The power lies in the people—and the government will recognize and respect that fact, long after any outside agency has departed.

It is *community organizing* that leads to transformation of a community, because it results in people's attitudes toward themselves being changed—they perceive themselves as being in control and competent—and that results in the government and outside agencies recognizing that the people are a legitimate force to be taken seriously. Organizing results in people building respect for themselves and the systems developing respect for them as well. That is truly transformational. Doing community organizing is always doing ministry "with" a community, never "to" or "in" a community.

What Actually Happened at Taquaril?

As the result of countless individual and house meetings conducted not only by Joana and James (the organizers) but by hundreds of emerging leaders of Taquaril and then three sector meetings, the people made the decision to confront the city government with the demand that they supply clean, sanitary, and adequate water to Taquaril through the building of three reservoirs. Out of that decision, the people chose specific residents to be their negotiating team with the government. That team negotiated for three months with the appropriate government officials. The result was a binding legal agreement between the city government and Taquaril that the city would provide all the material, supplies, and equipment for the building of the three reservoirs; the people of Taquaril would construct the three bases; the city would install the actual reservoirs on the bases, would hook up the reservoirs to the city's water system, and maintain the reservoirs, pumps, and equipment in perpetuity, and would treat and test the water on an agreed-upon schedule to maintain its purity. A final stipulation insisted upon by the people was that the Taquaril workers would get to keep all the tools supplied by the city so that they could start up their own businesses. The victory celebration of the people of Taquaril was something to behold!

The agreement was reached in July 1993. By September 1993, the people had completed construction of the first base; by January 1994 the second base was done; and by April 1994 the third base was complete. The city installed and hooked up the three reservoirs, and by June 1994, the first water poured from the reservoirs into the homes of the people of Taquaril.

Emboldened by the success they had experienced with the reservoirs, the people's organization of Taquaril then took on the Belo Horizonte school system. At the time, the Taquaril children had to ride a bus to the nearest school that was an hour's drive from the favela. An accountability meeting was held in the community of nearly 400 people with the school officials. The result was that a school building was built in Taquaril by the government and opened for classes in 1994.

As of 1995, it offered classes through the fifth grade (7 to 14 years old), with three shifts of children. The building is in use twelve hours a day.

That success led to another action—pressuring for adequate health care. The Brazilian "Statute of Children and Adolescents" clearly requires the city government to assume responsibility for the health care of all the city's children. So the organized people of Taquaril began pressuring for such health care. The government built a health clinic that now provides daily health care (with a doctor in residence) to the people.[4]

All of this came as the result of the people of Taquaril organizing to use their relational power to get the agencies of their city to work for the people rather than for themselves!

SUMMARY

The title of this chapter was, "What kind of transformation are we seeking?" That is a crucial question, because the answer you bring to it determines the essential ministry philosophy you will choose to embrace. If, for example, you believe that the work of transformation is solely the salvation of individuals, you will embrace the strategy of evangelism. If all you want to do is to minister to human need but not build people's capacity to stand on their own feet and change their situation, then you'll gravitate toward the provision of social services. If you want to have the ego satisfaction of defending the weak but could care less about equipping them to defend themselves, you'll assume an advocacy role.

You would not have gotten this far in this book, however, if you didn't have a strong yearning in your heart to see people take charge of their own lives and of society around them. You want people to no longer be "cowed, cringing, broken things" but instead people of strength, with "self-respect" and able to "stand on their feet and look even God in the eye."[5] So the two options truly open to you are community development and community organizing.

As I indicated earlier, there are distinct similarities between organizing and development. But each is its own unique discipline, with its own principles, objectives, and strategies. Both are legitimate for the task each is seeking to accomplish. Both contribute to the building of a people of power and to the transformation of a community. But, obviously, I prefer community organizing over community development (even though I am quite open to the use of community development strategies in an organizing effort). Why do I gravitate toward community organizing rather than development? Simply because I believe it addresses as its primary target what I believe is the real enemy of the poor, the powerless, the marginalized, and the exploited of the world.

At its heart, community development assumes that the real problem lies with the poor themselves. It believes that, without intervention, the poor have neither the capacity nor ability to compete in today's world—and because they aren't competitive, they lack the willingness as well. Therefore, most community development projects concentrate on the building of housing or the opening of businesses or the provision of educational or health facilities in the slums.

Community organizing sees it differently. It believes that the poor have great capacity and ability to alter both society and their neighborhoods. But they believe that the real problem lies not with the poor but with the political, economic, educational, social, and religious systems of society. The unbelievable living conditions of the urban poor—wretched housing, polluted water supplies, open sewers, a lack of balanced food, terrible health conditions—are essentially manifestations of a far deeper problem. And if we only address those manifestations, we are not seeking the transformation of the world that will really change society systemically and bring about shalom.

The primary problem in society is the distribution of power. A few have considerable wealth and political clout—and back up that clout with the laws of the state, their control of a city's, region's, nation's, or even world's economic machinery, and often with military hardware, guns, police dogs, and tanks. Unless the poor can find ways to confront and negotiate with the systems to effect an economic and political redistribution of power, all the efforts to feed, house, clothe them—or even to get them to build their own housing or their own businesses—will only be palliatives that will never significantly change their estate.

The task of the poor in the city is their own empowerment. The task of the church is to come alongside the poor and join with them in their struggle to deal with the forces that are exploiting their community. Society will never be changed if we do not take the battle to the powerful and demand of them responsible redistribution of wealth and power. That's what Moses did. That's what Israel's prophets did. That's what Jesus did. And that's what we're called to do, as well.

Our primary purpose is not to build up the institution of the church, or to build housing or educational or economic institutions for the poor. We are called to build the poor into a people of power. And the only discipline that is dedicated to that radical task is community organizing. That's why I choose community organizing as the means by which I seek the transformation of the world.

I had the privilege of spending a day in March 1994 in Taquaril. I got to see the bases for the reservoirs being built and the land that had been dedicated for the school. Earlier I had met with several government leaders who were visibly in awe of these people and more than willing to negotiate. Now I was having the opportunity to meet with the emerging leadership of Taquaril, apparently ordinary folk, many of whom couldn't even read, but who certainly knew how to think and to understand their task to get the powers to respond positively to their demands so that their community would be transformed and power redistributed. In my meeting with these leaders, I asked them what difference being involved in the organizing of their community had meant to them. I will never forget one woman's answer.

"Our community was suffocated by our suffering. We were silent, not knowing how to express our feelings or to act. By our work in the community organization, we now feel free to express our concerns and the issues that provoke us—and we know we will be listened to. We use to not have courage—the fear of violence was so great. But now we know we can speak out and we will be heard by the government. And then, changes will be made!"[6]

Isn't that what building a people of power is all about?

QUESTIONS

1. This chapter explores three approaches of the church in regards to the city: the church *in, to,* or *with* the city. Why is this an important distinction? How will one's determination of the appropriate role of the church toward the city affect the work he or she does in the city?

2. There are significant distinctives between community development and community organizing. What are some of those distinctives? How do you respond to these two disciplines for urban ministry?

3. The title of this chapter is, "What Kind of Transformation Are We Seeking?" How would you answer that question for yourself? How do you think your answer will affect the future directions of your ministry?

Chapter Twelve

BUILDING A CHURCH OF POWER

We are now approaching the end of our reflection together. But before it is complete, I would like us to consider the unique relationship between building a people of power in our community or city and the life and work of the church. Why should the church be involved in building power in its community? Why, of all institutions, should a body that names its Lord as "the Prince of Peace" fully participate in a community organization that confronts, resists the authorities, empowers the poor, and generally makes trouble?

THE CHURCH AND COMMUNITY ORGANIZATION

Let us consider the reasons why the church should be a committed participant in the building of a people of power through community organizing.

God Demands It

There is, of course, no Scripture that says, "Thou shalt be involved in community organizing!" But the themes of justice and of commitment to the building of a people of power (especially among the poor) dominate the Scripture.

God's intentions for all humanity is that we live in shalom communities—communities of peace, caring, support, prosperity, abundance, and oneness with God and humanity. God has created our political, economic, and social/spiritual systems to provide the structure and means for us to live in this paradise of shalom, thus bringing glory to God.

The religious system has been created by God to bring the nation, city, religious institution, or family into relationship with God and, consequently, into oneness with each other. That is why both corporate and individual life was created:

so that humanity might glorify God and enjoy God forever. The political system was created by God to bring a godly order to society—an order based upon equitable justice for all as the inevitable outworking of a corporate deepening of relationship with God and each other. The economic system was created by God to steward the resources of that nation, city, business, church, or family so that poverty would be eliminated. The Godly objective of economics was an equitable distribution of wealth so that economic justice could be maintained between all citizens.

Of course, we know society does not fit that description. Greed, avarice, the lust for power, and the need for prestige seem to dominate all individual and corporate relationships. The Bible is not shy about analyzing what went wrong. Whether describing the confrontation between Moses and Pharaoh, the gradual corruption of Israel's kings, the misuse of power by Nebuchadnezzar in Babylon, the coterie of priests and religious leaders who put Jesus to death, or the systems of Satan and God as represented in the whore, Babylon (Revelation 17–18) and the New Jerusalem (Revelation 20–21), the Bible analyzes the gradual corruption of the systems God has created and the abandonment of the shalom community.

Ezekiel contends that corruption begins with money. The economic leaders determine that they do not wish to be stewards of the people's wealth (commonwealth) but owners of an institution's wealth. Eventually they will only not seek honest gain but will find even illegal ways to build their own wealth, even if that means exploiting an increasingly vulnerable people (Ezekiel 22:12, 27). The political system, seeking to protect the wealth of the increasingly affluent (and thus protect the sources of the politician's own wealth and power) will create laws that oppress the people while protecting the powerful (Ezekiel 22:23–25). The religious system will then support this political and economic collusion by "blessing" it (for which they will be amply rewarded). This they will do by using their access to God by keeping the people from God, thus creating a religion of control while seeking their own power (Ezekiel 22:26). The voices of accountability—the prophets—will gradually be seduced by money, power, and prestige, and thus will be stilled (Ezekiel 22:28). The people, oppressed, exploited, and controlled by the systems created to serve them, will become the exploiters of each other (Ezekiel 22:29–31). Thus, the essential spiritual nature of the nation, city, business, church, or family that has been created by God will become implacably evil (Ezekiel 22:3–12).

Perhaps the most profound analysis of this corrupting power of systems was given by the apostle Paul. Faced with an increasingly oppressive Rome, Paul promulgated the doctrine of the "principalities and powers." The increasing evil in an institution, Paul taught, is not simply because of the evil that is within humanity. It occurs because the systems are particularly vulnerable to the demonic. Because they deal with the most primal realities of life, the systems can become demonically possessed. The struggle in the nation, city, business, church, or family is not simply "against flesh and blood." Instead, it is against "the rulers, the authorities, the powers of this dark world and against the spiritual forces of evil in the heavenly realm" (Ephesians 6:10–12). And that is why it is a particularly pervasive and intense battle.

Deeper than its social analysis, the Scriptures are particularly concerned about what the people of God are to do to challenge the corruption of the systems. The essential vocation of the church is to work for the shalom of its city (Jeremiah 29:7). It does this by calling the systems of its city to be what God created them to be rather than the demonic exploiters of people that they have become (Colossians 2:11–15). The church is to work for the transformation of the people and their institutions (Jeremiah 22:1–5, 13–17; John 9:1–39; Ephesians 3:8–12). Our model in doing this is none other than Jesus, our Lord and Master, who resisted the Jewish and Roman systems, called them to accountability, built an alternative community that would recapture shalom, and died and rose again to provide the means for transforming both the lives of people and their institutions.

What this means, in practical outworking, is that the church is to be on the side of the poor, the oppressed, the exploited. It is to work for their empowerment—both by the gospel and by their own self-determination. The Old Testament scriptures call Israel to this primary task (Deuteronomy 15:4–10; Isaiah 58:6–7; Amos 5:21, 24).

In the New Testament era, because of the overwhelming dominance by Rome of the political order and because of the church's exclusion from participation in that order, little is said in the New Testament regarding political justice. But the Christians did have control over their own pocketbooks. Therefore, the thrust of the New Testament's call to the church regarding the poor is in terms of economic responsibility. Jesus spoke more about money than any other subject except God because he perceived money as the most powerful vehicle either to keep a person away from God (Luke 18:18–27) or to enhance his relationship with God (Luke 19:1–10). But perhaps the most substantive call to the church to use the power given it (whether economic or spiritual) to work for humanity's liberation was sounded by Paul.

The book of Ephesians is about the liberation that comes to humanity through Christ (Ephesians 1:3–14; 2:1–22), who defeats both the heavenly principalities and their possession of the systems that organize humanity (1:15–23; 3:1–13). When the church becomes a body of believers committed to each other's liberation and empowerment in Jesus Christ (4:1–16), this will have a profound impact not only upon each other, but also on all society around them. It will radically alter the Christian's lifestyle into a pure, disciplined life (4:17–23). It will create a body of Christ that is truly liberating to all its members (5:1–20). It will profoundly change the relationships in marriage, empowering the women (in Paul's day, the legally disenfranchised party; 5:21–33) and protecting defenseless children (6:1–4). It will transform the economic institutions of society, especially protecting the right of the employees (6:5–9). Finally, it will equip the church to engage its city's or nation's political, economic, and religious systems in a spiritual warfare that will cause those systems to become what God intended them to be (6:10–17).

The primary way such commitment to the poor is to be lived out by the church is through working with the poor so that they become a people of power. God's people are called by Scripture to practice charity toward the poor (Deuteronomy 15:10–11), are to be concerned about deteriorating human conditions among the poor (Isaiah 61:1–9) and are to advocate the cause of the powerless before the systems of power (Jeremiah 22:13–27). But the greater emphasis throughout Scripture is commitment to the self-determination and self-initiative of the poor.

Thus, in the Old Testament, Pharaoh could only be faced down by a Jew who cried, "Let my people go." In the Promised Land, debts were to be periodically forgiven so that the poor could undertake the rebuilding of their lives (Deuteronomy 15:7–11), and the corners of a threshed field were not to be harvested so that the poor could gather grain for themselves (Deuteronomy 24:19–22; Ruth 2:1–23). Jeremiah instructed the Israelites enslaved in Babylon to build a life for themselves there (Jeremiah 29:1–7). Nehemiah called the defeated people of Israel not only to rebuild their walls (Nehemiah 2:16–20) but also their corporate life (Nehemiah 8–11).

In the New Testament, Jesus required the blind man to wash in the Pool of Siloam if he was to receive his sight (John 9). He consistently stated when he healed people, "Your faith has made you whole." Paul stressed that a person's initiative plays a strong role in his salvation; he cannot be helped by God unless he accepts for his own life what God has already provided for him through Christ (Romans 1:16–17; 12:1–2). The constant theme of Scripture—whether dealing with the liberation of the impoverished powerless or the salvation of the spiritually impoverished—is that of self-initiative, of empowerment through an intentional commitment to build power.

This is the biblical imperative for the church to be involved in the building of a people of power in the world and in the church. The organizing of communities to identify and address their own needs is simply another way of acting out the biblical injunction to "work out your own salvation with fear and trembling" (Philippians 2:13). Participation in community organization provides the church with the most biblically directed and most effective means for bringing about the transformation of a community through the Iron Rule: "Never do for others what they can do for themselves."

Self-Interest Requires It

There is a profound difference between self-interest and selfishness. Selfishness is the seeking of our own good, irrespective of and often to the exclusion of anyone else's good. Enlightened self-interest, on the other hand, is the seeking of our good in relation to seeking the good for others. It is the recognition that self-interest is a powerful motivating factor for every person and organization, and to deny that reality in ourselves is to deny what it means to be an authentic human being.

People and organizations act out of self-interest. They are concerned about their own effectiveness and success. It is self-interest that drives the compulsion to excel in business or in sports, to achieve the highest objectives, and to be considered successful by one's peers. It is actually a stronger motivation than the money one gets paid to excel in a job.

What gives self-interest a bad name are those people and organizations who have a compulsion to excel, no matter who they hurt or what they must do to reach their objectives. When self-interest is no longer enlightened by a concern for the effectiveness of others, then it turns into selfishness and becomes destructive in power.

A secret of effective community organization is to motivate the people and organizations of a community to discover that *it is in the serving of the interests of the community that the interests of each organization is better served.* In other words, one can more effectively make his organization successful by cooperating in the improvement of the entire life of the community than to seek solely the good of his own organization. This was never so clearly demonstrated to me than when I returned to my former Chicago neighborhood fifteen years after I had left it to go to Detroit.

I was in Chicago to attend a conference, and I decided to visit my former church. I telephoned the pastor to get his permission to visit (a requirement in the Presbyterian Church). He was delighted and told me he would gather together some of the church members who had been members when I had served there. Now it was my turn to be delighted!

As I got off the elevated train and started up Bryn Mawr Avenue, I was astounded by the changes I saw in my old neighborhood. No more trash lay in the gutters, trees were flourishing along the street where there formerly had been none, new sidewalks with brick inlays had been laid, the businesses I walked past were obviously thriving and had become definitely more up-scale, lovely fenced-in lawns lay where bare and trampled ground had once lay, apartment buildings were sand-blasted, tuck-pointed, and freshly painted. My immediate reaction, as I walked through an obviously transformed community was, "Gentrification! The rich have moved in, pushed out the poor and taken over." But I soon found out I was wrong.

Walking through this revived neighborhood, I arrived at the church I had once pastored. As I sat down with the church's present pastor and the members he had gathered, one of the "little old ladies" who had been part of the ONE community organizing effort eagerly asked, "Well, what do you think of Edgewater now?"

I replied, "I'm blown away! It's phenomenal! What happened to the neighborhood? It's so beautiful."

What had happened? It hadn't been gentrification at all. What my former church members and colleagues in organizing shared with me was the end result of good organizing. The people and institutions of that community—the shops, the businesses, the churches, the poor, the ordinary people—had banded together in that community organization I had helped to found nineteen years earlier, and together they rebuilt that community. They had set as their top priority the improvement of that community's quality of life. And they had set themselves to that task. The result was the slow, steady upgrading of that community. Each institution, each group, every individual in that community and their individual self-interests had been served, not by seeking their own good but by organizing together to seek the community's good. That is self-interest operating at its very best!

The church acts out of self-interest. It would deny this, with considerable embarrassment, but to deny it simply means that one does not understand the institutional nature of the church. Institutional needs must always be served, and such service can happen only by self-interest. It is in the self-interest of the church to seek to increase its membership, income, and worship attendance. To not admit that is simply to be deluding itself.

It is in the self-interest of the church to be involved in community organization. For example, visitors will not come to a church in a trash-filled, graffiti-sprayed neighborhood where muggings regularly occur. It is in the self-interest of the church to join forces with the other groups and people of that community to clean up both the crime and the litter on its streets. By doing so, the church has not only contributed to the welfare of its community; it has also made its building a more desirable destination for visitors and members to gather to worship God. It has wisely served its own interests by cooperating with other groups improving that entire community.

It has been clearly demonstrated in both third and first world cities that community organization has led to building a people of power out of the poor and, consequently, the improvement of their communities. But that has also led to the strengthening of the churches in those neighborhoods that have been active participants in its community organization. The wisest thing a church in a deteriorating neighborhood can do is to be active in the organizing of that community to deal with the problems threatening that neighborhood's quality of life. This is enlightened self-interest at its best.

Participation in Organizing Provides a Witness to the Church's Faith.

An important reason for the church to be involved in community organizing is an evangelical one. Commitment to community organizing provides the vehicle and relationships for the church to effectively witness to its faith in Christ. It carries out that witness in two ways.

First, a community organization has great potential. But that potential can be turned to evil as well as to good. Whenever people gain power, they can end up using that power for their own self-aggrandizement. The poor and middle class are no less likely to do this than are the rich, for we are subject to the same temptations as are the powerful. We only lack opportunity, and organizing gives us that opportunity. It is possible to use community organizing for corrupt ends as for virtuous ends.

But if God's people—the church—have really entered into the life and soul of that community, if they have identified with the people and worked side-by-side with them in the cause of justice, if they have been willing to undertake the most difficult and risky aspects of that work, if the church and its people give themselves away rather than profit from their involvement, then that church gains a profound credibility in that community. Because of its integrity, its willingness to risk, its freedom to ask the hard questions, and its lack of selfishness, the church can become the conscience both of that community organization and of the community. The first way the church can witness to its faith is through becoming the body that most shapes the spiritual grounding of that empowering effort.

But there is a second way the church can witness in that community organization. The church that has undertaken incarnational ministry and has placed itself on the line with the people is a church that gains a profound respect from that community. In being willing to lose its life, it saves it. That neighborhood knows the church did not have to risk its existence by joining common cause with them. But it did risk and did join and did work. In return the people will want to know what motivated the church to so commit itself to the people. They will want to hear about a Christ who also incarnated himself in our world, and they will often respond to that Christ. That is why today, throughout the world, the city churches that experience most growth are churches that are intensely involved in community organization.

Participation Can Build Up the Church

The application of community-organizing principles to the church can enrich the life of that church. Every principle presented in this book that contributes to the strengthening of a community can be equally used to strengthen a church. The members of the church can do individual meetings with each other, discovering what each other's issues and concerns are. House meetings can enable church members to listen to one another and to identify common concerns and common causes to organize around. Action teams can be formed in the church to address the interior problems of the church as well as community issues.

The pedagogy of action and reflection can be as effectively used in the church and its action teams as it can in a community organization's action-teams. Organizing those teams to set their objectives for the worship, education, pastoral care, outreach, stewardship, and building use—and then to carry out those objectives through their own self-determined actions—can place in the hands of the people the actual organizing of the life of that congregation.

The problem with most churches that get involved in broad-based or community organizing is that they involve themselves in it *distinct from the rest of the life and work of their church.* Rather than asking how they can use the principles of organizing to strengthen their own congregations, they treat organizing and the work of the church as two distinct entities. They put on their "organizing hat" when attending community organizing actions and their "church hat" when working at the church. They never perceive that the church is as much an institution to be organized as is their community.

But when you apply organizing principles to every facet of the interior life, mission outreach, and institutional development of your church, profound transformation occurs. You start to build a church of power! How to do that will be examined in the next major section of this chapter.

Of course, the application of community-organizing principles to the church will not succeed if the church is not also involved in its community organization. It is involvement in that organization that trains church members for congregational leadership, creates a vision for the church's community ministry through involvement in the community's issues, enables the clear articulation of the values upon which the church wants to form itself, and provides a model for organizing to that congregation. When the church builds its power on its experience in the community organization by using organizing principles in its own interior life, then the life and mission of that church will undergo profound transformation and empowerment.

BUILDING A CHURCH OF POWER

Your church can benefit in seven ways in the shaping of its interior life, its mission development, and its institutional development by building its ministry around the principles and strategies of community organizing. In essence, you can build a church of power by building a people of power within your congregation. If you do not fall into the trap that most churches do—that of perceiving community organizing as just another program in which the church is involved rather than a way of doing ministry—then you will find yourself building a church of power.

How can your church benefit from the discipline of community organizing? Let us count the ways:

1.   Strengthen the relational nature of your congregation.

I shared in chapter 5 about how my congregation in Chicago was turned around through organizing its leadership to conduct individual meetings throughout the community as well as the congregation. Within six months, those fifty-two church members had visited over one thousand community leaders and residents as well as most of our five hundred member congregation. This calling had built relationships throughout our neighborhood, deepened the congregation's commitment to one another, and given our leadership new insights into the directions the ministry of the church should go. It was the first step in the transformation of that congregation.

I learned an extremely valuable lesson from that experience. I learned how crucial having deep, intentional conversations with the members of my congregation and with the community could be in building the relationality of that congregation (as well as enabling it to gain new insights for its mission and increasing its credibility in the community). It was a lesson I never forgot.

As a result of that experience at Edgewater Church, I decided to make the conducting of individual and house meetings an integral part of my ministry. Since then, I have invested time in each church I have served, in my work with mission agencies, and in my teaching in academic institutions by simply spending time sitting down with people and finding out what really makes them tick. And that has made all the difference!

The church is both a relational body and an institution. My observation of the church is that its institutionality will continually overwhelm its relationality, unless it is checked. That is, the institutional concerns (raising money, maintaining the building, bringing more members into the church, paying the bills, operating programs, and chairing committees) will always take precedence over the fostering of both private and public relationships.

Yet it is the building of significant public relationships that empowers any church. Its impact upon the world or upon its members is not really built through its programs and projects. What makes a program appear successful are the relationships that have been engendered by working in or participating in that program.

One of the things I have stressed in each church I've pastored is that conducting individual and house meetings is not a task only for the pastor. It is everybody's right, responsibility, and privilege. Therefore, in my churches, I have used professional community organizers to teach people how to hold these one-on-ones or small group meetings. The people have quickly responded to the challenge and end up loving it. Relationships between people have been significantly deepened, sharing at substantive levels has occurred, clarity of mission has resulted, and the church has been built through relationship rather than solely as institution.

2. Develop leaders.

Community organizing makes a major investment of time and effort in the formation of leaders. One of the primary purposes of both individual and house meetings is to discern potential leadership, and then to call it out. The organizers will commit significant time to the training of those leaders. Through the pedagogy of action and reflection, the skills of leaders will be honed in conducting a meeting, speaking succinctly and powerfully at a public action or in a meeting with a government official, and in doing research. Considerable time will be committed not simply to hone a potential leader's skills, but to motivate him or her to think and act like a leader. In my "little old ladies" story in chapter 6, think of the time and effort Bob the organizer invested in those women that turned them into powerful leaders, which resulted in turning that community upside down.

But no organizer will confine himself to informal training. Every effective community organizing will provide a spectrum of formal training events where the vision of potential leaders is developed along with their skills. In chapter 8, I presented the spectrum of leadership training used by the broad-based organization that my present church belongs to—ONE LA-IAF. Formal leadership development activities run by ONE LA for its leaders and emerging leaders includes assigned reading, one- to ten-day training events, seminars and workshops, and leadership retreats.

The important thing for any pastor or church elder to keep in mind, however, is that it is *your* leaders and potential leaders who are being trained, developed, and skilled in this way. That training might occur to prepare and support them for leadership in the community organization of which your church is a member, but it won't stay there. Those leaders are learning lifetime skills and gaining a lifetime vision. If you choose, you can take advantage of that leadership training to strengthen your congregation. When I pastored churches, I intentionally used the leadership development work done by the local community organization as a way of building the people who I desired to see become leaders of our churches. I combined that with a formal training program of my own. (For example, in one of my churches, members couldn't be elected as an elder or deacon unless they had completed a two-year training program in Old Testament studies, introduction to the New Testament, theological studies, and Christian ethics). But I depended upon the leadership development efforts of our local community organization to build their leadership skills and vision for work in our congregation.

3. Enable congregational visioning and mission strategizing to occur.

By its very nature, organizing creates the future, and by that same nature, it can help congregations create their future as well. The very essence of organizing is captured in its training of community leaders how to analyze their situations, determine issues, set objectives, create plans of action, carry out those plans, and evaluate and reflect upon those plans and actions. Community organizings's highly developed capacity to vision and to act can be tapped for the life and ministry of its participating congregations as well.

Every church I pastored and every mission agency with which I worked has used essential principles of community organizing to envision their future and then to intentionally live into it. Very early on I discovered that the mission-study processes of my denomination were inadequate in providing my congregations with "a future and a hope" because they did not adequately engage the congregation in the discernment process—there was no ownership on the part of the congregation in its results.

Frustrated, I devised my own process, building it around the discipline of community organizing. It centers its research phase on the conducting of individual and / or house meetings throughout the congregation and its geographical community. Its discernment phase is built around a congregation-wide retreat, where all get to participate in determining the future for their church. In my thirty subsequent years of ministry, I have led more than 200 churches and mission agencies through this discernment process. Since the publication of these principles,[1] they have been used by an unknown number of other congregations and agencies. Let me share with you one example of its use.

The church I presently serve in the Los Angeles metropolis is the LaVerne Heights Presbyterian Church. I am a Parish Associate in that congregation, working under the leadership of its senior pastor, the Rev. Steve Metcalf. In the Presbyterian denomination, when a pastor retires (as I have), she or he has the option to continue in part-time ministry as a parish associate of a specific congregation.

My ministry at that church has always been in mission outreach. Twelve years ago, I led the congregation in discerning its unique mission, both in terms of its own life and in its outreach into the community of LaVerne, the larger Pomona Valley of which it is a part, the Los Angeles metropolis, and the world. That exploration on the part of the entire congregation began a mission development process that continues in that church to the present day.

LaVerne Heights Church is an upper middle class, primarily Anglo congregation in a relatively affluent community. The neighborhood immediately around
the church has a population of 16,736 in 3,683 households; it is 84 percent Anglo
and 13 percent Hispanic with 3 percent other races. Median family income in
2002 averaged $112,276 with Hispanic income averaging $102,133.[2] But voting
records are revealing as well. The average percentage of eligible voters who actually voted between 2000 and 2004 was only 48 percent. When you consider that
both the 2000 and 2004 presidential elections were highly contested and that these
two elections claimed 73 percent of the voting population, one is aware that the
number of citizens choosing to be engaged enough in public life to register votes
in primaries would have been significantly lower.[3]

The city next to LaVerne, within a few miles of LaVerne Heights Presbyterian
Church, is Pomona. Whereas LaVerne is essentially upper middle class, Pomona
is one of the poorest cities in the United States. The largest city in eastern Los
Angeles County, Pomona's median income for families was $30,000 in 2000 and
only $26,000 for a family headed by a female. Twenty-two percent of the popula-
tion lives below the poverty level. Pomona is 64.5 percent Hispanic, 10 percent
African-American, 7.2 percent Asian and 9.6 percent Anglo. Only 54.7 percent
of the couples heading families are married. Nearly 22 percent of all households
have neither a father nor mother present. Crimes against people (murders, rapes,
robberies, assault) are double the national averages. Half of all students are classi-
fied as having limited English proficiency, and nearly 50 percent drop out of high
school before graduation.[4]

As our congregation looked at ourselves, at our neighborhood, and of the
challenge of Pomona and of the entire Los Angeles metropolitan area (a metropolis of more than 10 million wider than the state of Indiana), we recognized that
God was calling us to move outside ourselves. Out of that mission discernment
process, the entire congregation worked together to produce a mission statement
that we still claim twelve years later:

> As a people committed to the Lord Jesus Christ and empowered by
> the Holy Spirit, we nurture and equip each other to be disciples, who
> perceive and carry out God's call to our mission: to share the Gospel
> and address community and world needs to the glory of God.[5]

The strategies we developed to implement that mission statement essentially
proved ineffective (see the next section). But the mission statement itself proved
inspired! The leadership of our church took that mission statement seriously—
even in our search for a pastor. It provided us with a clear sense of direction as a

congregation. It enabled us to articulate that what we really wanted to be about as a congregation was not being a friendly fellowship or a well run and adequately financed institution or even a center of great preaching. We wanted to be about enabling people to become disciples of Jesus Christ. We wanted to be a disciple-making factory! And we wanted to make disciples for one reason, and one reason only—"to share the Gospel and address community (read, "Pomona and the Los Angeles metropolis") and world needs to the glory of God." This clarity of mission came about because we applied the principles that community organizing had fostered—visioning and mission strategizing.

3. Organize congregation in new ways.

Perhaps one of the most delightful elements of community organizing is its capacity to get its leaders to think "outside the box." By its very nature, the process of action and reflection encourages people to approach the solving of issues in creative ways. Think of the creativity that lay at the heart of the picketing action of the "little old ladies" in their use of adapted Burma-Shave signs, wearing tennis shoes and featuring the motorcycle lady. It is developing a culture of thinking outside the box that is embraced by church leaders involved in a community-organizing effort. And when that culture of approaching issues that way is brought to the church, it can create the environment for some magnificent break-throughs.

The mission statement we had developed at LaVerne Heights Church pointed us in a dynamic new direction as a congregation. But we continued our old structures to implement a new mission statement. We were so used to doing church in a particular way (that is, through committees) that we couldn't envision a different way of carrying out mission. Soon we realized that our very structure was acting as a deterrent to our living out our mission.

A team of church leaders began working on our structure. We visited churches across the United States that we knew were creative in doing mission. We read books written by creative pastors in the United Kingdom, Australia, and New Zealand. We talked with community organizers all over this country. Gradually, a new structure for our mission as a congregation began to emerge.

Our church's leaders decided to do something very un-Presbyterian. We decided to eliminate our church's committees and to substitute ministry groups for them. Why eliminate committees? Because we realized that the very nature of a committee worked against what we were seeking to accomplish as a congregation.

Committees exist to generate programs and to preserve a structure as it is. We realized that we were not about perpetuating programs or maintaining an institution as much as we were about making disciples and finding ways to enable them to live out their discipleship in the world. For that, a new structure was needed—the structure of ministry groups.

What is a ministry group? *A ministry group is a small group of church members and friends who gather together for a period of time both to undertake a common mission and to build a strong life together.* Let's unpack that statement.

A ministry group "undertakes a common mission." If there are members and friends of LaVerne Heights Church who feel increasingly called to or concerned about a particular human need they want to address, they form a ministry group. A given ministry group is responsible for carrying out the church's ministry in its chosen area of mission and is approved and dedicated to that task by the Session (the ruling body of a local Presbyterian church). No other group is allowed to perform that mission on behalf of the church.

A ministry group is "a small group of church members and friends." A ministry group need not be large—just enough to plan and organize the ministry of that group. However, it may offer a chance to many more church members and friends to participate in that mission on a short-term basis.

A ministry group operates for "a period of time." The ministry continues only as long as the ministry group thinks it is profitable to continue. Each member of each ministry group is a member for only a year at a time. At the end of his/her year of service, each ministry-group member has the opportunity to decide whether she or he wishes to continue for the next year—and it's all right to drop out!

Each ministry group "builds a strong life together." Besides planning and implementing their mission, each ministry group spends time building the corporate spirituality of the group through prayer, Bible study, reflection, and sharing. The purpose of building that strong life together is both to sustain them in their mission and to strengthen and support them in the living of their lives.[6]

The ministry-group structure has provided the avenue by which the members and friends of our church discern God's call to them to reach out to the world around them or the world far off and thus carry out their discipleship. Today there are nine ministry groups and a number of other ministry areas in our church. Some of those ministry groups deal primarily with strengthening the interior life of our congregation (such as worship and children's and youth education). But others include very active membership in ONE LA-IAF (our metropolitan-wide, broad-based organizing effort), Pomona Hope (working with churches in Pomona to organize Hispanic families to address their most substantive needs), Providence Children's Home (building an AIDS orphanage in Nairobi, Kenya), and Outreach (praying for the neighborhood and reaching out through individual and house meetings).[7]

Ministry groups have become a powerful way in which the members and friends of LaVerne Heights Church have acted "outside the box" as a church and thus have empowered ourselves to live out what we perceive as our mission in the world. This has happened because, for many of us, organizing has taught us to organize our church in new ways.

4. Enhance evangelism.

Community organizing centers around the building of relational power, especially through individual and house meetings and through action around commonly identified issues. If those principles are applied to the evangelization effort of a congregation, they can have a profound impact on the capacity of the church to reach out to its community. There is no doubt that churches that are deeply involved in community organizing and apply those organizing principles to their church tend to become growing churches—even in communities where other churches are declining.

This was my experience in churches that I pastored. The first inner-city church I pastored, before I had discovered community organizing, experienced no growth the two years I was its pastor. It closed within a year of my resignation. On the other hand, the third church I pastored in a community far poorer and decayed than the neighborhood of my first church, thrived under the application of community organizing principles to its evangelistic efforts. Edgewater Church had lost nearly 1,000 members over a ten year period. But in only one year applying the principles of individual and house meetings to our evangelistic work, Edgewater Church added more members than it had lost over the previous six years combined. And 47 percent of those new members were adult converts to Christianity!

5. Increase income.

Think what would happen if you applied the technique of individual and house meetings to raise the finances of your church? If your congregation has concentrated upon the building of significant relationships, particularly in public life, and then uses those relationships to share the stewardship vision of your congregation, the results will likely be startling.

In the two churches I pastored where I used organizing strategies for fund-raising purposes, I discovered that a congregation accustomed to individual and house meetings and to building relationality would also be surprisingly receptive to a personalized approach toward their stewardship commitment. Through the use of such strategies, one of those churches increased its annual income by 56 percent in just two years, and in the other church, we built an endowment fund from nothing to over eight million dollars in less than two years.[8]

6.   Enable the congregation to become more effective in reaching its city and community.

This is the final benefit for the local congregation that not only gets involved in broad-based organizing but also intentionally uses the principles of organizing to strengthen their own congregation.

Organizing enables your congregation to become more effective in reaching its city and its neighborhood. It is a given that involvement in community organizing sensitizes the congregation to the world around it. If the members of the church are engaged with other congregations and other groups in working for the transformation of their city and community, it is inevitable that they will become more sensitized to the world around them, but they will also become more *effective* in impacting their community. That is, through organizing, you learn the skills of building relational power, of identifying issues, of selecting a target for your action, of bringing that target to a decision, of getting results. And because you become more skilled, you become more effective. And thus, your congregation becomes more powerful. When you apply organizing principles to your outreach to the world as well as every facet of the interior life, mission, and institutional development of your church, profound transformation occurs.

THE TALE OF TWO CITIES

I would like to end our reflection together with the tale of two Kenyan cities and their struggles to build a people of power.

The first tale deals with a squatter settlement in Nairobi, Kenya. The Soweto slum consisted of fifteen thousand people when World Vision Kenya's community organizers first came into the slum and began to organize it in 1990. Today, Soweto now numbers around twenty-three thousand.

I had the privilege of visiting Soweto many times. But when I visited it in 1994, I was particularly struck with how highly organized it had become in the four years World Vision had been working in that community. Our two organizers had moved into the squatter settlement with their families in 1990 and had, over the years, held countless individual and house meetings.

Out of that initial organizing, 30 action teams were created. Some of the action teams centered on income generation, designed to build an economic base under the community, not dependent upon outside decision-making. One such income generating action team is Soweto Woodwork. It consists of 20 carpenters and masons who build household furniture, desks for the public schools, and lecterns and tables for churches and halls. They eventually plan to open a vocational school to train unemployed youth in self-employed woodworking.

Besides income-generating action-teams, the people of Soweto have organized themselves to address other issues. The women of Soweto, concerned about poor sanitation and the refuse in the slum's streets, organized themselves to clean up the slum. Fifty of them gathered on one Saturday to clean several streets. The action was so effective that eighty turned up the following Saturday. Soon, the community began gathering weekly to clean the streets, remove trash and garbage, paint houses, and even plant flowers.

But this was just the beginning. Soon the Soweto women organized to get more equitable contracts from those supplying water and removing waste. That, in turn, led to actions upon the Nairobi city government that eventually resulted in the city supplying free water to Soweto and providing sanitary waste removal. When I visited with them in 1994, their next objective was to get the city to install public flush toilets, shower stalls, and the appropriate plumbing infrastructure by 1995. They accomplished that objective!

Another action of the people was to approach the Nairobi government with the demand that each family should have the opportunity to acquire the land upon which their home was built. The land belonged to the city. The people had simply moved into the area and were "squatting" on the city's land, building shanties and a community together. But because the land belonged to the city, the government could order them off the land whenever it chose. The resistance by the city to the organized demand was intense. But the Soweto people wouldn't give up. The end result was that the government finally conceded. They deeded the land to families that had a long-term residency in Soweto. And they made the opportunity available for more recent residences to purchase their plots at extremely favorable prices.

Since my visit, the organized people of Soweto have been successful in getting the Nairobi city government to deed over a large vacant area near the center of Soweto, level it, and turn it into a soccer field. Across the street, on one side of the quadrant, the city then built a school that now provides education for the children and youth. The people organized together to build a market on another side of the quadrant, and on the third side, their own hotel and restaurant.

As I visited with the people in their action teams, I was impressed with four things. First, I was struck by how effective they had been in turning Soweto into a decent place in which to live. Second, I was struck by the quality and quantity of their reflection, for the people see their deliberate talk together as the process by which they weigh the advantages and disadvantages of the action they are planning and thus come to reasoned and mature decisions. Third, I was pleased with the open displays of faith; for example, I discovered that the members of the action teams would insist that "born again" people open each meeting in prayer and resolve issues of personality clashes. Finally, what most impressed me were the people themselves. They were joyous, assertive, positive, and self-assured, feeling in control of themselves and of their community. They had become a people of power![9]

The second tale deals with another squatter settlement I visited in Kenya in 1994. This community was in the city of Mombassa, but it was a stark contrast to Soweto. My visit there was most depressing—not because of the squalor of the people as much as because of the naïveté of a humanitarian organization.

An international mission agency (not World Vision) entered this slum several years earlier. They did not like the poverty in which they saw the people living, so they decided to do something about it. They installed a drainage and sewer system underneath the slum, laid out and asphalted broad streets above the sewer lines, installed electric streetlights, and built a beautiful school and public buildings. Through their influence, they convinced the Mombassa government to sell the land upon which each squatter had built a shack to that person for twenty Kenya shillings (about one U.S. dollar). The agency then negotiated with several banks to make loans to these squatters at very generous terms so that these new owners of the land could build sound homes upon that land.

This Christian agency had done all they could do to empower these people, they thought. They had built a modern infrastructure under that community; they had made it possible for every squatter to own his land, and they had provided the means by which each squatter could build adequate, affordable housing for themselves.

The years passed. And what has happened to that development project? Well, the squatters went ahead and purchased their respective lots with their twenty shillings. They went ahead and borrowed the money from the bank to build their

homes. But they didn't build them. Instead, they used that money for other purposes. Soon, wealthy Kenyans came into the community and offered the squatters 20,000 Kenyan shillings for each plot. This was almost too good to be true,
thought the squatters. They had borrowed the money to build their homes. And
they were now being offered 20,000 shillings not to build them. They had more
money than they ever dreamed of having.

So they sold their land to these rich Kenyans. And these rich people built
grand homes upon the land, making use of the fine infrastructure installed by
that Christian development agency. That former slum is now in a gentrification
transition, as it becomes a settlement for the very rich.

Meanwhile, the formerly poor squatters had no idea how to handle so much
money, so they were quickly parted from it by swindlers, thieves, and frauds. The
squatters, now bereft of the only property they ever owned, moved down the road
and started another squatter settlement.

Were the poor residents of that slum simply irresponsible opportunists? Could
they not see the potential of owning their own home? Were they just helpless
victims of the rich?

Not really. It was simply that no one had actually *asked* them what they wanted to do with their community or with their lives. That international organization,
the government, and the banks all assumed that these people would want to be
permanent homeowners in that squatter settlement. But the people did not choose
this course of action; it was chosen for them. So they rejected it, and simply acted
pragmatically on the opportunity afforded them—and thus ended up worse off
than when they started.

As I drove through that Mombassa slum, I could not help but think of other
powerless people I have known—the Chicago people confronting the bank over
their red-lining of their community, the people of Taquaril getting their government to build reservoirs, a school, and a health center, the little old ladies stopping
crime in our Chicago neighborhood, the poor in Detroit convincing Chrysler Corporation to build a Dodge truck factory in their neighborhood and to employ and
train them to run it, the people in Nairobi's Soweto getting the city to sell them the
land they lived on and building an infrastructure for that community, even myself
as an orphan kid learning to stand up for my convictions.

I was reminded once again of the profound difference between enabling
people to build themselves into a people of power or simply providing for them.
For in each of the successful ventures of empowerment, the people decided what

they wanted to do, and they acted collectively to solve their own problems. Out of such self-determination a people of power is built. And it is only from a people of relational power that the economic, political, and religious systems can be called to accountability and made to work for the common good. For, as St. Paul so profoundly reminds us, "The kingdom of God depends not on talk but on power" (1 Corinthians 4:20). And the shalom community begins to be realized only when God's people willingly imitate their Savior by confronting the systems and working to build people of power who can work together for the transformation of this world into an earthly model of the kingdom of God.

QUESTIONS:

1. What did I find most helpful in this book—helpful in biblical/theological reflection, the conceptual framework of community organizing, or specific strategies or tactics I can use in my congregation?

2. What most spoke to me in this book? What do I want to be sure to carry away with me from this learning experience?

Next Steps in Building a People of Power

If you want to go farther in building a people of power . . .
consider the companion video/DVD course on
"BUILDING A PEOPLE OF POWER"

YOU'VE READ THE BOOK. NOW TAKE THE TRAINING!

The course, "Building A People of Power," was developed by Youth With A Mission and World Vision International for the training of urban workers throughout the world, and then adapted by Eastern University (Philadelphia, PA), Roberts Wesleyan College and Northeastern Seminary (Rochester, NY) and Vanguard University of Southern California (Costa Mesa, CA) to prepare students for urban ministry. The course is now available for use by churches and mission agencies in classes, small discussion groups, and for personal tutorials. It is available in either a video format or on DVD. The course is taught primarily by Dr. Robert Linthicum, supported by Marilyn Stranske and Mike Miller.

"Building A People of Power" presents a biblical framework for challenging and transforming the systems of power in your city. By taking this course, you will discover:

- A biblically-based analysis of how your city's or country's economic, political, and values-setting systems use their power to either empower or exploit the poor and middle class;

- The biblical vision of the shalom community (the kingdom of God);

- Biblical principles of how God's people can successfully work both for public justice and personal righteousness;

- Biblical models showing how God's people can bring about dramatic transformation in their city through the discipline of community organizing;

- Practical training in strategies and methodologies of community organizing.

You can purchase "Building A People of Power" in one of two ways.

- You can purchase the Base Package of 27 sessions on 14 videos or DVDs, as well as one copy each of the textbook, the student's workbook, and the facilitator's handbook at $300. Additional copies of the workbook and textbook can be ordered separately.

- You can order six shorter courses of "Building A People of Power," including a mini-workbook. Prices range from $40.00 to $75.00 (according to the number of sessions in the mini-course). The courses are as follows:

  - "The World As God Intended It To Be and As It Actually Is" (5 sessions)

  - "What Did Jesus Really Come To Do?" (4 sessions)

  - "Building A Church of Power" (6 sessions)

  - "Building Relational Power" (4 sessions)

  - "Using Power to Turn Things Upside Down" (3 sessions)

  - "How to Develop Powerful Leaders and Build Values" (5 sessions)

Please make further inquiry or place your order (including designating whether you want it in video or DVD) with:

Partners in Urban Transformation

25101 Bear Valley Road, PMB #44
Tehachapi, CA 93561-8311
Phone: (661) 821-0656
Fax: (661) 821-0676
Email: partnersoffice@surfbest.net
www.piut.org

Organizing Networks

The world of community and broad-based organizing is essentially built around networks of city-based organizations coming together to provide training, resources, and the preparation, supervision, and accreditation of community organizers. Most of these networks function primarily in the US, although a few function internationally and others organize exclusively outside the United States. The organizing networks are as follows:

ACORN (Association of Community Organizations for Reform Now)

1024 Elysian Fields Avenue
New Orleans, LA 70117
Phone: (504) 943-0044
www.acorn.org

Wayne Rathke, chief organizer

ACORN is unique among all organizing networks in that it is the only network to build its power around individual membership rather than institutional membership (all the other networks are "organizations of organizations," such as churches, religious institutions, schools, unions and community groups). ACORN organizes low- and moderate-income families in 850 neighborhood chapters in 75 cities in the United States, working for social justice and stronger communities. It publishes a monthly newsletter that is distributed at no cost by email. ACORN organizes in the United States, Canada, the Dominican Republic, and Peru.

DART (Direct Action and Research Training)

The DART Center
P.O. Box 370791
314 NE 26th Terrace
Miami, FL 33137-0791
Phone: (305) 576-8020
www.thedartcenter.org

John Calkins, director
Holly Holcomb, associate director
Dr. Jana Adams, training coordinator
Ben MacConnell, organizer recruiter

DART is a midsize network, primarily doing institutional organizing in southern states and in the Midwest of the United States. It tends to organize in midsize cities (e.g., Dayton, Columbus, Louisville, Jacksonville) rather than mega-cities. It has a very strong biblical training component that includes introductory training in how to read and use the Bible to do social analysis and to work for corporate and social reform in cities through community organizing. Its annual Clergy Conference is a continuing means for honing biblical interpretation and organizing skills of its pastors and church leaders.

Gamaliel Foundation

203 North Wabash, Suite 808
Chicago, IL 60601
Phone: (312) 357-2639
www.gamaliel.org

Gregory Galluzzo, director
Paul Marincel, associate director
John Norton, director of programs

Gamaliel is a network of 45 affiliates, concentrating on organizing in the United States and South Africa. It began in 1968 to support the Contract Buyers League, an African-American organization protecting homeowners on Chicago's Westside who were being discriminated against by banks and savings and loan associations. In 1986, it was reorganized to provide organizing resources to low income communities. Gamaliel has done some effective theological work, especially through their occasional theology papers and through pastors' conferences.

(IAF) Industrial Areas Foundation

220 West Kinzie Street
Chicago, IL 60610
Phone: (312) 245-9211
www.industrialareasfoundation.org

Edward T. Chambers, executive director
Ernesto Cortes, Jr., SW regional director
Michael Gecan, NE regional director
Arnold Graf, Midwest regional director
Margaret McKenzie, Pacific regional director

The IAF is the oldest and largest of the organizing networks in the United States, as well as doing organizing in Great Britain, Germany, and South Africa. The IAF was founded by Saul Alinsky in 1942 to coordinate his organizing work in the major cities of the US. It still continues that organizing task through four regional organizations working in 78 cities; those cities tend to be the largest of U.S. cities (e.g., New York, Los Angeles metropolis, Chicago metropolis, Houston, Philadelphia, Baltimore, Dallas, etc.). Organizing is broad-based and includes middle-class suburbs as well as inner cities. In its organizing, it has developed several national initiatives. These include the Nehemiah Homes (building affordable housing through organizing the poor in Baltimore, Boston, the Bronx, Brooklyn, Houston, Los Angeles, Philadelphia), the Alliance School Program (which organizes parents to be involved in the decision-making and the schooling of their children's schools) and Project QUEST (job creation, training, and placement).

(PICO) People Improving Communities through Organizing

171 Santa Rosa Avenue
Oakland, CA 94610
Phone: (510) 655-2801
www.piconetwork.org

Ed Bauman, executive director
Jose Carrasco, consultant/trainer
Scott Read, national director of organizing
Joselyn Coogler, executive program manager

PICO began as an organizing effort on the west coast, but is now organizing in U.S. cities as far east as Camden, New Jersey. It is the second largest organizing network in the United States. PICO brings people together to strengthen families and improve communities. Since 1972, PICO has created innovative strategies to increase access to health care, improve public schools, make neighborhoods safer, create housing opportunities, redevelop communities, and revitalize American democracy. PICO makes a major emphasis upon theological reflection and the building of a relational culture.

RCNO (Regional Congregations and Neighborhood Organizations)

> 738 East 92nd Street
> Los Angeles, CA 90002
> Phone: (323) 755-1114
> www.rcno.org
>
> Rev. Eugene Williams, executive director
> Cheryl A. Branch, director of training and development

RCNO is the smallest of the organizing networks, basically because it focuses in its organizing work on small to midsize African-American urban congregations. It believes that there is significant social capital and power in the small to midsize African-American church, which can generate considerable relational power that can be focused upon government and the business community. Consequently, RCNO seeks to fill this unique niche and to organize around relationships and issues unique to the African-American church. Because of its niche, RCNO concentrates on African-American theology and biblical reflection, within both the Protestant and Pentecostal church experience.

Servant Partners

> 1550 E. Elizabeth Street, Suite U-12A
> Pasadena, CA 91104
> Phone: (626) 584-5717
> www.servantpartners.org
>
> Derek Engdahl, executive director
> Tom Pratt, new site development director
> Osborne Joda-Mbewe, training director
> Will Niewoehner, field director
> Heather Stricklin, executive administrator

Servant Partners is committed to the building of the power of the urban poor in Africa, Asia, and Latin America. This is accomplished through the strategy of community organizing that results in community development, economic development, and the planting of churches. Organizing efforts are currently occurring in the slums and squatter settlements of major cities in China, Egypt, India, Kenya, Mexico, the Philippines, Senegal, Sudan, Thailand, and Venezuela.

Appendix C

Training and Resources

TRAINING

Each of the networks provides introductory and advanced training in both community and broad-based organizing and there are national and international organizations that concentrate upon training. Such training includes workshops and seminars for small groups, extended training for large organizations: consultation, laboratories, and mentoring. The primary independent training organizations in community and broad-based organizing are NTIC, OTC and PUT. NTIC basically concentrates upon secular organizing, PUT concentrates upon church-based and faith-based organizing, and OTC works with both groups.

National Training and Information Center (NTIC)

810 N. Milwaukee Avenue
Chicago, IL 60622
Phone: (312) 243-3035
www.ntic-us.org

Gail Cincotta, executive director

ORGANIZE Training Center (OTC)

442 Vicksburg Street
San Francisco, CA 94114
Phone: (415) 648-6894
Email: MikeOTC@aol.com

Mike Miller, executive director

Partners in Urban Transformation (PUT)

1236 Fairway Circle
Upland, CA 91784-1784
Phone: (909) 982-3676
Email: rlinthicum@surfbest.net
www.piut.org

Dr. Robert Linthicum, executive director

RESOURCES

Social Policy is the primary journal in the field of community- and broad-based organizing. Its masthead reads "Organizing for Social and Economic Justice and Democratic Participation." Social Policy is published quarterly by the American Institute for Social Justice in cooperation with the ACORN Institute and the Organizers' Forum. Besides keeping the reader informed on the latest activities in organizing going on around the world, it publishes think-pieces in church-based and faith-based organizing, community organizing, the labor movement, and in organizing among target groups (e.g., youth, women, etc.).

For subscription correspondence:

Social Policy
c/o The Institute for Social Justice
1024 Elysian Fields Avenue
New Orleans, LA 70117
Email: info@socialpolicy.org

Partners in Urban Transformation (PUT) is the major producer of organizing resources for evangelical, Holiness, Pentecostal, Protestant, and Roman Catholic churches in the United States. Those resources include books, videos and DVDs, papers and curricula. Through its executive director and its many associates, PUT also offers a wide spectrum of workshops, seminars, short-term and extensive training, laboratories and consultancies to churches, church clusters, regional denominational bodies, mission agencies, and community organizations.

The purpose of PUT is to equip faith-based institutions and their people to engage effectively in public life. It accomplishes this by basing its approach in the building of relationships, drawing people out of isolation and back into intentional communities, and enabling them to confront the problems that face them. Through this community-organizing process, Christians learn how to listen carefully to one another, to engage with each other around their shared faith, values, and concerns, and then begin to work corporately with each other to effect solid change in their neighborhoods, cities, and states.

Resources currently available on community and broad-based organizing include:

Books:

Building A People of Power: Equipping the Church to Empower the City's Poor (Authentic Media, 2006)

Transforming Power: Biblical Strategies for Making A Difference In Your Community (InterVarsity Press, 2003)

City of God; City of Satan: A Biblical Theology of the Urban Church (Zondervan, 1991)

Empowering the Poor: Community Organizing Among the City's 'Rag, Tag and Bobtail' (MARC Publications, 1991)

Signs of Hope in the City (MARC Publications, 1995)

Curricula for Churches:

How God's People Can Address Injustice (4 sessions of one hour each)

Who Is This Man? A Study of Jesus from the Four Gospels (Advent-Epiphany, 9 sessions)

The Gospel According to Ephesians: Paul and the Church in Public Life (8 sessions)

The Man Who Turned the World Upside Down: Paul in Acts (8 sessions)

How to Make A Difference: A Biblical Introduction to Community Organizing (choose between course 510 [10 sessions, three hours each] and course 520 [20 sessions, 90 minutes each])

Papers:

- "Why Some Churches Succeed and Others Don't"
- "The Shalom Community: The Thread That Ties the Bible Together"
- "Doing Community Organizing in the Urban Slums of India"
- "Building Heaven and Creating Hell: The Bible on Economic, Political and Religious Systems and Their People"
- "The Biblical Understanding of the World As It Actually Is"
- "Paul: The Man Who Understood Power"

- "We're Not in Kansas Anymore: Understanding the 21st Century Urban World"
- "One to Ones: A Way of Life and Ministry"
- "Relational Power: Bringing Morality Back Into Public Life"

Videos and DVDs:

- *Building A People of Power* (27 sessions, video or DVD)
- *The World As God Intended It to Be and As It Actually Is* (5 sessions, DVD)
- *What Did Jesus Really Come to Do?* (4 sessions, DVD)
- *Building A Church of Power* (6 sessions, DVD)
- *Building Relational Power* (4 sessions, DVD)
- *Using Power to Turn Things Upside Down* (3 sessions, DVD)
- *How to Develop Powerful Leaders and Build Values* (5 sessions, DVD)
- *The Book of Matthew: The Visual Bible* (word-for-word, English or Spanish, video only)
- *The Acts of the Apostles: The Visual Bible* (word for word, English only, video only)
- *Falling Fire: The Gift of the Spirit* (90-minute movie version of Acts, English, video)

All resources can be purchased from the PUT Business and Sales Office

25101 Bear Valley Road, PMB # 44
Tehachapi, CA 93561-8311
Phone: (661) 821-0656
Fax: (661) 821-0676
Email: partnersoffice@surfbest.net

Or any resource can be ordered from our website:

www.piut.org

Notes

CHAPTER ONE

1. I am indebted to Walter Brueggemann for his analysis of the two shalom traditions in Scripture—the traditions of liberation and of stewardship, and particularly his labeling of these two traditions as shalom for "haves" and "have-nots." Brueggemann's primary development of these two traditions is found in his book, *Peace* (St. Louis, MO: Chalice Press, 2001) 25–53.

2. We will develop this theme much more fully in chapters two and three of this book.

3. *Webster's Ninth New Collegiate Dictionary*, s.v. "Righteousness."

4. There are two Hebrew words that are translated "justice"—*mishpat* (used rarely) and *tsedeq* (the Hebrew word normally used that is translated "justice" or "righteousness").

5. Richardson, Alan, *A Theological Wordbook of the Bible* (NY: Macmillan, 1960) 202–204.

6. Richardson, 165–166. "Peace."

7. Linthicum, Robert C., *Transforming Power: Biblical Strategies for Making a Difference In Your Community* (Downers Grove, IL: InterVarsity Press, 2003) 24. For a thorough description and analysis of systems, how they interlock, and how they operate to set the directions and priorities of a society, see 23–26 of *Transforming Power*.

8. The most thorough study of Paul's theology of the "principalities and powers," as well as the political understanding of the contemporary Roman and Israelite worlds, has been made by Walter Wink in his trilogy, *The Powers*, all published by Fortress Press (*Naming the Powers*, 1984; *Unmasking the Powers*, 1986; and *Engaging the Powers*, 1992). His argument on the politicality of the "principalities and powers" was so cogently argued and so overwhelmingly documented that virtually no biblical scholar of today questions it.

9. This segment on Deuteronomy is taken from my book, *Transforming Power*, 31–35. Included in this segment in *Building a People of Power* is a section on the Jubilee that does not appear in the selection from *Transforming Power*. Jubilee was a well-estab-

lished principle and practice of Jewish economic policy that was intended to redistribute wealth; standard resources on Jubilee are included in the bibliography.

There are those who insist that Jubilee, though legislated, was never observed. There is significant biblical evidence to the contrary. Three examples of this evidence would include the indication in 2 Chronicles 36:21, Jeremiah 25:11–12, 29:10, and 34:4–5 that Judah would be in exile 70 years to compensate for the 70 sabbatical years (and thus 10 Jubilees) they did not observe. Computing from their final defeat in 586 BC, this would indicate that Israel stopped observing the Sabbatical Year and the Jubilee around 1076 BC, during the period of the Judges, while Gideon was the primary judge (about 50 years before Saul ascended to the throne). The assumption of Jeremiah and the author of Chronicles is that the sabbatical and jubilee were followed before 1076. The second and third evidences of the observance of the sabbatical/Jubilee were during the Deuteronomic reforms under Nehemiah (see chapter six) and the economic policies of the earliest Christian church.

10. Jesus used this verse from Deuteronomy when he said, "You always have the poor with you" (Matt. 26:11; compare Deut. 15:11). Those who wish to justify an increasing division of the impoverished and the wealthy or those who simply want to avoid their responsibility often use this statement. But to do so is to significantly misuse Scripture. Jesus quoted Deuteronomy within the context of the reality that he would not always be with Israel. It is illegitimate exegesis to use Jesus' quotation of Deuteronomy 15:11 as a means to justify poverty and a nation or church doing nothing to eliminate it.

11. Consider, for example, Ezekiel 22 (in fact, consider the entire book of Ezekiel, which is a profound social analysis from its first to its last chapter), Exodus 1:8–14; 3:7–10; 1 Kings 18:17–40; 21:1–24; Matt. 23:13–28; John 11:45–53; Acts 22:30–23:25; Rom. 13:1–3; Eph. 6:10–17; Rev. 18:1–24; 21:3–27. For a much more thorough study of the social analysis done in the Scriptures, see my books *Transforming Power,* 41–56 and *City of God; City of Satan* (Grand Rapids, MI.: Zondervan, 1991) 40–79.

12. The economic argument that appears in the text at this footnote should not be interpreted as a "zero-sum" argument. The essence of a capitalist economy is the continuous generation of new wealth through the operation of a capitalist economy—rather than simply redistribution of a static amount of wealth. Thus, through an expanding capitalist economy, more wealth is constantly created for more people. But that was not true of ancient Israelite society. For most of the life of the nation, from the period of the Judges through its decimation by Rome in 144 AD, theirs was a near-static economy. The primary way that a person, family, business, or even the crown could increase their wealth was to take it away from something or someone else. The Christian church desperately needs today to develop a "theology of economics" for a rapidly expanding society. But if we are to be faithful to our origins, we must begin by clearly and honestly understanding the biblical message on money for its economy, gather from that study the underlying principles that would be applicable to any Jewish or Christian society in any economy, and then "invent" for our economy operational strategies that would accomplish those principles in the peculiarity of our own twenty-first century adaptive capitalist economy. Thus, for example, one of those biblical principles is "there shall be no one in need among you." The question then becomes, what are the vehicles and operational strategies we need to make that an achievable objective for the entire world in the light of the capitalist

economy in which we now function? Once that question is answered, that would then give us Christians our economic marching orders.

CHAPTER TWO

1. Maus, Cynthia Pearl, *Christ and the Fine Arts* (New York: Harper and Brothers, 1938) 630.

2. Some of the most seminal research of the historical context of Israel and other agrarian cultures at the time of Jesus are reported in the following books:

Brueggemann, Walter. *The Prophetic Imagination* (Philadelphia: Fortress, 1978)

Carney, Thomas F., *The Shape of the Past: Models and Antiquity* (Lawrence, KS: Coronado, 1975)

Eisenstadt, Shmuel Noah, *The Political Systems of Empires* (New York: Free Press, 1963)

Eisenstadt and L. Roniger, *Patrons, Clients and Friends: Interpersonal Relations and the Structure of Trust in Society* (Cambridge: Cambridge University Press, 1984)

Herzog, William R. II, *Parables as Subversive Speech: Jesus as Pedagogue of the Oppressed* (Louisville: Westminster John Knox, 1994)

Kautsky, John, *The Politics of Aristocratic Empires* (Chapel Hill: University of North Carolina Press, 1982)

Kraybill, Donald B., *The Upside-Down Kingdom* (Scottdale, PA: Herald, 1990)

Lenski, Gerhard E., *Power and Privilege: A Theory of Social Stratification* (New York: McGraw-Hill, 1966)

Lenski, with Jean Lenski, *Human Societies: An Introduction to Macrosociology,* 4th ed. (New York: McGraw-Hill, 1982)

Malina, Bruce, *The New Testament World: Insights from Cultural Anthropology* (Atlanta: John Knox Press, 1981)

Malina and Richard Rohrbaugh, *Social-Science Commentary on the Synoptic Gospels* (Minneapolis: Fortress, 1992)

Moxnes, Halvor, *The Economy of the Kingdom: Social Conflict and Economic Relations in Luke's Gospel* (Philadelphia: Fortress, 1988)

Neusner, Jacob, et.al., *The Social World of Formative Christianity and Judaism* (Leiden: E.J. Brill, 1988)

Trocme, Andre, *Jesus and the Nonviolent Revolution* (Eugene, OR: Wipf & Stock, 1998)

Wink, Walter, *Engaging the Powers: Discernment and Resistance in a World of Domination* (Minneapolis: Fortress, 1992)

Wink, Walter, *The Powers That Be: Theology for a New Millennium* (New York: Doubleday, 1998)

3. Green, Joel B., *The Gospel of Luke* (Grand Rapids: William B. Eerdmans Publishing Co., 1997) 433–437.

4. I am particularly indebted to Paul Hertig and the research he has done on the marginalization of Jesus in the gospel of Matthew, both in conversations we have had and in his monograph, "The Multi-Ethnic Journeys of Jesus in Matthew: Margin-Center Dynamics" in *Missiology: An International Review, the Quarterly Journal of the American Society of Missiology* 26, no. 1 (1998): 23–35.

5. Mark and Luke present abbreviated statements of the Jewish leaders' statements. Mark states, "He saved others; he cannot save himself. Let the [Christ], the King of Israel, come down now from the cross, that we may see and believe" (15:31–32). Luke states, "He saved others; let him save himself, if he is the [Christ] of God, his chosen one!" (23:35) The theological significance of the Matthean statement, as developed in the text, can be developed only from the full statement that alone occurs in Matthew.

6. The word *savior* had, in the ancient world, an economic as well as religious meaning, still captured today in our use of the word "save" to refer to accumulating or putting aside into a reserve fund or storehouse.

7. I am particularly indebted to the research done by Athol Gill, author of *Life on the Road: The Gospel Basis for a Messianic Lifestyle* (Homebush, Australia: Lancer Books, 1989), and Ched Myers, author of *Binding the Strong Man: A Political Reading of Mark's Story of Jesus* (Maryknoll, NY: Orbis Press, 1988), on the gospel of Mark, particularly the conversations I had with Dr. Gill at the House of the Gentle Bunyip in Melbourne, Australia, in 1988 just months before his tragic premature death.

8. Myers, Ched. *Binding the Strong Man: A Political Reading of Mark's Story of Jesus* (Maryknoll, NY: Orbis Press, 1988) 142.

9. I am indebted to the seminal study of the gospel of John done by Wes Howard-Brook in his book, *Becoming Children of God: John's Gospel and Radical Discipleship* (Maryknoll, NY: Orbis Books, 1994) for many of the insights expressed in this summary of John's gospel.

10. Throughout the gospel of John, the Greek word "Judaos" is translated "Jews" in most English translations of the Bible (e.g., see 2:13, 18, 20 in the NRSV). It is unfortunate because it gives the wrong impression of what John was likely seeking to communicate with the use of this word throughout the entirety of his gospel. To twenty-first century thinking, the word Jew means "a person belonging to a continuation through descent of the ancient Jewish people" or "one whose religion is Judaism" (*Webster's Ninth New Collegiate Dictionary* s.v. "Jew"). In other words, today a Jew is seen as a person who belongs to a specific ethnic group and/or the dominant religion of that ethnic group. The Greek word Judaos was not a reference to either that ethnic group, its dominant religion, or that nation. It was, instead, a reference to a particular group within the larger Jewish people.

As we developed earlier in this chapter, the Jewish people at the time of Christ were divided into three national entities. The nation of Israel consisted of Judea (the area surrounding Jerusalem), which was governed by a procurator of Rome (in this case, Pontius Pilate), Galilee (an area north of Judea), which was ruled by the puppet king, Herod Antipas, and Trans-Jordan (an area east of Galilee) ruled by the tetrarch

Philip. The only unifying elements among this politically divided "nation" were its common religious heritage, its religious aristocracy, and the domination of Rome. The continuing reference throughout the gospel of John to the "Judaos" was a reference, not to the Jewish people as a whole but to the "Judeans"—that portion of the nation ruled by the Roman procurator and, specifically, the dominating political, economic, and religious structure of the Judaos—the religious aristocracy of priests, elders, Pharisees, and Sadducees.

This differentiation is important because if we translate Judaos as Jews, that implies the gospel writer is referring to the Jewish nation or the Jewish people—when, in fact, he is referring to the Israelite religious establishment that also held the economic and political reins of that nation. By translating Judaos consistently as Jews, it therefore becomes easy to accuse the Jewish people of being "Christ-killers." But they were not! In fact, by-and-large, in the gospel of John, the ordinary Jewish people are portrayed as supporters of Jesus. They were deceived by their own rulers.

Jesus' enemies were not "the Jews" but "the Judeans"—the political, economic, and religious elite of Israel working in collusion with Rome to control the nation for their own political and economic benefit. The writer of the gospel of John is very careful to make that distinction from the prologue all the way through the stories of Jesus' betrayal, trial, crucifixion, burial, and resurrection! Consequently, throughout this synopsis of the gospel of John, I will exclusively use the word Judeans instead of Jews and will thus intentionally correct the translation I am using.

CHAPTER THREE

1. See Linthicum, Robert C., *City of God; City of Satan: A Biblical Theology for the City* (Grand Rapids, MI: Zondervan, 1991) 25–26 for a full explanation of the etymology of the name, "Jerusalem."

2. e.g., Knight, George A.F., *A Christian Theology of the Old Testament* (Richmond, VA: John Knox Press, 1959) 306–8; Richardson, Alan (ed), *A Theological Wordbook of the Bible* (New York: Macmillan, 1960) 106–108; note references to "Sheol" and "Gehenna."

3. It is important to keep in mind that at the time of Paul, there was not the clear differentiation into distinct entities of the political, economic, and religious systems as there is today. The king was the personification of all three systems—for he was not only the ruler of the nation but ultimately held all the wealth of the nation under his hegemony. He granted to individuals and to combines the responsibility of managing that wealth and even being secondary "owners" of that wealth, but in the final analysis it was his to claim. Likewise, he was the chief "religious" of his country; in some nations, he was the chief priest of that nation's cult; in other countries, he was the personification of the chief deity of that nation (as in Egypt) or a god (as in Rome). Therefore, all three systems were finally centered in the monarch and, consequently, in the political system.

4. George Frideric Handel, "The Hallelujah Chorus," *The Messiah: An Oratorio, 38th Edition* (New York: G. Schirmer, Inc., 1912) 197 (first published and performed in 1742).

5. The Federal Reserve Survey of Consumer Finances as reported by Edward Wolff,

Shifting Fortunes: The Perils of the Growing American Wealth Gap (United for a Fair Economy, 1999).

6. *U.S. News* and *World Report*, Sept. 26, 2000 issue.

7. As compiled from the United Nations *Development Report of 1997* and the World Health Organization's annual report of 1998.

CHAPTER FOUR

1. Much of this chapter appears in my book, *Transforming Power: Biblical Strategies for Making a Difference in Your Community* (Downers Grove, IL: Inter Varsity Press, 2003) 71-90 and is used by permission of the publisher.

2. In reality, Judah was not in captivity for seventy years. This prophecy was written near the beginning of the first invasion by Nebuchadnezzar that resulted in the bulk of Israel's leadership being taken into captivity; that occurred in 597 BC. The final defeat of Judah and the second deportation occurred in 586 BC. Cyrus conquered the Babylonian Empire in 539 BC, and the edict that returned the Israelite exiles to Judah was in 538 BC. Computing from the first deportation to Cyrus' edict, the Israelites were in captivity 59 years. So what explanation can be made regarding the seventy years? The first explanation is that Jeremiah was wrong! The second is that the number is meant to be symbolic. The third is that the period of time from the destruction of the Temple (which occurred in 586) to the completion of its rebuilding in 515 BCE was a period of 70 years. I prefer the third explanation, because the destruction of the Temple would have been perceived by Judah as the destruction of Israel's nationhood, and its restoration would be perceived as the rebirth of the nation.

3. The Hebrew word is *galah*; that word contains within it both the component of "exile" (i.e., forced removal from the land) and of "going forth," "emigrating," or "being sent"—as in an ambassador; see Brown, Driver and Briggs, *Hebrew and English Lexicon of the Old Testament* (Oxford, England: Oxford University Press, 1959) 162-163.

4. The New International Version, the Living Bible, the New Revised Standard Version, the Jerusalem Bible.

5. "Red-lining" is the illegal practice of a bank, fiduciary institution, or any other business or government agency to withhold home-loan funds or insurance or to otherwise discriminate against people in housing or insurance who live in neighborhoods considered poor economic risk. To "red-line" a community is to initiate an action that, if not stopped, will inevitably bring about decline in the neighborhood's housing stock (because people can't get loans to repair, renovate, or protect their property from calamity), resulting in decay and eventual collapse of the community.

6. I am indebted to the Industrial Areas Foundation and particularly its formulation of power as found in the teachings of Ernesto Cortes, Sr. Marybeth Larkin, and Sr. Christine Stephens in the IAF ten-day training given on July 7–16, 1998. The IAF's understanding of power forms the foundation upon which my observations of power are built.

CHAPTER FIVE

1. Much of the material in this chapter on Nehemiah was taken from my book, *Transforming Power: Biblical Strategies for Making a Difference in Your Community* (Downers Grove, IL: InterVarsity Press, 2003) 93-98.

2. Much of the material detailing an individual meeting is from four sources: my personal experience in doing individual meetings most of my ministry; my book, *Transforming Power,* ibid., 139-147; my book, *Empowering the Poor* (Monrovia, CA: MARC Publications, 1991) 43-51; and Marilyn Stranske, "The Individual Meeting: A Way of Life and Ministry" in the *Student Workbook* of the video course, *Building a People of Power* (Colorado Springs: Crown Publications, 2000) 41-43.

CHAPTER SIX

1. *Transforming Power*, 91-93.

2. The wording of Nehemiah 2:10 is ambiguous. It is unclear whether Sanballat and Tobiah had heard from third sources of Nehemiah's journey to Jerusalem and its purpose or whether they heard of it because of Nehemiah's direct visit to them. The latter makes the most sense, because it would have been proper protocol for Nehemiah to at least make a courtesy visit upon the governor of the province in which he would be at work on assignment from the emperor. And such a visit would have given Nehemiah opportunity to determine whether Sanballat would be cooperative or resistant.

3. *Transforming Power*, 98-100.

4. The book of Nehemiah is divided into two parts. Chapters one through six deal with Israel's organizing to address their most immediate problem—their broken-down walls and sense of vulnerability. Chapters seven through thirteen deal with Israel's organizing to address their deepest spiritual problem—their broken-down corporate life and their re-embracing of the shalom community. We examine the first part of the book of Nehemiah in this and the previous chapter. We will examine the second part in chapter 10.

5. *Transforming Power*, pp.100-107.

6. Ibid., 110-111.

CHAPTER SEVEN

1. Much of this chapter is built on a paper written by this author and appearing in the book, *Leadership and Team Building: Transforming Congregational Ministry through Teams*. Edited by Roger Heuser (Matthews, NC: Christian Ministry Resources Press, 1999) ch. 11, "Biblical Examples and Principles in Team Building." For another excellent resource on intentionally growing leaders, see *The Making of a Mentor: Nine Characteristics of Effective Christian Leaders* by Dr. Ted Engstrom and Dr. Ron Jenson (Waynesboro, GA: Authentic, 2005).

CHAPTER EIGHT

1. Source unknown.

2. *Webster's Ninth New Collegiate Dictionary*, s.v. "Pedagogy."

3. Jim Colling, "The 10 Greatest CEOs of All Time." *Fortune*, (2003):64, quoting "What the Doctor Ordered," *TIME*, August 18, 1952.

4. Grosse Pointe Woods Church's leadership had come to that commitment, not because of altruism or liberal generosity, but both out of a growing awareness of the demands of the Gospel and of the biblical commitment to the poor, as well as out of self-interest on their part. That is, they realized that if that poor neighborhood did not gain significant economic viability, it would continue to decline and its growing crime, violence, and anger would inevitably spill over the single street barrier that stood between that neighborhood and our wealthy suburb—and that, in turn, would bring about the inevitable decline of that suburb.

5. As quoted by Arnie Graf in the video, *The Democratic Promise: Saul Alinsky and His Legacy* (Chicago: The Chicago Video Project, 1999).

6. Paulo Friere, *Pedagogy of the Oppressed* (New York: Herder and Herder, 1972) 19.

7. See the bibliography at the end of this book for a listing of contemporary biblical theologians who are making valuable contributions to a biblical theology of public life.

8. Origen, *Contra Celsus*.

CHAPTER NINE

1. *Transforming Power*, 171-173.

2. Tajra, Harry W., *The Trial of St. Paul: A Juridical Exegesis of the Second Half of the Acts of the Apostles* (Tubingen: J.C.B. Mohr, 1989) 68.

3. For a thorough discussion of the legal rights of a Roman citizen, see Rapske, Brian, *The Book of Acts and Paul in Roman Custody* (Grand Rapids, MI: William B. Eerdmans Publishing Co., 1994) 139-146. Also see Barclay, William, *The Acts of the Apostles* (Philadelphia: Westminster Press, 1976) 163.

4. See Acts 21:32–36; 22:22–29; 23:9–10, 12–22.

5. *The Trial of St. Paul*, 113, 144–147.

6. Ibid., 171.

7. Much of this material on Paul is taken from a more extensive paper written by Robert Linthicum that appears as chapter 25, "The Apostle Paul's Acts of Power" in the following book: Gallagher, Robert L. and Paul Hertig, *Mission in Acts: Ancient Narratives in Contemporary Context* (Maryknoll, NY: Orbis Books, 2004) 297–312.

8. Some translations translate the Hebrew word *anav* as "humble" (NRSV, NIV, NKJV) while others translate it "meek" (RSV, KJV). The actual Hebrew word has the sense about it of humility, rather than of mildness, timidity, or of being easy-going.

9. Cf., *The New Interpreter's Study Bible: The Revised Standard Version with the Apocrypha* (Nashville, TN: Abingdon Press, 2003) 90–91; Bernard Anderson, *Understanding the Old Testament* (Englewood Cliffs, NJ: Prentice-Hall, 1966) 37–42; George A.F. Knight, *A Christian Theology of the Old Testament* (Richmond, VA: John Knox Press, 1959) 40–51.

10. Excerpted from my book, *The People Who Met God* (Tucker, GA: Lay Renewal Publications, 1980) 34–37.

CHAPTER TEN

1. It is intriguing that the very same reaction to the reading of Deuteronomy occurred when it was first discovered in the wall of the temple four hundred years earlier. King Josiah, when hearing it read, (2 Kings 22:11–13), also wept, tore his clothes in mourning, and repented. Perhaps this response of tears was due to the disparity that both king and people recognized lay between the way the nation was currently conducting its life and the Deuteronomic ideal it ought to have been following.

2. The stipulation in 10:34 is more complicated than this, but I have summarized it in my own words in order to get to its essence, which is the support and care of the temple.

3. Nehemiah 10:35–39 is again stated in a much more thorough way than summarized here; this action was to re-establish the celebrations of the three major festivals required in Deuteronomy: First Fruits, Passover, and Booths (also known as the Feast of Tabernacles) at which every Israelite male was required to make an appearance.

4. Nehemiah 10:28–39; 11:1–2; Besides excerpting the critical verses, I have also paraphrased some of the commitments either because they were too lengthy to include in their entirety or because of the use of cultic language that makes them initially obscure. These agreements are based upon commands appearing in Deuteronomy and not necessarily appearing in other books of the Pentateuch (e.g., # 1: Deuteronomy 25:1–10; # 2: Deuteronomy 5:12–15; # 3: Deuteronomy 15:1–19; # 4: Deuteronomy 15:1–19; # 5: Deuteronomy 12: 1–19; # 6: Deuteronomy 14:22–29; # 7: Deuteronomy 16:1–17; 26:1–16; #8: Deuteronomy 14:22–29). The apparent dependency of this covenant upon the stipulations of Deuteronomy is what gives credence to the argument that the "book of the law" referred to in Nehemiah 8 and 9 is Deuteronomy.

5. The first session of the commission was held on the first day of the tenth month (December 29) and ended on the first day of the first month (March 27). In other words, the commission hearings took three months, and in that time investigated all the men who had married foreign women. The reason why elders and judges were present from the town of each accused man was so that they would share with Ezra responsibility for the forthcoming divorces and the consequences of those divorces. In reality, according to the figures given in the book of Ezra, the number was not great. Only 110 men actually divorced their wives. This is 0.58% of the clergy and about 0.67% of the laity, based on the figures given in Ezra 2. Cf. Klein, Ralph W., "Ezra," *The New Interpreter's Study Bible: New Revised Standard Version with the Apocrypha* (Nashville, TN: Abingdon Press, 2003) 667–668.

6. At the time this study was done, the Presbyterian Church held to eight confessional standards: the Nicene Creed, the Apostles' Creed, the Scots Confession, the Heidelberg Catechism, the Second Helvetic Confession, the Westminster Confession of Faith, the Theological Declaration of Barmen and the Confession of 1967. Since then, the Westminster Shorter Catechism, The Larger Catechism, and A Brief Statement of Faith—Presbyterian Church (USA) have been added.

7. Some of this material appears in my book, *Transforming Power* (Downers Grove, IL: InterVarsity Press, 2003) 175.

8. Ibid., 184–185.

9. Ibid., 185.

10. Ibid., 185–186.

11. Ibid., 188–189.

CHAPTER ELEVEN

1. Much of the material on Taquaril was taken from the unpublished paper, "Evaluation Report: Brazil Urban Advance Projects" (Monrovia, CA: Office of Urban Advance, World Vision International, Dec. 15, 1994) 26–30.

2. Source unknown.

3. Isaiah 1:10–11, 14–17, *The Holy Bible, New Living Translation* (Wheaton, IL: Tyndale House Publishers, 1996).

4. "Evaluation Report: Brazil Urban Advance Projects," 33–34.

5. Origin, *Contra Celsus.*

6. "Evaluation Report: Brazil Urban Advance Projects," 34.

CHAPTER TWELVE

1. Robert Linthicum, *Church: Discover Your Calling* (Los Angeles: Partners in Urban Transformation, 1993). Available from Partners in Urban Transformation, PMB # 44; 25101 Bear Valley Road, Tehachapi, CA, 93561-8311; phone: (661) 821-0656; fax: (661) 821-0676; email: partnersoffice@surfbest.net.

2. U.S. Census Bureau statistics, data gathered by ONE LA-IAF.

3. State of California Voting Records, 2000-2004, data gathered by ONE LA-IAF.

4. Statistics gathered from the 2000 population report of the US Census Bureau, Pomona Unified School District report (ici.umn.edu/all/awardsite14.html); Claritas (a marketing survey group); Percept Group; Neighborhood Knowledge California (nkca. ucla.edu); nationmaster.com/encyclopedia/Pomona%2c-CA; Pomona.areaconnect. com/statistics.htm; www.cde.ca.gov/sp/el/t3/immdemogaphics.asp; Pomona.areaconnect.com/crime1.htm.

5. *1992 Mission Study of the LaVerne Heights Presbyterian Church* (LaVerne Heights Presbyterian Church, 1040 Baseline Avenue, LaVerne, CA. 91750, 1992) 3.

6. Paper, "What Is A Ministry Group?" LaVerne Heights Presbyterian Church, 1995.

7. Ibid.

8. This was endowment income, not budgetary income. That is, it was binding commitments made by members of our congregation to leave a percentage of their estates to our church. Therefore, because it required the person to die before the endowment would come our way, we hadn't raised the $8,000,000 in two years. Rather, we had

binding commitments for the $8,000,000. But that wouldn't have happened without the prior building of relationships.

9 "The Nairobi Urban Advance Evaluation" (Monrovia, CA: World Vision International, September 20, 1994) 21-23.

Bibliography

BIBLICAL THEOLOGY

Bakke, Ray. *A Theology As Big As the City*. Downers Grove, IL: InterVarsity Press, 1997.

Brueggemann, Walter. *Hope Within History*. Atlanta: Westminster-John Knox Press, 1987.

Brueggemann, Walter. *Peace*. St. Louis, MO: Chalice Press, 2001.

Brueggemann, Walter. *The Prophetic Imagination*. Philadelphia: Fortress Press, 1978.

Elliott, Charles. *Praying the Kingdom: Towards a Political Spirituality*. New York: Paulist Press, 1985.

Gill, Athol. *Life On the Road: The Gospel Basis for a Messianic Lifestyle*. Homebush, Australia: Lancer Books, 1989.

Green, Joel B. *The Gospel of Luke*. Grand Rapids, MI: Eerdmans, 1997.

Hertig, Paul. "The Multi-Ethnic Journeys of Jesus in Matthew: Margin-Center Dynamics." *Missiology: An International Review*. Vol. XXVI, No. 1 (January 1998). Scottdale, PA: American Society of Missiology,

Howard-Brook, Wes. *Becoming Children of God: John's Gospel and Radical Discipleship*. Maryknoll, NY: Orbis Press, 1994.

Kinsler, Ross and Gloria Kinsler. *The Biblical Jubilee and the Struggle for Life*. Maryknoll, NY: Orbis Press, 1999.

Kraybill, Donald B. *The Upside-Down Kingdom*. Scottsdale, PA: Herald Press, 1978.

Linthicum, Robert C. *City of God; City of Satan: A Biblical Theology of the Urban Church*. Grand Rapids, MI: Zondervan, 1991. (Out-of-print; available only from PUT)

Linthicum, Robert C. *Transforming Power: Biblical Strategies for Making a Difference In Your Community.* Downers Grove, IL: InterVarsity Press, 2003.

Mitchell, Henry and Nicholas Cooper-Lewis. *Soul Theology: The Heart of American Black Culture.* NY: Harper, 1986.

Mouw, Richard J. *When the Kings Come Marching In: Isaiah and the New Jerusalem.* Grand Rapids, MI: Eerdmans, 2002.

Myers, Ched. *Binding the Strong Man: A Political Reading of Mark's Story of Jesus.* Maryknoll, NY: Orbis, 1988.

Tonga, Benjamin. *Gospel for the Cities.* Maryknoll, NY: Orbis Press, 1985.

Trocme, Andre. *Jesus and the Nonviolent Revolution.* (Eugene, OR: Wipf and Stock Publishers, 1998.

Ucko, Hans, ed. *The Jubilee Challenge: Utopia or Possibility.* Geneva, Switzerland: WCC Publications, 1997.

Vincent, John J. *The Secular Christ: A Contemporary Interpretation of Jesus.* Nashville, TN: Abingdon, 1968.

Wink, Walter. *Engaging the Powers: Discernment and Resistance in a World of Domination.* Minneapolis, MN: Augsburg Fortress, 1992.

Wink, Walter. *The Powers That Be: Theology for a New Millennium.* New York: Doubleday, 1998.

COMMUNITY ORGANIZING

Alinsky, Saul D. *Reveille for Radicals.* New York: Vintage Books, 1980.

Alinsky, Saul D. *Rules for Radicals.* New York: Vintage Books, 1972.

Bobo, Kim, Jackie Kendall, and Steve Max. *Organizing for Social Change: A Manual for Activists in the 1990s.* Santa Ana, CA: Seven Lock Press, 1991.

Boff, Leonardo. *Ecclesiogenesis: The Base Communities Reinvent the Church.* Maryknoll, NY: Orbis Press, 1986.

Cambers, Ed. *Roots for Radicals: Organizing for Power, Action and Justice.* London: Continuum Press, 2003.

Cochran, Clarke E. *Religion in Public and Private Life.* New York: Rutledge, 1990.

Dorrien, Gary J. *Reconstructing the Common Good.* Maryknoll, NY: Orbis Press, 1990.

Freeman, Samuel G. *Upon This Rock: The Miracles of a Black Church.* New York: Harper Collins, 1993.

Friere, Paulo. *Pedagogy of the Oppressed.* New York: Herder and Herder, 1972. New York: Continuum, 1984.

Gecan, Michael. *Going Public: An Organizer's Guide to Citizen Action.* New York: Anchor Books, Inc., 2002.

Holland, Joe and Peter Henriot. *Social Analysis: Linking Faith and Justice.* Maryknoll, NY: Orbis Press, 1983.

Horwitt, Sanford. *Let Them Call Me Rebel: Saul Alinsky – His Life and Legacy.* New York: Random House, 1989.

Jacobsen, Dennis. *Doing Justice: Congregations and Community Organizing.* Philadelphia: Fortress Press, 2001.

Kretzmann, John P., and John L. McKnight. *Building Communities from the Inside Out: A Path toward Finding and Mobilizing a Community's Assets.* Evanston, IL: Center for Urban Affairs and Policy Research, Northwestern University, 1993.

Linthicum, Robert C., Mike Miller, and Marilyn Stranske. *Building A People of Power: A Workbook and Urban Reader.* Colorado Springs, CO: Procla-Media Productions, 2002.

Linthicum, Robert C. *Empowering the Poor: Community Organizing Among the City's 'Rag, Tag and Bobtail.'* Monrovia, CA: MARC Publications, 1991, 1999.

Pierce, Gregory F.A. *Activism That Makes Sense: Congregations and Community Organization.* Chicago: ACTA Publications, 1984.

Reich, Charles A. *Opposing the System.* New York: Crown Publishing, 1995.

Rogers, Mary Beth. *Cold Anger: A Story of Faith and Power Politics.* Denton, TX: University of North Texas Press, 1990.

Villa, Dana. *Socratic Citizenship.* Princeton, NJ: The Princeton University Press, 2001.

Warren, Mark R. *Dry Bones Rattling: Community Building to Revitalize American Democracy.* Princeton, NJ: The Princeton University Press, 2001.

Williams, Cecil. *No Hiding Place: Empowerment and Recovery of Our Troubled Communities.* New York: Harper and Row, 1992.

URBAN MINISTRY

Bakke, Ray and Sam Roberts. *The Expanded Mission of City Center Churches.* (Chicago, IL: International Urban Associates, 1998.

Branch, Taylor. *Parting the Waters: America in the King Years 1954-63.* New York: Simon and Shuster, 1988.

Claerbaut, David. *Urban Ministry in the New Millennium.* Waynesboro, GA: Authentic, 2005.

Conn, Harvie M. *A Clarified Vision for Urban Mission.* Grand Rapids, MI: Zondervan, 1987.

Cosby, N. Gordon. *By Grace Transformed: Christianity for a New Millennium.* (New York: Crossroads Publishing, 1999.

Dulles, Avery. *Models of the Church.* Image Books, 1978.

Fluker, Walter E. *They Looked For A City: A Comparative Analysis of the Ideal Community in the Thought of Howard Thurman and Martin Luther King, Jr.* University Press of America, 1989.

Gornik, Mark R. *To Live in Peace: Biblical Faith and the Changing Inner City.* Grand Rapids, MI: Eerdmans, 2002.

Gunder, Darrell. *The Missional Church.* Grand Rapids, MI: Eerdmans, 1998.

Kim, Young-Li, *Knowledge, Attitude and Experience: Ministry in the Cross-Cultural Context.* Nashville: Abingdon Press, 1992.

King, Martin Luther, Jr. *Why We Can't Wait.* New York: Signet, 1963.

Kunjufu, Jawanza. *Black Economics: Solutions for Economic and Community Empowerment.* African Image, 1991.

Newbigin, Lesslie. *The Gospel in a Pluralistic Society.* Grand Rapids, MI: Eerdmans, 1989.

Ortiz, Manuel. *The Hispanic Challenge: Opportunities Confronting the Church.* Downers Grove, IL: InterVarsity Press, 1993.

Regele, Mike. *Death of the Church,* Grand Rapids, MI: Zondervan, 1995.

Sample, Tex. *Blue Collar Ministry: Facing Economic and Social Realities of Working People.* Philadelphia: Judson Press, 1987.

Sample, Tex. *U.S. Lifestyles and Mainline Churches: A Key to Reaching People in the 90's.* Louisville, KY: Westminster Press, 1990.

Schaller, Lyle E. *Center City Churches: The New Urban Frontier.* Nashville, TN: Abingdon, 1993.

Schwarz, Christian A. *Natural Church Development: A Guide to Eight Essential Qualities of Healthy Churches.* Carol Stream, IL: ChurchSmart Resources, 1996.

Scott-Meyers, Eleanor. *Envisioning the New City: A Reader on Urban Ministry.* Louisville, KY: Westminster, 1992.

Smith, Donald P. *Congregations Alive: Practical Suggestions for Bringing Your Church to Life Through Partnership in Ministry.* Louisville, KY: Westminster, 1981.

Tillapaugh, Frank R. *Unleashing the Church: Getting People Out of the Fortress and Into Ministry.* Ventura, CA: Regal Books, 1982.

Villafane, Eldin. *Seek the Peace of the City: Reflections on Urban Ministry.* Grand Rapids, MI: Eerdmans, 1995.

Walker, Wyatt Tee. *The Soul of Black Worship.* New York: MLK Fellow Press, 1984.

Yamamori, Tetsunao, Bryant L. Myers, and Kenneth L. Luscombe. *Serving With the Urban Poor.* Monrovia, CA: MARC Publications, 1998.

Younger, George D. *From New Creation to Urban Crisis: A History of Action Training Ministries 1962-1975.* Austin, TX: Center for the Scientific Study of Religion, 1987.

URBANISM AND URBANIZATION

Bessenecker, Scott. *Quest for Hope in the Slum Community: An Urban Reader.* Waynesboro, GA: Authentic, 2005.

Dogan, Mattei and John D. Kasarda. *Mega-Cities: The Metropolis Era.* Beverly Hills, CA: Sage Foundation, 1988.

Dogan, Mattei and John D. Kasarda. *A World of Giant Cities.* Beverly Hills, CA: Sage Foundation, 1988.

Drake, St. Clair and Horace Clayton. *Black Metropolis, Vol. 2: A Study of Negro Life in a Northern City.* Phoenix, AZ: Harbinger Books, 1962.

Friedman, Thomas L. *The Lexus and the Olive Tree: Understanding Globalization.* New York: Anchor Books, 2000.

Fulton, William *The Reluctant Metropolis: The Politics of Urban Growth in Los Angeles.* Point Arena, CA: Solano Press Books, 1997.

Gibbs, Jewell Taylor. *Young, Black and Male in America: An Endangered Species.* Auburn House, 1988.

Gitlin, Todd. *The Twilight of Common Dreams: Why America Is Wracked by Culture Wars.* New York: Metropolitan Press, 1995.

Greider, William. *Who Will Tell the People? The Betrayal of American Democracy.* New York: Simon and Schuster, 1994.

Handy, Charles. *The Age of Paradox.* Boston: Harvard Business School Press, 1994.

Jacobs, Jane. *Cities and the Wealth of Nations.* New York: Random House, 1984.

Jewell, K. Sue. *Survival of the Black Family: The Institutional Impact of the US Social Policy.* New York: Prager, 1988.

Kawachi, Ichiro and Bruce Kennedy. *The Health of Nations: Why Inequality Is Harmful to Your Health.* New York: The New Press, 2002.

Linthicum, Robert, ed. *Signs of Hope In the City.* Monrovia, CA: MARC Publications, 1995.

McElroy, John Harmon. *American Beliefs: What Keeps A Big Country and a Diverse People United.* Chicago: Ivan R. Dee, 1999.

Mumford, Lewis. *The City in History: Its Origins, Its Transformations, and Its Prospects.* New York: Harcourt, Inc., 1961.

Palen, J. John. *The Urban World, 2nd Edition.* New York: McGraw-Hill Book Co., 1981.

Rief, David. *Los Angeles: Capital of the Third World.* New York: Simon and Schuster, 1991.

Sandel, Michael J. *Democracy's Discontent: America in Search of a Public Philosophy.* Cambridge: Belknap Press of Harvard, 1996.

Sassen, Saskia, *The Global City.* Princeton, NJ: Princeton University Press, 1991.

Siegel, Fred. *The Future Once Happened Here: New York, D.C., L.A. and the Fate of America's Big Cities.* New York: The Free Press, 1997.

Wallerstein, Immanuel. *Utopistics: Historical Choices of the Twenty-First Century.* New York: The New Press, 1998.